In Spirit and in Truth

Analyzing Theology Series

In Spirit and in Truth

Analytic Essays in Pentecostal and Charismatic Theology

Edited by
D. T. Everhart
Joanna Leidenhag
Christopher Woznicki

Foreword by Veli-Matti Kärkkäinen

 CASCADE *Books* • Eugene, Oregon

IN SPIRIT AND IN TRUTH
Analytic Essays in Pentecostal and Charismatic Theology

Analyzing Theology

Cascade Books
An Imprint of Wipf and Stock Publishers
199 W. 8th Ave., Suite 3
Eugene, OR 97401

www.wipfandstock.com

PAPERBACK ISBN: 979-8-3852-1046-6
HARDCOVER ISBN: 979-8-3852-1047-3
EBOOK ISBN: 979-8-3852-1048-0

Cataloguing-in-Publication data:

Names: Everhart, D. T., editor. | Leidenhhag, Joanna, editor. | Woznicki, Christopher G., editor. | Kärkkäinen, Veli-Matti, foreword.

Title: In spirit and in truth : analytic essays in pentecostal and charismatic theology / edited by D. T. Everhart, Joanna Leidenhag, and Christopher Woznicki ; foreword by Veli-Matti Kärkkäinen.

Description: Eugene, OR : Cascade Books, 2026 | Series: Analyzing Theology | Includes bibliographical references and index.

Identifiers: ISBN 979-8-3852-1046-6 (paperback) | ISBN 979-8-3852-1047-3 (hardcover) | ISBN 979-8-3852-1048-0 (ebook)

Subjects: LCSH: Philosophical theology. | Pentecostalism. | Analysis (Philosophy).

Classification: BT40 .I47 2026 (paperback) | BT40 (ebook)
03/13/26

The cover art was designed and painted by Joanna Leidenhag. It is a depiction of John 4:1–42, from where the title of this volume is derived.

To David and April Wagner, who taught me how to worship in Spirit and in truth, and that truth can come off rather bland without the Spirit.

—D. T.

To Alison and Harry Macdonald, Toby and Carol Foster, and William J. Abraham, all of whom encouraged me to be both a rigorous thinker and a Spirit-filled Christian.

—Joanna

To my Mom, whose love and faithfulness to the Lord led me to embrace a Spirit-led life.

—Chris

God is Spirit, and those who worship him
must worship in spirit and truth.

—JOHN 4:24 ESV

Contents

Key Doctrines

Practices and Spirituality

Analyzing Theology

The 1980s witnessed a sea change in the academic, philosophical study of Christian doctrines on the heels of a renewal in philosophy of religion initiated by such prominent figures as Alvin Plantinga, Marilyn McCord Adams, William P. Alston, Eleonore Stump, and Nicholas Wolterstorff. At the turn of the second millennium, interest in the analysis of Christian doctrine only grew more profound as analytic philosophers and systematic theologians began to interact in more substantive ways. These interactions eventuated in the rise of analytic theology, an explicitly constructive theological program equipped with the tools and methods of analytic philosophy.

Despite its significant promise for driving theology forward in both the academy and the church, much of analytic theology remains outside the grasp of nonspecialists. One of the fundamental goals of this series is to broaden analytic theology's audience and influence.

Analyzing Theology is a series of books in Christian theology that showcases cutting-edge work in analytic and systematic theology. Monographs in the series are aimed at: (i) introducing cutting-edge analytic and systematic theology, (ii) providing a platform for original contributions in analytic and systematic theology, and (iii) connecting questions of theoretical significance to theology with the practices of actual theological communities.

Analytic theology is an emerging methodology that draws from the tools and methods of contemporary analytic philosophy to serve the ends of constructive systematic theology. Those methods make use of contemporary logical and conceptual analysis, emphasize the virtues of clarity and concision (as employed within the analytic philosophical tradition), and typically include a commitment to the objectivity of truth, goodness, justice, and rationality.

The monographs in the series span a range of Christian traditions and encompass a range of subject matter. This includes discussions of the method of analytic theology, exploring its engagements with other theological disciplines (such as biblical studies), as well as exemplifying this method by addressing underexplored theological topics from an analytic perspective.

Contributors

MATTHEW CHURCHOUSE, curate, St. Martin's Church, Birmingham

CLIFTON CLARKE, professor of African descent and black theological studies, Pentecostal Seminary

JOSHUA COCKAYNE, lecturer in mission and evangelism, Cranmer Hall

MELISSA DAVIS, postdoctoral fellow, Regent University

D. T. EVERHART, programme leader and lecturer in theology, London School of Theology

KIMBERLEY KROLL, assistant professor of biblical and systematic theology, Trinity Evangelical Divinity School

JOANNA LEIDENHAG, associate professor in theology and philosophy, University of Leeds

CHRISTA MCKIRLAND, lecturer in systematic theology, Carey Baptist College

MATTHEW MCKIRLAND, student and course media coordinator, Carey Baptist College

J. P. MORELAND, distinguished professor of philosophy, Talbot School of Theology, Biola University

STEVEN NEMES, instructor, North Phoenix Preparatory Academy

JULIANY GONZÁLEZ NIEVES, adjunct professor, Trinity International University

CHRISTOPHER STEPHENSON, assistant professor of systematic theology, Lee University

CHRISTOPHER WHYTE, admissions counselor, Life Pacific University

CHRISTOPHER WOZNICKI, affiliate assistant professor in theology, Fuller Seminary, and research fellow, The Jonathan Edwards Center at Gateway Seminary

Foreword

"Truth and Spirit"

Veli-Matti Kärkkäinen

In the Annual Meeting of the Society for Pentecostal Studies in 2021, I gave a presentation entitled "The Pentecostal Meets the Pannenbergian" in which I engaged the theology of Pentecostalism (through one of its ablest proponents, my current Fuller colleague Prof. Amos Yong) from the perspective of the late Lutheran giant Wolfhart Pannenberg. I was inspired to pursue this somewhat unexpected comparison by recalling one of the most surprising, if not even counterintuitive, claims of Pannenberg, namely "theology as doxology"! When summing up his mature understanding of the nature and task of theology, the Lutheran scholar known for uncompromising rational argumentation and brilliant analytic skills stated that, ultimately,

> our talk about God becomes doxology in which the speakers rise above the limits of their own finitude to the thought of the infinite God. In the process the conceptual contours do not have to lose their sharpness. Doxology can also have the form of systematic reflection.[1]

1. Pannenberg, *Systematic Theology*, 1:70.

Pannenberg was drawn to this conclusion when negotiating between the Scylla of modern theology's retreat to subjective experience as the criterion of religious talk and the Charybdis of premodern theology's insistence on the Scripture Principle or the experience of God as the criterion of divine truth. An example of the former is Schleiermacher, for whom "the sole criterion of dogmatic presentation was the faith consciousness,"[2] thus making "beliefs and dogmatics [no more than] . . . an expression of pious states."[3] A well-known example of the latter is Calvin's making of Christian (biblical) truth a matter of the Holy Spirit's inner testimony.

To be fairer to Pannenberg's highly nuanced position, he of course was not critical of modern theology's desire to save academic theology from the authoritarian enforcement of truth claims.[4] Nor was he against rediscovering the importance of experience, whether human experience at large or individual experience; he just wanted to avoid making any particular experience—even a most deeply convinced religious experience—the ultimate platform for deciding truth.

But what on earth has all of this to do with the manuscript at hand? Pannenberg was neither Pentecostal nor an analytic theologian (although, as I have presented elsewhere, if there ever was a theologian who embodied the best virtues of analytic theology's methodology, he certainly fits the description!). In my mind, the connection lies in Pannenberg's capacity to combine doxology, the "worship"[5] of God, with the strictest analytic and rational pursuit of truth. Hence, I believe that reference to Pannenberg helps situate and ground this set of essays that investigate the promise, potential, and limitations of analytic theology in relation to Pentecostal-charismatic phenomenon and its theology and spirituality.

Analytic theology is prone to raise this very question with which Pannenberg struggled throughout most of his highly productive academic career: the relationship between human experience and God's truth.

2. Pannenberg, *Systematic Theology*, 1:57.

3. Pannenberg, *Systematic Theology*, 1:56.

4. "The promotion of experience as distinct from the objectivism and authoritarianism of the older doctrine of inspiration was not misguided in and of itself. In fact we can validate and appropriate as true only that which our own experience confirms. More dubious was the tendency, influenced by Pietism and Revivalism, to limit the principle of experience to one very specific experience, i.e., that of conversion. Most fateful of all, however, was the desire to use this experience, as earlier the doctrine of inspiration, to achieve a guarantee of the truth of Christian doctrine prior to all discussion of the individual themes" (Pannenberg, *Systematic Theology*, 1:62).

5. The quotation marks remind us that "doxology" for Pannenberg—as for much of Christian tradition at large—means more than the current somewhat limited term "worship." Yet, it still communicates the basic idea for the sake of my argumentation.

Pentecostalism usually frames the same dynamic in terms of "Spirit and Truth." That is, what kind of experience of the Spirit of God best facilitates the "assurance of salvation," or confidence in the truthfulness of the gospel? What if these are not alternatives but are mutually conditioned in some complex way?

Would it be possible for Pentecostals and charismatics to continue cherishing the primacy of spiritual experience—call it "ecstatic" or "mystical" or "doxological"—while at the same time honing their analytic and rational skills in the pursuit of the "foundation" of truth claims? To put it otherwise: What if Pentecostals first considered the question of "Truth and Spirit" and only thereafter "Spirit and Truth"?

Similarly to all other renewal movements throughout history, Pentecostals and charismatics did not pursue the question of truth with the help of analytic and rational reasoning. Nor did many of them seek wisdom and learning primarily from books and treatises—although in recent decades a formidable academia has emerged among highly educated members of the movement. Originally, Pentecostals relied on the more or less direct, unmediated experience of the Spirit of God. In doing so, they aligned themselves with the mainstream of Christian tradition, beginning from the New Testament and extending all the way to our own times. This is all good and right. But it is not all that is needed.

With the growth of the movement and the rise of a new generation of charismatics, a need to test the authenticity and implications of the experience of the Spirit has arisen. This is a natural result of institutionalization and growth, of passing the faith to the next generation. One promising way, although not the only one, for Pentecostals and charismatics to pursue the "foundation" of their spiritual experience and its rooting in the truth of God is the methodology of analytic theology. In fact, analytic theology is particularly apt for such a work because, unlike many other most recent theological trends (say, Radical Orthodoxy or post-liberalism), it is more or less "neutral" when it comes to the "content" of theology; analytic theology in my understanding puts method[ology] into the forefront. Therefore, one may practice analytic theology from a "conservative" or a "liberal" position or, for example, from a Christian or Muslim faith tradition. In other words, while of course never totally "neutral," analytic theology gives much leeway for Pentecostals and charismatics to test and hone various tools in analysis and argumentation.

The book at hand, *In Spirit and in Truth: Analytic Essays in Pentecostal and Charismatic Theology* is an ideal forerunner for such a project. It provides a needed platform to get the work started. It also gives the wider theological community an opportunity to critique, challenge, and debate the potential of this particular theological approach to analyzing charismatic experience and its theological and spiritual implications.[6]

Veli-Matti Kärkkäinen

Bibliography

Pannenberg, Wolfhart. *Systematic Theology. Vol. 1.* Translated by Geoffrey Bromiley. Online edition by Alexander Street. Grand Rapids: Eerdmans, 1991.

6. I am grateful for my PhD student Mike Smith at Fuller Seminary's Center for Advanced Theological Studies for his careful editorial work.

1

Inhabiting the Land Between Two Streams

An Introduction to Analytic and Pentecostal-Charismatic Theology

Joanna Leidenhag and Christopher Woznicki

The contributors to this volume inhabit the land between two streams. While this imagery might bring up images of fruitfulness, productivity, and fertile grounds—e.g., the Fertile Crescent of Mesopotamia or Indian *doabs*—the fruitfulness of this particular interfluve has been left largely unconsidered or has been plainly dismissed. It is the editors' conviction that this is an unfortunate oversight. The editors—D. T. Everhart, Joanna Leidenhag, and Christopher Woznicki—share the conviction that the space occupied by the fourteen contributors to this collection holds promise for matters of utmost importance. To extend this metaphor, we might say that this space is like a tree planted by streams of water, which yields its fruit in season and whose leaf does not wither (Ps 1:3). What are these two streams? The first is Pentecostal and charismatic theology; the second is analytic philosophy and theology.

The Pentecostal-Charismatic Stream

Histories of Pentecostalism and subsequently charismatic renewal among mainline churches and non-denominational churches abound. These histories help to distinguish between historic Pentecostalism and charismatic renewal movements among a variety of churches. In this volume, however, we adopt the Society of Pentecostal Studies' self-understanding as defined in its constitution. "Pentecostal" includes "charismatic."[1] Amos Yong explains that this is "recognition of the fact that the work of the Holy Spirit includes the streams of renewal in mainline Protestant, Roman Catholic, Orthodox, and other churches and movements around the world."[2] He concludes that "this 'charismatic' dimension of Pentecostal studies should not be under-emphasized."[3] We agree. Therefore, all contributors have either been members of a Pentecostal denomination or would self-identify with the practices and aims of charismatic renewal.

"Waves" in Pentecostal movements seem to come in three. The first wave of the Pentecostal movement consists of Azusa Street and the foundation of the historic Pentecostal denominations. The second wave consists of the spread of charismatic experiences and practices in the 1960s and 1970s. The third wave includes the widespread incorporation of charismatic practices into evangelicalism. Amos Yong, likewise, identifies three waves in Pentecostal theological scholarship.[4] These waves, however, don't correspond to the previous waves and actually begin in the 1960s. In this first wave, a generation of Pentecostals began pursuing PhDs in history. Their desire was to preserve the firsthand accounts of those who participated in the initial revival. Their hope was to understand and tell the story of God's action in the world. The second wave of Pentecostal scholars began to undertake their doctoral work in biblical studies in the 1970s. While this group of scholars were initially drawn to the background of the texts and historical-grammatical exegesis pertaining to texts that concerned charismatic gifts (e.g. Gordon Fee), a shift eventually took place. Increasingly, Pentecostal biblical scholars developed a Pentecostal hermeneutic which was grounded in the conviction that "the Spirit who raised Christ from the dead is the same Spirit who spoke to and through the biblical authors and who makes

1. Society of Pentecostal Studies, *Bylaws SPS 3.2.19*. Throughout the rest of this essay "Pentecostal" will refer to "Pentecostals proper, charismatic Christians, and pentecostal penumbra." See, Wariboko and Oliverio, "Society for Pentecostal Studies at 50 Years," 329.

2. Yong, "Pentecostal Scholarship," 161.

3. Yong, "Pentecostal Scholarship," 161.

4. Yong, "Pentecostalism and the Theological Academy," 245–48.

available to human beings today the life described in the scriptures."[5] The third wave has its origins in the early 1990s and is composed of those who earned their PhDs in theology. Yong argues that even these theologians have been primarily occupied by pneumatological concerns, e.g., a theology of glossolalia and charismata. Time has passed since this Yong's identification of three waves. It is no longer true that Pentecostal systematic theologians focus on these narrow sets of issues. Christopher Stephenson has identified six broad types of ways that Pentecostals are pursuing the theological task. These ways include: 1) Theology as Bible Doctrines (also a reflection of the earliest stage in this wave); 2) Theology and Spirituality; 3) Theology in Light of the Kingdom of God; 4) Philosophical and Fundamental Theology; 5) Theology as Full Gospel; and 6) Theology for a Pluralistic World.[6] The variety of types of Pentecostal systematic theology indicates the increasing maturity of the discipline in this tradition.[7] Nimi Wariboko and Bill Oliverio have argued that part of this maturing includes—at least since the 2010s—"Pentecostal scholars producing philosophical theologies and philosophies that are increasingly set within broad frameworks that engage the wider academy and multiple philosophical traditions."[8] It is this philosophical turn that garners our interest in this volume. We will return to this stream in due course.

The Analytic Stream

Brian Lieter once quipped, "I don't think anyone knows what 'analytic philosophy' is."[9] While this tongue-in-cheek comment might be amusing, the reality is that the definition of analytic philosophy (if there can even be a definition) is hotly contested. One definition of analytic philosophy states that

> analytic philosophy is characterized above all by the goal of clarity, the insistence on explicit argumentation in philosophy, and

5. Yong, "Pentecostalism and the Theological Academy," 247.

6. Stephenson, "Systematic Pentecostal Theology," 7–15.

7. Three waves in Pentecostal theological scholarship would correspond neatly to the three waves of the Pentecostal movement, however, Nimi Wariboko and Bill Oliverio have identified two additional waves. See Wariboko and Oliverio, "Pentecostal Scholarship," 1–2.

8. Wariboko and Oliverio, "Pentecostal Scholarship," 1.

9. Leiter, "What Is 'Analytic' Philosophy?"

> the demand that any view expressed be exposed to the rigours of critical evaluation and discussion by peers.[10]

One could easily poke holes in this definition. Don't other approaches to philosophy value clarity? Explicit argumentation? Rigor and discussion? Hans-Johan Glock has observed that analytic philosophy has often been used as an *honorific title*.[11] It is used by analytic philosophers to express what is "good" philosophy as opposed to "bad" philosophy. Analytic philosophy is a value-laden term. Yet surely it is more than that! Others have suggested that "analytic philosophy" is a concept too wide to be captured by a set of necessary and sufficient conditions. Rather it is more helpful to consider analytic philosophy as being "characterized in terms of overlapping circles of family resemblances."[12] It has also been suggested that analytic philosophy be considered from a genetic perspective. Sluga comments, "Following common practice, I take analytic philosophy here as originating in the work of Frege, Russell, Moore, and Wittgenstein . . . as well as their worldwide affiliates and descendents."[13] The genetic approach emphasizes the influence of particular philosophers of the past upon later generations and thinks of analytic philosophy as a tradition. By my lights (Woznicki), Dean Zimmerman's modification of the genetic/tradition approach is especially illuminating. I quote Zimmerman at length:

> The distinctive thing about analytic philosophers is that they see themselves as the rightful heirs of Russell and Moore, or of philosophers who saw themselves as the rightful heirs of Russell and Moore, or . . . "Analytic" so understood, is an adjective grounded, rather loosely, in the way philosophers think about their debts to their predecessors active at the beginning of the twentieth century. To be an analytic philosopher is to accept a version of the history of philosophy according to which the heroes at the beginning of the last century were Frege, Russell, and Moore—not Bradley, Bosanquet, and Bergson. It is to admire the philosophical impact of the analytic revolutionaries, and to hope to be a similar "force for good" in one's own time.[14]

Zimmerman's characterization emphasizes self-definition—we aren't doing *that*—family resemblance, and historical connections.[15]

10. Quoted in Beaney, "What Is Analytic Philosophy?," 3.
11. Glock, *What Is Analytic Philosophy*, 206.
12. Sluga, "What Has History to Do with Me?," 107.
13. Sluga, "Frege on Meaning," 17n1.
14. Zimmerman, "Metaphysics After the Twentieth Century," xv.
15. Dainton and Robinson, "Coda A," 574.

Understanding the historical connections is important for understanding contemporary Christian analytic philosophy and analytic theology. In light of this history Nicholas Woltersforff has narrated how analytic philosophical theology—and as a result analytic theology—has become possible. He begins this narrative with the logical positivism of the late 1950s that made philosophical theology difficult. If logical positivism were true, he explains, then "genuine talk about God could occur only under conditions that were most unlikely ever to be satisfied."[16] The collapse of logical positivism and shifting epistemologies, however, opened the door for a new generation of philosophers interested in philosophical-theological questions.[17] While the early stages of analytic philosophy may have been conceptually unfriendly toward Christianity, these shifts opened the door for figures like Plantinga, Alston, and Leftow to make significant contributions to non-theological fields of philosophy as well as to Christian thinking about philosophical questions. These philosophers—among others—paved the way for the mainstreaming of Christians doing philosophical theology. It was a small leap from that point to the point where we began to see analytic philosophers engage with questions specific to Christian doctrine—as opposed to theism in general—and theologians engage with philosophical literature.[18] While some Christians continue to consider their own work to be analytic philosophy of religion or philosophical theology there are others who consider their work to be analytic theology.[19]

The term "analytic theology" was coined in a 2009 publication by Michael Rea and Oliver Crisp. There, Rea described analytic theology as theology which conforms to the following prescriptions:

> P1. Write as if philosophical positions and conclusions can be adequately formulated in sentences that can be formalized and logically manipulated.
>
> P2. Prioritize precision, clarify, and logical coherence.
>
> P3. Avoid substantive (non-decorative) use of metaphor and other tropes whose semantic content outstrips their propositional content.

16. Wolterstorff, "How Philosophical Theology Became Possible," 156.

17. Wolterstorff, "How Philosophical Theology Became Possible," 162.

18. Woznicki, "Plea to Christian Philosophers," 212.

19. On what makes distinguishes analytic philosophy of religion from analytic theology see, for example: Baker-Hytch, "Analytic Theology and Analytic Philosophy"; Chignell, "As Kant Has Shown"; Rutledge, "Separating the Theological Sheep"; Torrance, "Possibility of a Scientific Approach."

P4. Work as much as possible with well understood primitive concepts and concepts that can be analyzed in terms of those.

P5. Treat conceptual analysis (insofar as possible) as a source of evidence.[20]

Analytic theology is just the activity of approaching theological topics with these ambitions and prescriptions that are distinctive of analytic philosophy.[21]

The Land Between the Streams

Is the land between the streams of Pentecostal-charismatic theology and analytic philosophy-theology barren or fertile? A brief look at the nature of Pentecostal theology would suggest the former. In the prolegomena to Pentecostal doctrine Wolfgang Vondey suggests that Pentecostal theology "demands a 'logic' that runs askew to the ordering of traditional doctrinal expectations, and the dominant theological systems are often ill-fit for expressing a functional Pentecostal theology."[22] Pentecostal theology, Vondey argues, exudes a spirit of "play." It eschews precise rules, boundaries, and systems; it emphasizes imagination, spontaneity, enthusiasm, and improvisation.[23] He explains that "play is a primal way of accepting the freedom of the Spirit in an attempt not to analyze the logic of Pentecost before participating in its experience."[24] The hesitancy toward analysis—before participation—and the elusive nature of the Spirit, in other words the spirit of *play*, might seem to be ill at ease with P2, P4, and P5. This spirit of *play*, however, is not the only thing that might indicate a lack of fruitfulness. Vondey goes on to argue that "Narrative is widely considered the native expression of Pentecostal and charismatic spirituality."[25] He elaborates explaining that

> rather than representing elements of propositional doctrine or a system of doctrines, identifying the full gospel as a narrative for articulating meaningful experiences and spirituality suggests

20. Rea, "Introduction," 5.

21. Treatments of what constitutes analytic theology abound. See for example: Davis, "Analytic Theology"; Wood, *Analytic Theology and the Academic Study of Religion*; Arcadi, "Introduction"; McCall, *Invitation to Christian Analytic Theology;* Woznicki, "Analytic Theology and Jonathan Edwards."

22. Vondey, *Pentecostal Theology*, 12. See also, Dabney, "Saul's Armor," 115–46.

23. Vondey, *Pentecostal Theology*, 13.

24. Vondey, *Pentecostal Theology*, 14.

25. Vondey, *Pentecostal Theology*, 21.

> that these theological accents build the core motivation for Pentecostal theology.[26]

Again, this emphasis on narrative might *seem* to be ill at ease with the analytic emphasis on formulation of propositions. Narratives, it would *seem*, contain content that goes beyond the capturability in propositions. Finally, Vondey addresses the role of affections in Pentecostal theology claiming that "the present experience and participation in the story of God proceeds by way of the affections rather than intellect, reason, and knowledge."[27] There is no such thing as non-affective, neutral, detached, and rational Pentecostal theology. Pentecostal theology is a matter of affections toward God because Pentecostal theology is about an encounter with God's Spirit. A purely rational and "objective," approach to theological matters—which the analytic tradition purportedly aims for—is completely undesirable for the Pentecostal theologian. These factors—1) play; 2) narrative; and 3) affections—in Pentecostal theology might sway readers towards thinking that the land between the streams is barren.[28] Yet, as I mentioned above, there is a trend in the third wave of Pentecostal theological scholarship that emphasizes philosophical thought.[29] May this be a way forward for analytic Pentecostal philosophy and theology?

J. Aaron Simmons would likely respond, "No." He points to the "official" beginning of Pentecostal philosophy to around 1999–2000 when Smith and Yong proposed the "Philosophy Interest Group" within the Society for Pentecostal Studies.[30] He then traces the key turning points in Pentecostal philosophy. These include the publication of Joseph Byrd's "Paul Ricoeur's Hermeneutical Theory and Pentecostal Proclamation," Amos Yong's "The Demise of Foundationalism and the Retention of Truth: What Evangelicals Can Learn from C. S. Peirce," Hittenberger's "Toward a Pentecostal Philosophy of Education," Smith's "Advice to Pentecostal Philosophers" along with his subsequent *Thinking in Tongues*, as well as Nimi Wariboko's engagement with critical theorists like Žižek and Lacan and psychoanalysis. What this list reveals is that Pentecostal philosophy has primarily been either continental

26. Vondey, *Pentecostal Theology*, 21.

27. Vondey, *Pentecostal Theology*, 25.

28. For more on the affective, narrative, and personal themes in Pentecostal epistemology of theology see Smith, *Thinking in Tongues*, 12 as well as Simmons, "Philosophy," 402–5.

29. A classic text on Pentecostal philosophy is Smith's "Advice to Pentecostal Philosophers." Regarding why Pentecostals have been hesitant to embrace philosophy in the first place see Simmons, "Prospects for Pentecostal Philosophy," 175–78 and Shin, "Advice to Pentecostal Philosophers," 157–67.

30. Simmons, "Prospects for Pentecostal Philosophy," 185.

or pragmatic. "For better or worse," he says, "the generally postmodern/continental/pragmatic approaches to pentecostal philosophical work are starkly at odds with the dominant analytic approach of most of the work of contemporary Christian philosophy."[31] While Simmons acknowledges the value of a variety of approaches to philosophy—including analytic philosophy—he thinks there are better and worse fits for Pentecostal philosophy. Continental philosophy is a natural fit because of its "embrace of metaphor, poetics, and dare we say it, the playfulness of linguistic dance."[32] This "fit" is the reason for so much fruitfulness in Pentecostal philosophy and philosophical theology over the last several decades. Does this fruitfulness on the continental side imply bareness on the analytic side? The authors of these essays would argue that it does not. It is each author's conviction that the land between the Pentecostal-charismatic stream and the analytic stream is fertile enough to plant a tree that will "yield fruit in season." These essays that follow are the firstfruits of what we hope will be an abundant crop.

Summaries

The essays in this volume are organized into three thematic sections: "Sources and Materials," where contributors bring analytic and Pentecostal/charismatic theological methods and epistemologies into dialogue; "Key Doctrines," where contributors use resources from analytic theology to discuss key Pentecostal and charismatic doctrinal topics; and "Practices and Spirituality," where contributors use analytic methods and literature to discuss Pentecostal and charismatic spiritual practices. Of course, this tripart organization is an imperfect heuristic, and some essays could have fit equally well in more than one section. More significantly, many of the essays go beyond discussion of analytic and Pentecostal charismatic theology to also include other dialogue partners, such as developmental psychology (Cockayne), Radical Orthodoxy (Davis), phenomenology (Nemes), and sociology (González Nieves), which helpfully stretch the two streams that this volume focuses on in new, pressing, directions.

In characteristically gentle and clear erudition, J. P. Moreland discusses how Pentecostal and charismatic Christians can know that their religious experiences—miracles, prophecies, encounters with God, angels or demons, etc.—are either genuinely supernatural in cause and/or veridical in content. By introducing some clear epistemological distinctions and

31. Simmons, "Prospects for Pentecostal Philosophy," 191. A recent counterexample is Christopher Stephenson's "Should Pentecostal Theology Be Analytic Theology?"

32. Simmons, "Prospects for Pentecostal Philosophy," 200.

debates, Moreland not only provides a means of philosophical justification for Pentecostal and charismatic claims, but also offers rational guidance to help Pentecostal and charismatic Christians avoid the pitfalls of *ad hoc* justifications, being gullible, skepticism, or abuse.

D. T. Everhart explores the role that charismatic experiences of the Spirit in Pentecostal and charismatic worship play in theological method. To do this, Everhart considers the common critique from Protestant evangelical theologians, that the use of charismatic experiences in one's theological method undermines the sufficiency of Scripture. Everhart uses literature in analytic philosophy of science, particularly the pragmatic representational view of how data relates to scientific modelling, to argue that spiritual experiences and Scripture are not in competition, but have different purposes within Pentecostal and charismatic theology. More precisely, drawing on recent work in analytic theology, Everhart argues that charismatic spiritual experiences are theological data primarily for the purpose of granting worshipers practical and personal knowledge, rather than factual knowledge, about God.

Whereas the first two essays in this section employ analytic philosophy to clarify and defend Pentecostal and charismatic theology, Stephenson and Clarke focus on the opposite direction of influence—that is, they consider how Pentecostal theology can contribute to analytic theological methods.

Clifton Clarke demonstrates how African Pentecostal theology and epistemology can provide constructive, critical insights for analytic theologians. Using the five characteristics stated in Michael Rea's and Oliver D. Crisp's (2009) *Analytic Theology* to structure his essay, Clarke not only critiques the Western rational tradition upon which analytic theology stands, but uses African Pentecostal Christology to offer a collaborative way forward—a theology that incorporates the West's analytic rigor with the dynamic embodied knowledge systems of African and non-Western theological traditions.

Christopher Stephenson argues that the Pentecostal practices of glossolalia and spiritual reading should be considered facets or modes of the kind of speculative theology that typically characterizes analytic theology. Stephenson's argument is that glossolalia and spiritual reading offer the speculative theologian moments of apophatic and affectively moving mental rest during the strenuous discursive work of analytic thinking. This argument also contains a challenge for Pentecostals who do not often consider their practices of glossolalia and spiritual reading to be connected to speculative theology. Stephenson thereby uses the concept of speculative theology as a bridge between the two streams of Pentecostal and analytic theology.

Part two offers essays on a range of key Christian doctrines, including the doctrine of God, creation, Christology and anthropology, pneumatology, ecclesiology and eschatology, and Mariology.

Churchouse offers not only a proposal and proto-exemplar of Pentecostal analytic theology but also provides this volume's first extended discussion of doctrine. Churchouse shows how Pentecostals use analytic tools to excavate the nature of Pentecostals' doctrine of God. Although Churchouse disagrees with scholars who have suggested that Pentecostals are best described as panentheists, he describes the Pentecostal practice as leading to an immamentist doctrine of God where the Spirit is not only active and interactive, but able to be more or less present in particular times and places.

Melissa Davis considers the God-world relationship from the perspective of the doctrine of creation, a doctrine which although historically neglected in Pentecostal and charismatic theology has received recent attention. Going beyond analytic interlocutors, Davis uses the work of James K. A. Smith and Simon Oliver to argue that, when read through a Pentecostal/charismatic lens which emphasizes the role of the Holy Spirit, the doctrine of *creatio ex nihilo* provides fertile ground for a Trinitarian-participatory ontology of creation.

Chris Woznicki offers a Pentecostal twist to the work of one of the founders of analytic theology, Oliver D. Crisp, by arguing for a Spirit-Christological anthropology. According to Woznicki, what it means for humans to image God is revealed and modelled by Jesus's relationship with the Holy Spirit. Woznicki draws on the early (or proto-) analytic theology of Thomas Morris's "Two-Minds Christology" to argue that, although Christ never gave up his divine nature as the Son, Christ performed miracles through the power of Holy Spirit—just as Pentecostal and charismatic Christians do today by following Christ's example. In this, Woznicki not only provides detailed discussion of a Pentecostal and analytic Christology, but also offers a Pentecostal doctrine of the image of God, which is simultaneously christological, pneumatological, and functional.

Kimberely Kroll further explores the indwelling relationship, which Woznicki has highlighted as so central for both Christology and anthropology. Kroll's essay exemplifies the quiet confidence and maturity of analytic theology by showing how the tools and style of analytic theology can be used to point out its own limitations. Kroll argues that the distinct charismatic experience of the Holy Spirit post-regeneration cannot be modelled or precisely articulated but remains irreducible to its parts and necessarily ambiguous.

In their essay, Christa L. McKirland and Matthew McKirland evaluate the place of the Holy Spirit in both egalitarian and hierarchical models of (early) church authority. McKirland and McKirland begin their essay drawing on analytic philosophers on the nature of authority before summarizing key debates in biblical studies on the nature of authority in early Christian communities. They use an eschatological lens to argue for an overall egalitarian view whereby, although some hierarchy remains in the church's present existence, because we all share in one Spirit as siblings of Christ, all Christians are called to mature in leadership and imitation of Christ.

Drawing our attention to gender-based violence against women in Latin America, Juliany Nievez Gonzalez implicitly poses the question: What resources can analytic feminist philosophy and Pentecostal and charismatic Mariology offer to the urgently important and under-examined realities of *feminicidio*. She outlines the historical context within which Mariology was introduced to Latin American and the Caribbean, considers how traditional depiction of Mary have been correlated to gender-based violence, and offers three imperatives for Christian communities in Latin American and the Caribbean as a result before ending with an imprecatory psalm by Puerto Rican reggaetón icon Ivy Queen.

Although analytic theology initially focused on questions of doctrinal coherence and consistency, it has since significantly expanded to consider, not what Christians claim to believe, but what Christians actually do, particularly in communal gatherings. In the final section of this volume, contributors expand this literature further to consider Pentecostal and charismatic worship practices.

Joshua Cockayne paves the way for this expansion by providing an account of charismatic liturgy. For many "liturgy" and "charismatic worship" seem to be incompatible; charismatic worship is typically spontaneous and informing, being led by the perception of the Holy Spirit, rather than following a prescribed liturgical text. Borrowing from Anglo-Catholic theologian, Evelyn Underhill, Cockayne argues that attention and habit is at the heart of all liturgy. He then draws on both developmental psychology of joint attention and analytic philosophy of joint action to argue that at the heart of charismatic liturgy is a kind of joint action that strives to attend to the presence of the Holy Spirit and to become quiescent to the work of the Spirit in the midst of the community.

Steven Nemes argues for a radical theology of the Eucharist for Pentecostals. He argues that this position is "radical" for two reasons. First, by drawing on the phenomenological tradition, his account pushes the understanding of the Eucharist in a more sacramental direction than is typically found in evangelical and Pentecostal theologizing. Second, in typically

Pentecostal manner, his account contests the inherited presuppositions of the Catholic tradition (such as a metaphysical account of Real Presence), and strives to be true to Scripture and the freedom of God by seeing the Eucharist as an invitation to express one's belief in Jesus alongside other Christians from whom one's beliefs might diverge.

Joanna Leidenhag brings practices of glossolalia into dialogue with analytic philosophy of language—two topics which, respectively, have been central to the origins and identity of Pentecostal-charismatic Christianity and analytic philosophy. Eschewing questions of whether the general phenomenon of glossolalia counts as a form of evidence, she asks instead whether and how glossolalic utterances can be deemed meaningful speech. To do this, Leidenhag first argues for a biblical distinction between xenolalia and private-prayer glossolalia. She pairs xenolalia with Tyler Burge's anti-individualist externalism and private prayer glossolalia with both expressivism and J. L. Austin's speech-act theory, preferring the latter because it helps us to predict how the practice of private prayer glossolalia can sometimes go wrong.

Chris Whyte's essay closes this volume with a discussion of the complex issues around claiming spiritual authority in Pentecostal-charismatic Christianity. His analysis focuses on what it means to name a particular action as an act of the Spirit or claim the Spirit's help, either as a request for a future action or present reality. Using historical and biblical examples, Whyte sensitively addresses the problem of how naming and claiming the Spirit has been weaponized by individuals and communities to reinforce racial privilege, but argues that agnosticism about the Spirit's work is an inadequate response to this problem. Instead, Whyte defends an ethical model of discerning the Spirit's presence, which emphasizes listening to the voices of the least.

Given the paucity of work explicitly drawing together analytic theology and Pentecostal and charismatic Christianity, these essays represent a ground-breaking contribution to these two streams. As ever, there remains much more work to be done. Although a few essays discuss topics such as race/racism, equality in leadership and gender-based violence, if analytic theology is to expand in service of the global church, then these ethical topics need continual attention. There are some other more obvious omissions in this collection, such as Asian Pentecostal-charismatic theology, disability theology, and—although most chapters include extended engagement with biblical scholarship—the doctrine of Scripture. We see no reason in principle for these lacunas, and we hope they are quickly filled in forums beyond the pages of this volume.

Bibliography

Arcadi, James. "Introduction." In *T&T Clark Handbook of Analytic Theology*, edited by James M. Arcadi and James T. Turner, 1–5. London: Bloomsbury, 2021.

Baker-Hytch, Max. "Analytic Theology and Analytic Philosophy of Religion: What's the Difference?" *Journal of Analytic Philosophy* 4 (2016) 347–61.

Beaney, Michael. "What Is Analytic Philosophy?" In *The Oxford Handbook of the History of Analytic Philosophy*, edited by Michael Beaney, 3–29. Oxford: Oxford University Press, 2013.

Chignell, Andrew. "'As Kant has Shown: Analytic Theology and the Critical Philosophy." In *Analytic Theology: New Essays in the Philosophy of Theology*, edited by Oliver D. Crisp and Michael C. Rea, 117–35. Oxford: Oxford University Press, 2009.

Dabney, D. Lyle. "Saul's Armor: The Problem and the Promise of Pentecostal Theology Today." *Pneuma* 23 (2001) 115–46.

Dainton, Barry, and Howard Robinson. "Coda A: What *Is* Analytic Philosophy?" In *The Bloomsbury Companion to Analytic Philosophy*, edited by Barry Dainton and Howard Robinson, 569–74. London: Bloomsbury, 2014.

Davis, Aaron Brian. "Analytic Theology." *Philosophy Compass* 17 (2023) 1–11.

Glock, Hans-Johan. *What Is Analytic Philosophy?* Cambridge: Cambridge University Press, 2008.

Leiter, Brian. "What Is 'Analytic' Philosophy? Thoughts from Fodor." *The Leiter Report*, October 21, 2004. https://leiterreports.typepad.com/blog/2004/10/what_is_analyti.html

McCall, Thomas. *An Invitation to Christian Analytic Theology*. Downers Grove, IL: InterVarsity, 2015.

Rea, Michael. "Introduction." In *Analytic Theology: New Essays in the Philosophy of Theology*, edited by Oliver D. Crisp and Michael C. Rea, 1–30. Oxford: Oxford University Press, 2009.

Rutledge, Jonathan. "Separating the Theological Sheep from the Philosophical Goats." *Journal of Analytic Theology* 9 (2021) 205–22.

Shin, Yoon. "Advice to Pentecostal Philosophers Redux: A More Confessionally Determinate Philosophy." In *Advice to Christian Philosophers: Reflections on the Past and Future of Christian Philosophy*, edited by Christopher Woznicki, 157–67. Raleigh: Hanover, 2024.

Simmons, J. Aaron. "Prospects for Pentecostal Philosophy: Assessing the Challenges and Envisioning the Opportunities." *Pneuma* 42 (2020) 175–200.

Sluga, Hans. "Frege on Meaning." In *The Rise of Analytic Philosophy*, edited by Hans Johan Glock, 17–34. Oxford: Blackwell, 1997.

———. "What Has History to Do with Me? Wittgenstein and Analytic Philosophy." *Inquiry* 41 (1998) 99–121.

Smith, James K. A. "Advice to Pentecostal Philosophers." *Journal of Pentecostal Theology* 11 (2003) 235–47.

———. *Thinking in Tongues: Pentecostal Contributions to Christian Philosophy*. Grand Rapids: Eerdmans, 2010.

Society of Pentecostal Studies. *Bylaws SPS 3.2.19*. https://sps-usa.org/download/Bylaws_SPS_3.2.19.pdf.

Stephenson, Christopher. "Should Pentecostal Theology Be Analytic Theology?" *Pneuma* 36 (2014) 246–64.

———. "Systematic Pentecostal Theology: A Typology." In *The Routledge Handbook of Pentecostal Theology*, edited by Wolfgang Vondey, 7–17. London: Routledge, 2020.

Torrance, Andrew. "The Possibility of a Scientific Approach to Analytic Theology." *Journal of Analytic Theology* 7 (2019) 178–98.

Vondey, Wolfgang. *Pentecostal Theology: Living the Full Gospel*. London: Bloomsbury, 2017.

Wariboko, Nimi, and Bill Oliverio. "Pentecostal Scholarship: A Shift has Occurred." *Pneuma* 42 (2020) 1–4.

———. "The Society for Pentecostal Studies at 50 Years: Ways Forward for Global Pentecostalism" *Pneuma* 42 (2020) 327–33.

Wolterstorff, Nicholas. "How Philosophical Theology Became Possible within the Analytic Tradition of Philosophy." In *Analytic Theology: New Essays in the Philosophy of Theology*, edited by Oliver D. Crisp and Michael C. Rea, 155–68. Oxford: Oxford University Press, 2009.

Woznicki, Christopher. "Analytic Theology and Jonathan Edwards in a Baptist Context." *Journal of Baptist Theology and Ministry* 20 (2023) 117–39.

———. "A Plea to Christian Philosophers: From One Who Cares About Philosophy but Is Not One of You." In *Advice to Christian Philosophers: Reflections on the Past and Future of Christian Philosophy*, edited by Christopher Woznicki, 207–17. Raleigh: Hanover, 2024.

Wood, William. *Analytic Theology and the Academic Study of Religion*. New York: Oxford University Press, 2021.

Yong, Amos. "Pentecostal Scholarship and Scholarship on Pentecostalism: The Next Generation." *Pneuma* 34 (2012) 161–65.

———. "Pentecostalism and the Theological Academy." *Theology Today* 64 (2007) 244–50.

Zimmerman, Dean. "Metaphysics After the Twentieth Century." In *Oxford Studies in Metaphysics*, edited by Dean Zimmerman, ix–xxii. Oxford: Oxford University Press, 2004.

Sources and Materials

2

Epistemological Foundations of Charismatic Religious Experience

J. P. Moreland

Christians of all stripes have religious experiences of various sorts. But the role of such experiences is central to charismatic, Pentecostal, and Third-Wave Christianity (hereafter, CC). Sadly, these branches of Christianity have a reputation for being goofy, gullible, and anti-intellectual. People differ as to whether and to what degree this reputation is true. But there can be little question that this perception is ubiquitous. This matters for at least two reasons. (1) It weakens the ability of CC advocates to spread their ideas to the broader body of Christ. (2) Revivals seldom last if they are not accompanied with significant theological and general intellectual activity.

This chapter aims to provide help in correcting this situation. In what follows, I will, first, distinguish between two fundamental types of religious experiences, specifically, Christian religious experiences. Second, I will provide a general set of key components of knowledge and justified belief that are relevant to religious experience. Finally, I will apply the insights gained to both types of Christian religious experience.

Before we launch into our investigation, I want to make two preliminary points. First, it is better if one's epistemic justification for distinctively

Christian knowledge claims to be at home in and flow naturally from one's overall epistemology than to have a general epistemology that undermines or, at least, leaves no room for those claims. In the latter case, one may "justify" the rationality of them by an appeal to blind faith or by committing the fallacy of special pleading and employing *ad hoc* stipulations to one's general epistemology when it comes to one's Christian truth claims.

Consider this example. Years ago, a literature professor at a Christian college adopted a postmodern epistemology according to which we have no direct access to reality, including texts; rather, we bring our presuppositions, conceptual schemes, gender, etc. to the hermeneutical task and can only report our community's interpretation of a constructed text. Thus, the text itself (if there is such a thing) is forever inaccessible to us. I asked her if that was her view of biblical interpretation. No, she said. Regarding Scripture, the Holy Spirit gives us the text's meaning. It should be clear that her approach to Scripture was not at home in her overall postmodern epistemology, and her appeal to the Holy Spirit was an *ad hoc Deus ex machina*. This is far from satisfying. It would be much more epistemologically preferable to reject a postmodern epistemology and adopt an alternative that entailed we have direct access to texts—biblical or otherwise—and our presuppositions et al. influence us but do not constitute what we see.

Second, while this chapter is strictly philosophical, I would be remiss if I did not make one theological point. In my opinion, the fundamental theological support for CC is not a rejection of cessationism by which I mean the rejection of the so-called miraculous gifts of the spirit after the death of the apostles. Rather, it is the presence of a new form of the kingdom of God initiated by Jesus of Nazareth—the now, not yet of the kingdom—that warrants contemporary expectations of miracles and the supernatural. That said, let us begin our investigation in earnest.

Two Fundamental Types of Christian Religious Experience

There are two very different kinds of Christian religious experience—*causal* and *phenomenological*:

> *Causal Religious Experience* (CRE): A person has a causal religious experience if and only if that person experiences some event or phenomenon such that an appeal to divine action is the best explanation for that event or phenomenon.

> *Phenomenological Religious Experience* (PRE): A person has a phenomenological religious experience if and only if that person is directly aware of a supernatural being—God, an angel, or a demon—or some communication from a supernatural being.

Cases of CRE would be specific answers to prayer or a divine healing. In these cases, one witnesses some event and based in an inductive inference to the best explanation (IBE), it is more reasonable to explain that event by postulating God's action as its cause vs. suspending judgment or disbelieving the inference to a divine cause. In a later section, I will offer criteria for discerning the difference between a genuine miracle (divine act of intervention) vs. a serendipitous improbable coincidence.

Cases of PRE would be a direct awareness of God's manifest presence or of a demon/angel, a direct awareness of God's speaking to one outside but under the authority of the Bible. Again, below I will give additional insight about epistemic considerations regarding PRE.

General Components of Knowledge Applied to Christian Religious Experience

In this section, I discuss two crucial components of the epistemology of knowledge (and justified belief) that are relevant to issues surrounding Christian religious experience: three kinds of knowledge and the debate between Particularists and Methodists.

Three Kinds of Knowledge

First, we need to get clear about what knowledge is. There are at least two kinds of knowledge. The first is knowledge by direct awareness or *experience* and the second is *propositional* knowledge. The first type of knowledge is achieved by directly experiencing something—being aware of it. For example, a little child can experience the color red while looking at an apple even if the child has no concept of redness or ability to use the word "red." Thus, the child can be aware of red without being able to form the thought "this is red." Knowledge by direct awareness goes well beyond the five senses. For example, I have direct introspective awareness of what is going on in my mind or emotions, or a direct awareness of wisdom and love and other concepts or feelings. As we will see, people often know God, a demon, or an angel is present by being directly and experientially aware of the being in question. Knowledge by direct awareness plays a big role in PRE.

The second kind of knowledge is propositional knowledge. One has this knowledge if *one has a true belief about something based on adequate reasons or grounds.* For instance, I know that my foot is hurting now because: (1) I believe it is hurting; (2) that belief is true; and (3) I have adequate grounds for holding to the belief (e.g., I feel the pain and throbbing in my foot or I can see it is swollen and inflamed). I know Jesus rose from the dead for a number of reasons, but among them is adequate evidence. Thus, I believe Jesus rose from the dead, that belief is true, and my evidence for this belief is more than adequate for it to count as knowledge.

Propositional knowledge plays a big role in CRE. Here's an example. During an appointment with my Christian doctor, our conversation turned to the topic of miracles. As we talked, I asked him if he could recall an answer to prayer that he knew—without a doubt—was miraculous. He thought for a bit, and then shared (in his own words) this story with me: "Our daughter, Ashley, was about ten years old at the time. She had two parakeets and one of them had just died. So she told her mother she wanted to get another one so she would have a couple again. Her mother, however, had had enough of pets for the time being, and she told Ashley that we weren't going to get another parakeet right now. Ashley had a mind of her own though. She said she was going to pray to God for another parakeet. And she did. The very next day, Ashley was playing outside with her friends when one of the kids saw there was a bird in the tree. They all knew that Ashley had just lost her pet. And it turned out to be a parakeet, even the very same color as the one she had just lost! We asked around, and no one could remember ever having found a parakeet in the neighborhood before. Keep in mind, this occurred the very next day after she began to pray. You can imagine her sense of triumph as she brought the bird—an exact duplicate of the one that had just died—into the house on her finger and announced that God had answered her prayer!"

Was this an answer to prayer? How would one know? Besides the fact that this case seems pretty obvious, I clearly have propositional knowledge that it was a miracle. How? Well, the account is true (the doctor wasn't a liar), I trust and therefore believe the account, and I have adequate grounds for believing it (I know the doctor well, he is a man of character and a credible witness). Alternative explanations (it was pure chance) are far less plausible than appealing to divine intervention. So, I have a true belief based on adequate reasons.

Once we grasp there are two kinds of knowledge, there is a second point we need to understand, though it may sound confusing at first: *one can know something without knowing how they know.*

Let me explain. In my field of philosophy, there is a sub-branch called epistemology that studies the nature of knowledge or reasonable beliefs, along with the ways we gain or possess such knowledge and beliefs. Most experts in this field accept the idea that there are clear cases in which one can know something without knowing *how* one knows it.

Don't get me wrong. Knowing how one knows something—e.g., that a certain interpretation of a biblical text is the correct one—is usually needed. I am making the mere point that it is not *always* needed, and there are clear cases where we know something without knowing how. This matters because we sometimes know that God spoke to us, that an event was an answer to prayer, or that a demon was present without knowing *how* we know these things. We just do.

The third point follows on this second point, and it is the notion that *one can know something without being absolutely certain that one is right.* Recall that propositional knowledge is a true belief based on *adequate*—not completely certifying—grounds. What counts as adequate grounds for something to be a genuine claim to knowledge will vary from field to field. It will be different in literature, chemistry, history, art, mathematics, ethics, theology—even in the "field" of hearing God's voice. Determining what is adequate to justify knowing something is true varies from case to case—one size does not fit all! The reasons for believing a demon is present will be different from those justifying the idea that dogs are mammals, yet both claims can be knowledge claims.

One can know something—for example, that one's youngest son left his room a mess—while at the same time admitting one might be wrong. You may even have some unanswered questions or doubts about what you know. This happens often and when it does, we still have knowledge. This means we can know something is supernatural while admitting we might be wrong and still have unresolved questions. In such a case, the possibility we are mistaken does not discount the solid grounds we have for claiming knowledge. To illustrate this, let's suppose a true belief needs a certainty of 80 percent to be counted as knowledge. If our question is "Did God really speak to me when I was praying?," you would need enough reasons for your belief to be 80 percent confident it's true.

But let's further suppose that you only have 60 percent or 70 percent confidence in your belief that God was speaking to you. Should you reject that belief? Of course not. While you would no longer be able to say you *know* it was God's voice, it is still more reasonable to accept that it was God's voice than to reject the idea.

This simple conceptual tool should bring one relief and freedom. There are many, many times in my life when I did not know *for certain* an event was an answer to prayer, a demon was involved in someone's problems, or that it was God who was directing me. But if, as we are assuming, I have reason to be 80 percent confident in my belief, then I know it's true without being certain. But so often in those very cases, I was 55 percent, 60 percent, or 75 percent sure these were supernatural occurrences. And in those cases, I *should* have believed them to be just that. Why? While I don't *know* they were supernatural events, it is more reasonable to take them as such vs. disbelieving or being agnostic about them.

So far, we have looked at two types of religious experiences and applied two types of knowledge to them. As a result, we know have some idea as to what we might mean to claim that we know some religious experience was genuinely supernatural. But this raises a question: Do we actually *have* such knowledge? What is needed for to possess such knowledge? In the next two section, I will address these questions, starting with the issue of whether we need to know how we know something, e.g., that God just spoke to me, before we can know it.

Skepticism, Particularism, and Methodism

Obviously, there are skeptics about claims based on religious experience. So, to provide a defense of the rationality of such claims, we must address skepticism. And a good way to begin an evaluation of skepticism is to focus on what is called the problem of the criterion. We can distinguish two different questions in epistemology. First, we can ask, what is it that we know? This is a question about the specific items of knowledge we possess and about the extent of our knowledge. Second, we can ask, how do we decide in any given case whether we have knowledge in that case? What are the criteria for knowledge? This is a general question about *how we have* knowledge. For example, to have knowledge, do we have to have scientific confirmation, do we need to test our alleged knowledge with our five senses, or satisfy some other criterion?

Suppose that people wish to sort all of their beliefs into two groups—the true or justified ones and the false or unjustified ones—in order to retain the former and dispose of the latter in their entire set of beliefs. Such a sorting would allow them to improve their epistemic situation and grow in knowledge and justification.

But now a problem arises regarding how one is able to proceed in this sorting activity. One would need an answer to one of the two questions above in order to proceed. But before one can have an answer to the first question about the extent of knowledge, one would seem to need an answer to the second question about criteria for knowledge. But before one can have an answer to the second question, it seems that one needs an answer to the first question. This is the problem of the criterion.[1]

Suppose someone claims to know that a demon is present in the room. To know that this claim is a case of genuine knowledge, it would seem that the individual would need to tell others how it is that he/she knows this to be true. In other words, he/she needs some criterion for deciding whether this case count as knowledge or not. But what criterion or criteria would one use? Where would the criteria come from and how would one know it was the correct criterion? To answer these questions, it seems that one would need to already know clear cases of demonic presence and clear cases where we don't know a demon is present. On that basis, one could decide on the right criteria by seeing which of a set of competing criteria get it right. That is, the right criteria are those that correctly imply that the cases in which we know demons are present are properly considered as knowledge, and the cases in which we don't have such knowledge.

There are three main solutions to the problem of the criterion as illustrated in the demonic case. Do we start by knowing specific things and go on to formulate criteria for knowledge that is consistent with what we already know without the criteria? First, there is skepticism. The skeptic claims, among other things, that no cognitivist solution to the problem exists and thus there is no knowledge. The next two solutions are advocated by cognitivists who claim that people do have knowledge. Methodism is the name of the second solution and it has been advocated by philosophers such as John Locke, René Descartes, logical positivists, and others. According to Methodism, one starts the enterprise of knowing with a criterion for what does and does not count as knowledge, in other words, one starts with an answer to question two and not question one. Methodists claim that before one can know some specific proposition P (e.g., there is a tree in the yard), one must first know some general criterion Q and, further, one must know that P is a good example of or measures up to Q. For example, Q might be "If you can test some item of belief with the five senses, then it can be an item of knowledge," or perhaps, "If something appears to your senses in a certain way, then in the absence of defeaters, you know that the thing is as it appears to you."

Unfortunately, Methodism is not a good epistemic strategy because it leads to a vicious infinite regress. To see this, note that in general, Methodism implies that before one can know anything, P, one must know two other things: Q (one's criterion for knowledge) and R (the fact that P satisfies Q). But now the skeptic can ask how it is that one knows Q and R, and the

1. See Chisholm, *Problem of the Criterion*.

Methodist will have to offer a new criterion Q′ that specifies how he knows Q, and R′ that tells how he knows that Q satisfies Q′. Obviously, the same problem will arise for Q′ and R′, and a vicious regress is set up.

Another way to see this is to note that there have been major debates about what are and are not good criteria for knowledge. Locke offered something akin to the notion that an item of knowledge about the external world must pass the criterion that the item of knowledge must be derived from simple sensory ideas or impressions (roughly, testing it with the senses). By contrast, Descartes offered a radically different criterion: the item of knowledge must be clear (precise, not fuzzy) and distinct (not confused with other ideas) when brought before the mind. If one is a Methodist, how is one to settle disputes about criteria for knowledge? The answer will be that one will have to offer criteria for one's criteria, and so on. It would seem, then, that Methodism is in trouble.

There is a third solution to the problem, known as Particularism, advocated by philosophers such as Thomas Reid, Roderick Chisholm, and Dallas Willard. According to Particularists, people start by knowing specific, clear items of knowledge: that one had eggs for breakfast this morning, that there is a tree before one or, perhaps, that one seems to see a tree, that 7 + 5 = 12, that mercy is a virtue and so on. One can know some things directly and simply without having to have criteria for how one knows them and without having to know how or even that one knows them. People know many things without being able to prove that they do or without fully understanding the things they know. People simply identify clear instances of knowing without applying any criteria for knowledge or justification. One may reflect on these instances and go on to develop criteria for knowledge consistent with them, and then use these criteria to make judgments in borderline cases of knowledge. But the criteria are justified by their congruence with specific instances of knowledge, not the other way around.

For example, one may start with moral knowledge (murder is wrong) and legal knowledge (taxes are to be paid by April 15) and go on to formulate criteria for when something is moral or legal. One could then use these criteria for judging borderline cases (intentionally driving on the wrong side of the street). In general, we start with clear instances of knowledge, formulate criteria based on those clear instances, and extend our knowledge by using those criteria to resolve borderline, unclear cases.

The skeptic can raise two basic objections against the Particularist. First, Particularism allegedly begs the question against the skeptic by simply assuming the point at issue—whether people have knowledge. How does the Particularist know that people have this? Is it not possible in the cases cited above that the Particularist is wrong and he only thinks that he has knowledge?

Particularists respond to this objection in at least four ways. First, if the skeptical question is the result of an argument, then this argument must be reasonable before it can be held as a serious objection against knowledge. However, if one did not know some things one could not reasonably doubt anything (e.g., the reason for doubting one's senses now is one's knowledge that they have misled him in the past). Such skepticism is not a rationally defensible position, and the skeptical question cannot be rationally asserted and defended without presupposing knowledge that the skeptics reasons for rejecting knowledge are objectively rational.

Second, the skeptic tries to force the Particularist to be a Methodist by asking the "how do you know?" question since the skeptic is implying that before one can know, one must have criteria for knowledge. And the skeptic knows he can refute the Methodist. But the Particularist will resist the slide into Methodism by reaffirming that he can know some specific item without having to say how he knows it.

Third, the Particularist argues that just because it is logically possible that he is mistaken in a specific case of knowledge, that does not mean he is mistaken or that he has any good reason to think he is wrong. And until the skeptic can give him good reason for thinking his instances of knowledge fail, the mere logical possibility that he is wrong will not suffice.

The Particularist and skeptic have very different approaches to knowledge. For the skeptic, the burden of proof is on the cognitivist. If it is logically possible that one might be mistaken, then knowledge is not present because knowledge requires certainty. Of the two main tasks of epistemology (obtaining true or justified beliefs and avoiding false or unjustified beliefs), the skeptic elevates the latter and requires that his position be refuted before knowledge can be justified.

Moreover, if one asks what it means to have "a right to be sure" that one has knowledge, two different senses of this phrase are involved: (1) One can dogmatically assert that one has knowledge and refuse to look at further evidence; or (2) One can have the right to rely on the truth of the belief in explaining things and in forming other beliefs while remaining open to further evidence in the future. The skeptic claims that the Particularist assertion of knowledge is an example of the former sense of the right to be sure, not the latter.

By contrast, the cognitivist places the burden of proof on the skeptic. Just because it is logically possible to be mistaken in a given case, it does not follow that one might be mistaken in an epistemic sense. There is a distinction between a logical "might" and an epistemic "might" in "you might be mistaken." The former means that there is no logical contradiction in asserting that a knowledge claim is in error. The latter means that there are good reasons for thinking that one actually is mistaken in a knowledge claim. The particularist claims that all the skeptic provides is the logical possibility of error in certain clear cases of knowledge, but not the epistemic possibility of error (good reasons for thinking one actually is in error), and it is the latter that is required to defeat a knowledge claim. The Particularist holds that (1) knowledge does not require certainty; (2) the burden of proof is on the skeptic, that all the Particularist needs to do is rebut, not refute the skeptic; (3) of the two main tasks of epistemology, having true or justified beliefs takes precedent over avoiding false, unjustified beliefs; and (4) the appropriate notion of the "right to be sure" is the second one.

There is one final point the Particularist makes in his defense. The Particularist claims that his view has advantages over the other two positions. Regarding Methodism, the Particularist avoids a vicious infinite regress. Regarding skepticism, Particularism accords and skepticism does not accord with the fact that, after all, people do know many things.

We are now in a position to understand the dialectic between skeptics and Particularists about a second major skeptical objection to Particularism. Simply put, the objection is that Particularism might easily be abused. One could just go around and assert that he or she knows all kinds of things and sanction this intellectual irresponsibility by claiming to be a Particularist.

In light of what we have seen above, the Particularist response should be clear. Just because it is logically possible to abuse Particularism, it does not follow in a particular case that one is actually abusing it. Instead of focusing on generalities and mere logical possibilities, one should look at specific cases of knowledge claims and require that the skeptic give good reasons for thinking that Particularism is being abused in that very case. The mere possibility that such an abuse is going on is not sufficient to prove the skeptic's case, and the Particularist does not need a criterion for telling when Particularism itself is and is not being abused before he can adopt a Particularist standpoint in a specific instance of knowledge.

One Sunday, my wife and I took a couple with us to church. After the service, they went forward for prayer and we accompanied them. A respected, prophetically gifted brother in the church began to pray for the wife. Suddenly, he broke out into a expressing a series of prophetic words about her childhood, her family system, and some current issues she was facing. Our lady friend began to weep, acknowledging that everything he prophesied was true! At that point, I asked the brother how he knew these things and how he know it was God who was speaking to him? His answer was a perfect expression of Particularism: "I just know in my knower," he said. "I just know it was the Lord and that's it." Setting abuses of Particularism aside, in this case, he was right: He knows these things without knowing how he knew them. The woman's husband was a bit skeptical about what had happened, but without knowing it, the prophetic brother was spot-on in his reply. Why? Because Particularism is the best solution to the problem of the criterion.

This section has provided important insights relevant to claims to know certain things via religious experience. But there is more to learn here: How does one distinguish between a real miracle and a lucky coincidence? How do you assess the eyewitness testimony of someone who claims to have seen a miracle? To these questions we now turn.

Further Reflections on CRE

How to Distinguish a Miracle from a Mere Coincidence

William Dembski has presented a clear, successful way to determine when it is legitimate to conclude that some phenomenon is the result of a purposive, intelligent act by an agent and when such a conclusion is unwarranted.[2] Among other things, Dembski analyzes cases in which insurance employees, police, and forensic scientists must determine whether a death was accidental (there was no intelligent cause) or brought about intentionally (it was done on purpose by an intelligent agent).

According to Dembski, whenever two factors are present, investigators are rationally obligated to draw the conclusion that the event was brought about intentionally for a purpose by an intelligent agent:

> The event was a very unlikely one; it had a small probability of happening.
>
> The event is capable of independent characterization. In other words, it is capable of being identified as a special occurrence besides the simple fact that it did, in fact, happen. There is some independent description of the event itself that implies that if an event satisfies that description, then the event is a special one.

To illustrate these two points, consider a game of bridge in which four people receive a hand of thirteen cards each. The winner gets $500. To simplify matters, let's focus on just two of the four players—Person A and the Dealer. What would you think if, on the first deal, Person A gets a random

2. Dembski, *Intelligent Design*, 127–49. I have adopted Dembski's discussion for our present purposes.

set of cards while the Dealer gets a perfect bridge hand? If that happened, everyone would infer that the dealer had somehow cheated. But what justifies our suspicion?

It cannot be a matter of probability since Person A and the Dealer have the same number of cards (thirteen) and each hand is equally improbable. So, the small probability of an event is not sufficient in itself to raise suspicions that the Dealer cheated. Still, small probability is *necessary* to be confident that the result (the dealer getting a winner on the first deal) was done on purpose.

To see this, suppose that Person A and the Dealer were the only two players in a different game. In this game, each person is dealt three cards, and the winner must have at least two black cards out of the three dealt to him. Person A gets two red cards and one black card. The Dealer gets a winning hand with two black cards and one red one. If this happened, no one would suspect the Dealer of rigging the deck. Why? Because getting two black cards and one red card does not have a small probability of occurring. In fact, it is fairly likely and, thus, it can easily be explained by pure chance.

By itself, the small probability of the Dealer in the bridge game getting a perfect hand is not enough to charge him with cheating. Highly unlikely coincidences happen all the time. Something else is needed to infer intentional agency, and the second criterion makes this clear: *The perfect bridge hand can be described as special independently of the fact that it happened to be the hand that came about, but this is not so for Person A's hand.* Person A's hand can be described as "the improbable hand Person A happened to get." Now that specification applies to all hands whatever and does not mark out as special any particular hand that occurs. Thus, Person A's hand is no more special than any other random deal.

But this is not so for the perfect bridge hand. This hand can be characterized as a special sort of combination of cards by the rules of bridge, quite independently of the fact that it is the hand that the dealer received. It is the combination of small probability (this particular arrangement of cards was quite unlikely to have occurred), and independent describability or "specialness" (according to the rules, this is a pretty special hand for the dealer to receive, and we know that independently of the fact that it happened to be the hand the dealer got) that justifies us in accusing the dealer of cheating. To sum it up: *small probability + independent specialness = done on purpose by an intelligent agent.* Let's call this the *Intelligent Agent Principle (IAP).*

What does any of this have to do with distinguishing between a genuine miracle and a mere coincidence? Let's recall what we have learned about the Intelligent Agent Principle (IAP): *Small probability + independent specialness = done on purpose by an intelligent agent.* If the Agent is God (or a demon/

angel) we have a miracle (or some sort of supernatural event if we don't want to call acts by angels/demons "miracles"). The IAP is almost never wrong, and you can be assured if some event or phenomenon satisfies it, it is miraculous. Small probability alone is insufficient. By way of application, if one prays for some improbable but important thing to happen, if it does, it is both improbable and special (it was exactly what one was praying for).

Consider this case. Shortly after my conversion in November 1968, I heard a talk about learning to pray for things specifically, and I wove that instruction into my prayer life. Upon graduation from college, I joined the staff of Campus Crusade for Christ (now called Cru) and was assigned to work at the Colorado School of Mines in Golden, Colorado, starting in the fall of 1971. After a summer of training in Southern California, I drove to Colorado alone to start looking for a place to live with one roommate for that year. I began to pray specifically that God would provide me and my roommate with a white house that had a white picket fence and a grassy front yard around two to three miles from campus costing no more than $115/month (this was 1971!).

After two weeks of daily prayer for this, I arrived in Golden and looked for three days for a place to live. I must have visited fifteen different places, but I found nothing at all in Golden. There was a two-bedroom apartment available located ten miles away in Denver for $130/month. Frustrated, I told the manager I would take it. She informed me that the apartment was the only one left, a couple had seen it that morning, and still had that day to decide to move in. If they did not take it, it was mine. She called me around 5 p.m., informing me that the couple had moved in. I was back to square one.

That evening, I received a call from a fellow Crusade staff member, Kaylon Carr. Keep in mind that no one, not even my roommate, knew anything about my prayer request. Kaylon asked if I still needed a place to live, which I clearly did. She went on to share how that very day she had gone to Denver Seminary, looked on their bulletin board, and spotted a pastor who wanted to rent a house in Golden to a Christian. I met the pastor at the house the next morning around 9 a.m. And would you believe it! As I drove up, I saw a white house with a white picket fence. It was located two miles from campus and rented for $110/month! My roommate, Ray Womack, and I lived there for the year, and it was the perfect home for inviting students over as part of our ministry to the campus.

Was this a miracle—a specific answer to prayer—or a mere coincidence? To answer this question, we no longer have to rely on mere commonsense intuition, as helpful as that can be. Now we have a scientifically tested and proven way to tell the difference. IAP will do the job. Was the discovery of that specific sort of house (white with a white picket fence, etc.) highly improbable? Yes, given all the specifications for the house mentioned in my prayer. Was the discovery of that specific house special independently of the fact that it happened to be the house we rented? Wow, you bet! Prior to finding the house, I had been praying for some house or other that satisfied a certain description—white house, white picket fence, grassy front yard, two to three miles from campus, renting for no more than $115/month! And it was perfect for meeting our ministry needs. This specific house was highly improbable and independently describable or special. So, it is safe to assume its provision was brought about by an Intelligent Agent.

The Epistemology of Eyewitness Testimony

Second, if the eyewitness testimony satisfies a set of criteria for judging credibility, then it should be accepted. Modern detective work has been around for two centuries, and during that time, detectives have refined their skills. Especially relevant to this chapter, detectives have developed tools and techniques for assessing the credibility of an alleged eyewitness's report. J. Warner Wallace is a leading figure in this area of expertise,[3] a cold-case detective for several years with the Los Angeles police department who has appeared frequently on Dateline NBC as well as other programs. According to Wallace, when certain criteria are met it makes a strong case for trusting the eyewitness's testimony:[4]

1. How well could the witness see, hear, or otherwise perceive the things about which the witness testified?
2. How well was the witness able to remember and describe what happened?
3. Was the witness's testimony influenced by a factor such as bias or prejudice?
4. How reasonable is the testimony when you consider all the other evidence in the case?
5. What is the witness's character for truthfulness?
6. Is the witness known for his/her integrity or engaged in other conduct that reflects on his or her believability?

3. Wallace, *Cold Case Christianity.*

4. Wallace, *Cold Case Christianity*, 69–78. I have selected six out of fourteen criteria Wallace provides because they are the most relevant ones for present purposes. I have also modified some principles to make them clearer when applied to answers to prayer.

This leaves us with point 3: *Was the witness's testimony influenced by a factor such as bias or prejudice?* Skeptics often claim that believers are plagued with confirmation bias, the tendency to search for, notice, and recall only the things that confirm one's previous beliefs, while disregarding or failing to notice disconfirming evidence. They will say that believers only notice and remember the times when their prayers "were (allegedly) answered," and fail to notice or remember all the times when prayer was impotent.

Two things should be said in response. First, the skeptic's claim is beside the point. When the Intelligent Agent Principle (IAP) has been satisfied, then the alleged bias of the believer is irrelevant. In and of itself, the satisfaction of the IAP is sufficient to show a divine intervention has taken place without needing to rely on the bias on the believer to arrive at the claim that a genuine miracle has occurred. The principle is so reliable that it is almost impossible for its application to generate a false positive (taking an event to result from the action of an intelligent agent when it did not).[5]

Secondly—and to be blunt—the skeptic needs to hang around with a different group of friends! Anyone who has been around good churches and genuine believers will know that one of the big challenges Christians face is noticing and remembering all the times when our prayers *were not* answered! Indeed, this problem is one of the reasons I'm writing this chapter. Around 25–30 percent of the psalms are laments or complaints against God for being indifferent to requests and not doing anything. The Christians I know are honest about life and fully aware of the times God does not seem to "show up." Confirmation bias? If anything, it is the skeptic who engages in naturalistic confirmation bias, projecting that onto believers. The skeptic approaches miracle claims with a commitment to the idea that miracles just don't happen and that's the end of the story. Period. This commitment is often an expression of a naturalistic worldview. Thus, for any miracle claim, the skeptic's commitments bias him/her to remember only prior miracle claims that were bogus and explainable in purely naturalist terms to the skeptic's satisfaction. He/she suppresses the memory of cases that were so strong that the miracle-hypothesis was the most reasonable one. By constantly taking all miracle claims to be bogus and capable of a natural explanation (even if he/she doesn't have one), the skeptic is guilty of the sort of confirmation bias he/she wrongly attributes to those who believe in miracles.

5. Dembski, *Intelligent Design*, 139–48.

Further Reflections on PRE

The Argument

In a believer's life, it often happens that one seems to be aware of a demon, an angel, God himself, or a communication from God. In this section I provide arguments that these experiences can be evidence for the claim that it is beyond reasonable doubt that these experiences are veridical. To show this, I will start by specifying some relevant epistemic principles:

> *Prima Facie* justification (PFJ): For some subject S, if it seems to S that Y, then in the absence of an awareness of overriding defeaters, S is *prima facie* justified in believing that Y. Y would be some state of affairs, e.g., an object's being round, a lemon's tasting sour, a demon's being malevolent, God's being kind, some event's being an answer to prayer.
>
> Overall justification: ff PFJ is satisfied for some subject S, then if S reflects carefully on his overall epistemic situation and PFJ still seems to be satisfied, then S is overall justified in believing that Y.

By "reflecting carefully" I mean that S carefully reexamines his experience, taking into account his epistemic justification or lack thereof of previous relevantly similar experiences, the support S has from external confirming principles (e.g., other mature believers have had similar kinds of experiences that turned out to be veridical), and the strength of relevant defeaters (e.g., one's tendency to hallucinate or be gullible in similar situations).

> If S has overall justification for believing that Y, then it is beyond reasonable doubt that Y.
>
> Y is *beyond reasonable doubt*: Believing Y is more reasonable than believing not-Y or withholding (being agnostic about) belief that Y.

Given these background principles, here is an argument for the claim that certain cases of religious perception (awareness, experience) are beyond reasonable doubt. Call this the Religious Perception Argument (RPA):

1. In cases of sensory perception, if S has overall justification for believing Ψ (e.g., that the apple S sees is red), then it is beyond reasonable doubt for S that Ψ.

2. Sensory perception bears a close, relevant similarity to religious perception.

Therefore, in cases of religious perception, if S has overall justification for believing Y (e.g., that God is speaking to me to witness to Kathleen) then it is beyond reasonable doubt for S that Y.

Premise 1 would be denied by extreme skeptics, but if one adopts Particularism, then while our sensory beliefs based on sensory experience are defeasible, if we have overall justification for them, then we simply find those beliefs to be beyond reasonable doubt. So let us set aside extreme skeptics regarding the aptness of our senses to provide us with sensory beliefs whose truth is beyond reasonable doubt.

Premise 2 is the one that will be subject to criticism and those criticisms need to be taken seriously. In what follows, I will provide a defense of 2.

Defense of Premise 2

Sensory Perception

At least seven features characterize normal acts of sensory perception. First, certain conditions must be met, both in and out of the perceiving subject, if the perception is to be possible. The perceiving subject must not be blind or even colorblind, must have his eyes open and be concentrating, and so forth. Concerning conditions outside the subject, the lights must be on, there must be no other objects between the subject and the alleged object of perception, the subject must be within, say, a mile of the object to see it, and so on.

Second, sensory perception possesses intentionality. Such experiences have intentionality; that is, they are *about* or *of* objects which usually exist independently of the experience itself. Some philosophers contrast experiences with intentionality with those which lack it. An (alleged) example of the latter would be an experience of pain or depression, which is not an experience of some object which is taken to exist.[6] Experiences with intentionality (e.g., visual experiences) are experiences *of* objects which are taken to exist outside the subject and which usually do exist. Note, that when one sees a red apple, one does not *interpret* one's sensory experience to be of the red apple. Rather, if one pays attention to the sensory experience itself, one

6. For a list of at least sixteen traits of religious experience with an emphasis on the object of such experiences, see Jones, "Mysticism, Human and Divine," 17–24.

simply *finds* or *becomes aware of* its being of the red apple. This *ofness* is just as much a feature of the experience as is the appearing of red.

Third, sensory perception exhibits what is called a fulfillment structure.[7] Among other things, a fulfillment structure includes law-like relations which obtain between and among successive experiences of the object which lead one from a vague experience to a clear experience of that object. The exact nature of these law-like sequences is dependent, in part, on the nature of the object which offers itself through different modes of presentation to the subject, depending on how it is viewed.

An illustration may help clarify what is meant here. Suppose a person is seeing a table from a half a mile away. At that distance, he may see an object but not be able to tell that it is a table. As he approaches the table, the successive experiences he has of the table replace one another in normal (lawlike) ways appropriate to acts of seeing a table. The table is seen as larger and larger, the color becomes brighter, and so on. Once one is at the table, it may appear as a circle viewed from overhead, an ellipse from an angle, and a straight line with legs from the side. These different experiences replace one another in law-like ways appropriate to the perception of a table. As one moves one's head from overhead to the side of the table, the circle should pass through the ellipse and into the line. These are some of the different modes of presentation that the table possesses. Given that the object is a table, there will be a regular, lawlike series of experiences one will have in going from a vague to a clear perception of the table. It should not be a part of this sequence that one suddenly sees the table moving its legs. Such an experience is not a part of the proper lawlike series of experiences involved in viewing a table.

Fourth, sensory experiences should be approached by the preliminary principles I laid out above just prior to stating RPA.

Fifth, sensory experience exhibits a public aspect and a private aspect. The objects of such experiences are public in the sense that tables are mind-independent entities which can be seen by several people at the same time. On the other hand, no one else can have my experience of the table. The having-of-the-experience is private and cannot be shared; the object of the experience is public and can be seen by many simultaneously.

Sixth, sensory perception admits of a part/whole distinction in the object of perception. One need not see all of the table to genuinely see the table. For example, one cannot see the back side of the table. But just because one can see only part of the table, it does not follow that the table

7. See Willard, *Logic and the Objectivity of Knowledge*, 205–55; Rickabaugh and Moreland, *Substance of Consciousness*, 191–233.

cannot be truly grasped in perception. One need not exhaustively see an object in its entirety to see it truly. Furthermore, one need not see some part of the object correctly to be justified in claiming to see the object itself. For example, one may mistakenly see the top of a round table as an ellipse, or one may see the red leg as slightly orange, yet one would still be seeing the table. There is a line to be drawn here. If one claimed that the table was running and barking, or that it was a round square which was red and green all over at the same time, then one's claim to see a table would be better understood as a hallucination.

Finally, there are public checks for sensory perception. One can ask others if there is a table in the room, one can have someone else describe the color, and so on. A variety of means exist whereby one could check his perception and have it confirmed or disconfirmed.

Religious Perception

I agree with a number of scholars who argue that religious perception exhibits the same features which characterize sensory perception. For one thing, religious experience involves conditions within and outside of the subject. In most cases, the subject must be "looking" for God, he must be seeking, and he must be willing to respond. He must try to still himself and not be in a frenzy or hurry (Ps 46:10). He must develop, through practice and discipline, an ability to "recognize" God's voice, and so on. Conditions outside the subject are important as well. Most mystical writers state that places of quiet or solitude are helpful, certain kinds of music can facilitate an awareness of God, certain forms of group prayer where people are genuinely seeking God can allow one to be aware of God directly.

Second, religious perception exhibits intentionality; that is, it is described by those who have it in intentional terms such that "the sense of immediacy or objectivity of what is apprehended in mystical experience comes across very strongly in mystical writings and mystics stress that it persists long after the experience is over."[8] In religious experiences themselves, there is a constant claim that the experiences are *awarenesses of* an object which is given in the perceptual acts. They are more like experiences of an apple than experiences of pain. When one attends to the latter, one does not find that the pain is of or about an intentional object, though one may know what caused it. But when one attends to the former, one finds—not interprets—the experience to be of or about an object. The same is true of religious perception and the intentional "object" of which it is. *It is a feature of the*

8. Moore, "Mystical Experience," 125.

perception itself that it is of or about a real object. Obviously, in both sensory and religious perception, one can be wrong about whether there is such an object or what that object is like. But this problem is addressed above in the preliminary principles provided before the RPA.

Here's the crucial point to keep in mind: In an experience of God, that very experience alerts us to what it is about—God himself. We don't have an experience for which we have no idea of its alleged object such that we have to interpret what to experience is about. This matters because we would have no idea about what interpretation to use without first having a direct, uninterpreted experience of an object (God) that provides us an interpretation-free access to the object that allows us to determine correct vs. incorrect interpretations of the experience's object.

Third, religious experiences show a fulfillment structure where law-like relations obtain among sequences of apprehension and the Object of the perceptions exhibits different modes of presentation. In one kind of religious perception, the initial stage of an awareness of God frequently involves an awakening of the self to a vague sense of God's presence accompanied by intense feelings of joy and exaltation.[9] This is often followed by a clearer apprehension of God's beauty and holiness with a concomitant awareness of one's own sin and guilt. Eventually, perception becomes clearer to the point that spiritual work is done on the self in that it becomes more unified, whole, and at peace. Further, God has several attributes. So, it is possible to apprehend different modes of presentation with God. Just as a table could appear circular from one angle and elliptical from another, so religious perception can fasten onto different aspects of God as he is experienced in different ways in different conditions (grief, celebration, guilt).

Fourth, the epistemic principles presented before the RPA would seem to apply to religious experience. In the absence of any special conditions (use of drugs, nitrous oxide, alcohol) the experience itself carries some presumption of evidence in favor of the veridicality of the experience. And under the conditions I specific above, evidence from a religious perception places the associated belief beyond reasonable doubt.

Fifth, religious perceptions show a public and private aspect. There is no sufficient reason for taking these experiences as private in a way that sensory experience is not private. In religious awareness, the having-of-the-experience is private in the sense that no one else could have my experience of God. But it does not follow that the object of such an awareness in private in any sense relevant to epistemological considerations. Others may experience the same Object at the same time I do, whether they are in the same

9. See Underhill, *Mysticism*, 169.

group as I am or somewhere else. Objects of religious awareness can be attended to by several persons at once, and in this sense, is just as public as a table.

Sixth, the Object of religious awareness enters into those experiences in a part/whole way. One need not exhaustively perceive God to be genuinely aware of him. One can truly apprehend God's attribute of love even if that apprehension does not fully experience that love and even if it does not experience some other attribute of God at that time.

Further, different degrees of vagueness may explain the different descriptions given to the Object of religious experience. It may well be that God is experienced in some cases of religious experience in different world religions (there is a clear tendency in monistic meditation to describe the Object of such awareness in impersonal terms). This does not mean that such awarenesses are veridical and it certainly does not mean that they would bring salvation. Christianity teaches that salvation comes only through faith in Christ. But just as a red table is being experienced by a person even though he is colorblind and describes the table as a brown ellipse, so God may be the real object of some religious experiences (one could not rule out other spiritual beings such as demons as appropriate objects in these cases) even though the descriptions are not completely accurate.

At some point, a line would be crossed where we would no longer say that God is being perceived. If one ascribes barking and a tail to the table we would say that the subject is hallucinating. Similarly, if one ascribes contradictory or monistic properties to God, we would not say that God is not being attended to accurately in these cases but rather that he is not being attended to at all.

Finally, there seem to be several public checks available to the subjects of religious experiences by which one can validate the truthfulness of those experiences. We should not expect these tests to be identical to those used in visual sensory perception. The nature of the object of perception and the faculty used in perception (the eyes as opposed to a faculty of spiritual apprehension) should determine the nature of the relevant tests for veridicality. At least seven tests have been offered to distinguish true from false perceptions of God.[10]

First, if the experience is about an internally contradictory object (such as a Being who is both personal and impersonal) or if the experience is somehow self-refuting (such as the experience that I am not a real self

10. See Evans, *Philosophy of Religion*, 92–95; Gutting, *Religious Belief and Religious Skepticism*, 141–77.

who can have experiences), then the object does not exist (compare this with the denial of the existence of square circles in visual perception).

Second, do the experiences show similarities with those of mystics who are considered to be exemplars of religious apprehension (e.g., Isaiah, Moses, Saint Francis, or Saint Teresa of Avila)? These people demonstrated themselves to have been seeking God and trying to see him; to have mastered certain disciplines or skills which are important conditions for religious perception (fasting, solitude, various kinds of prayer); to embody those character traits which are important preconditions of religious perception (such as purity of heart, devotion, kindness). In cases where these preconditions are not met (e.g., when God appeared to Abraham before he had any idea of who God was), we can carefully study the nature of the experiential aspects of these cases, the circumstanced in which they occurred, and the religious significance of them. Based on factors like these, we can compare our experiences (e.g., when an unbeliever experiences God) to see how well they comport with acknowledged veridical cases of the same sort.

Third, if an experience of God is veridical, one would expect certain other experiences to usually follow: those having such experiences would be likely to have them again; other individuals should be found who have had similar experiences (especially when the same skills are mastered and the same character traits are present); those having such experiences will be aided in their efforts to lead morally better lives.[11]

Fourth, the consequences of such experiences should be good for the mystic in the long run (such as edifying to his outlook on life, unifying to his personality, empowering to his devotion to God and others).

Fifth, the consequences of such experiences should be good for others. Do his experiences tend to cause him to build others up and help them, or do they make him self-centered?

Sixth, the depth, the profundity, the "sweetness" of the experience counts as evidence for its genuineness. On the other hand, the insignificance or silliness of the experience counts against it.

Seventh, does the experience conform to an objective body of revelation, Holy Scripture, which can in turn be validated by means other than religious claims (fulfilled prophecy, historical arguments) to keep from arguing in a circle?

In sum, it seems that there are several reasons for holding that there is a close analogy between sensory perception and religious perception. And

11. For a discussion of tests similar to the second and third tests mentioned here but on the topic of petitionary prayer, see Woznicki, "Did God Answer That Prayer," 115–33.

since we know that the former is (usually) veridical, there is good reason to take the latter as (usually) veridical.[12]

I acknowledge that people can abuse religious experience. However, this can occur in two ways—by being too gullible and too skeptical. In this chapter I have attempted to provide rational guidance and support for the credibility of claims based on religious experience. I hope this helps my brothers and sisters to avoid being gullible or skeptical and, instead, to be wise in employing and assessing this part of the Christian life.

Bibliography

Chisholm, Roderick. *The Problem of the Criterion*. Madison: Marquette University Press, 1973.

Dembski, William. *Intelligent Design*. Downers Grove, IL: InterVarsity, 1999.

Evans, C. Stephen. *Philosophy of Religion*. Downers Grove, IL: InterVarsity, 1985.

Gutting, Gary. *Religious Belief and Religious Skepticism*. Notre Dame: University of Notre Dame Press, 1982.

Jones, C. P. M. "Mysticism, Human and Divine." In *The Study of Spirituality*, edited by Cheslyn Jones et al., 17–24. Oxford: Oxford University Press, 1986.

Moore, Peter. "Mystical Experience, Mystical Doctrine, and Mystical Technique." In *Mysticism and Philosophical Analysis*, edited by Stephen T. Katz, 125–42. New York: Oxford University Press, 1978.

Moreland, J. P. *A Simple Guide to Experiencing Miracles*. Grand Rapids: Zondervan, 2021.

Rickabaugh, Brandon, and J. P. Moreland. *The Substance of Consciousness: A Comprehensive Defense of Contemporary Substance Dualism*. Oxford: Wiley Blackwell, 2023.

Underhill, Evelyn. *Mysticism*. New York: New American Library, 1955.

Wallace, J. Warner. *Cold Case Christianity: A Homicide Detective Investigates the Claims of the Gospels*. Colorado Springs: David C. Cook, 2013.

Willard, Dallas. *Logic and the Objectivity of Knowledge: Studies in Husserl's Early Philosophy*. Athens: Ohio University Press, 1984.

Woznicki, Christopher. "Did God Answer that Prayer: Spiritual Perception and the Epistemology of Petitionary Prayer." *Pneuma* 43 (2021) 115–33.

12. For a general defense of contemporary miracles, see Moreland, *Simple Guide to Experiencing Miracles*.

3

Word and Worship

Charismatic Spiritual Experience as Theological Data

D. T. Everhart

This chapter explores the role of experience and worship in theological method. Charismatic and Pentecostal traditions tend to place a high value on God's revelation of Godself and God's will for humanity through experiencing God in worship. These experiences usually center on a work of the Spirit in indwelling individuals in worship. Such experiences involve unique gifting, called *charismata*, in which God's presence and power are demonstrated through some outward and graciously given sign in order to unite the rest of the congregation in loving and knowing God.[1] For instance, one member of the congregation may receive a word of prophecy from the Spirit in the midst of worship. This word might relate to some truth about God to be meditated or focused upon for a season. Or perhaps it is something particular that the congregation is being called to do. The same goes for speaking in tongues, gifts of healing, and so on; these gifts count as experiences of God that tell the congregation something about God and his will for them in a particular context or season.

One common objection to these charismatic expressions of the Christian faith is that they are valued for their theological content over and against other sources, devaluing or decentering important sources like Scripture,

1. Leidenhag, "For We All Worship," 80–81.

tradition, and reason. In extreme cases, charismaticism is accused of *replacing* the revelation of God in Scripture with these experiences.[2] As Grudem explains this objection, "To add any more words from continuing prophetic utterances would be, in effect, either to add to Scripture or to compete with Scripture. In both cases the sufficiency of Scripture itself would be challenged, and, in practice, its unique authority in our lives compromised."[3] While I am not convinced that such accusations find any purchase, defenders of charismatic worship as a source for theology are notably vague about how valued the content of these spiritual experiences is understood to be when juxtaposed with things like the Christian Scriptures, the tradition, history, reason, or other experiences that occur in the Christian life. Understanding what kind of information about God is being learned in these experiences and how that information relates to other sources of revelation or knowledge of God can better help the Christian to understand what role charismatic experiences play in building models of God and the Christian life.

The analytic philosophy of science is well positioned to help us think about the relationship between these different kinds of sources precisely because the theologians leveraging this objection already make analogies to "the data of Scripture" or "models of God" in this criticism. I thus will first lay out the role that charismatic spiritual experience plays in theological method in Pentecostal and charismatic communities, as well as this particular objection to its use in theological method. I then draw on the pragmatic representational view of data from the philosophy of science to distinguish between these sources as different kinds of data collected for different purposes and in different contexts. These distinctions will determine what role these different sources of data can play in constructing models of God, thus preserving the Protestant emphasis on the uniqueness of Scripture as a source for theology and leaving space for a role for charismatic experience. Finally, I argue for a particular role which experience of God in worship plays in model building in relation to other sources of theological data. This role need not compete with these other important sources and yet remains indispensable to theological model construction.

Understanding Gifts From the Spirit: Charismatic Spiritual Experience and Theological Method

In the first place, we need to understand what is meant by charismatic spiritual experience and the role it plays in Pentecostal and charismatic worship.

2. See for instance, Middlemiss, *Interpreting Charismatic Experience*, 24.

3. Grudem, *Systematic Theology*, 1039.

From here, it will be easier to compare that role with other sources, such as Scripture. In charismatic and Pentecostal spirituality, the gifts of the Spirit play a central role in worship and practice. Worship services give prominent space for the Holy Spirit being poured out and the congregation responding to this outpouring with the practice of the *charismata*.[4] These gifts may include healing, speaking in tongues, gifts of prophecy, or words of knowledge. These spiritual practices are important not only in the rituals of worship, but also play a prominent role in Pentecostal and charismatic theological method. One might assume that gifts of knowledge or prophecy would be especially prominent in theological methodology. After all, the Holy Spirit revealing knowledge directly to a person seems a convenient way to learn about God. However, these practices in Pentecostal and charismatic communities tend to be valued not for the knowledge or prophecy given by the Holy Spirit, but for the experience of the Holy Spirit's presence they provide.[5]

Still, it is hard to imagine a Christian spirituality so informed by practices such as prophecy and gifts of knowledge in which these practices do *not* inform theological method and the generation of theological knowledge. But the question remains, how do these practices relate to doctrinal formation? For Pentecostal and charismatic Christians, the Spirit's gifts are construed as direct experiences of God of which doctrine helps make sense. As Vondey observes, "Pentecostals have highlighted the centrality of Jesus Christ as the messiah anointed with the Holy Spirit. In turn, the outpouring of this Spirit on the world marks the proper frame for all subsequent formulations of Pentecostal doctrine."[6] When the Spirit is poured out during worship, Christians receive the Spirit's gifts and experience the presence of God.

Rather than trying to shape experiences in worship which fit already formed systems of doctrine, Pentecostal theology will often form doctrines in response to these experiences. "Pentecostal theology is born out of the need to narrate the experiences of the salvific work of God in Christ and the Spirit and to do so in terms that do justice to their experiences rather than to official formulations of doctrine."[7] Doctrine, in other words, can act as models which make sense of various information about God; for Pentecostals and charismatics it is vitally important that doctrines account accurately for these particular kinds of experiences of the Spirit being poured out.

Experience of God in particular acts or events takes a central role; what matters to our understanding of God here is how we come to know

4. Cartledge and Swoboda, *Scripting Pentecost*, 2; Vondey, *Beyond Pentecostalism*, 219.

5. See, Leidenhag, "For We All Worship," 79.

6. Vondey, *Pentecostalism*, 70.

7. Vondey, *Pentecostalism*, 71.

God through tangible encounters.[8] The Spirit can give knowledge about the world, ourselves, or something that God is calling us to through these particular gifts. But knowledge about God acquired through this outpouring is derived from the experience of what God is like in the giving of these gifts.[9] Thus, knowledge of God acquired through charismatic spiritual experiences is not limited to gifts of knowledge or prophecy. Christians experiencing gifts of healing, speaking in tongues, or any other charismatic gifting would also be experiencing the presence of God. The emphasis, therefore, on the role that these charismatic experiences play in theological methodology is on knowledge of what God is like, what it is like to experience God's presence, and what it is like to interact with God in worship.

One might, therefore, expect Scripture and other sources to have very little place in such theological models of God. If doctrine is about building models that can accurately account for these experiences, then experience seems the only sort of informational input (or perhaps, theological data) which matters in Pentecostal and charismatic theology. On the contrary, Scripture actually plays an essential role in interpreting these encounters, and can even be part of the particular word or picture given by the Spirit.[10] Vondey gives the example of Luke and Acts and the role they play in Pentecostal theology: "Most Pentecostals find in Luke-Acts, in particular, an experiential pattern for the formulation of Christian beliefs that possesses a theological integrity in its own right and which is indicative of the development of Pentecostal doctrine."[11] Scripture can serve as a specific and trusted record of experiences of God, with Gospels being the most tangible instances of encountering God in human flesh.

On the one hand, we only know that these experiences of the Spirit in worship need to be accounted for in our doctrinal models of God because of the experiences chronicled in Scripture and how they inform early believers' understanding of God. On the other, because these chronicled experiences are a trusted basis for our own today, the doctrinal models of God based on current experiences of the Spirit in worship need to also align with this trusted chronicle of experiences.[12] This is further evidenced by the role that Scripture often plays in charismatic experiences, such as when the Spirit gives a particular passage of Scripture to a worshiper as part of a prophetic

8. Warrington, *Pentecostal Theology*, 17–27; Miller and Yamamori, *Global Pentecostalism*, 129–59.

9. Vondey, *Beyond Pentecostalism*, 43–44.

10. Leidenhag, "For We All Worship," 79.

11. Vondey, *Pentecostalism*, 70.

12. Vondey, *Pentecostalism*, 88–89.

word or gift of knowledge. Experiential knowledge of God acquired in these instances begs to be aligned with depiction of God from the text. It would not make sense for God to give experiential knowledge of himself that contradicts the prophetic word being given. The kind of experiential knowledge of God acquired in charismatic spiritual experiences already aligns itself with the Protestant emphasis on the authority of Scripture.

If these charismatic experiences of God in worship are not obviously contradictory to the knowledge of God acquired from Scripture, than how do these two kinds of sources fit together in theological method? If these experiences do not conflict with the authority of Scripture, are they simply repeating knowledge already acquired from Scripture? Or are they adding something to the knowledge of God acquired through Scripture?

These questions lie at the heart of the objection to the use of charismatic spiritual experiences in theological method explored below. To answer these questions and address this objection, we first need to establish what it is that we think charismatic spiritual experiences actually do to increase our knowledge and understanding of God. If Pentecostal and charismatic theology formulates doctrine in ways that consciously account for these experiences, what do these experiences bring to the table of doing theology that we wouldn't have otherwise?

In a basic sense, charismatic and Pentecostal worship is meant to cultivate our relationship with God. This is probably true of most worship, in point of fact, not just charismatic or Pentecostal worship. As Benton puts it,

> If we suppose that learning how to do all of [these worship activities] involves learning the practical skill of relating to God through such practices, and that cultivating such practices is part of how one learns to recognize God's responsive actions to us, we can think of liturgy as facilitating both perceptual recognition and personal knowledge-how, and ultimately, interpersonal knowledge.[13]

Worship, in other words, is meant to cultivate our knowledge of what God is like (knowledge by acquaintance), how to interact with God (knowledge-how), or knowledge through personal interaction (interpersonal knowledge). This lines up with how charismatic and Pentecostal Christians perceive their own worship activities. In charismatic worship, "the 'common sense' understanding of participants was that, with reference to the Spirit, it was God who was being addressed and God who acted among the worshiping congregation."[14] Charismatic and Pentecostal Christians experiencing

13. Benton, "God and Interpersonal Knowledge," 17–18.

14. Steven, *Worship in the Spirit*, 178.

the Spirit's presence are, at least by their own lights, interacting with God in a personal and practical way. Leidenhag makes this argument particularly about charismatic spiritual experiences, arguing that "charismatic gifts may be a means of gaining second-personal knowledge of the Holy Spirit as well as of fellow human participants, which enables greater unity within the gathered community."[15] Leidenhag's uses the example of a gift of knowledge given to one member of the congregation for the benefit of another to show how these gifts provide opportunities to not just learn new facts about God—which we would call propositional knowledge—but to come to know God and other worshipers better through interpersonal interaction. This kind of interpersonal knowledge, whether construed as acquaintance, practical knowledge, or something unique to the knowledge of persons, may be the key to understanding the role that charismatic spiritual experience ought to play in theological methodology.

Competing Sources: The Sourcehood Objection to Charismatic Gifts and Experience as a Source for Theology

Since these charismatic experiences of God are in fact treated as sources in theology, something which systems of doctrine ought to account for, then it will help our purposes to clearly outline at least one objection to the use of these experiences as theological source. Addressing this objection will help to clarify how charismatics and Pentecostals can and should use charismatic experiences in theological methodology. While there are many objections to the *practice* of charismatic gifts, it is the particular objection that these experiences undermine biblical authority that interests this essay. Addressing this objection, while beneficial in its own right for Pentecostal and charismatic communities, ultimately serves to elucidate the distinctive roles that both Scripture and experience can play in theological methodology.

The objection that the use of charismatic gifts, particularly those which might include God revealing something to believers such as gifts of prophecy or knowledge, undermines biblical authority has its origins in B. B. Warfield's *Counterfeit Miracles*,[16] but has undergone development and challenge since.[17] In brief, this objection to the use of charismatic gifts argues that they constitute a revelatory alternative to the source of Scripture

15. Leidenhag, "For We All Worship," 79.

16. Warfield, *Counterfeit Miracles*, 27.

17. Ruthven, *On the Cessation of the Charismata*, 76.

in theological method which at best undermines the sufficiency of Scripture and at worse replaces the role of Scripture entirely. As Gaffin argues, "While [Pentecostal and charismatic theology] affirms the authority of Scripture, it denies its sufficiency. Or, to be fairer, their view has an inadequate and too restricted understanding of its sufficiency."[18] In his interpretation of Pentecostal theological method, Gaffin takes the reliance on the gifts of the Spirit for revelation to violate one of the four principles of a Protestant doctrine of Scripture. If Scripture alone is sufficient revelation of who God is, he reasons, than why should we need any additional revelation through prophecy or words of knowledge?

On Gaffin's reading of Pentecostal doctrines of Scripture, Scripture is but one source among many—the constant invocation of the Spirit to come and give gifts indicates a reliance on these gifts for knowledge of God rather than on Scripture. When Pentecostals and charismatics pray in an open sense for the Spirit to come during worship, we fail to ascertain the appropriate limits of the Spirit's work today. According to Gaffin, the proper limits of the Spirit's revelatory or illuminative work today is in the Spirit's leading us towards or in reflection on Scripture: "Prayer is not a blank check . . . the desire to speak in tongues and to receive other revelatory word gifts would become appropriate only after it could first be convincingly established by sound, Spirit-led reflection on Scripture, that God intends for these gifts today."[19] In other words, according to this particular criticism of charismatic and Pentecostal worship, God's revelation through words, prophecy, or gifts of knowledge, can at most be a reiteration of Scripture's revelation of God. Otherwise, they would be additional to Scripture in a way that questions its sufficiency. Any "additional revelations" to Scripture are by definition redundant or a challenge to sufficiency.

More extreme versions of this objection also exist, though these are not typically defended with rigorous arguments or evidence. Appealing to the "slippery slope" of slight theological deviations from the sole authority of Scripture, popular author John MacArthur argues that "the uniqueness and central authority of the Word have thus been lost, and charismatics have developed a mystical brand of Christianity that may eventually have little biblical content or substance."[20] On this stronger, more populist account of theological knowledge imparted through charismatic gifts, charismatic and Pentecostal Christians have replaced the authority of Scripture entirely with personal revelations given by the Spirit.

18. Gaffin, "Cessationist Conclusion," 337.

19. Gaffin, "Cessationist Conclusion," 336.

20. MacArthur, *Charismatic Chaos*, 83.

At stake in this objection, whether in stronger or weaker form, is the fear that use of charismatic experience as a source in theology supplants the role of Scripture in theology. The stronger form probably fails because Pentecostal and charismatic Christians also use Scripture in their theology, often in conjunction with charismatic experiences like a word of knowledge that includes reference to a particular Scripture. So at face value, Pentecostals and charismatics do not see an obvious competition between the authority of Scripture and the role of charismatic experience in theology. But if these sources are not competing with one another, then how is it that charismatic experience can be drawn upon in a non-redundant way without challenging the sufficiency of Scripture.

Baked into this objection seems to be an assumption about the sufficiency of Scripture which has not been adequately questioned: for what purpose is Scripture sufficient? This objection appears to assume that Scripture and charismatic experience play the same function or contribute the same kind of knowledge to theological understanding. This assumption about the sufficiency of Scripture has been addressed by non-charismatic Christians wrestling with the relationship between Scripture and tradition, reason, and other domains of inquiry such as the natural sciences and psychology. Vanhoozer, for instance, argues for reasonable limits to the sufficiency Scripture set by its purpose: Scripture is sufficient "ruling the church's social imaginary" and "understanding extra-biblical knowledge in the framework of biblical narrative," but probably won't tell us much about clinical psychology or string theory.[21] If Scripture's sufficiency is for a particular purpose in knowing God, than perhaps it is the case that charismatic experiences serve a different purpose or function in the generation of theological knowledge. Scripture and experience, in other words, might provide different kinds of input in theological method.

Experience as Theological Data Fit for Purpose

This way of treating charismatic experiences as providing valuable input for theological models of God and the Christian life would benefit greatly from engagement with the philosophy of science, particularly from engaging philosophies of data and how data helps us build models of reality. Insofar as we are treating Scripture and charismatic experiences as different kinds of inputs into theological method which might serve different functions in the generation of knowledge about the divine, we can make an analogy to scriptural and experiential "data" which matches the common of analogy of

21. Vanhoozer, "Sufficiency of Scripture," 218–19.

treating systems of doctrine like scientific "models" of God. Models, in this sense, serve as systemic explanations of the information, whether scriptural or otherwise, gathered about a phenomenon or object in the world, in this case, God. It seems at least intuitively the case that charismatic and Pentecostal traditions of the Christian faith treat spiritual experiences *as well as other sources* as valuable data for knowing who God is and how to love him. However, these various sources appear to be treated as different kinds data relevant for different purposes.[22] By better understanding what kind of data these spiritual experiences count as and how different kinds of data should relate to one another, we can better understand the role they play in theological model-building. For this, we will turn to the philosophy of science and how it helps us to better understand the relationship between data of different kinds and explanatory models.

So what do we mean by data and how do they help us to build models? There is some debate among philosophers of science as to exactly what data is, and the view one takes has a significant impact on how one uses data to build models. On the one hand, there is the assumption that data is "given"; that we simply encounter data out in the world in raw form and build models to help us make sense of that data.[23] So in a geology lab, the rocks collected for study simply are the data, and geologists build models of, say, a geological process which explains how the rocks came to be the way they are. Data simply exists, and the best model builder is the one who best explains the data.

But this explanation of data and how they work to build models isn't how most scientists work when they study natural phenomena. Scientists usually collect and record data for a specific purpose, and that purpose shapes the record of observations. For instance, a geologist studying the density of the particular rock probably won't record much about the color or size of the rock. There could be a range of colors and sizes, but these probably won't make it into the scientist's charts and graphs when reporting their findings; they will focus instead on the relevant factors of their study like density and how the rock responds to pressure. And thus, any scientists drawing on this study for their own work would get an abstracted or edited version of the data fit for the purpose it was collected. Scientists aren't being dishonest when they do this, but are trying to communicate clearly and effectively for the purpose of their study.

Thus, Bokulich and Watkins instead argue for a representational view of data, defining it "as *records* of a process of inquiry involving a physical

22. Fee, *Empowering Presence*, 164; Yong, *Spirit Poured Out*, 294.

23. Bokulich and Watkins, "Data Models," 214.

interaction between the researcher, measuring instrument, and the world: it is only the results of observations or measurements performed . . . that count as data. . . . Data necessarily involve a level of abstraction. Data involve replacing the thing in the world with a number, a photograph, or a recorded description."[24] Data is always collected with a purpose and that purpose always shapes the record of the data in some fashion.

Certainly, scientists will collect and keep what is often called "raw data," which may include irrelevant information like the color and size of the rock from our geologist example (perhaps they will photograph each rock used in the study). But even this distinction between raw and processed data is often questioned. As Bokulich and Watkins observe,

> Such immediate outputs are not yet in a form that is useable by scientists. This can occur for a wide variety of reasons: first, the data-collection process might involve some obvious errors resulting in a certain portion of "bad" data that should be excluded from the data set; second, there could be a source of "noise" in the data signal that needs to be filtered out or subtracted; third, the output of the instrument might be of a quantity (measurand) that is closely related, but not identical, to the data quantity of interest, and hence must be converted before being useful; fourth, data are often discrete samples of a continuous quantity, hence need to be smoothed or interpolated; and, fifth, data often need to be organized or ordered before patterns can emerge.[25]

In other words, the data that scientists use has always been processed in some way, from the instruments measuring it to organizing it into something that can meaningfully be modelled. So while there is some meaningful sense in which we might refer to "raw" data as being uninterpreted or neutral, pragmatically we never really use data in this way.

Most important for our purposes is Bokulich's and Watkins's third observation about "raw" data. Across all their observations, but especially this third one, is a recognition that the data is collected in an attempt to make sense of a particular phenomenon and build an explanatory model that can account for the data. This is, practically, how data is used. Scientists rarely walk out into the world with a handful of instruments just to take in information at random which can later be used to build a comprehensive model of the world. Scientists engage in careful, controlled experiments designed to isolate one or two features of the thing they are studying with a mind for building a coherent model to explain the observations of those features.

24. Bokulich and Watkins, "Data Models," 213.

25. Bokulich and Watkins, "Data Models," 216.

Data, in other words, is collected with model-building in mind. So not only is data best understood as representational, but it is pragmatic in the way that it is collected.

This pragmatic view of data as a representation of things out in the world—aptly named the pragmatic representational view of data—was developed by Alisa Bokulich and Wendy Parker to account for the purposefulness of data collection.[26] Data, they argue, is always collected a certain way with a certain goal in mind. They write, "What data are taken to provide evidence about can change from context to context, depending on the interests, background knowledge, and other resources available to researchers."[27] The process of inquiry and the reason for which the data is being collected determine to some extent the adequacy of that data for a given purpose.[28] Data is always collected by an instrument or observer for a specific purpose, and those factors will limit for what the data can be used. This is true first and foremost because

> even "raw" data are "made" through a process of inquiry, which itself is often carefully and deliberately designed . . . data are the product of an *interaction* between a measuring device (or observer) and the world, and that both these, along with background conditions and the means by which data are recorded, can influence the content and character of the data produced. Data collection procedures are often carefully designed to manage these interactions so that sought-after information is obtained.[29]

Let us be clear: Bokulich and Parker are not advocating a radically subjective view of data in which "data are purely made-in-the-mind" but simply demonstrating that a sense of "raw data" in which the data itself is contextless with regards to its collection simply doesn't exist.[30] Neither do they mean that data can only be used for its original collection purpose. Rather, the value of the data is judged based on "whether they represent their targets with *sufficient* accuracy in the respects that are *relevant*, given the *purpose* at hand. What matters, on this view, is that a model is *adequate for the purpose of interest*."[31] By analogy, our theological "data" ought to be viewed with

26. See the definition of data as minimally representational and drawn from particular forms of inquiry offered by Bokulich and Parker, "Data Models," 31.

27. Bokulich and Parker, "Data Models," 30.

28. Leonelli, "What Distinguishes Data," 22.

29. Bokulich and Parker, "Data Models," 35.

30. Bokulich and Parker, "Data Models," 40–41.

31. Bokulich and Parker, "Data Models," 32.

respect for the context in and purpose for which it is collected, even if that original context is not the particular purpose for which we are using said data.

This would allow us to distinguish between the kinds of data that spiritual experiences, Scripture, and other theological data are by highlighting their adequacy for various purposes. A particular charismatic experience may seem very adequate for building a model of the Holy Spirit's work in the world today, but might be less helpful for building a model of, say, the hypostatic union. Analyzing the adequacy of charismatic experiences for various purposes will help us to better understand how it ought to function as data in theological work. More importantly, we might better be able to distinguish it from other kinds of theological data like Scripture and leave space for Scripture to be sufficient for a particular context and purpose.

Purposeful Spiritual Experience: Rethinking the Role of Charismatic Experiences in Theological Method

This way of viewing Scripture and charismatic spiritual experience as different kinds of theological data fit for particular purposes promises some interesting challenges for how we think about theological methodology and model-building. First, if taken seriously, the pragmatic representational view of data challenges approaches to the sufficiency of Scripture that view its sufficiency without limits or attempts to treat *prima facie* readings of the Bible as "raw data." All data, even Scripture, is delivered to us interpreted and commented through the eyes of others. As McCaulley observes in his defense of an African American hermeneutic, "Everybody has been reading the Bible from their own locations, but [black theologians and biblical scholars] are just honest about it."[32] Most theologians read the Bible in their own language, meaning it has come to them "processed" through the work of a translator. But even the ambitious theologian who reads in the original Hebrew and Greek is usually reading compiled manuscripts that have simplified complexities and inconsistencies across copies of manuscripts, and is coming to the text with particular questions, concerns, and assumptions.

Second, Scripture itself is already used in a way reflective of the pragmatic representative approach to data; it is "collected" differently for different purposes. Biblical scholars, for instance, are usually interested in using the text of Scripture to get into the minds of ancient Hebrew and first-century authors to explain what they meant to their original audience. Systematic and constructive theologians, on the other hand, will have more

32. McCaulley, *Reading While Black*, 20.

interest in how the words of ancient authors apply to Christians today, and historical theologians will often look at how Scripture was used by previous generations of Christians. So Scripture itself is already collected in a variety of pragmatic ways which are fit for a particular purpose. And it seems that these purposes are what we ought to think Scripture is sufficient for.

Third, this leaves room for other kinds of data to be collected for other purposes which might aid the task of theology without undermining the sufficiency of Scripture for its particular purposes. Suppose we take the earlier example of Scripture being a trusted record of early Christians' experiences of the Holy Spirit against which to measure our own practices and experiences—it may be sufficient for other purposes too, but it is at least fit and sufficient for this purpose. This would mean that the kind of experiential knowledge of God acquired through interactions with the presence of the Spirit in charismatic worship is neither attempting to accomplish the same purpose, nor is it fit for that purpose. In fact, many charismatic and Pentecostal traditions have ways of testing a particular revelation from God given in worship, and caution humility and discernment in the exercising of gifts of knowledge and prophecy.[33] Such experiences do not seem to hold the same amount of trust as the chronicle of experiences of the Spirit held in Scripture. At a pragmatic level, charismatic spiritual experience functions differently from Scripture, and even relies on it in order to accomplish its purpose.

So what is this distinct purpose for which charismatic spiritual experience is fit? As already alluded, charismatic worship seems to be focused on tangible encounter with the Holy Spirit that cultivates relationship with God. I have argued with Joshua Cockayne elsewhere that worship is unique in the way that it cultivates relationship with God, and thus plays an indispensable role in the task of theology by giving us knowledge of how to interact with God.[34] So where Scripture seems to give us facts or truths about God and the narrative of salvation history, or perhaps tells us about God's relationship with his people in the past, charismatic spiritual experiences give us a personal kind of knowledge about God in the here and now. Where this may be guided, or even limited, by reflection on Scripture, it seems a distinct kind of knowledge.

So what kind of knowledge are we generating in worship distinct from the particular purposes for which Scripture is sufficient? This seems to be not factual knowledge—for example, direct revelations about God delivered by the Spirit—but a personal or practical knowledge that cultivates our

33. For instance, Wimber and Wimber, *Everyone Gets to Play*, 154.

34. Everhart and Cockayne, *Engaging Liturgy*, 13.

relationship with the same God described in Scripture. One way of delineating these kinds of knowledge is the distinction between propositional and personal knowledge. Propositional knowledge is sometimes referred to as "knowledge-that"; it is knowledge associated with facts or propositions which we may know to be true or false.[35] This does not seem to be the kind of knowledge we acquire in charismatic experiences. Certainly, propositions are being acquired, typically in the content of the word of knowledge or prophecy given. But the role that these experiences play in theological method seems to be more focused on the interaction with the Spirit's presence and what it tells us about how we interact with God, rather than on the content of word given.

In contrast, personal knowledge or interpersonal knowledge is the kind of knowledge that we have of other persons. "Roughly, interpersonal knowledge is had when two individuals know each other personally, as subjects, from the second-person perspective."[36] Interpersonal knowledge is usually distinguished from propositional knowledge in the following way: I can know a lot of propositions or facts about a celebrity by reading their Wikipedia page, but this is different than how I know a close personal friend; I know facts about that friend, but I also know how to interact with them, or how they might respond to something I do.[37] There is something pragmatic about personal knowledge which cultivates the relationship between persons that propositional knowledge does not share. It might be the case that Scripture gives us both propositions about God and about God's relationship with his people throughout salvation history. And it might be that this kind of knowledge will aid us in our cultivation of relationship with God in worship, especially as a trusted account of relationship with God against which to check our own experiences. But Scripture does not directly do the same kind of thing that the data of charismatic experience does. It is fit for a different purpose.

That purpose seems to be to cultivate relationship with God, thus to give us a personal knowledge of what God is like and how we relate to or interact with him. What role would such personal knowledge, then, play in theological method? Again, this seems to be distinct from the role played by Scripture as a trusted chronicle of salvation history and God's relationship with his people in the past. First, we could characterize the role of this personal knowledge in terms of acquaintance. Knowledge by acquaintance is distinguished from knowledge-that or propositional knowledge by

35. Benton, "Epistemology Personalized," 820–21.

36. Benton, "God and Interpersonal Knowledge," 1.

37. Everhart and Cockayne, *Engaging Liturgy*, 12.

signalling the qualitative difference between having facts about something and having a first-person experience of it. Stump uses the example of Mary, who, never having met her mother, knows *that* she has a mother and *that* her mother loves her, but comes to know something new in meeting her mother and experiencing that love first hand.[38] Stump argues that Mary's awareness of her mother's love prior to meeting her is distinct from Mary's direct experience of that love. She writes, "Mary's mind is opened to all that we learn and experience in face-to-face contact, the complex give-and-take of personal interactions."[39] So it might be that charismatic experience adds to our propositional knowledge of God the knowledge of what God's presence is like during worship. We can read about that presence in Scripture, but we can add to our understanding by actually experiencing the Spirit's outpouring and its effects during worship.

Another way to characterize this contribution of personal knowledge is as practical knowledge, or knowledge-how. Cuneo makes the distinction between propositional and practical knowledge by distinguishing how they get "upgraded." Knowledge-that can be upgraded to certainty, whereas knowledge-how gets upgraded to mastery instead. For instance, it makes sense to say, "I not only know *that your mother's maiden name is 'Smith,' but I'm also certain of it*," but it does not make sense to say "I not only know how to perform [the musical piece] 'Giant Steps,' I am also certain of it."[40] Instead, we would say that we know how to perform "Giant Steps" well. In the case of relationships, practical knowledge involves growing in understanding how to interact with another person. So by worshiping God and partaking in the gifts of the Spirit, we are learning through experience how to better interact with God. This is another way that charismatic experiences can cultivate relationship with God in a way distinct from the role of Scripture. Scripture can tell us how others have interacted with God, or how we *should* interact with God, but it cannot cause us to grow in the practical knowledge of interacting with God. That can only come through practice.

We need not commit ourselves to both or either of these ways of understanding the personal knowledge acquired in charismatic spiritual experience in order to show that such experiences can act as a different kind of data than Scripture in theological method. These data have been collected, interpreted, and are even used for distinct purposes for which they are adequately fit. There is room for both to play a role in theological method without charismatic spiritual experiences undermining the sufficiency of

38. Stump, *Wandering in Darkness*, 50–53.

39. Stump, *Wandering in Darkness*, 53.

40. Cuneo, "Ritual Knowledge," 371.

the role scriptural data plays in theology; Scripture is sufficient for its role, and need not be in competition with the role of experience. I have proposed two ways of characterizing a distinct role for charismatic spiritual experience in cultivating relationship with God through worship, but there may indeed be more.

Conclusion

In treating charismatic spiritual experience and Scripture as data, we come to understand that each is fit for a particular purpose or purposes. Those purposes shape the role that each kind of data plays in theological method. Good theology, like good science, can attempt to account for both data sets, while recognizing that the sets are collected for distinct and mutually beneficial purposes. But this does not mean that theology must collapse the data sets, or that one data set is somehow better than another. It only means that there are reasonable limits to how each data set can be used without further work of recontextualizing and translating those sets across contexts and purposes. Scripture, as a particular and unique authority in Protestant Christianity, need not be set in competition with charismatic spiritual experience.

Rather, I have proposed that Scripture can be treated as a propositional data set intended specific purposes, such as being a trusted chronicle of God's people and their experiences of God. This trusted data set is fit for the purpose of being a "norm that norms": experiences of God and propositions about him against which we might check our own experiences of God. This need not compete with the purpose for which charismatic experiences are fit: these experiences can provide us with practical or personal knowledge of what God is like and how we should interact with his presence. Where Scripture can provide a trusted guide for knowing about God and his story with his people, charismatic spiritual experience provides us with personal knowledge of God through worship that cultivates relationship with him.

Maintaining this distinction is important, even where Scripture provides the content for charismatic spiritual experience (such as words of knowledge referencing particular passages), and at other times the act of reading Scripture can be the occasion for an experiential encounter with the Holy Spirit (such as reading a particular passage leading a spontaneous worship). So even though both kinds of theological data can overlap, this distinction regarding their purposes in granting different kinds of knowledge helps us to see how they relate to one another harmoniously.

In considering the role that theological data play in model-building, it seems intuitively the case that both kinds of data and the purposes for which they are fit belong in the task of theology. Theology should seek to make propositional claims about God which align with his history with the ancient Hebrews and early Christians, but it should also seek to understand what God is like and how we should relate to him in worship. Both have a proper place in the task of theology, in how we know and relate to God. This tells us not only that charismatic spiritual experience has a role to play in theology, but suggests that it has a particular role to play in informing how we relate to God through the outpouring of the Holy Spirit.

Bibliography

Benton, Matthew. "Epistemology Personalized." *The Philosophical Quarterly* 67 (2017) 813–34.

———. "God and Interpersonal Knowledge." *Res Philosophica* 95 (2018) 421–47.

Bokulich, Alisa, and Aja Watkins. "Data Models." In *SAGE Encyclopedia of Theory in Science, Technology, Engineering, and Mathematics*, edited by James Mattingly, 214–22. Thousand Oaks, CA: SAGE: 2022.

Bokulich, Alisa, and Wendy Parker. "Data Models, Representation, and Adequacy-For-Purpose." *General Philosophy of Science* 11 (2021) 1–26.

Cartledge, M. J., and A. J., Swoboda, eds. *Scripting Pentecost: A Study of Pentecostals, Worship, and Liturgy*. London: Routledge, 2016.

Castillo Brache, Leticia, and Alisa Bokulich. "Models, Data Models, and Big Data." In *The Routledge Handbook of Philosophy of Scientific Modeling*, edited by Tarja Knuuttila et al., 245–55. Abingdon: Routledge, 2024.

Cuneo, Terence. "Ritual Knowledge." *Faith and Philosophy* 31 (2014) 365–85.

Everhart, D. T., and Joshua Cockayne. *Engaging Liturgy Engaging, God, Community, and Tradition*. Eugene, OR: Cascade, forthcoming.

Fee, Gordon. *Empowering Presence: The Holy Spirit in the Letters of Paul*. Grand Rapids: Baker Academic, 2009.

Gaffin, Richard. "A Cessationist Conclusion." In *Are Miraculous Gifts for Today? Four Views*, edited by Wayne Grudem, 334–40. Downers Grove, IL: InterVarsity, 1996.

Grudem, Wayne. *Systematic Theology: An Introduction to Biblical Doctrine*. Grand Rapids: InterVarsity, 1994.

Leidenhag, Joanna. "For We All Worship in One Spirit." *Theologica* 4 (2020) 64–87.

Leonelli, Sabina. "What Distinguishes Data From Models?" *European Journal for Philosophy of Science* 11 (2021) 1–27.

MacArthur, John. *Charismatic Chaos*. Nashville: Thomas Nelson, 1993.

McCaulley, Esau. *Reading While Black: African American Biblical Interpretation as an Exercise in Hope*. Downers Grove, IL: IVP Academic, 2020.

Middlemiss, David. *Interpreting Charismatic Experience*. London: SCM, 2012.

Miller, Donald, and Tetsunao Yamamori. *Global Pentecostalism: The New Face of Christian Social Engagement*. Oakland, CA: University of California Press, 2007.

Ruthven, Jon Mark. *On the Cessation of the Charismata: On the Protestant Polemic on Post-Biblical Miracles*. Tulsa, OK: Lord and Spirit, 2011.

Steven, James H. S. *Worship in the Spirit: Charismatic Worship in the Church of England*. Elizabethton, TN: Send the Light, 2003.

Stump, Eleanore. *Wandering in Darkness: Narrative and the Problem of Suffering*. Oxford: Oxford University Press, 2010.

Vanhoozer, Kevin J. "The Sufficiency of Scripture: A Critical and Construction Account." *Journal of Psychology and Theology* 49 (2021) 218–34.

Vondey, Wolfgang. *Beyond Pentecostalism: The Crisis of Global Christianity and the Renewal of the Theological Agenda*. Grand Rapids: Eerdmans, 2010.

———. *Pentecostalism: A Guide for the Perplexed*. Edinburgh: T&T Clark, 2012.

Warfield, B. B. *Counterfeit Miracles*. Edinburgh: Banner of Truth, 1976.

Warrington, Keith. *Pentecostal Theology: A Theology of Encounter*. Edinburgh: T&T Clark, 2008.

Wimber, John, and Christy Wimber. *Everyone Gets to Play*. Garden City, ID: Ampelon, 2013.

Yong, Amos. *The Spirit Poured Out on All Flesh: Pentecostalism and the Possibility of Global Theology*. Grand Rapids: Baker, 2005.

4

Analytic Theology and African Pentecostal Epistemology

An African Christological Reflection

CLIFTON R. CLARKE

In this chapter,[1] I aim to put analytic theology in conversation with Pentecostal theology. My primary focus will be on African Pentecostal epistemology—including its manifestations and expressions in the black transatlantic world—and the methods of analytic theology. I aim to facilitate a dialogue between analytic and African Pentecostal theology, specifically emphasizing Christology. This exploration demonstrates how African Pentecostal theology and epistemology can provide constructive critique, engagement, and insights into analytic theology.

I will not rehearse the rise and merits of analytic theology here as its proponents have done so extensively elsewhere.[2] My engagement with analytic theology through the lens of African Pentecostal theology and epistemology will involve examining the five prescriptions (5P) that Michael

1. Scripture quotations in this chapter are taken from the New International Version.

2 Plantinga and Wolterstorff, *Faith and Rationality*; Lindbeck, *Nature of Doctrine*; Morris, *Divine and Human Action*; Crisp and Rea, *Analytic Theology*; Crisp, *Retrieving Doctrine*.

Rea outlines as characteristics of analytic philosophy's rhetorical approach.[3] Since analytic philosophy is the epistemic foundation upon which analytic theology stands, understanding its rhetorical tendencies is essential for a thorough critique of analytic theology.

> P1. Sentential Formulation: The assumption that philosophical positions and conclusions can be captured in sentences suitable for logical analysis and manipulation.
> P2. Clarity and Precision: The prioritization of clear definitions, unambiguity, and rigorous logical coherence.
> P3. Minimal Metaphor: Avoid metaphors and tropes where the semantic content extends beyond direct propositional meaning.
> P4. Conceptual Foundations: Building arguments upon well-understood primitive concepts or concepts rigorously definable in those terms.
> P5. Conceptual Analysis as Evidence: Employing the analysis of concepts as a primary source of evidence for philosophical conclusions.

Before I proceed, two key caveats are worth noting. First, it is not my intention in this critique to portray analytic theology as a form of sterile rationalism or rigid reductionism; I am aware that there are inroads to addressing more nuanced approaches that transcend the rational-mystical dichotomy. Scholars like Sarah Coakley, for example, advocate for incorporating insights from mystical traditions and religious experiences into analytic theology.[4] In addition to Coakley's contribution, other innovative areas within analytics are exploring ways to integrate diverse knowledge production forms. For instance, some scholars are drawing on insights from virtue ethics and narrative theology to expand the scope of analytic theological inquiry.[5] Additionally, there is growing interest in exploring the intersections of theology and science, including biological theology and the cognitive science of religion.[6] I mentioned these areas of innovation—and there are many others—within analytic theological developments because they portray far more sophisticated and complex approaches to analytic theology than a cursory engagement might give it credit. These areas of expansion and enlargement are not overlooked in this critique; they open further avenues for dialogue and interchange with African Pentecostal theology and epistemology. While these insights provide the breadth and

3. Rea, "Introduction," 3–4.

4 Coakley, "Dark Contemplation," 280–312.

5. For an example of virtue ethics in theology, see Hauerwas, *Character of Virtue*.

6 Haught, *God After Darwin*.

diversity of analytic theology, analytic theology remains a Western rationalistic theology deeply rooted in the Enlightenment tradition.

My second caveat is that it is crucial for us to distinguish between the non-rational (an aspect of faith transcending pure reason) and the irrational (which contradicts logic or evidence) within theology.[7] While this is not the time to explore this in grave detail, understanding the roots of analytic theology requires grappling with the misconception that rationality is an exclusively Western phenomenon or invention. Ancient African civilizations such as Egypt demonstrated sophisticated analytical systems of thought that appeared long before the rise of classical Greece.[8] Their written records and pursuit of knowledge across science, ethics, and religion reveal highly sophisticated empirical and philosophical traditions.[9] Philosophical discourse has deep roots in Africa, particularly among civilizations such as ancient Egypt, in which sophisticated thought systems emerged long before the modern Western distinctions between rational and irrational were formulated. African philosophy (and, by extension, African Pentecostal epistemology) operates on a more integrated level, transcending mere rationality to encompass a profound understanding of meaning-making in the world.

P1. Sentential Formulation

Let's begin with Rea's first claim about the analytical method, namely, philosophical positions and conclusions can be adequately formulated sentences that can be formalized and logically manipulated.[10] Sentential formulation, a cornerstone of analytic theology, asserts that written sentences can capture philosophical truths.[11] The idea that sentential formulation can capture philosophical truth has been well-attested among philosophers.[12] The notion that philosophical or theological truths are confined to sentences on a page and can be unlocked solely by decoding sentential meaning contrasts sharply with Pentecostal beliefs. For Pentecostals, truth is primarily rooted in personal experience rather than abstract reasoning or textual analysis

7. For a deeper exploration of the non-rational/irrational distinction, see, Hick, *Interpretation of Religion*.

8. To explore the Egyptian mystery religion, see Assmann's *Search for God*.

9. One example is the Rhind Mathematical Papyrus, demonstrating advanced Egyptian mathematical concepts: Imhausen, *Mathematics in Ancient Egypt*.

10. McCall, *Invitation to Analytic Christian Theology*, 17.

11. See Rea's discussions of sentential formulation in *World Without Design*.

12. See, Wittgenstein, *Tractatus Logico-Philosophicus*; Russell, *Principles of Mathematics*; Ayer, *Language, Truth, and Logic*; Carnap, *Logical Structure of the World*.

and is akin to a more mystical approach to theology than dogmatic prolegomena.[13] Jürgen Moltmann captures this well when he notes,

> Mystical theology aims to be wisdom drawn from experience, not doctrinal wisdom. It is not the theology that is mystical. It is mystical only because it tries to put mystical experience in words. By mystical, we do not mean exceptional supernatural experiences here. We suggest the intensity of the experience of God in faith, so in this sense, we are talking about the deep dimension of every experience of faith. Mystical experiences cannot be conveyed through doctrinal tenets. So, the theology of mystical experience always talks only about the way, the journey, the crossing over to that unutterable experience of God that no one can tell or communicate.[14]

Written doctrine and theological propositions undoubtedly play a significant role in Pentecostal theology, but the personal experience with God precedes and informs any doctrinal formulation. For Pentecostals, the encounter and experience with the Holy Spirit are foundational starting points for understanding and articulating truth.[15] Pentecostal theology does not begin with an encounter with words on a page but with encountering God through the power of the Holy Spirit. The sentential formulation is the corollary of an encounter with God. When sentential formulations are the starting point of theological construction, the words fall to the ground and are lifeless. Jesus said it best:

> It is the Spirit that gives life; the flesh profits nothing; the words that I speak to you are Spirit, and they are life. (John 6:63)

Before theological formulation can be "captured in sentences," it must itself be precipitated by the divine encounter. This idea of encounter is a point of departure between Pentecostal theology, particularly in the Global South, and other forms of theology. Keith Warrington, the author of *Pentecostal Theology: A Theology of Encounter*, notes,

> That which is central to their [Pentecostals] faith and practice are the concepts of "encounter" and "experience." They aim to know God experientially, whether via an intellectual recognition of his being or an emotional appreciation of his character. This often makes them functionally different within the Christian tradition. . . . Indeed, Pentecostal theology may be best

13. Albrecht and Howard, "Pentecostal Spirituality," 235–53.

14. Moltmann, *Spirit of Life*, 198.

15. Warrington, *Pentecostal Theology*; Land, *Pentecostal Spirituality*, 32.

> identified as a theology of encounter—encounter with God, the Bible, and the community.[16]

Veli-Matti Kärkkäinen notes, "Any theological formulation can hardly capture the essence of Pentecostalism; spirituality and spiritual experience is primary."[17] Scott Ellington adds, "It is not a teaching which must be believed or a proof which can be deduced and defended against all challenges, but a God who must be reckoned with in direct encounter.[18]

Pentecostal theologian Wolfgang Vondey states it well in this extended quote from his book *Pentecostal Theology: Living the Full Gospel*:

> Because it traverses a spirituality manifested in a foundational experience of the Holy Spirit, Pentecostal theology cannot simply use doctrine as an end of theology disassociated from the original experience. In other words, Pentecostal theology does not seek doctrine as an end. Still, it upholds the possibility of the continuing actualization of the encounter with God, which makes articulating the experience as doctrine principally unnecessary.[19]

The sentential formulation does not capture "truth," for Pentecostal truth is captured by the encounter that is subsequently expressed through sentential articulation.

Sentential Formulation and African Pentecostal Christology

As I have noted above, Pentecostal theology takes the personal encounter with the Holy Spirit as a starting point in contrast to the sentential approach of analytical theology. However, African Pentecostalism and black Pentecostalism across the black transatlantic world represent an even more extreme focus on encounter and experience, prioritizing direct, personal encounters with the divine to a greater extent than Western Pentecostal approaches. In another work, I have argued that the African Pentecostal theological method is characterized by the "call and response" where I define call-and-response as an ongoing dialectic between the Holy Spirit (the call) and the existential experience of African people (the response).[20] African Pentecostal theology contrasts with Western sentential theological

16. Warrington, *Pentecostal Theology*, 21.
17. Kärkkäinen, "Pentecostal Theological Education," 13.
18. Ellington, "Pentecostalism and the Authority of Scripture," 17.
19. Vondey, *Pentecostal Theology*, 12.
20. Clarke, *Pentecostal Theology in Africa*, 28.

approaches in two essential areas: the *emphasis on experience rather than formal analysis* and the *abstract rather than the concrete.*

First, experience versus formal analysis. Whereas the analytic approach theology adopts a more formal study, prioritizing logical structure and formal sentences to articulate and analyze theological concepts, African Pentecostalism embraces an experiential epistemology. Great emphasis is placed upon personal experience, community ritual, and direct encounters with the divine over formal analysis. In his book *African Pentecostal Theology: An Introduction*, the late Ogbu Kalu captures the essence of African Pentecostal theology as it relates to this discussion when he notes,

> Pentecostalism represents a paradigm shift that unshackles theology from rationalistic/scientific thinking and expands the understanding of the spiritual dimensions of reality and the operation of the invisible world. It posits that there are three different ways of knowing—intellectual, observational, and experiential—and accords new emphasis to the realm of human experience. It says that the power of Scripture does not reside in the letter; rather, God is behind the law.[21]

An essential aspect of the experiential nature of African Pentecostal hermeneutics is its emphasis on orality and narrative. For African Pentecostals, the "text" is not merely something to be analyzed but a vibrant, living expression of divine power and presence that actively shapes and transforms the believer's experience and understanding through the power of the Holy Spirit. Ghanaian Pentecostal theologian Kwabena Asamoah-Gyadu asserts,

> The performance effect of the spoken word in African pneumatic movements is yet further evidence of the resonances between primal ideas and Christian innovation. In the traditional context, words translate into action; therefore, the power of blessing and curse is very important, especially from figures of authority.

Therefore, African Pentecostals have a different relationship with the text, making a purely sentential analytical approach problematic.

Second, abstract versus concrete. The text is not an unearthed and disconnected set of abstract theoretical constructs for African Pentecostalism. Instead, the text engages directly with the believer's real-life experiences. African Pentecostals embrace a tangible manifestation of divine presence manifested through healing, deliverance, miracles, and prophetic encounters integral to the text. Logical constructs often overlook the practical, experiential dimensions of faith. African Pentecostal challenges sentential

21. Kalu, *African Pentecostalism*, 250.

analysis by asserting that proper understanding comes from engaging with the text in ways that directly impact and transform the reader's concrete reality.

African Pentecostal Christology and Sentential Analysis

Sentential formulation as a tool of analytic theology presents significant challenges when applied to African Christology. Let's take the doctrine of the incarnation, which is explained in detail by analytic theologians such as Oliver Crisp. In his writing, Crisp seeks to demonstrate the rationality and coherence of the traditional doctrine of the incarnation, which is a profoundly mysterious and supernatural event where the eternal Son of God takes on human form. This event, which is profoundly enigmatic and extraordinary, is creatively explained by Crisp using the philosophical tools of analytic theology. Through the deployment of the tools of philosophical reason, Crisp attempts to show the intellectual defensibility of the incarnation, making it accessible within contemporary philosophical discourse.[22] Although a detailed engagement with Crisp's analysis is beyond the scope here, it's worth noting that for African Pentecostals, such an analysis may not fully address their deep experiential and epistemological needs. This analytical approach overlooks the rich, lived experiences and communal reality that shape African theological understanding. Though not a Pentecostal, Karl Barth provides insight into why this approach for many does not connect with the worldview Africans inhabit. Barth emphasized God's transcendent nature and human understanding's limitations in grasping the mysteries of the divine. He argued that human efforts to comprehend God through rational means or theological systems ultimately fall short. Barth captures the importance of divine revelation as the primary means God discloses himself to humanity.[23] Although rational efforts to clarify the mysteries of the incarnation are critical for the theological task, one must also be aware that this central mystery defies strict sentential definition, and efforts to confine it within precise propositions risk oversimplification or even heresy. For African Pentecostals, doctrines such as the incarnation do not exist in isolation from the faith community. Divine speech about Christ is lived out and expressed within the community of the faithful, moving through shared spaces such as communal worship and fellowship. For African Pentecostals, the language of faith is inseparable from the practice of faith.

22. Crisp, *God Incarnate.*

23. Barth, *Church Dogmatics, Vol. II/1.*

P2. Clarity and Precision

Clarity and Precision—prioritizing clear definitions, unambiguity, and rigorous logical coherence—is the second of Rea's analytic philosophical prescriptions. In *An Invitation to Analytic Christian Theology*, Thomas McCall uses Rea's five prescriptions to explain what he understands analytic theology is or should be. In his attempts to provide Precision to what P2 or the second of Rea's prescription means, McCall is at pains to debunk misconceptions of what Clarity and Precision mean within the scope of analytic theology.[24] Although McCall and others deserve recognition for their efforts to define "clarity and precision" in the context of analytic theology, it remains that analytic theology is significantly rooted in the principles of Western Enlightenment philosophical epistemology. Despite their attempts to adapt these philosophical principles to suit Christian theology, analytic theology better remains closely wedded to the constraints and limitations of intellectual discourse. The connection to its philosophical origins reveals the challenges of integrating analytic theology's rigorous methods with the broader historical and theological traditions of Christianity. Indeed, the quest for precision, clarity, and logical coherence is valuable in theological and philosophical discourse. This is especially true when pursuing doctrinal soundness, engaging in dialogue with other faith traditions, and safeguarding against heretical teaching. While there is clear value in precision, clarity, and logical coherence, it is equally essential to be open to the mystery of faith that transcends cognitive processes and the limits of human reason to grasp divine truth. For African Pentecostals, clarity is not just a matter of intellectual rigor but rather something that comes to us through the intelligence of the Holy Spirit. This type of clarity and precision does not only appear in the form of well-crafted prose and theoretical constructs but also through lived experience, symbols, communal narratives, and vibrant worship. For African Pentecostals, narratives, symbols, and communal rituals carry the theological weight that may not align with analytic theology's more abstract and propositional reasons. African Pentecostal epistemology is multidimensional in that the visible and the invisible, the concrete and the abstract, the spiritual and the material exist simultaneously. Clarity and Precision are therefore clarity and precision should not be selected over and above more mystical interpretations or vice versa; rather, clarity arises from lived experiences with God in everyday life. Precision is not so much about strict and precise articulation as it is about the faithful witness and articulation of God's presence in the world.

24. McCall, *Invitation to Analytic Christian Theology*, 18.

Clarity and Precision and African Pentecostal Christology

We will focus on Christology to provide more concrete examples of the contrast between African Pentecostal theology and the quest for Clarity and Precision in analytic theology. As noted, analytic Christology prioritizes precise definitions and propositional truths about Christ's nature and works through clearly articulating principle doctrinal statements and concepts. For African Pentecostals, knowledge of Christ is centered on personal and communal encounters.[25] In this context, great emphasis is placed on lived experiences and the transformative power of the Holy Spirit over abstract theological reasoning. Worship is a critical practice as far as this is concerned. Whereas the analytic theological approach might focus on doctrinal teaching about Christ, emphasizing intellectual engagement and clarity, African Pentecostal worship is characterized by music, dance, and a direct encounter with Christ. In this context, Scripture is not static but a dynamic living text that interacts with the worship experience. John 16:13–14 is a well-attested passage often quoted in African Pentecostal services:

> But when the Spirit of truth comes, he will guide you into all the truth. He will not speak on his own; he will speak only what he hears and tell you what is yet to come. He will glorify me because it is from me that he will receive what he will make known to you.

This verse captures the African Pentecostal orientation toward truth. For them, the encounter with the Holy Spirit ultimately reveals the truth of Christ. For African Pentecostals, the truth of Christ is seen in the clarity of sentential formulae and in Christ's ability to demonstrate his power in the here and now. Christ's power to cast out demons, heal the sick, raise the dead, and break the chains of poverty demonstrates with clarity and precision that he is indeed the Christ. This does not mean African Pentecostals inhabit an anti-intellectual posture; numerous universities and colleges founded and led by Africans abound. Instead, the ultimate clarity of Christ is seen in his ability to transform lives, bring hope, and transform individuals and communities in the face of adversity. What I have stated in another work is worth repeating here:

> The driving force behind African Pentecostal hermeneutics is not "unquestioning" literalism, which is one of the hallmarks of Western fundamentalism, but rather a pragmatic need to "concretize" and appropriate the Bible to "living faith. . . . This

25. Clarke, *African Christology*.

> coloristic approach to biblical hermeneutics seeks to apply the Bible to real-life situations or ordinary people.[26]

Clarity and Precision have their place in theology; however, overemphasizing these elements can advance a narrow understanding of Christology, particularly within African contexts.

P3. Minimal Metaphor

Another of Michael Rea's analytic theological prescriptions emphasizes "minimal metaphor," which means avoiding metaphors and tropes whose semantic content extends beyond direct propositional meaning.[27] According to McCall, minimizing metaphors is difficult because metaphors are tricky to spell out and clarify in a manner suitable for analytic theological discourse.[28]

McCall is correct in pointing out the limitation of metaphor in theological discourse, as there are challenges with its overuse. Such limitations include context dependence, potential for misinterpretation, and reductionism, as they often reduce intricate theological concepts to simplistic terms, just to name a few.[29] Conversely, there are also severe restrictions and limitations to using the language of theological inquiry. Language as a means of theological discourse can lead to ambiguity due to different cultural or linguistic backgrounds; limitations can often fall short when trying to articulate the complexities of divine realities and spiritual experiences; and the evolution of language means that the meaning of words changes over time, along with other limitations.[30] McCall—and I believe the various schools of analytic theologians would agree—does not entirely outlaw metaphor's use in theological discourse. However, they caution that it should be used sparingly as a clear indication that there is a preference for articulation through language, preferably written, over other means of communicating meaning. Pentecostal theologians are far more optimistic

26. Clarke, *Pentecostalism*, 67.

27. Crisp and Rea, *Analytic Theology*.

28. Crisp and Rea, *Analytic Theology*, 20.

29. For further reading about the limitations of metaphors see, Rorty, *Philosophy and the Mirror of Nature*; Lakoff and Johnson, *Metaphors We Live By*; Capps, *Reinterpreting Religious Experience*; Plantinga, *Warranted Christian Belief*; Vanhoozer, *Drama of Doctrine*; Adams, *Horrendous Evils*; Dillard, *Pilgrim at Tinker Creek*.

30. For further discussion of the limits of language in theological discourse, see Rorty, *Philosophy and the Mirror of Nature*; McFague, *Metaphor and Religious Language*; Vanhoozer, *Drama of Doctrine*.

about the potential of symbolic language, placing them more in line with the worldviews of the biblical writers.

The rich and frequent use of symbolic language—and other aspects of dynamic and experiential dimensions of Christian faith—distinguishes Pentecostal theology from analytic and other philosophical theologies. While metaphors may distract analytic theologians who prefer using less nebulous interpretive tools, Pentecostals believe that symbolic language, such as metaphors, can illuminate the profound mysteries of God's engagement with the world. An excellent example of this is the metaphor of Spirit baptism, whose meaning is complex to capture using purely philosophical analytic tools. Even the physician Luke, the writer of Acts of the Apostles, saw it necessary to engage metaphorical language, such as fire, wind, and divided tongues, in his graphic description of the baptism of the Holy Spirit on the early believers.[31] Pentecostal theologians such as Frank Macchia, Amos Yong, Cheryl Bridges Johns,[32] and others are enthusiastic about Spirit baptism's potential as more than a theological event. On the contrary, it metaphorically depicts the kissing of divine power with human frailty, bringing about spiritual transformation and renewal for the beleaguered post-resurrection believers in a language that needs divine assistance.

The use of metaphor is therefore generously employed for Pentecostal theology because, as Wolfgang Vondey asserts, "A different logic holds together Pentecostal theology to that of philosophical theology." In Vondey's case, Pentecostal theology employs play as a theological metaphor. Vondey notes,

> The notion of play can be used as a heuristic metaphor for a way of doing theology that eludes precise rules, boundaries, and stems even though it can make us of them. For the purpose of identifying Pentecostal theology, play is understood as a redemptive method of living and interpreting the logic of reality by transforming and transcending its existing structures. It demands the realm of alternative expectation motivated by an unlimited imagination.[33]

Vondey further notes,

> Play is the (Pentecostal) pursuit of that divine imagination, which often contradicts existing theological interpretation and dominant articulation of reality. In a methodological sense, play

31. Acts 21–24.

32. See, Macchia, *Baptism in the Spirit*; Yong, *Spirit Poured Out;* Johns, *Pentecostal Formation.*

33. Vondey, *Pentecostal Theology*, 12.

> engages the world not exclusively through doctrine but also materially, physically, spiritually, aesthetically, morally, and socially.[34]

In addition to the ideas of Spirit baptism and play, Pentecostal theologians have employed various ways in which metaphors contribute to capturing theological Precision and meaning.[35]

Metaphors in African Christology

Metaphors are the language of African Christology. In the African symbolic universe, theological discourse finds clear expression through metaphor. According to S. K. Langar, "Metaphor is the most striking evidence of African abstractive seeing. Every new experience or idea about things first evokes some metaphorical expression."[36] African Pentecostals view the world in symbolic, not scientific terms. However, as I noted in my introduction, symbolic representation within African Pentecostal epistemology does not indicate some prehistoric thought process but constitutes coherent thinking and logical thought processes. African Philosophy Kwame Gyekye states it well when he notes,

> African philosophical thought is expressed both in the oral literature and in the thoughts and actions of the people. Thus, much philosophical material is embedded in the proverbs, myths, folklore, fold songs, rituals, beliefs, customs, and symbols.[37]

Although scholarship and academic pedagogy in the Western hemisphere penalize symbolism and ridicule metaphors, African Pentecostalism cannot dispense with the symbolic languages Western scholasticism eliminated from Christian theology. In many ways, it is somewhat ironic that the first Christians and the early church fathers did not hold to a minimum metaphor to express their faith and make it intelligible to others. What is seen in African Pentecostal Christology is a re-actualization of the significance of Christ within a cultural structure of orality, where symbolism expresses the destiny of humanity through metaphor of the banality of everyday life. At

34. Vondey, *Pentecostal Theology*, 12.

35. A few more examples include Nimi Wariboko's engagement of the metaphors of music and dance in his theological discourse; see Wariboko, *Thinking Through the Spirit* and Yong, *Hospitality and the Other*. In this book, Amos Yong develops a theology from the event of Pentecost that engages the issue of a Pentecostal approach to interfaith dialogue.

36. Langer, *Philosophy in the New Key*, 141.

37. Gyekye, *Essay on African Philosophical Thought*, 13.

the core of this approach to Christology is that we cannot attain Christ by lifting ourselves out of the world or isolating ourselves from time and space to reach God in pure abstraction. Instead, we find Christ concretely at the human level, in the tangible existence where salvation takes on flesh, and every aspect of Christ crucified penetrates the most physical aspects of our daily lives.[38] According to Ashon T. Crawley, "Blackpentecostalism is an intellectual practice grounded in the fact of the flesh, flesh unbounded and liberating, flesh as vibrational and always on the move."[39]

In summary, African Pentecostal theological traditions provide a powerful lesson on the indispensable role of metaphors in theological discourse. By harnessing the evocative power of metaphorical language, African Pentecostals remind us of the inherent limitations of human expression, bridge the gap between the divine and the human, and open new avenues for understanding the profound mysteries of faith. Their approach to christological discourse is a sobering reminder that theological language, at its best, is not merely descriptive but also evocative, participatory, and transformative.

P4. Conceptual Foundations

The fourth of Michael Rea's analytic philosophical prescription emphasizes "conceptual foundations." This means building arguments upon well-defined, primary concepts or concepts rigorously defined by those primary terms. For centuries, philosophers and theologians have debated various conceptual Christologies concerning the mysteries of the incarnation of Christ. Classical Western and Eastern scholars have sought to dissect the mysteries of the Incarnation in search of a clear and rationally defensible explanation. While this approach reflects a desire for clarity within Western thought, it risks overlooking the unique character of how knowledge and understanding are conveyed within biblical and other non-Western traditions. This tendency overlooks the profound ways the biblical narrative portrays Jesus. Biblically, Jesus is not a concept to be analyzed but a person to be encountered. His teachings, miracles, and even his horrific death and glorious resurrection are not merely events to be categorized but revelations of God's character and promises unfolding within human history. For Pentecostals, this lived, unfolding revelation is the bedrock of living faith, not the bane of philosophical reasoning.

38. For more on African Christology and metaphors, see my book, *African Christology*, ch. 4.

39. Crawley, *Black Pentecostal Breath*, 4.

Therefore, Rea and the analytic school's search for clear conceptual foundations echoes Western thought's tendency to prioritize rationality and definition over embodied expressions of faith and experience. If taken too far, it can lead to a sterile understanding of biblical concepts. For example, miracles, healings, and instances of the Spirit's work—all central themes in the Bible—have suffered under the analytical gaze of Western epistemology. Attempts to force them into neat categories miss how they function as expressions of God's power within the world, signs intended to disrupt expectations and demonstrate new possibilities. Western theology has a history of decoupling biblical ideas from their original context—the lived realities of the people and places within the text to abstract concepts.[40] This approach misses the vitality of the "primitive voice" embedded within the Biblical narrative.

African Pentecostal Epistemic Christology and Conceptual Foundation

African Pentecostal ways of knowing offer a powerful counterargument to the approach offered by the analytic theology school. African Pentecostal theological engagement with the biblical text helps us re-engage with the Bible as grounded in lived experiences, relationality, and the acceptance of paradox and mystery.[41] This approach offers African Pentecostals a more faithful and epistemologically relevant understanding of engagement with the biblical text, honoring the dynamic nature of the Bible's stories, teachings, and experiences beyond the conceptual foundational framework. This alternative approach allows for a richer and more dynamic understanding of the depth and beauty inherent within the foundational text of Christianity. Therefore, foundational concepts fly in the face of African Pentecostalism because foundational concepts appear fixed and static, and African

40. The works of Jennings, *Christian Imagination* and Carter, *Race*, do a superb job of demonstrating the move from theology connected to people, language and land to abstract reasoning couched in whiteness and Western European hegemony.

41. *Power, Principalities, and the Spirit* by Dr. Esther Acolatse is an example of hermeneutical boldness and biblical sagacity arising out of the Global South in the twenty-first century. She argues that the rise of religion in the Global South—characterized by a burgeoning Pentecostal and charismatic fervor—demands a fresh biblical hermeneutical outlook. The monopoly of Western enlightenment epistemological interpretation of the biblical text comes under serious scrutiny in this work. The Western suspicion of the mythological and enchanted worldview favored by African peoples is brought into creative dialogue through theological scholarship. See Acolatse, *Power, Principalities, and the Spirit.*

Pentecostal theology is pneumatic and dynamic. According to Kwabena Asamoah-Gyadu,

> There is an inseparable connection between the Bible as text and the Bible as sacred material that must be handled with referential respect. The dynamism of Christianity in contemporary Africa is partly due to the sacredness or supernatural character of the Bible that has been maintained in the African Christian imagination.[42]

A conceptual framework's necessity emphasizes the need for a predefined structure system of thought and philosophical rigor in understanding and interpreting theological truths. However, this is not the way African Pentecostals do theology. There are three distinct reasons why this idea of beginning with a conceptual foundation clashes with African Pentecostal approaches.

1. Christ Revealed in Experience Over Abstract

In African Pentecostalism, theology is not built upon abstract concepts or systematic doctrines but is informed by how Christ is experienced in everyday life through healing, deliverance, and worship.[43] As Vondey makes the following assertion about Pentecostal theology, which is also valid for African Pentecostals:

Pentecostal theology begins as a spirituality consistent with the Christian mystical tradition. The Pentecostal tradition is rooted deeply in the experience of Pentecost. The belief practices, sensibilities, and values of Pentecostal spirituality are defined as the core by the experience of God. Pentecostal theology as a form of mystical theology demands the constant availability to be practiced and thus makes speculative theology as a purely intellectual or theoretical endeavor impossible.[44]

For African Pentecostals, a rigid conceptual framework can seem obstructive and sterile. As I explained earlier, African Pentecostal Christology focuses on how Christ transforms individuals and communities, and there is little need to fit that transformation into predefined intellectual categories.[45]

42. See Asamoah-Gyadu, *Sighs and Signs of the Spirit.*

43. Clarke, *Pentecostal Theology in Africa*; Kalu, *African Pentecostalism*; Burgess et al., *Pentecostalism in Africa.*

44. Vondey, *Pentecostal Theology*, 15–16.

45. For more on African Pentecostal hermeneutics, see Nel, *African Pentecostal Hermeneutics.*

2. Spontaneity Over Systematization

African Pentecostal theology emphasizes spontaneity and openness to Christ's revelation against intellectual rigidity. The imposition of a proper conceptual framework would limit the ability of African Pentecostals to be open to the movement of Christ through the Holy Spirit. The Scriptures say in John 3:8, "The wind blows where it chooses, and you hear the sound of it, but you do not know where it comes from or where it goes, so it is with everyone who is born of the Spirit." In line with this biblical text, African Pentecostals emphasize Christ's ongoing and unpredictable action through the Holy Spirit. Therefore, theology is not understood as something that can be contained or tamed within static concepts but as an ongoing journey with Christ.[46]

3. Communal Over Isolationist Activity

In the Spirit of Ubuntu (I am because we are)[47] African Pentecostals understand theology as a communal activity where Christ emerges from within the worship activity of the faithful, not something done in isolation. The need for a proper conceptual framework often removes the theological task from within the worship context of the faithful. It puts it into the purview of the professional class of scholars.[48] African Pentecostal theology does not understand faith as something that can be compartmentalized into neat categories or frameworks; instead, it integrates theology with everyday life and spirituality. Black Pentecostals, therefore, engage theology in an intuitive, organic, and often interdisciplinary, seamlessly integrating faith, worship, and praxis.

These are just a few short snippets and responses to the idea of conceptual foundation in theological inquiry from an African Pentecostal perspective. They have sought to explain that theology in this tradition is born out of real-life encounters with the living Christ, deeply embedded in communal life and the spontaneity of the Spirit's work.

46. In my edited volume, *Pentecostal Theology in Africa*, I have constructed an African Pentecostal theological method based upon the African rhythmic tradition of "call and response." There, I define call and response as an ongoing dialectic between the Holy Spirit (the call) and the existential experience of the African people (the response). See Clarke, *Pentecostal Theology in Africa*, ch. 1.

47. For a good read on the meaning and significance of Ubuntu, see Desmond Tutu's *No Future Without Forgiveness*. See my joint essay with Dr. Marcia Clarke, "Church Unity and the Spirit of Ubuntu."

48. For more on the impact of the Bible when read by the scholar class and from the perspective of the ordinary reader in Africa, see West and Dube, *Bible in Africa*.

P5. Conceptual Analysis as Evidence

We come now to the last of Rea's 5Ps: Conceptual Analysis as Evidence. Analytic theologians understand conceptual analysis to refer to the importance of building theological reason on consistent theological analysis. If the analysis is internally inconsistent, then its evidence must be rejected, and conversely, if the analysis is consistent, then its evidence must be taken as valid.[49] From a broader Pentecostal perspective, "conceptual analysis" as a source of evidence collides with the Pentecostal emphasis on experience, immediacy, and the active role of the Holy Spirit as the primary source of evidence.[50] For Pentecostals, conceptual validity is not based upon the human subject as the chief hermeneut but on the Holy Spirit, who is the author and interpreter of the text.[51] Therefore, Pentecostals advocate for a theology that is open, fluid, and responsive to the divine rather than one that is limited to human rational processing and sagacity.

The African Pentecostal critique of conceptual analysis continues with the objection to Rea's P4 prescriptions. As mentioned there, African Pentecostals place the work of the Holy Spirit and the lived experience of the believers at the center of theological inquiry. For Pentecostals, internal consistency is not the litmus test of theological truth. On the contrary, spiritual truths are validated through experiential confirmation of the Holy Spirit and not the logical coherence across all contexts. As noted earlier, rigid adherence to conceptual consistency risks neglecting the immediate and unpredictable move of the Holy Spirit. The additional critique area for the conceptual analysis is outlined in the treatment of Rea's P.4 and aspects of his other prescriptions, so I will not repeat them here. Suffice it to say that the African Pentecostal critique of conceptual analysis as evidence centers on the method's reliance on rational consistency, which often conflicts with the dynamic, Spirit-empowered, and experience-based approach of African Pentecostalism. While conceptual analysis seeks to build theology on clear, coherent concepts, African Pentecostals prioritize the empowering work of the Holy Spirit and the lived experience of the faith community, often accepting theological fluidity that responds to divine revelations. For African Pentecostals, theology is more than the ability to craft theological conceptual precision; it is more about encountering God in transformative ways that the cerebral cortex cannot always grasp.

49. McCall, *Analytic Christian Theology*, 21.

50. Vondey, *Pentecostal Theology*, 15.

51. See the introductory chapter of Yong, *Hermeneutical Spirit*, 27–71.

Conclusion

The analytic theology school's philosophical approach, which focuses on precise definitions and logical rigor, offers a valuable lens for examining theological truths. In an age when scientism's apologists, such as Richard Dawkins with his best-selling book *The God Delusion*, relegate faith to the realm of intellectual laziness and a convenient escape from the rigorous demands of rational inquiry, and the thirst for a reasoned-orientated answer to the mystery of the Christian faith is unabating, analytic theology is a powerful apologetic weapon.

An African Pentecostal critique of analytic theology is not just a critique of a theological method. Still, it critiques a Western rational tradition at the core of analytic theology. The history of this tradition must not be ignored or left without robust critique and dialogue. The legacy of Western rationalist thought was used to promote scientific racism, the transatlantic slave trade, and Western colonialism. This Western rationalist tradition played a part in the elevation of whiteness as the standard and normative goal of Christian imagination, as Willie Jennings astutely identifies as "a diseased social imagination."[52] I raised these issues not to stain the valuable service that analytic theologians are contributing to the Christian tradition but to highlight the potential danger of the analytic theological tradition gradually resuming the dominant place of its senior brother, Western philosophical rationalism. This Western philosophical enlightenment tradition created a theological stranglehold on non-Western expression of faith, particularly in the Global South.[53]

The future of theological inquiry lies in dialogue between analytic rigor and the dynamic, embodied knowledge systems of African epistemologies and other non-Western theological traditions. Imagine a theological landscape where careful dissection of concepts walks hand-in-hand with ethnographic studies of faith communities. Here, stories and personal testimonies hold as much weight as logical propositions. The result would be a deeper, more inclusive Christology that resonates with the experiences of believers worldwide while responding to the Western cultural despiser of the Christian faith.

52. Jennings, *Christian Imagination*, 6.

53. Sanneh explores how Western missionaries engaged in Bible translation and interpretation, impacting both local cultures and Western hermeneutics. See Sanneh, *Translating the Message*.

Bibliography

Acolatse, Esther E. *Power, Principalities, and the Spirit: Biblical Realism in Africa and the West.* Grand Rapids: Eerdmans, 2018.

Adams, Marilyn McCord. *Horrendous Evils and the Goodness of God.* Ithica, NY: Cornell University Press, 1999.

Albrecht, Daniel E., and Evan B. Howard. "Pentecostal Spirituality." In *The Cambridge Companion to Pentecostalism*, edited by Cecil M. Robeck Jr. and Amos Yong, 235–53. New York: Cambridge University Press, 2015.

Asamoah-Gyadu, J. Kwabena. *Sighs and Signs of the Spirit: Ghanaian Perspectives on Pentecostalism and Renewal in Africa.* Minneapolis: Fortress, 2015.

Assmann, Jan. *The Search for God in Ancient Egypt.* Ithaca, NY: Cornell University Press, 2001.

Ayer, A. J. *Language, Truth and Logic.* London: Victor Gollancz Ltd, 1936.

Barth, Karl. *Church Dogmatics, Vol. II/1: The Doctrine of God.* Edited by G. W. Bromiley and T. F. Torrance. Translated by T. H. L. Parker et al., New York: T&T Clark, 1957.

Burgess, Richard, et al., eds. *Pentecostalism in Africa: Presence and Impact of Pneumatic Christianity in Postcolonial Societies.* Leiden: Brill, 2012.

Capps, Donald. *Reinterpreting Religious Experience: Expressing the Ineffable.* Athens: University of Georgia Press, 1995.

Carnap, Rudolf. *The Logical Structure of the World: Pseudoproblems in Philosophy.* Translated by R. A. George. London: Routledge, 1928.

Carter, Kameron. *Race: A Theological Account.* Oxford: Oxford University Press, 2008.

Clarke, Cliffton R. *African Christology: Jesus in Post-Missionary African Christianity.* Eugene, OR: Pickwick, 2011.

———. *Pentecostalism: Insights from Africa and the African Diaspora.* Eugene, OR: Cascade, 2018.

———, ed. *Pentecostal Theology in Africa.* Eugene, OR: Pickwick, 2014.

Clarke, Cliffton R., and Marcia Clarke. "Church Unity and the Spirit of Ubuntu: Insights from the Global South." In *Pentecostal Theology and Ecumenical Theology*, 333–58. Leiden: Brill, 2019.

Coakley, Sarah. "Dark Contemplation and Epistemic Transformation: The Analytic Theologian Re-Meets Teresa of Avila." In *Analytic Theology: New Essays in the Philosophy of Theology*, edited by Oliver Crisp and Michael Rea, 280–312. Oxford: Oxford University Press, 2009.

Crawley, Ashon T. *Black Pentecostal Breath: The Aesthetics of Possibility.* New York: Fordham University Press, 2016.

Crisp, Oliver D. *God Incarnate: Explorations in Christology.* London: T&T Clark, 2007.

———. *Retrieving Essays in Reformed Theology.* Downers Grove, IL: InterVarsity, 2010.

Crisp, Oliver D., and Michael C. Rea, eds. *Analytic Theology: New Essays in the Philosophy of Theology.* Oxford: Oxford University Press, 2009.

Dillard, Annie. *Pilgrim at Tinker Creek.* New York: Harper & Row, 1974.

Ellington, S. A. "Pentecostalism and the Authority of Scripture." *Journal of Pentecostal Theology* 9 (1996) 16–38.

Gyekye, Kwame. *An Essay on African Philosophical Thought: The Akan Conceptual Scheme.* Cambridge: Cambridge University Press, 1987.

Hauerwas, Stanley. *The Character of Virtue: Letters to a Godson.* Grand Rapids: Eerdmans, 1997.

Haught, John F. *God After Darwin: A Theology of Evolution.* 2nd ed. Boulder, CO: Westview, 2008.

Hick, John. *An Interpretation of Religion.* New Haven: Yale University Press, 2004.

Imhausen, Annette. *Mathematics in Ancient Egypt: A Contextual History.* Princeton: Princeton University Press, 2016.

Jennings, Willie. *The Christian Imagination: Theology and the Origins of Race.* New Haven: Yale University Press, 2010.

Johns, Cheryl Bridges. *Pentecostal Formation: A Pedagogy among the Oppressed.* Sheffield: Sheffield Academic Press, 1993.

Kalu, Ogbu. *African Pentecostalism: An Introduction.* Oxford: Oxford University Press, 2008.

Kärkkäinen, Veli-Matti. "Pentecostal Theological Education in a Theological and Missiological Perspective." EPTA conference paper, Iso Kirja, Sweden, 2006.

Lakoff, George, and Mark Johnson. *Metaphors We Live By.* Chicago: University of Chicago Press, 1980.

Land, Steven J. *Pentecostal Spirituality: A Passion for the Kingdom.* Sheffield: Sheffield Academic Press.

Langer, S. K. *Philosophy in the New Key.* Cambridge, MA: Harvard University Press, 1942.

Lindbeck, George A. *The Nature of Doctrine: Religion and Theology in a Postliberal Age.* Louisville, KY: Westminster John Knox, 1984.

Macchia, Frank. *Baptized in the Spirit.* Grand Rapids: Zondervan, 2006.

McCall, Thomas. *An Invitation to Analytic Christian Theology.* Downers Grove, IL: InterVarsity, 2015.

McFague, Sallie. *Metaphor and Religious Language.* Oxford: Oxford University Press, 1993.

Moltmann, Jürgen. *The Spirit of Life.* London: SCM, 1992.

Morris, Thomas V. ed. *Divine and Human Action: Essays in the Metaphysics of Theism.* Ithaca, NY: Cornell University Press, 1988.

Nel, Marius. *An African Pentecostal Hermeneutics.* Eugene, OR: Wipf & Stock, 2018.

Plantinga, Alvin. *Warranted Christian Belief.* Oxford: Oxford University Press, 2000.

Plantinga, Alvin, and Nicholas Wolterstorff, eds. *Faith and Rationality: Reason and Belief in God.* Notre Dame: University of Notre Dame Press, 1983.

Rea, Michael C. "Introduction." In *Analytic Theology: New Essays in the Philosophy of Theology*, edited by Oliver D. Crisp and Michael C. Rea, 1–30. Oxford: Oxford University Press, 2009.

———. *World Without Design: The Ontological Consequences of Naturalism.* Oxford: Clarendon, 2002.

Rorty, Richard. *Philosophy and the Mirror of Nature.* Princeton: Princeton University Press, 1979.

Russell, Bertrand. *Principles of Mathematics.* London: George Allen & Unwin, 1919.

Sanneh, Lamin. *Translating the Message: The Missionary Impact on Culture.* Maryknoll, NY: Orbis, 2009.

Tutu, Desmond. *No Future Without Forgiveness.* New York: Image, 2000.

Vanhoozer, Kevin J. *The Drama of Doctrine: A Canonical-Linguistic Approach to Christian Theology.* Louisville, KY: Westminster John Knox, 2005.

Vondey, Wolfgang. *Pentecostal Theology: Living the Full Gospel.* London: Bloomsbury, 2017.

Wariboko, Nimi. *Thinking Through the Spirit: The Pentecostal Principle.* Grand Rapids: Eerdmans, 2011.

Warrington, Keith. *Pentecostal Theology: A Theology of Encounter.* London: T&T Clark, 2008.

West, Gerald O., and Musa W. Dube, eds. *The Bible in Africa: Transactions, Trajectories, and Trends.* Leiden: Brill, 2000.

Wittgenstein, Ludwig. *Tractatus Logico-Philosophicus.* London: Routledge, 1921.

Yong, Amos. *The Hermeneutical Spirit.* Eugene, OR: Wipf & Stock, 2011.

———. *Hospitality and the Other: Pentecost, Christian Practices, and the Neighbor.* Maryknoll, NY: Orbis, 2008.

———. *Spirit Poured Out on All Fresh.* Grand Rapids: Baker, 2005.

5

Glossolalia and Spiritual Reading as Speculative Theology

Common Ground for Analytic Theology and Pentecostal Theology

CHRISTOPHER A. STEPHENSON

Although analytic theology has only recently begun to examine spiritual practices, there is a growing number of works devoted to such topics.[1] The consideration of analytic theology itself *as* a spiritual practice, however, has received less attention.[2] Important work on this front remains to be done, and I want to contribute to that initiative with some suggestions that both bring together and challenge analytic theology and Pentecostal theology through a consideration of speculative theology. By broadening the typical boundaries of the scope of speculative theology, I attempt to create an interface between analytic theology and Pentecostal theology in connec-

1. Wolterstorff, *Acting Liturgically*; Wolterstorff, *God We Worship*; Cuneo, *Ritualized Faith*. See also the following essays in Arcadi and Turner, *T&T Clark Handbook of Analytic Theology*: David Efird, "Analytic Spirituality," 439–50; Nathaniel Gray Sutanto, "Christian Baptism," 451–61; James M. Arcadi, "On the Intelligibility of Eucharistic Doctrine(s) in Analytic Theology," 463–75; Joshua Cockayne, "Analytic Theology and Liturgy," 477–88; Scott A. Davison, "Prayer," 489–97.

2. Wood, *Analytic Theology*, 175–90; Inman, "Theology in the Second Person"; Stephenson, "Should Pentecostal Theology Be Analytic Theology," 246–64; Stephenson, "Analytic Theology," 97–115.

tion with the spiritual practices of glossolalia and spiritual reading. Both of these practices involve using words—one speaking and one reading—and both of the practices have perlocutionary qualities. One of the things that the words of glossolalia and spiritual reading *do* is to suspend discursus and rouse affections. If analytic theologians will recognize spiritual practices that generate affections as a potential part of the method of speculative theology and if Pentecostal theologians will acknowledge that their propensity towards these affect-inducing practices is already the nascent form of a positive disposition towards speculative theology that implicitly encourages them to carry out more traditional exercises of speculative theology more intentionally than they generally do, then analytic theologians and Pentecostal theologians will have come a little bit closer to each other.

Speculative Theology as a Bridge Between Analytic and Pentecostal Theology

The potential for analytic theology and Pentecostal theology to be allies is probably not obvious. Perhaps one way to bring together analytic theology and Pentecostal theology is through speculative theology. The connection between analytic theology and speculative theology is uncontroversial, especially given the analytic tradition's propensity for speculative metaphysics. To focus on analytic philosophy of religion, for example, consider the common distinction between a defense and a theodicy in relation to the problem of evil. Constructing a defense is an exercise in probabilities that does not require one to claim that this or that possible reason is the actual reason that God permits evil. Thus, it is possible for a defense to be a purely speculative enterprise offered as a defeater for the charge that God and evil cannot coexist, but without making a definitive claim about why God in fact allows evil to continue. While the connection between analytic theology and speculative theology may be clear, the connection between Pentecostal theology and speculative theology is likely less clear. Connecting Pentecostal theology to speculative theology takes a little more effort, since Pentecostal theology has a history of avoiding speculative theology. Pentecostal theology is ready-made for integration with spiritual practices, but it has not taken up speculative theology to the same degree to which it has taken up other theological approaches or to the degree to which other theological traditions have taken up speculative theology. For example, one kind of Pentecostal systematic theology rarely strays beyond explicit statements in Scripture and attempts to do no more than gather data under topical headings through an inductive study of the Bible. It rarely employs deductive reasoning, and it acknowledges no developmental process to move from Scripture to doctrine, since doctrines are thought to be contained in Scripture itself.[3]

However, a connection between speculative theology and Pentecostal theology can be made through spiritual practices, which are paramount for Pentecostal identity. I will make that connection by means of affectivity. Affections are integral to Pentecostal worship and life,[4] and some affective practices may be well-suited to become avenues for speculative theology. Two such practices are glossolalia and spiritual reading. Analytic traditions excel at discursive thinking and precision, and Pentecostal traditions excel at making affectivity a source for theological reflection. While logical rigor aids the articulation of theological speech, glossolalia and spiritual reading often entail a turn away from discursive thought and the utterance of intelligible words. It may be that logical rigor and affectivity are not as far removed from each other as it first seems. It may also be that analytic theology and Pentecostal theology are not as far removed from each other as it first seems, even if each needs to assist the other regarding its own tendencies concerning speculative theology. If I have any success, it will become clearer that speculative theology can be a bridge between analytic and Pentecostal theology.

By "speculative theology," I mean making theological claims other than the truths that God has revealed or the truths that follow necessarily from the truths that God has revealed. Speculative theology is common in the history of Christian theology, and differences of belief in the area of speculative theology are some of the material parts of the doctrinal lines of demarcation that distinguish and, at times, divide different church traditions. However, what I propose here requires analytic theologians to expand the traditional boundaries of speculative theology and Pentecostal theologians to acknowledge that they might be primed for speculative theology after all. On the one hand, speculative theology is most frequently a discursive exercise predicated largely on the cognitive use of the intellect and reason; it does not usually entail spiritual practices closely associated with affectivity. On the other hand, speculative theology does not usually factor into the self-understanding of those who take up practices closely associated with affectivity; that is, it is not what those practitioners—even the academic theologians among them—generally understand themselves to be doing when they perform those practices. Nonetheless, glossolalia and spiritual

3. I underscore that this is only one kind of Pentecostal theology. See Stephenson, *Types of Pentecostal Theology*, 11–27; Vondey, "Pentecostal Theology."

4. The *locus classicus* on Pentecostal affections is Land, *Pentecostal Spirituality*, 122–81.

reading can invite and promote the kind of imaginative thinking that speculative theology involves, and to take up those two practices is already to take a step towards speculative theology, even if one is not fully aware of the step.

Furthermore, part of my goal is an understanding of speculative theology that has apophatic dimensions, not only cataphatic ones. For my purposes, here "cataphatic" refers both to making positive claims about who God is and to using images, analogies, and models to do so. "Apophatic," however, refers only to a posture before God that seeks to elevate affectivity over speaking intelligible words and over reading words that communicate information primarily in order to increase the reader's knowledge base. My use of the term "apophatic" does not mean negative theology in the sense of statements of who God is *not*. While negative theology in this sense is indispensable to theological discourse, it is not my primary concern here.

Glossolalia as an Affective and Apophatic Part of Speculative Theology

Glossolalia, speaking in unknown tongues, is almost synonymous with Pentecostalism. Although glossolalia does not have exactly the same functions among all of the three major demographics of Pentecostals that scholars tend to recognize,[5] its close association with global Pentecostalism abides. The association is due both to the phenomenon on the day of Pentecost recorded in Acts of the Apostles 2 and to the fact that many Pentecostals of all kinds continue to cling to the practice, whether as an indication that one has been baptized in the Holy Spirit or as a form of charismatic prayer.

Affections often accompany glossolalia. At times, one may simultaneously manifest signs of exuberance or ecstasy, and sometimes one may sense calmness or serenity while speaking in tongues. One might speak as a form of mystical prayer, which one cannot initiate at will without extraordinary assistance from the Holy Spirit and divine grace, or as a form of ascetical prayer, which one can initiate at will with ordinary assistance from the Holy

5. The three demographics are: (1) Pentecostal denominations with origins in the US or fruits of their worldwide missionary activity ("classical Pentecostals" or just "Pentecostals"); (2) those who embrace charismatic phenomena but remain in their Catholic, Protestant, Anglican, or Orthodox Churches ("charismatics"); and (3) those who embrace charismatic phenomena but are not part of Pentecostal denominations or the church traditions who constitute "charismatics," including evangelical independent congregations inside the US and countless indigenous independent congregations outside the US. For the sake of simplicity, I employ "Pentecostals" as a single referent to all three of these demographics, but it is the Pentecostals in demographics (1) and (2) who are most likely to need encouragement to engage in speculative theology explicitly and to take analytic theology seriously.

Spirit and divine grace that is always available. Whatever the case, glossolalia is a kind of "un-speaking," that is, an intentional turning away from intelligible words while continuing to use words. Glossolalia is a kind of "letting go," a ceding of control. It amounts to a surrender of one's prerogative to assert oneself through rational communication. One who speaks in tongues implies that she lacks sufficient intelligible words for the gravity of that particular moment, but rather than remaining silent, she speaks anyway without knowing exactly what to say. Tongues-speech is a kind of humble confession that one does not have adequate words at a particular time. Whereas silence could give the impression that she is simply choosing not to share any number of wise and discerning words, to speak in tongues is to admit, "I do not know what to say right now." Although intelligible words fail, affections prompt a verbal response instead of a wordless one. In this regard, some interpret Paul's words about the Holy Spirit interceding for believers when they do not know how to pray (Rom 8:26) to refer (at least) to glossolalia.[6]

Calling glossolalia an ascetic practice that one can initiate without extraordinary operations of the Holy Spirit and divine grace is an initial move towards thinking about glossolalia as a means of speculative theology. When one refrains from praying with understanding, he exercises his volition in order for another kind of speech to take place temporarily. He initiates glossolalia and speaks with divine assistance. If glossolalia is sometimes an ascetic form of prayer that he can initiate, it can be a spiritual discipline that he can exercise to promote spiritual growth. Restraining from more familiar patterns of known speech is already an expression of the kind of self-control that spiritual disciplines both require and promote. Glossolalia is a spiritual discipline of training speech and thought, and exercising this kind of self-chastening can result in greater sensitivity to the Holy Spirit.[7]

However, a potential relationship between glossolalia and speculative theology is not yet established. Indeed, it may seem that the two are at odds with each other due to speculative theology's dependence on crafting intelligible words, often in large amounts. Speculative theology usually consists of filling the mind with a myriad of theological possibilities—sometimes in great detail—in order to try to understand the truth, but glossolalia is a form of self-emptying that bypasses understanding. Speculative theology is usually an active and intentional form of thought that enlivens the faculties of the mind, but glossolalia is a form of praying without the mind

6. For example, Macchia, "Sighs Too Deep for Words," 47–73.

7. On glossolalia and asceticism, see Stephenson, "Un-Speaking in Tongues," 88–101.

(1 Cor 14:14) that renders the mind more passive than it would be if it were praying or thinking with understanding.

Yet, there seem to be good reasons to link glossolalia to speculative theology. As a form of affective prayer, glossolalia might benefit the speculative theologian by giving her moments of mental rest before, during, or after strenuous theological work. By utilizing times of discursive thought along with times of glossolalia, she might keep from pushing her intellect to the point of exhaustion.[8] To take an analogy from aerobic exercise, glossolalia might allow her to "warm up" before and "cool down" after a session of focused theological thought. Perhaps she might benefit also from something like "interval training," in which there are intense periods of discursive work that are punctuated with breaks for glossolalia, set cycles of alternating between the mind being more active and then being more passive. Perhaps while the mind is more passive, it will also be more receptive.[9]

In addition to providing mental rest, glossolalia as a more apophatic than traditional facet of speculative theology has the potential to strengthen the more traditional cataphatic facets of speculative theology. One goal of speculative theology is the creation of conceptual models that are syntheses of a large amount of information that may be particularly detailed and/or complex,[10] and glossolalia could be a tool for evaluating and constructing models. Sometimes it is necessary to modify or remove entrenched paradigms of thinking. When a model is valuable it becomes part of the lens through which we view and interpret realities themselves. There can be little doubt that models can become so firmly established that we lose either the ability to imagine that a different model might be superior or perhaps even forget that the model is only a medium for understanding rather than the totality of the reality itself. When a theologian works with models, glossolalia could help him gain some distance from a model in order to return eventually to evaluating it critically. Instead of rushing to assume the details of a model or to make claims about its current form and value, glossolalia could be one of the ways that he attempts to "begin again" with considering and evaluating a model. Not only can praying with unintelligible words

8. On the possibility of varying forms of praying in order to reduce strain on the intellect, see Kavanaugh and Rodriguez, *Collected Works of St. Teresa of Avila*, 1:128–30.

9. For the suggestion that glossolalia decreases frontal lobe activity, see Newberg et al., "Measurement of Regional Cerebral Blood Flow," 67–71. For and analytic-theological consideration of glossolalia amid other charismatic gifts, see Arcadi and Turner, *T&T Clark Handbook of Analytic Theology*, 281–94.

10. This is not to say that model-building is always speculative theology. On models in analytic theology, see Crisp, "Importance of Model Building."

bring rest to the theologian's mind, it can also help him withdraw from the assumption that the model is beyond improvement in its current form.

As an exercise in self-emptying that deprives the theologian of understandable expressions, glossolalia can help create the disposition necessary to reexamine something that has become so familiar that the critical distance necessary to picture it otherwise is diminished. Glossolalia, thus, becomes a gesture of fallibilism, an acknowledgment that our theological ideas are subject to improvement through reevaluation. Of course, it is possible to have such an outlook apart from glossolalia, but as a practice of spiritual discipline glossolalia can help cultivate the disposition of openness to the need for correcting and revising theology. The ultimate goal is not to shift permanently from the cataphatic mode of making positive claims in preference for saying less about a specific theological matter. To the contrary, apophatic moments of un-speaking in the form of glossolalia might help the theologian become more sensitive to the existence of previously unrecognized room for additional cataphatic statements. Apophatic forms of prayer are ends in and of themselves and should not be reduced to their instrumental value. Nonetheless, glossolalia also can be a means by which one is transformed and equipped to say more than one was able to say before a period of apophatic withdrawal from intelligible thought and speech.

It has been suggested that glossolalia can make theological speech more humble by resisting logocentrism, that glossolalia is an acknowledgment that we cannot fully do justice to God with our talk about God.[11] This is an important claim that is worthy of consideration, but it is not exactly the same as what I have in mind here, although it seems to be compatible with my claims. I am suggesting glossolalia neither as a way to reinforce the limitations of human language for speech about the divine per se—although such limitations exist—nor as an apophatic practice in the sense of negative theology asserting who God is not like—although such theological statements are necessary. Glossolalia may very well have value in both of these areas. Instead, my interest here is in considering glossolalia as a spiritual practice for clearing one's mind. As an apophatic form of prayer, glossolalia can be accompanied by a volitional withdrawal from intelligible thinking in order to break out of the ruts of thinking that sometimes hinder the theological and philosophical imagination, just as glossolalia itself entails breaking out of established patterns of intelligible speech.[12] Tongues speech might be a way to address writer's block, a way to become more docile for the Holy

11. For example, Castelo, *Pentecostalism as a Christian Mystical Tradition*, 175–77.

12. Of course, glossolalia is not always volitional. At times, it has mystical qualities that rely on extraordinary operations of divine grace and the Holy Spirit.

Spirit to inspire new insights that come from a well that is far deeper than that of one's own creativity. Glossolalia can help cultivate a disposition of openness and of listening, not in order to remain silent but in order to try to speak more extensively and more accurately than before.

Furthermore, glossolalia might help create the distance between the theologian and her topic of concern that is necessary for her to view the topic in a different light. To the extent that false theological ideas can function like idols, removing them by purging misconceptions amounts to a kind of sanctifying of the mind. If praying in the Holy Spirit can help reorder disordered desires, then it might also chasten the mind by redirecting it away from theological error. Of course, theological ideas do not have to be outright false to function like idols. Theological notions that we have simply lost the ability to question might be idolatrous or interest in questioning. Some might worry that this could lead to the substantial revision of fundamental theological truths, but it need not take that form. Rather, exercising glossolalia in the hope of achieving a fresh perspective on a matter might be a significant move towards seeing anew an opportunity for the further unfolding of the faith once delivered to the saints (Jude 3). Scrutiny and critical analysis can be ordered towards construction not only towards deconstruction, towards building oneself up in the most holy faith—which Jude 20 places alongside praying in the Holy Spirit—and further extrapolating details of that faith.[13] Indeed, as an ascetic practice, glossolalia can mitigate against solipsistic temptations to canonize any and every personal view or individual self-expression or experience. There is no necessary reason that glossolalia as a spiritual exercise for theological work should not be governed by whatever standards of authority that guide other forms of theological reflection.

Glossolalia can have a perlocutionary quality. It can do something that surpasses the strict semantics of the words spoken.[14] The meaning of those words are generally unknown to the speaker, and, at least at times, the words may have no literal meaning at all. Thus, while the speech act value of such talking might be continuous with the phonetic utterances of glossolalia themselves, the value cannot be reduced to those utterances. Glossolalia in this mode can function as speculative theology by urging the one who speaks to stray temporarily both from established speech patterns and from presuppositions that might hinder further theological reflection. The retreat

13. On praying in the Holy Spirit, following evil desires, and contending for the faith, see the New Testament letter of Jude.

14. On glossolalia and speech act theory, see Smith, *Thinking in Tongues*, 123–50.

from intelligible speech is temporary in order to actualize its instrumental value for analytic theology by means of a mode of speculative theology.[15]

It is axiomatic that a Christian theologian should pray, and one might enumerate any number of reasons that she should. If glossolalia can function the ways that I claim, then one implication is that a theologian should not pray only because there are centuries of historical precedent within the Christian tradition for considering growth in prayer as a primary means of measuring growth in the spiritual life—although she, no doubt, should pray for this reason. She should also pray in order to be a better theologian. In this regard, the often cited words of Evagrius Ponticus come to mind, namely, that one who is a theologian truly prays and that the one who truly prays is a theologian.[16] My claim also implies, in addition, that the theologian should pray because prayer can be a vital part of theological method[17] and that glossolalia is particularly suited to be a form of prayer through which affectivity can ultimately promote discursive theological work. One way, then, for speculative theology to be an activity guided by the Holy Spirit is through glossolalia, a charismatic dimension to theological method. Thus, one incentive for crafting a thorough theology of tongues-speech is consideration of the importance of tongues for theology.

Spiritual Reading as an Affective and Apophatic Part of Speculative Theology

Many church traditions maintain that, in addition to being a privileged source of information for revealed truths, Christian Scripture is also a medium through which spiritual formation takes place. Pentecostals affirm this understanding, with an emphasis on Scripture as a place for divine encounter. While they have not been quick to use terms like "spiritual reading" or *Lectio Divina*, they practice them extensively.[18] According to one Pentecostal scholar, spiritual reading is not concerned first and foremost with determining the meaning of biblical texts but with hearing the texts call us to God. Spiritual reading is for the purpose of rousing affections in

15. By highlighting this instrumental value, I am not suggesting that glossolalia has *only* instrumental value.

16. Evagrius, "On Prayer," 1:62.

17. On prayer as part of the method of systematic theology, see Coakley, *God, Sexuality, and the Self*.

18. On the importance of Scripture for Pentecostal thought and life and the ways that Pentecostals engage Scripture, see Archer, *Pentecostal Hermeneutic*; Oliverio, *Theological Hermeneutics*, 31–82; Warrington, *Pentecostal Theology*, 180–205.

the heart, not for gaining information. Spiritual reading is ordered towards creating dispositions in the reader. Scholars in particular are conditioned to read primarily for information, to analyze the texts, without listening for God to speak through them. More important than the kind of Christian texts that one reads is the way that one reads them, and with enough proficiency, one can read theological texts, in addition to Scripture, spiritually.[19] The lives of the saints can also rouse and intensify love or other affections on a path of sanctification towards perfection. Whatever the specific content, spiritual reading should lead to prayer so easily that one might not notice that he has made the transition from reading to prayer.[20]

Due to its aim to create affect in the reader more than to relay information, spiritual reading's ability to stimulate analytic theology is not apparent. Consider, however, this example from Eleonore Stump's interaction with John Henry Newman's reflections on Christ's prayer in Gethsemane. Newman's account is complete with colorful descriptions and rhetorical questions that are moving. Stump describes Newman's rendering as more melodramatic than that with which she is comfortable, but she still builds on Newman's rhetorical flourish for her own articulation of Christ's anguish in Gethsemane and Satan's use of that moment to suggest to Christ that Christ's upcoming suffering is unendurable. Stump also provides a reading of the birth narratives in Matthew and Luke. She points out details in these stories that reinforce Christ's vulnerable condition during his entrance into the world and states that the lack of such details would have bearing on the stories' ability to move one's heart. These observations about Christ's passion and birth might be somewhat banal on their own, but Stump uses them for part of her larger argument for why Christ's passion is necessary within a broadly Thomistic framework, namely, that the stories of these events are tools through which God can melt hardened hearts that will to be lonely.[21] In short, Stump offers a kind of spiritual reading of an evocative theological text (Newman) and of moving portions of Christian Scripture as part of the impetus behind her prosecution of philosophical and theological claims that bear her characteristic analytic style, all in pursuit of a speculative theology of the atonement.

Spiritual reading, then, has potential to play a role in a mode of speculative theology by creating in the reader affections that fund theological reflection. Evocative literature can spur a kind of "brainstorming" in which one makes an initial attempt to bring together inchoate ideas in order to

19. Chan, *Spiritual Theology*, 159–63.

20. Aumann, *Spiritual Theology*, 377–78.

21. Stump, *Atonement*, 275–79, 288.

assess whether one can turn them into a sound and thorough display of theological ideas that become more logically rigorous and exact as the theologian continues to meditate on them. Spiritual reading might render beginning formulations of ideas that ultimately become more precise than they are in their original evocative form. If so, then it seems to follow that spiritual literature—which rarely contains the sophisticated content and formal style of the analytic tradition—can nonetheless stir the affections and the intellect in ways that lead directly to analytic theological reflection that pursues precision and clarity as intellectual virtues and tries to give more careful expression and nuance to underdeveloped ideas.

Spiritual reading can have a perlocutionary quality. It can do something that surpasses the strict semantics of the words read. The meaning of those words may be communicated through poetry, exaggerations, or even sweeping generalizations. Thus, while the speech act value of spiritual reading might be continuous with the meaning of the actual words read, it cannot be reduced to those words. Spiritual reading in this mode can function as speculative theology by prompting the reader to stray temporarily from reading primarily to gain information. The rousing of one's affections in response to something more than the literal meaning of the words read can move the reader towards basic insights that can still be distilled from a text used for spiritual reading, and it can do so in ways that she might not be moved without evocative language that calls to her in addition to or even instead of increasing her knowledge by reporting information to her. The retreat from more academic forms of reading is temporary in order to actualize its instrumental value for analytic theology by means of a mode of speculative theology.[22]

In addition to spiritual reading fueling analytic theology by means of speculative theology, perhaps also texts in analytic theology could be used for spiritual reading. Such a view challenges traditional assumptions about the sophistication and style of texts suitable for spiritual reading, which tend to be devotional and to rely on prose that is directed more towards readability than towards fastidiousness. This view also challenges the assumption that one should choose between reading for a high degree of understanding and spiritual reading. And yet, attempts to understand can rouse the reader's affections. When at its best, analytic theology is an attempt to set before the reader theological truth for contemplation. An intricate articulation of the truth can rouse affections in the reader similarly to the way that a work of art might do the same. After all, the truth is beautiful, and it can be so

22. By highlighting this instrumental value, I am not suggesting that spiritual reading has *only* instrumental value.

in meticulous analytic splendor. Logical rigor can be a thing of beauty that exhibits patterns and symmetry in the process of reaching conclusions. If so, then using analytic theological literature for spiritual reading has potential to help overcome a polarizing tendency to think that texts can be either academic or spiritual but not both, even if intellectuals are more likely to be able to use academic literature for spiritual reading than others are able to do so.

For example, soon after I published *Types of Pentecostal Theology*, I received an unexpected response from one of its readers. It was not a published review or a message from fellow scholars. Rather, it was a note that recounted the brief testimony of a married couple. The husband reported that although they were part of a church tradition that historically did not talk much about baptism in the Holy Spirit, reading my book played a role in their becoming more open than they had been to this idea. Their openness was on both an intellectual and an experiential level, and they eventually were baptized in the Holy Spirit. I continue to rejoice at this news, but I admit that it is not among the possible consequences of writing the book that I imagined in advance. The book is not an apologetic for baptism in the Holy Spirit in Pentecostal perspective and it is not popular writing. While I teach, preach, and perform other activities that I pray might sometimes make a small contribution to results like this, it had not been an intentional goal for writing this book. Also, while I do not describe the book as "analytic theology," it has many of the marks of a monograph that originated as a PhD dissertation in theology or philosophy. That is, the book is a thoroughly researched and copiously documented study that fills a lacuna in previous scholarship through logical reasoning and careful presentation, not devotional literature aimed primarily at non-specialists. Nonetheless, something in the book made two of its readers want to pray, draw closer to God, and open their hearts in a particular way.

Conclusion

Analytic theology and Pentecostal theology might seem too disparate to be brought together. However, if analytic theologians and Pentecostal theologians can learn from each other and can benefit from each other's approaches to speculative theology, then speculative theology can help bring together analytic theology and Pentecostal theology. Analytic theology challenges Pentecostal theology to make its use of speculative theology more formal, intentional, and explicit. Often Pentecostal theology's use of speculative theology is informal, accidental, and implicit through practices like glossolalia and spiritual reading. Pentecostal theology encourages analytic theology to consider the potential of practices like glossolalia and spiritual reading for being part of the mode of speculative theology. Such a realization could contribute to the notion of analytic theology itself *as* a spiritual practice. An understanding of speculative theology that is broadened to include glossolalia and spiritual reading gives analytic theology two additional tools that it might not ordinarily use and helps Pentecostal theology become more aware of the implications of two of its spiritual practices for theological method.

Analytic theology stands to benefit from understanding glossolalia as a facet of speculative theology. Glossolalia can provide opportunities of mental rest during theological work. As an apophatic practice that rouses the affections, it can strengthen cataphatic theology by encouraging theologians to withdraw temporarily from and then return to abiding theological questions and answers in order to see them in a new light. A gesture of fallibilism, glossolalia can clear the mind and promote docility to the Holy Spirit to lead into all truth and away from error. Analytic theology stands to benefit from spiritual reading as a facet of speculative theology. Spiritual reading can function similarly to a brainstorming session. As an apophatic practice that rouses the affections, it can produce initial and cursory ideas that one can later scrutinize, modify, and sharpen. By temporarily deemphasizing the search for information in a text, the theologian can listen for what the voice of God might evoke in him through the text that he reads. None of this assumes that analytic theologians do not already practice glossolalia and spiritual reading per se, but it is uncommon to practice them with the understanding that they are modes of speculative theology as I have described.

Pentecostals, who readily practice glossolalia and spiritual reading, stand to benefit from understanding the two practices as facets of speculative theology. Although, again, it is uncommon to practice glossolalia and spiritual reading as modes of speculative theology, this insight could help Pentecostals realize that speculative theology might have more value than they tend to give to it. Pentecostals often resist speculation for several reasons. One reason is pessimism about being able to do any more than repeat truths that are already revealed by God without falling into error. It is better, they assume, to say less than to risk saying too much. They also incline to resist speculation because of residuals of select Protestant polemics against scholasticism. The negative influence, both direct and indirect, of Charles Hodge's inductive method on many Pentecostal thinkers cannot be overstated on this score.[23] Fear of being "impractical" is another reason

23. Stephenson, *Types of Pentecostal Theology*, 22–24.

that Pentecostals sometimes bypass speculation. The pragmatist impulses in Pentecostal discourse at both popular and some academic levels remain strong. They sometimes shun and dismiss as "hairsplitting" those ideas whose cash value is not immediately obvious. Part of the irony here is that these standards for theological discourse and concomitant antagonism towards speculation seem to conflict with what might be called the frivolity of Pentecostal spiritual practice. After all, glossolalia and spiritual reading themselves exhibit elements of play, inasmuch as they deviate from established norms of speaking and reading. Understanding these two spiritual practices as modes of speculative theology could help Pentecostals set aside stereotypes of speculation as arid and sterile logic-chopping. They could embrace the etymological root of "speculate," namely, "to see." Through speculative theology, they could attempt to *see* God, with the mind's eye, at least, if not also the soul, and to contemplate the truth. If glossolalia and spiritual reading rouse the affections of Pentecostals, then perhaps more traditional forms of speculative theology associated with discursus predicated largely on the cognitive use of the intellect and reason, too, might stir the affections of Pentecostals.

Speculative theology can have apophatic and cataphatic dimensions. I have emphasized "apophatic" as refraining from speaking and reading words in and for discursus in order to speak and read words in ways that are especially suited for rousing the affections, but I have not emphasized apophatic theology as negative theology. The retreat from the cataphatic to the apophatic is temporary and is taken up in part to fuel a return to the cataphatic. In this regard, the apophatic and the cataphatic are distinct from each other but are not separated from each other. They are not two elements that coexist without interacting. Rather, apophatic theology—in the form of practices like glossolalia and spiritual reading—funds cataphatic theology.

Analytic theology is readily associated with the cataphatic dimensions of speculative theology, and Pentecostal theology is readily associated with affectivity in relation to apophatic practices like glossolalia and spiritual reading but without an explicit connection between the practices and speculative theology. However, speculative theology becomes additional ground upon which analytic theology and Pentecostal theology can meet if analytic theology will grant an expansion of the traditional boundaries of speculative theology and Pentecostal theologians will grant that two of their spiritual practices both count implicitly as speculative theology and, thus, prompt them to be more open than they sometimes are to speculative theology. The theological imagination needs to be directed by the Holy Spirit, and glossolalia and spiritual reading are two practices through which the

Spirit works.[24] Both analytic theologians and Pentecostal theologians would do well to recognize the implications of these two practices for speculative theology and, in turn, for the relationship between analytic theology and Pentecostal theology.

Bibliography

Arcadi, James M., and James T. Turner Jr., eds. *T&T Clark Handbook of Analytic Theology*. London: Bloomsbury, 2021.

Archer, Kenneth J. *A Pentecostal Hermeneutic for the Twenty-First Century: Spirit, Scripture, and Community*. London: T&T Clark, 2003.

Aumann, Jordan. *Spiritual Theology*. London: Continuum, 2006.

Castelo, Daniel. *Pentecostalism as a Christian Mystical Tradition*. Grand Rapids: Eerdmans, 2017.

Chan, Simon. *Spiritual Theology: A Systematic Study of the Christian Life*. Downers Grove, IL: InterVarsity, 1998.

Coakley, Sarah. *God, Sexuality, and the Self: An Essay on the Trinity*. Cambridge: Cambridge University Press, 2013.

Crisp, Oliver D., et al., eds. *Analyzing Prayer: Theological and Philosophical Essays*. Oxford: Oxford University Press, 2022.

———. "The Importance of Model Building in Theology." In *T&T Handbook of Analytic Theology*, edited by James M. Arcadi and James T. Turner Jr., 9–19. London: Bloomsbury, 2021.

Cuneo, Terence. *Ritualized Faith: Essays on the Philosophy of Liturgy*. Oxford: Oxford University Press, 2016.

Evagrius. "On Prayer." In *The Philokalia*, edited and translated by G. E. H. Palmer et al., 1:55–71. London: Faber and Faber, 1979.

Inman, Ross D. "Theology in the Second Person." In Analyzing Prayer: Theological and Philosophical Essays, edited by Oliver Crisp et al., 116–35. Oxford: Oxford University Press, 2022.

Kavanaugh, Kieran, and Otilio Rodriguez, trans. *The Collected Works of St. Teresa of Avila*. 3 vols. Washington, DC: ICS, 1987.

Land, Steven J. *Pentecostal Spirituality: A Passion for the Kingdom*. Sheffield: Sheffield Academic Press, 1993.

Macchia, Frank D. "Sighs Too Deep for Words: Toward a Theology of Glossolalia." *Journal of Pentecostal Theology* 1 (1992) 47–73.

Newberg, Andrew B., et al. "The Measurement of Regional Cerebral Blood Flow During Glossolalia: A Preliminary SPECT Study." *Psychiatry Research* 148 (2006) 67–71.

Oliverio, L. William, Jr. *Theological Hermeneutics in the Classical Pentecostal Tradition: A Typological Account*. Leiden: Brill, 2012.

Palmer, G. E. H., et al., eds. *The Philokalia: The Complete Text*. 5 vols. New York: Faber and Faber, 1979.

Smith, James K. A. *Thinking in Tongues: Pentecostal Contributions to Christian Philosophy*. Grand Rapids: Eerdmans, 2010.

24. For a pneumatological perspective on the theological imagination, see Yong, *Spirit-Word-Community*.

Stephenson, Christopher A. "Analytic Theology: Postliberal, Performative, and Pentecostal." *Criswell Theological Journal* 19 (2021) 97–115.

———. "Should Pentecostal Theology Be Analytic Theology." *Pneuma* 36 (2014) 246–64.

———. *Types of Pentecostal Theology: Method, System, Spirit*. Oxford: Oxford University Press, 2013.

———. "Un-Speaking in Tongues: Glossolalia as Ascetical Prayer." *Journal of Spiritual Formation and Soul Care* 13 (2020) 88–101.

Stump, Eleonore. *Atonement*. Oxford: Oxford University Press, 2018.

Vondey, Wolfgang. "Pentecostal Theology." *St. Andrews Encyclopaedia of Theology*. https://www.saet.ac.uk/Christianity/PentecostalTheology.

Warrington, Keith. *Pentecostal Theology: A Theology of Encounter*. London: T&T Clark, 2008.

Wolterstorff, Nicholas. *Acting Liturgically: Philosophical Reflections on Religious Practice*. Oxford: Oxford University Press, 2018.

———. *The God We Worship: An Exploration of Liturgical Theology*. Grand Rapids: Eerdmans, 2015.

Wood, William. *Analytic Theology and the Academic Study of Religion*. Oxford: Oxford University Press, 2021.

Yong, Amos. *Spirit-Word-Community: Theological Hermeneutics in Trinitarian Perspective*. Burlington: Ashgate, 2002.

Key Doctrines

6

How Could (Some) Pentecostal Theology Be Analytic Theology?

A Proposal, Proto-Exemplar and an Example in the Doctrine of God

Matthew Churchouse

In a 2014 edition of *Pneuma*,[1] Christopher Stephenson wrote to introduce and commend analytic theology to (charismatic-)Pentecostals.[2] In a work that helped pave the way for the thought expressed in this subsequent compendium, he contended that Pentecostal theology would benefit from both analytic theology's style of clarity and precision but also its potential for encouraging prayer and meditation; he therefore suggested that some Pentecostal theology should be carried out as analytic theology (AT) as Pentecostal thought becomes more sophisticated philosophically.[3] Since his

1. *Pneuma* being the *Journal of the Society for Pentecostal Studies*. In this article I use the term "Pentecostal" to mean the same thing as this compendium's slightly fuller term "charismatic-Pentecostal."

2. Stephenson, "Should Pentecostal Theology Be Analytic Theology?," 246–64.

3. Although the method of analytic theology had been gradually developing in status prior, particularly the 2009 publication entitled *Analytic Theology: New Essays in the Philosophy of Theology* (Crisp and Rea [eds.]) was a landmark in the field and a book that launched the discipline to international prominence. For early response to that book, see for instance the critically endorsing reviews in the *International Journal of Systematic Theology* 12.4 (2010); for subsequent response, see main text above.

writing that article, the discipline (or more specifically, "method/style") of AT has continued to flourish and mature, now sporting centers around the world at institutions no less than the University of Notre Dame, University of St. Andrews, and Fuller Seminary. The growing interest it has garnered—from theologians and philosophers alike—is further demonstrated by the scholarly "invitations" to the discipline in recent years,[4] plus the development of the disciplinary specific *The Journal of Analytic Theology*—all of which giving considerable grounds for Stephenson's proposal and indeed the case of this following compendium. However, while potentially agreeing with the modest proposal that *some* Pentecostal theology could beneficially be carried out as AT, Pentecostals might validly raise the questions as to just *how* AT might be implemented *by* Pentecostals and what it would look like for their theologizing due to the uniqueness of approach in Pentecostal theology. Such questions bely latent difficulties for some Pentecostals with the usage of AT within the discipline of Pentecostal theology,[5] potentially impeding their employment of AT and stemming their enacting of the proposal. But in what follows I seek to examine the two disciplines and address these questions—allaying the latent difficulties and seeking to smooth the way for Pentecostals considering the analytic approach—specifically by way of the following: After drawing out the potential issues that Pentecostal theological method might (appear to) have with the analytic method, through closer inspection I propose, firstly, a way in which AT might be beneficially and consistently implemented by Pentecostals. I then, secondly, point to James K. A. Smith as an example of a Pentecostal theologian who, though not terming it as such, has already hinted at the potentiality of the method I suggest, functioning as an exemplar of a "proto-analytic approach" in areas of his Pentecostal work—a particular instance being evident in his work on Pentecostal ontology and the related doctrine of God. Thirdly, in continued dialogue with Smith but, in addition, with Pentecostal theologians more widely, I seek to give a fuller example of AT (employing it within Smith's already-existent Pentecostal theological method but extending his proto-analytic approach into a fuller analytic theology) by excavating the nature of Pentecostals' doctrine of God. As such, I give a proposal, a proto-exemplar and an example of AT to address the question of *how* (some) Pentecostal theology could be AT, so facilitating and modelling what it might look like for Pentecostal theology to beneficially employ AT.

4. For instance, McCall, *Invitation to Analytic Theology*.

5. I am grateful to Professor Mark Cartledge for drawing my attention to this point in a stimulating conversation we had following the publication of Stephenson's article.

Pentecostal Implementation of Analytic Theology?

The potential doubt for some Pentecostals as to the value of AT for Pentecostal theology is easily drawn out by comparing the methods of AT and Pentecostal theology.[6] On the one hand, there is AT, described by Rea as

> the activity of approaching theological topics with the ambitions of an analytic philosopher and in a style that conforms to the prescriptions that are distinctive of analytic philosophical discourse.[7]

The analytic ambitions Rea has in mind are (for thinkers) to:

1. Identify the scope and limits of our powers to obtain knowledge of the world.
2. Provide such true explanatory theories as we can in areas of inquiry (metaphysics, morals, and the like) that fall outside the scope of the natural sciences.[8]

And the analytic style he refers to is to:

a. Write as if philosophical positions and conclusions can be adequately formulated in sentences that can be formalized and logically manipulated.

b. Prioritize precision, clarity, and logical coherence.

c. Avoid substantive (non-decorative) use of metaphor and other tropes whose semantic content outstrips their propositional content.

d. Work as much as possible with well-understood primitive concepts, and concepts that can be analyzed in terms of those.

e. Treat conceptual analysis (insofar as it is possible) as a source of evidence.[9]

6. It should be clarified that although it is the methods of analytic theology and Pentecostal theology that make them distinctive, the meaning of "method" is different for each of these. As will be seen, for AT, the "method" is more one of a rhetorical *style* of articulating theology, and as such is theologically neutral. For Pentecostal theology, the "method" is integral to the distinctive *content* of the theology and as such is theologically saturated.

7. Rea, "Introduction," 7. Note, both Rea and Crisp—the editors of the book—are deliberate in pointing out that the discipline is not wedded to a certain view of truth (e.g., correspondence theory) or epistemological theory (e.g., foundationalism). It is simply a method of doing theology.

8. Rea, "Introduction," 4.

9. Rea, "Introduction," 5–6.

Other concise definitions have arisen from further advocates such as William Abraham,[10] but the following from Crisp brings a particularly succinct and complimentary understanding to that of Rea, defining AT as "the theological appropriation of the tools and methods of analytic philosophical theology for properly theological ends."[11]

One can see much benefit in this AT style.

However, on the other hand and in apparent contrast to AT, there is the approach of Pentecostal theology, which, as is regularly affirmed arises from Pentecostal *spirituality* and as such takes a somewhat different form to traditional systematic theology—its primary form being that of a *narrative* theology.

As Vondey has articulated, Pentecostal theology proceeds from the Pentecostal spirituality (or Pentecostal "lived experience of faith") in which believers seek on-going encounter experiences with the Spirit of Christ, which are then recounted in the form of testimony, in turn shaping the affections (of the "heart"), and becoming embodied in the worshiping practices and lifestyle of the believer.[12] In this spirituality, because the encounter is a Spirit-spirit encounter (difficult to convey in propositions),[13] the preferred form of expressing such is by oral *testimony* and *narrative*, Pentecostals using songs, tongues, stories, poetry, as some of their vehicles of expression for their experienced encounter with God—the theology being embedded in such forms. This articulation of the theology is somewhat foreign to the Western style of prose and propositions that theologians are used to finding in academic journals; however, it is a lot more encompassing of the styles of expression found in the non-Western world. Relatedly, this oral form of expressing themselves, which in turn shapes their affections (or "desires of the heart"[14]), means that Pentecostals are less interested in their theology being systematic—in the sense of being a logically ordered system of beliefs—but

10. Abraham prefers to define AT as "Systematic Theology attuned to the deployment of the skills, resources, and virtues of analytic philosophy. It is the articulation of the central themes of Christian teaching illuminated by the best insights of analytic philosophy." (Abraham, "Systematic Theology as Analytic Theology," 54).

11. Crisp and Rea, "Analytic Theology."

12. Vondey, *Pentecostal Theology*, 13.

13. For an exposition of Pentecostalism's being a (Divine-human) Spirit-*spirit* encounter see Churchouse, *Spiritual Soul.*

14. See for instance, Smith, *Desiring the Kingdom*. (A slightly more nuanced articulation of the relation between the desires and the affections [resulting from an analytical consideration of mental states {in the philosophy of mind}] is provided in Churchouse, *Spiritual Soul*, ch. 6).

more in it being an "aesthetic" logic of the heart,[15] lived out in embodied practice and everyday life. Presenting it starkly, Cartledge admonishes that.

> It [Pentecostal Theology] is concerned with the witness of life rather than the intricacy of arguments, allowing space for the Spirit to change hearts and lives . . . [In contrast to the rationality employed by many Evangelicals, Pentecostals] are less concerned with the issue of proof and propositions, even if they are just as concerned with issues of truth. In the Pentecostal worldview, truth is offered as 'witness' in and through a transformed lifestyle. Therefore, the primary vehicle is not western rational argumentation.[16]

Again, there is clearly much benefit in the Pentecostal method. But particularly focussing here on its inclusiveness of believers around the globe and their theological expressions, and its emphasis on the heart, it is easy to see why Pentecostal systematic theology has naturally embraced, and demonstrated a preference for, *continental* philosophy.[17] With its emphasizing of first-person experience and the *contextualized* nature of human thought, the appeal of continental philosophy is clear and indeed very evident in a lot of Pentecostal systematic theology, often resulting in much discussion concerning hermeneutics (since the postmodern "linguistic turn") as a result of its influence.

However, recognizing this influence and the approach of Pentecostal theology, when compared with the approach of AT it is easy to understand why some might consider Pentecostal theology to be at loggerheads with AT. Essentially, AT is interested in conceptual, propositional argumentation, Pentecostal theology is primarily interested in narrative, affections, and praxis. With these apparently divergent sets of interests, is there any benefit at all that AT can offer Pentecostal theology? And how could the latter implement the former?

While recognizing the differences, on closer inspection, the seeming conflict of interests is not as actual as might first appear. Though recognizing

15. Smith, *Thinking in Tongues*, 80–85.

16. Cartledge, "Text-Community-Spirit," 132, 136.

17. While scholars have found it difficult to give a precise definition of continental philosophy (in distinction from analytic philosophy), what follows in the main text above identifies some of the key features of the continental approach. (For a general and more popular definition of continental philosophy, there is value in the following—understanding continental philosophy as a Hegelian-influenced approach to philosophy emphasizing the historical, social, and cultural contextualizing factors of human life, and in turn often seeking to bring emancipation for societies and individuals from forms of injustice. See "Continental Philosophy."

that Pentecostal theology's *primary* vehicle of expression is oral narrative and testimony, Pentecostal scholars are evidently now using the forms of rational argumentation prevalent in Western academia as a means of articulating that theology—even if that is in (what Cartledge terms) a "chastened" sense due to the over-arching Pentecostal approach.[18] This means that systematic and speculative theology is a valid possibility for Pentecostals while recognizing it as subordinated to the pneumatic life-transformative practices of the Pentecostal spirituality, and as such in this secondary sense, re-opens the door for Pentecostals to implement the benefits of AT after all—when applied to their Western academic theology in prose and propositional form.

What that might look like is an interesting question. Informed by the continental tradition of philosophy, there are a number of Pentecostal systematic theological methods employed by Pentecostal scholars: examples such as the pneumatological theological hermeneutics of Yong,[19] or Kärkkäinen's renewal (and Pannenbergian), transversal approach,[20] further, Macchia's (Barthian and) pneumatological, post-liberal methodology,[21] are just a selection of the Pentecostal systematic theological methods being employed.[22] Yet I suggest that none of the variety of Pentecostal theological methods needs be altered to implement the benefits of AT. Rather, like Pentecostal systematic theology—occurring, as it does, chastened and *within* the wider narrative form—such AT could also be carried out *within* the already operational continental-colored Pentecostal methods thinkers are working with, and employed for certain subjects of systematic theology—particularly those that have a specific metaphysical focus that would benefit from AT's approach.[23]

Interestingly, all the Pentecostal theologians cited as examples above have, to a degree, carried out something of what might be called "analytic-leaning" theology in their work when touching on, for instance, the topics of divine sovereignty and free will, the constitutional ontology of humanity, and the nature of heaven and hell. However, for the purposes of spelling out and illustrating the contention that AT could be beneficially employed *within* an already operating Pentecostal method, James K. A. Smith will be illumined as a proto-exemplar of this suggestion—a *continental* philosopher and theologian but who has shown hints of an analytic theological approach

18. Cartledge, "Text-Community-Spirit," 136.

19. See primarily Yong, *Spirit-Word-Community.*

20. See Kärkkäinen, *Creation and Humanity*, 1.

21. See Macchia, *Baptized in the Spirit.*

22. See further, Stephenson, *Types of Pentecostal Theology.*

23. Remembering the "ambitions" of Rea.

within his more continental method. After briefly outlining his continental philosophical-theological method, his Pentecostal ontology and related doctrine of God will receive focus as a proto-example of the viability (and benefit) of Pentecostal usage of AT *within* an already existing continental approach. Employing the approach, then, more fully—having highlighted by this point the potentiality of AT within Pentecostal theological method—the chapter will proceed from Smith's particular Pentecostal ontology and related doctrine of God to addressing the doctrine of God more widely to give a fuller example of what AT might look like when applied to this specific area of Pentecostal thought. Maintaining dialogue with Smith on the issue, but considering Pentecostal thinkers more broadly, the chapter will ask the question as to whether Smith and Pentecostals' theology is panentheistic—a question that is theologically provocative but analytically sufficient for excavating Pentecostals' doctrine of God, so demonstrating more fully the suitability and benefit of applying the analytic approach within already-existent Pentecostal theological method(s).

Smith's Methodology in Proposing His Pentecostal Ontology

Smith's (self-defined) identity as a continental philosopher of religion is demonstrable from his writings; Having authored extensively on such topics as hermeneutics, postmodernism, and liturgy—engaging particularly with such thinkers as Husserl, Heidegger, and Derrida—Smith's continental credentials are clear.[24] This preference for continental philosophy has shaped Smith's theological method, leading him to distinguish between (what he calls) theology1 and theology2—theology1 being a community's spirituality or their set of "worship practices," theology2 being their reflection on the beliefs entailed in such practices.[25] Comparable to Wittgenstein's thinking (and sounding similar tones to the thought of George Lindbeck[26]) this approach affirms that doing theology is like speaking a language—one learns how to participate in the language first, then reflects on the language's grammar later.[27] What theology2, then, is (the discipline that "theologians" are

24. See Smith: *Fall of Interpretation*; "Taking Husserl at His Word"; "Confessions of an Existentialist"; *Hermeneutics of Charity*; *Jacques Derrida*; *Who's Afraid of Postmodernism?*; *Hermeneutics at the Crossroad*; *Devil Reads Derrida*; *Desiring the Kingdom*; *Thinking in Tongues*; *Imagining the Kingdom*; *Awaiting the King*.

25. Smith, *Introducing Radical Orthodoxy*, 166–79.

26. Cf. Lindbeck, *Nature of Doctrine*.

27. Or, in Wittgenstein's own terminology, one participates in the language-game

particularly engaged in[28]) is a retrospective reflection on the beliefs entailed in those worshiping practices—it being second-order reflection on (the practice of) theology1. Smith's methodology puts a clear stress on believers' spirituality (or their "lived experience of faith"), which resonates with the continental philosopher's interest in the (first-person) subjective experience. As such, his philosophy of religion and philosophical theology tends to focus on the areas of hermeneutics, liturgy, and postmodern thought—displaying the continental interest in the first-person subjective experience. However, while focussing specifically on these topics (and while still employing his method above as his overarching approach) Smith has intriguingly gained an interest in (Pentecostalism and) the natural sciences—an arena more commonly the focus of those in the *analytic* tradition. With the sciences' natural accent on the third-person empirical approach for acquiring knowledge about the world, Smith's engagement in this scientific venture has led him to draw on methods more favored by philosophers of the analytic tradition. This has, therefore, further led him to engage with their associated questions of interest such as how (given the world's existence, and the regularities of its laws) one can believe in the existence of God, or how (given God's existence) might God relate to the world. Indeed, as one reads through his work(s) it becomes evident that many of Smith's dialogue-partners on the issue are those more commonly identified as being *analytic* philosophers.[29] Yet, in engagement with these dialogue-partners, Smith has expounded his own particular ontology—indeed, a unique *Pentecostal* ontology (and entailed description of God's relationship to the world). As such, he functions, I would suggest, as a proto-exemplar of a thinker who beneficially employs the analytic tools within a more continentally colored, over-arching Pentecostal method.

There is much to be praised in Smith's ontological project—indeed the project in its entirety serves as a valuable model of Pentecostal philosophical theology. Yet, appreciating its creativity, it could be contended that additional use of the tools of the analytic tradition might potentially enhance this work. As articulation of his position will show, Smith distinguishes his Pentecostal ontology (from related ontologies of others) terming his view

---

first, and then reflects on the rules of the language-game later.

28. Smith is content to add "Christian philosophers" into this category too—in that both are both are second-order disciplines for reflecting on the first-order lived experience of faith; however, there is nuance in Smith's thinking between the relationship of theology and Christian philosophy (see further Smith, *Thinking in Tongues*, 3–7).

29. Smith, "Is the Universe Open," 879–96 (cf. Smith, "Is There Room," 34–49, ch. 2 in Smith and Yong, *Science and the Spirit* and ch. 4 of his *Thinking in Tongues*).

specifically as that of an "Enchanted Naturalism"[30]—the world being one that is "En-spirited."[31] His view of the world as such means that, while affirming the physical world—with its regular laws of nature—he likewise affirms its enchantment—namely its being filled with spirit(ual) beings.[32] The use of the word "Enchanted" is a literary, colorful description that helpfully appeals to the imagination but it is not particularly precise as to the relationship of God to the world; additional analytic employment could have proffered him further clarity. So while applauding Smith's endeavor—indeed wanting to highlight such work as serving as a fore-runner/proto-exemplar of Pentecostal-analytic-engagement—the chapter will seek to address his ontology and doctrine of God more fully (in dialogue with Pentecostal scholars more widely), and through asking the sufficient question, bring the chapter to a juncture of providing a fuller analytic understanding as to Pentecostal thought on the God-world relation. Indeed, the analytic process of such will more fully excavate Pentecostals' doctrine of God—(with a nod to Smith's methodology) the doctrine of God that is inherent in Pentecostal spirituality.

Smith's "Enchanted Naturalism" Ontology and the Pentecostal Doctrine of God

In articulating more fully the Pentecostal ontology of Smith, it is helpful to recognize its starting from a *rejection* of the Enlightenment's idea that the world is an autonomous entity; Smith finds thoroughly inadequate the contention that the world exists as an independent entity whose laws God has to "interrupt" (even "violate") in order to perform his actions within the natural world. By contrast, Smith advocates a *participatory* ontology in which the world can exist in being "only insofar as it *participates in* or *is suspended from* the transcendent Creator."[33] Put in other words, Smith affirms clearly that "Creation *is* (and 'nature' *is*) insofar as it participates in and is indwelled by God, in whom we live and move and have our being."[34] This participatory ontology is one he formed originally in dialogue with the

30. Smith, *Thinking in Tongues*, 89 and ch. 4.

31. Smith, *Thinking in Tongues*, 103–5.

32. The *Holy* Spirit's relation to the world being the primary focus of Smith's exposition.

33. Smith, *Thinking in Tongues*, 100 (emphasis mine).

34. Smith, *Thinking in Tongues*, 100 (emphasis his). Put alternately, Smith clarifies "being is a *gift* from the transcendent Creator such that things exist only insofar as they participate in the being of the Creator—whose Being is Goodness" (Smith, *Thinking in Tongues*, 100; emphasis his).

Radical Orthodoxy Movement, but, in a manner particularly of interest to Pentecostals—with their on-going expectation of the Spirit's manifestations in the world—is one he subsequently pneumatologically enhanced through conversation with Amos Yong. Yong offered Smith's ontology a "pneumatological assist" by suggesting that he considered the agent in whom the world is suspended as being *the Holy Spirit* in particular,[35] an assist which Smith gladly accepted. Yet Smith decided to take the assist in his own direction by advancing an ontology of differing *intensities* with which the world participates in the Spirit—suggesting that the world as God intended it enjoys a *directional* participation in the Spirit, but in their fallen sense, humans (and fallen angels) experience merely a structural participation in the Spirit.[36] As this relates to the aforementioned ontology of Smith, the assist has clearly Pentecostalized his participatory ontology, this color being prominent in what he states in the following passage:

> The *Spirit* is understood [by Pentecostals] to be the Trinitarian person in which creation lives and moves and has its being. So, nature, in a sense, is "suspended" in the Spirit of creation; or we might say that creation is "charged" with the Spirit's presence.[37]

As regards the God-world relationship—and what he suggests then is the view inherent in Pentecostal spirituality—he further expounds, stating:

> Nature is always already suspended in and inhabited by the Spirit such that it is always already *primed* for the Spirit's manifestations. Pentecostal spirituality and practice don't merely expect that God could "interrupt" the so-called "order" of nature, rather they assume that the Spirit is always already at work in creation, animating (and reanimating) bodies, grabbing hold of vocal cords, taking up aspects of creation to manifest the glory of God.[38]

(While the language of "grabbing hold of" may be not quite as others would express it,) Smith's describing the world as "primed," "charged" or "suffused" (the latter being the terminological preference of Yong) is language commonly shared by Pentecostal scholars to describe the world's being full of the Spirit's presence and his work as manifested in many ways in and

35. Yong, "Radically Orthodox, Reformed, and Pentecostal," 233–50.

36. A structural participation that, in the case of human beings, can be restored to a directional participation through the means of redemption in Christ (Smith, "Spirit, Religions and the World," 251–61).

37. Smith, *Thinking in Tongues*, 40 (emphasis mine).

38. Smith, *Thinking in Tongues*, 101.

through creation. As such it is common for Pentecostals to describe the world as being one that is "sacramental" in nature.[39] But in considering the "place" of the world as being *in* the realm of Spirit (the one "in whom we live, move and have our being"[40]), would it be additionally accurate to regard Smith's, and indeed Pentecostal theology as a whole, as being *panentheistic* in nature? Such a question is in some ways provocative and a question that divides Pentecostal scholars.[41] However, the question is provocatively helpful in its being philosophically sufficient for analytically excavating Pentecostals' distinctive understanding of God. In proceeding towards this goal, therefore, the following initially gives exposition of the meaning and position of panentheism, to then question its appropriateness as a description of Smith's and Pentecostals' theology; the process of such being sufficient for analytically excavating Pentecostals' distinctive doctrine of God and so giving a fuller example of the employment of AT to the benefit of Pentecostal theology.

Pentecostals and Panentheism

In wanting to define, analytically, the meaning of the (broad) term "panentheism," it would be helpful to begin with the unanimous contention that is held by panentheists across the (broad) spectrum: panentheists are united in their rejection of classical theism's account of the relation of God to the world, asserting that it does not do adequate justice to God's immanence *in* creation.[42] While classical theists want to affirm God's being present *to* all of creation they are often reluctant to affirm that he is *in* creation, and so by contrast panentheists distinctively affirm that the world is *in* God and God *in* the world—wanting to assert a particularly strong view of the immanence of God (while affirming at the same time his transcendence). Indeed, panentheism has been defined as:

39. Vondey, "Between This and That," 243–64; Green, *Towards a Pentecostal Theology of the Lord's Supper*; Cartledge, *Mediation of the Spirit*; Vondey, "Pentecostal Sacramentality," 94–107.

40. See the title of Clayton's and Peacocke's well-known compendium on Panentheism *In Whom We Live and Move and Have Our Being: Panentheistic Reflections on God's Presence in a Scientific World.*

41. Smith's (and also Yong's) shaping of a Pentecostal ontology that sees the world as "in" the realm of the Spirit—forged in relation to panentheistic thinkers—not surprisingly brings out such a question, on which there is not a unanimous answer among Pentecostals.

42. An immanence they contend is argued in Scripture, philosophy, and science.

> The belief that the Being of God includes and penetrates the whole universe so that every part of it exists in Him, but (contra Pantheism) that his Being is more than, and not exhausted by, the universe.[43]

Elaborating the understanding more fully, a complimentary definition has been given by philosopher Chad Meister who states,

> Unlike pantheism . . . in which God is *identical* to the world, and unlike theism, in which God is *present to* but *ontologically* distinct *from* the world, for panentheism, the world is in God and God is in and beyond the world. God contains the whole world within Godself, but God is also more than the world.[44]

While the exact sense of what it means for the world to be "in" God is disputed,[45] and so the category of "panentheist" acknowledged as wide, a scale has been proposed by leading panentheist Philip Clayton to highlight what he sees as the differing *degrees* of panentheism. On Clayton's scale below (between classical theism [at 1] and pantheism [at 7]), he proposes categories 2–6 as varieties of the pan*en*theist via media—ranging from

43. Cross and Livingstone, "Panentheism," 1213 (emphasis mine).

44. Meister, "Ancient and Contemporary Expressions," 1 (emphasis his).

For a further complimentary delineation, see Göcke who prefers:

On theism, God and reality are essentially ontologically distinct. Theistic models of God often assume that God is an everlasting, omniscient, omnipotent, and morally perfect person who creates the world ex nihilo.

On panentheism, reality is (completely) in God. The being of the world is supposed to be completely in God while not exhaustive of the divine being.

On pantheism, God and reality are identified. Pantheistic models of the God-world relation often argue that because there can only be one substance, the universe has to be identified with this substance that we call God.

Göcke, "Concepts of God," 5. (Note, the ordering above inverts Göcke's original order [which has theism as number 1, pantheism as number 2, an additional category—"theistic emergentism"—as number 3, and panentheism as number 4).

45. Göcke provides the following list of interpretations of the meaning of "in" in differing views of panentheism: the world is "in" God because (a) that is its literal location; (b) God energizes the world; (c) God experiences or "prehends" the world (process theology); (d) God ensouls the world; (e) God plays with the world (Indic Vedantic traditions); (f) God "enfields" the world (J. Bracken); (g) God gives space to the world (J. Moltmann drawing on the zimzum traditions; A. Peacocke); (h) God encompasses or contains the world (substantive or locative notion); (i) God binds up the world by giving the divine self to the world; (j) God provides the grounds of emergences in, or the emergence of, the world (A. Peacocke, P. Davies, H. Morowitz, P. Clayton); (k) God befriends the world (C. Deanne-Drummond); (l) all things are contained "in Christ" (from the Pauline *en Christo*); and (m) God graces the world (P. Clayton). Göcke, "Concepts of God," 11n25.

weak panentheist (at 2) through to strong panentheism (at 6)—his scale (of panentheisms) being as follows:

1. God created the world as a distinct substance. It is separate from God in nature and essence, although God is present to the world.
2. God is radically immanent in the world.
3. God is bringing the world to Godself.
4. The world is in God—at least metaphorically, and perhaps also in a stronger sense.
5. God's relation to the world is in some sense analogous to the relationship between mind and body.
6. The world and God are correlated (contingently for some authors, necessarily for others).
7. The world and God are "nondual," or there is only one substance that can be called "nature" or "God."[46]

If Clayton's scale is granted, the pertinent question then becomes as to whether Smith and Pentecostals more widely might map their ontology and doctrine of God onto this scale at any point. Plausibly sensing resonances with what is expressed in category 2 (so being those that Clayton would term *weak* panentheists), Pentecostals Yong and Gabriel have answered the question in the affirmative being content to describe themselves as *trinitarian* panentheists.[47] While both are clear to distinguish themselves from *process* (or "strong" forms of) panentheism, both are content—with this caveat—to take the *trinitarian* panentheist label, describing the world as being *in* specifically the person of *the Holy Spirit*. Pertinently, the description of trinitarian panentheism is one that is particularly associated with Clayton himself—his having expounded the position in an article of 1998 and propagated the view in his subsequent work.[48] Indeed, given Yong's interactions with Clayton's work (and Yong's influence in Pentecostal theology),[49] it appears that Clayton has done much to engender Yong and

46. Clayton, "Panentheism Today," 251–52.

47. Yong, "Science and the (Super) Natural," n6. Cf. Gabriel, *Lord Is the Spirit*, 142–25.

48. See Clayton, "Case for Christian Panentheism," 201–8; Clayton, "Panentheism Internalism," 208–15; Clayton, "Kenotic Trinitarian Panentheism," 250–55.

49. Clayton's influence on Yong is particularly apparent in Yong, *Spirit of Creation*. Yong's influence in Pentecostal scholarship is displayed particularly by the appreciative compendium Vondey and Mittelstadt, *Theology of Amos Yong*.

Gabriel's identifying with the view and adopting the label for themselves—being content to assume the description of being (Pentecostal) trinitarian panentheists.

Smith, by contrast, does not—in any sense of the word—affiliate with the term "panentheist." While sometimes expressing sympathies with those he terms "nonreductionist materialists"—panentheists Peacocke, Clayton, and Griffin—he yet maintains a certain level of distance from their panentheism(s) as he forges his own (participatory) ontology[50]—underlining the distinction and uniqueness of his Pentecostal enspirited ontology.[51] This distinction and uniqueness becomes apparent when, in commenting on the panentheism that underpins Clayton's *Mind and Emergence* project, he states, "[Clayton's panentheism] does not start from a sufficiently dynamic sense of the *contingency* of the 'laws' of nature."[52] Giving further insight to his thought and expanding his critique more generally (to encompass the panentheists Peacocke and Griffin in addition), he elaborates:

> The panentheism that usually attends . . . [the nonreductive materialist position of Peacocke, Griffin as well as Clayton] emphasizes the *immanence* of God to the world as the *world's dynamic principle*. This differs from the Pentecostal ontology insofar as the "God" internal to the world, as it were, does not, would not, and cannot act outside of the "laws" of nature. In short, the key difference between [the 2 views] is the question of miracles.[53]

Notably, Smith's articulated concern here is not with the *trinitarian* nature of Clayton (et al.)'s panentheism(s),[54] rather his concern is regarding the contingency of the laws of nature, fearing that God (on panentheists' views) collapses into just the dynamic principle of the world. As such, he wants to maintain a distance from Clayton's view and indeed any form of panentheism. Smith's diagnosis of Clayton's view in this sense sounds similar and

50. See Smith, "Spirit, Religions and the World," 191n17 and Smith, *Thinking in Tongues*, 102n38.

51. Smith, *Thinking in Tongues*, 96–103.

52. Smith, *Thinking in Tongues*, 102–3n38 (emphasis his).

53. Smith, *Thinking in Tongues*, 97 (emphasis of "imminence" his, emphasis of "world's dynamic principle" mine). Following the reading of this book and in wanting to clarify exactly where Smith stands as regards to panentheism, in a personal correspondence I asked him whether he might map his ontology onto Clayton's scale of panentheisms (anywhere between #2–6). In reply Smith clarified that he did not feel entirely comfortable with any panentheistic affiliation.

54. As a scientific and philosophical treatise, in *Mind and Emergence* for example, Clayton does not emphasize the *trinitarian* aspect in the work—though such being consistent with the panentheism he (there) espoused.

related tones to what panentheists themselves have sought to convey (about the panentheistic God–world relation) by way of the mind-body analogy: On this (oft-cited) analogy, just as the mind brings about effects in the body and gains understanding and knowledge *through* the body, so God brings about effects in the world and gains understanding and knowledge *through* the world; this indicating a more *interactive/interdependent* relation of God to the world than traditional theism espouses.[55] Indeed, while Clayton might want to counter that he *does* in fact affirm the contingency of the laws of nature [*in* God] and want to re-assert that only from his category 5 onwards would a panentheist want to espouse such an analogy, even as a self-identified *trinitarian* panentheist, he too wants to affirm this "interdependent" relation (of God and the world) that the analogy draws attention to.[56] As such (while being a critique of degree), one can see why Smith is not fully satisfied that the contingency (of the laws of nature) is sufficiently dynamic on Clayton's view. In truth, being consistent with the definition(s) of panentheism given above, Clayton's stress on "interdependence" (or "mutuality" as it is sometimes termed[57])—indeed panentheists' contention that God's being *includes* the world—carries *ontological* implications, lucidly revealed by Stenmark:

> Since [on panentheism] the world constitutes a part of God, God is *ontologically* affected by changes in the world. . . . Since the world is a part of God but not identical with God . . . [panentheists] reject the doctrine of ontological distinction and embrace instead . . . the doctrine of *ontological inclusion*.[58]

With this feature being common to panentheism as a collective, one can see why Smith and other Pentecostals might not want any panentheistic affiliation. Pentecostals are largely traditional theists in the sense of espousing the aseity of God and creation ex nihilo. In contrast, once it is affirmed that God and the world are mutually *inter*-dependent, the doctrine of God's

55. The word "classical" has been exchanged here for "traditional" because a number of non-panentheistic Christian thinkers identify with theism in its Christian traditional sense while not terming themselves classical theists. Sometimes revising, for instance, the doctrine of the impassibility of God, such thinkers remain in the traditional theistic category (as opposed to moving to Open Theism or panentheism). For further discussion see Cooper, *Panentheism*.

56. Clayton, "Panentheism in Metaphysical and Scientific Thought," 83.

57. Cf. Meister, "Ancient and Contemporary," 8.

58. Stenmark, "Panentheism and Its Neighbours," 26–27 (emphasis mine). He goes on to spell out more starkly—of panentheism as a collective—"the essential difference is that traditional theists think that God is (ontologically) distinct from the world and does not depend on it for God's own existence, whereas panentheists believe that God (ontologically) includes the world and depends on the world for God's own existence" (41).

aseity quickly disappears, and a number of panentheists also go onto deny creation ex nihilo[59] (affirming instead a "self-transformation in the divine being" because creation *proceeds from within him*[60]). While Yong and Gabriel appear to find their own (trinitarian) niche within the panentheist household, the connotations of the movement as a whole, as indeed of some trinitarian proponents, may not be those that Pentecostals find particularly attractive.

Pentecostals' Doctrine of God

Having suggested, then, that it may not be a favorable or accurate description to describe Pentecostal theology as panentheistic, how does one then conceive of the Pentecostal doctrine of God and the God–world relation? The asking of this question and exploration into ontology has revealed that Smith and Pentecostals generally *do* affirm a very intimate relationship between God and the world. Indeed, Pentecostals' understanding of the immanence of God (and specifically of his Holy Spirit) makes it distinctive in its doctrine of God from other traditional theologies—in which God's immanence is commonly downplayed (even lost) in such models' emphasis on transcendence. As such, while Pentecostals fully maintain the transcendence of God in their theology, their (what might be termed as an) "immanentist" view of God provides some push back on certain traditional views that have lost sight of the immanence of God (and so which potentially contribute to the rise in the caricaturing of classical theism[61]). Indeed, while being helpful to delineate that Pentecostals affirm creation's being distinct from, but dependent upon (the Spirit of) God, it is fair to say further that they want to affirm that the Spirit is present to *and within* creation—bifurcating Clayton's categories 1 and 2 and expressing a degree of immanence commonly missing in traditional models. This distinct and liminal understanding of God—what I have termed the Pentecostal "immanentist" view—then, is one that prizes open traditional models of God creating more space for God's (specifically the Spirit's) immanence than is usually maintained. While resisting the category of panentheism, then, the raising of this provocative question has been analytically sufficient for excavating the Pentecostal doctrine of God inherent in Pentecostal practice. As such, within Smith's continental

59. Peters, "Models of God," 285.

60. Göcke, "Concepts of God," 7.

61. It has become all too common in the modern era to hear classical theism being presented as a position which espouses a static view of God who is unaffected by anything that happens in the world—a position that falls far short of the classical theism expounded through church history.

theological approach, the tools of analytic theology have been employed to advance Pentecostals' understanding of God but of course in a manner that brings edification to Pentecostals in their spiritual practice. Beyond the example Smith alluded to as regards miracles, the understanding of the Spirit's immanence to and within the world brings spiritual insight as to what is happening in Pentecostals' "Come Holy Spirit" times during their worship gatherings. In asking the Spirit to "come," Pentecostals are asking/expecting the Spirit immanent within the world to "intensify" his presence,[62] or (employing alternate terminology) to "surge" more fully in that particular place.[63] So, the use of AT here facilitates a deeper understanding for Pentecostals as to what is happening in their Spirit-filled worship gatherings and so enriching their theological-spiritual understanding and practice. As such, this analytic discussion has brought excavation of Pentecostals' doctrine of God and highlighted a variety of implications, displaying the benefit the analytic method can bring to certain areas of Pentecostal theology.

Conclusion

In what has been argued, this chapter has sought to address and indeed model how (some) Pentecostal theology might be carried out as *analytic* theology. While recognizing that Pentecostal theological method tends to be a discipline more influenced by continental philosophical method, it has been argued that the methods of AT and Pentecostal theology are not at loggerheads as is sometimes assumed. Rather, for *some* topics of discussion, the tools of analytic theology can be helpfully applied *within* those wider Pentecostal continental theological methods. The continental philosopher and Pentecostal theologian James K. A. Smith has been presented as a proto-exemplar of this suggestion with his work on Pentecostal ontology and the related doctrine of God given prominence in order to model this contention. Having employed the tools of AT to consider his Pentecostal ontology and doctrine of God more fully, Pentecostals' immanentist doctrine of God has been more clearly excavated and its implications revealed. As such the benefit of AT to Pentecostal theology has been displayed and through giving the proposal, proto-exemplar and example from the doctrine of God it has,

62. To use the wording of Smith (for example, *Thinking in Tongues*, 102). (This description of the "intensification" of the Spirit raises another and related question which analytic theology might bring additional insight to, namely the view of the Trinity that is inherent in Pentecostal practice.)

63. Consider the lyrics to the popular Pentecostal song "Holy Spirit you are welcome here, come flood this place and fill the atmosphere." (Torwalt and Torwalt, "Holy Spirit You Are Welcome Here."

the chapter has addressed the question of *how* (some) Pentecostal theology might be carried out as analytic theology.

Bibliography

Abraham, William. "Systematic Theology as Analytic Theology." In *Analytic Theology: New Essays in the Philosophy of Theology*, edited by Oliver D. Crisp and Michael C. Rea, 54–69. Oxford: Oxford University Press, 2009.

Cartledge, Mark J. *The Mediation of the Spirit: Interventions in Practical Theology*. Grand Rapids: Eerdmans, 2015.

———. "Text-Community-Spirit: The Challenges posed by Pentecostal Theological Method to Evangelical Theology." In *Spirit and Scripture: Exploring a Pneumatic Hermeneutic*, edited by Kevin L. Spawn and Archie T. Wright, 130–44. London: T&T Clark, 2011.

Churchouse, Matthew J. *The Spiritual Soul: Towards an Enhanced Pentecostal (-Charismatic) Philosophical-Theological Doctrine of Human Constitution*. Eugene, OR: Pickwick, forthcoming.

Clayton, Philip. "The Case for Christian Panentheism." *Dialog* 37 (1998) 201–8.

———. "Kenotic Trinitarian Panentheism." *Dialog* 44 (2005) 250–55.

———. "Panentheism in Metaphysical and Scientific Thought." In *In Whom We Live, Move and Have our Being*, edited by Philip Clayton and Arthur Peacocke, 73–93. Grand Rapids: Eerdmans, 2004.

———. "Panentheism Internalism: Living within the presence of the Triune God." *Dialog* 40 (2002) 208–15.

———. "Panentheism Today." In *In Whom We Live, Move and Have our Being*, edited by Philip Clayton and Arthur Peacocke, 249–64. Grand Rapids: Eerdmans, 2004.

Clayton, Philip, and Arthur Peacocke, eds. *In Whom We Live and Move and Have our Being: Panentheistic Reflections on God's Presence in a Scientific World*. Grand Rapids: Eerdmans, 2004.

"Continental Philosophy—Wittgenstein and Analytic Philosophy." http://science.jrank.org/pages/8829/Continental-Philosophy-Wittgenstein-Analytic-Philosophy.html.

Cooper, John, W. *Panentheism: The Other God of the Philosophers—from Plato to the Present*. Grand Rapids: Baker Academic, 2006.

Crisp, Oliver D., and Michael C. Rea, eds. "Analytic Theology: Interview with Editors Crisp and Rea (part 1)." Evangelical Philosophical Society, January 8, 2010. http://blog.epsociety.org/2010/01/analytic-theology-interview-with.asp.

———. *Analytic Theology: New Essays in the Philosophy of Theology*. Oxford: Oxford University Press, 2009.

Cross, F. L., and E. A. Livingstone, eds. "Pantheism." In *Oxford Dictionary of the Christian Church*. 3rd ed. Oxford: Oxford University Press, 2005.

Gabriel, Andrew. *The Lord Is the Spirit: The Holy Spirit and the Divine Attributes*. Eugene, OR: Pickwick, 2010.

Göcke, Benedict P. "Concepts of God and Models of the God-World Relation." *Philosophy Compass* 12 (2017) 1–15.

Green, Chris E. W. *Towards a Pentecostal Theology of the Lord's Supper: Foretasting the Kingdom*. Tennessee: CPT, 2012.

Kärkkäinen, Veli-Matti. *Creation and Humanity*. A Constructive Christian Theology for the Church in the Pluralistic World 3. Grand Rapids: Eerdmans, 2015.

Lindbeck, George. *The Nature of Doctrine: Religion and Theology in a Postliberal Age*. Philadelphia: Westminster John Knox, 1984.

Macchia, Frank. *Baptized in the Spirit: A Global Pentecostal Theology*. Grand Rapids: Zondervan, 2006.

McCall, Thomas. *An Invitation to Analytic Theology*. Downers Grove, IL: IVP Academic, 2015.

Meister, Chad. "Ancient and Contemporary Expressions of Panentheism." *Philosophy Compass* 12 (2017) 1–12.

Peters, Ted. "Models of God." *Philosophia* 35 (2007) 273–88.

Rea, Michael A. "Introduction." In *Analytic Theology: New Essays in the Philosophy of Theology*, edited by Oliver D. Crisp and Michael C. Rea, 1–30. Oxford: Oxford University Press, 2009.

Smith, James K. A. *Awaiting the King: Reforming Public Theology*. Cultural Liturgies 3. Grand Rapids: Baker Academic, 2017.

———. "Confessions of an Existentialist: Reading Augustine After Heidegger." *New Blackfriars* 82 (2001) 273–82 (Part 1) and 335–47 (Part 2).

———. *Desiring the Kingdom: Worship, Worldview, and Cultural Formation*. Grand Rapids: Baker Academic, 2009.

———. *The Devil Reads Derrida: and Other Essays on the Church, the University, Politics, and the Arts*. Grand Rapids: Eerdmans, 2009.

———. *The Fall of Interpretation: Philosophical Foundations for a Creational Hermeneutic*. Downers Grove, IL: InterVarsity, 2000.

———. *Hermeneutics at the Crossroad: Interpretation in Christian Perspective*. Edited with K. Vanhoozer and B. E. Benson. Bloomington: Indiana University Press, 2006.

———. *The Hermeneutics of Charity: Interpretation, Selfhood, and Postmodern Faith*. Edited with H. Venema. Grand Rapids: Brazos, 2004.

———. *Imagining the Kingdom: How Worship Works*. Cultural Liturgies 2. Grand Rapids: Baker Academic, 2013

———. *Introducing Radical Orthodoxy: Mapping a Post-Secular Theology*. Grand Rapids: Baker Academic, 2004.

———. "Is There Room for Surprise in the Natural World? Naturalism, the Supernatural and Pentecostal Spirituality." In *Science and the Spirit: Questions and Possibilities in the Pentecostal Engagement with Science*, edited by James K. A. Smith and Amos Yong, 34–49. Bloomington: Indiana University Press, 2010.

———. "Is the Universe Open for Surprise? Pentecostal Ontology and the Spirit of Naturalism." *Zygon: Journal of Religion and Science* 43 (2008) 879–96.

———. *Jacques Derrida: Live Theory*. London; Continuum, 2005.

———. "The Spirit, Religions and the World as Sacrament: A Response to Amos Yong's Pneumatological Assist." *Journal of Pentecostal Theology* 15 (2007) 251–61.

———. "Taking Husserl at His Word: Towards a New Phenomenology with the Young Heidegger." *Symposium: Journal of the Canadian Society for Hermeneutics and Postmodern Thought* 4 (2000) 89–115.

———. *Thinking in Tongues: Pentecostal Contributions to Christian Philosophy*. Grand Rapids: Eerdmans, 2010.

———. *Who's Afraid of Postmodernism?: Taking Derrida, Lyotard, and Foucault to Church*. Grand Rapids: Baker Academic, 2006.

Smith, James K. A., and Amos Yong, eds. *Science and the Spirit: Questions and Possibilities in the Pentecostal Engagement with Science*. Bloomington: Indiana University Press, 2010.

Stenmark, Mikael. "Panentheism and Its Neighbours." *International Journal of Philosophy of Religion* 85 (2019) 23–41.

Stephenson, Christopher A. "Should Pentecostal Theology Be Analytic Theology?" *Pneuma* 36 (2014) 246–64.

———. *Types of Pentecostal Theology: Method, System, Spirit*. Oxford and New York: Oxford University Press, 2013.

Torwalt, K., and B. Torwalt. "Holy Spirit You Are Welcome Here." 2012. https://www.youtube.com/watch?v=ktsPuZvH-rQ.

Vondey, Wolfgang. "Between This and That: Reality and Sacramentality in the Pentecostal Worldview." *Journal of Pentecostal Theology* 19 (2010) 243–64.

———. "Pentecostal Sacramentality and the Theology of the Altar." In *Scripting Pentecost: A Study of Pentecostals, Worship and Liturgy*, edited by Mark J. Cartledge and A. J. Swoboda, 94–107. Grand Rapids: Eerdmans, 2016.

———. *Pentecostal Theology: Living the Full Gospel*. London: Bloomsbury T&T Clark, 2017.

Vondey, Wolfgang, and Martin W. Mittelstadt, eds. *The Theology of Amos Yong and the New Face of Pentecostal Scholarship*. Leiden: Brill, 2013.

Yong, Amos. "Radially Orthodox, Reformed, and Pentecostal: Rethinking the Intersection of Post/Modernity and the Religions in Conversation with James K. A. Smith." *Journal of Pentecostal Theology* 15 (2007) 233–50.

———. "Science and the (Super) Natural: Can Pentecostals Mediate Any Conversation."—Yong's response to a review symposium regarding his book *The Spirit of Creation*: "A Review Symposium on Amos Yong The Spirit of Creation: Modern Science and Divine Action in the Pentecostal-Imagination." *Australian Pentecostal Studies* 15 (2013). https://aps-journal.com/index.php/APS/article/view/122/119.

———. *The Spirit of Creation: Modern Science and Divine Action in the Pentecostal-Imagination*. Grand Rapids: Eerdmans, 2011.

———. *Spirit-Word-Community: Theological Hermeneutics in Trinitarian Perspective*. Aldershot: Ashgate, 2002.

7

Creation ex Nihilo, Participation, and the Sanctification of Matter

Melissa Davis[1]

The doctrine of *creatio ex nihilo* arose in the second century as a philosophical-theological response to the then-current challenges to Christianity—Platonism, Stoicism, and Gnosticism. While not explicitly stated in Scripture, it is a "*biblically compelled* piece of metaphysical theology."[2] A general misconception concerning the doctrine is that it is primarily concerned with the material origins of the universe and thus "stands or falls on the interpretation of Genesis 1."[3] However, while material origins are part of the conversation, as Janet Soskice asserts, "*Creatio ex nihilo* is not a teaching about the cosmos but about God."[4] *Creatio ex nihilo* is not Greek philosophy in Judeo-Christian guise. It engages Scripture to answer philosophical questions about God arising from a Hellenistic context. The doctrine has three central topics: the identity and nature of the Creator, his act of creating, and from this, the nature and *telos* of created things.[5]

1. Scripture quotations in this chapter are taken from the English Standard Version.
2. Soskice, "*Creatio Ex Nihilo*," 25.
3. Anderson, "*Creatio Ex Nihilo* and the Bible," 22.
4. Soskice, "Why *Creatio Ex Nihilo*," 38.
5. Webster, "Love Is Also a Lover of Life," 157, 160–61.

However, it is appropriately criticized for focusing on the Creator or God without nuancing the Trinity.

Pentecostal-charismatic theology is particularly interested in articulating explicitly trinitarian doctrine, with particular attention to the work of the Holy Spirit. However, while Pentecostals and charismatics have traditionally affirmed God as the Creator of the universe, the doctrine of creation was secondary in concern.[6] Studebaker, Lamp, and Chan link the deprioritization of creation to two primary theological commitments. First, many early Pentecostals followed evangelicals by holding a dispensational premillennial eschatology that anticipated Christ's imminent return and the resulting destruction of this world in the New Creation.[7] Second, they held a dualistic worldview, prioritizing the spiritual over the created order and an anthropocentric reading of the creation narratives.[8] In this paradigm, creation becomes the backdrop to God's "real work" of salvation, but not part of the action.

Recently, the doctrine has received renewed interest among Pentecostal-charismatic scholars. Scholars have explored creation by reframing the doctrine in pneumatological terms,[9] in conversation with the Fivefold Gospel,[10] science and natural history,[11] or through ecotheology and creation care.[12] For the most part, these scholars treat the term creation as

6. Many Pentecostal theologies do not contain an entry for the doctrine of creation. Richie, *Essentials of Pentecostal Theology*; Warrington, *Pentecostal Theology*; Menzies, *Bible Doctrines*; Duffield and Van Cleave, *Foundations of Pentecostal Theology*.

7. Peter Althouse argues that early Pentecostals held to a covenantal "latter rain" eschatology before moving to evangelical premillennialism in the mid-twentieth century. See Althouse, "'Left Behind.'"

8. Lamp, "Ecotheology," 357–59; Studebaker, *From Pentecost to the Triune God*, 241–42; Chan, *Pentecostal Ecclesiology*, 19. Grace Milton notes that until recently, Pentecostal soteriology understood humankind as the primary, if not sole, object of salvation. Creation, while impacted by human sin, was left largely untreated. Recent Pentecostal ecotheologies have sought to address this lacuna, arguing that the renewal and restoration of the eschaton will bring wholeness to all created things—human and non-human. Milton, "Salvation," 232.

9. Williams, *Renewal Theology*, ch. 5; Lamp, "Wisdom Pneumatology and the Creative Spirit," 39–56; Althouse, "Implications of the Kenosis of the Spirit," 155–72.

10. Vondey, *Pentecostal Theology*, 155–74; Studebaker, *From Pentecost to the Triune God*, 240–68; Studebaker, "Creation Care," 248–64; Lamp, "Jesus as Sanctifier," 152–68; Lamp, "New Heavens and New Earth," 64–80; Clifton, "Preaching the 'Full Gospel,'" 117–34; Macchia, *Baptized in the Spirit*; Griffiths, "Spirit-Baptised Creation," 46–60.

11. Yong, *Renewing Christian Theology*, ch. 7; Yong, "*Ruach*, the Primordial Chaos," 183–204; Badger and Tenneson, "Does the Spirit Create," 92–116.

12. Lamp, "Ecotheology," 357–66; Chandler, "Creation Care," 112–28; Willams, "Greening the Apocalypse," 205–29; Swoboda, "Looking the Wrong Way," 231–47; Studebaker, "Creation Care," 248–64.

coterminous with the natural world. However, as James Mays notes, the contemporary notion of "creation" is at odds with its scriptural antecedents.

> The term [creation] has come to mean no more than the natural world in the vocabulary of New Age religion, nature romanticism, environmental enthusiasm, artistic aestheticism, and even in unselfconscious traditional religion and liberal piety. There is no term or text in the Psalms, or indeed in the entire Bible, for creation in this sense.[13]

While Mays overstates his case—he notes in the Psalms that creation refers to YHWH's creative action *and* its results—his point is well put. Scripturally and theologically, creation encompasses more than the created world. Creation includes the Creator, his creative work, and the created world. Thus, contemporary theological use of "creation" is often too narrow. As such, the traditional doctrine of *creatio ex nihilo* is often assumed and left undeveloped, bypassed, or denied.

Reformed-Pentecostal philosopher James K. A. Smith has developed a pneumatological, or "enchanted," naturalism. Smith's approach combines themes from Radical Orthodoxy (RO), the Pentecostal-charismatic worldview, and science. His participatory ontology seeks to be trinitarian and engages with many of the themes of *creatio ex nihilo* without expressly engaging with the doctrine.

In this chapter, I will argue that when read through a Pentecostal/charismatic lens, *creatio ex nihilo* provides fertile ground for a trinitarian-participatory ontology of creation. My argument will proceed through three stages. I will begin by outlining *creatio ex nihilo* with particular attention to its relationship with Scripture, its significance for the Creator/creature distinction, and its divine participation by engaging with Thomas Aquinas and Simon Oliver. Then, I will draw Smith's enchanted naturalism into the conversation. Finally, I will bring these two together to argue that creation is sanctified through its participation in the Father (*Archē*), Son (*Logos*), and Spirit (*Dunamis*).

Creatio Ex Nihilo

The doctrine of *creatio ex nihilo* finds its genesis in the Hellenistic context of Second Temple Judaism. According to Greek Philosophers, something has always existed. In the late sixth century BC, Parmenides articulated the

13. Mays, "Maker of Heaven and Earth," 75.

philosophical maxim *ex nihilo, nihil fit*, "out of nothing, nothing comes."[14] Thus, in the *Timaeus*, Plato argued that a divine demiurge formed the world by ordering pre-existent material chaos,[15] Aristotle argued that the universe has always existed,[16] and the Neoplatonist Plotinus argued in his *Enneads* that all things emanate from the "One."[17] As Robert Wilken notes, according to Greek Philosophy, while God or the gods dwelt above the earth, they were nonetheless part of the cosmos, subject to the same natural laws as the rest of creation.[18] For the Judeo-Christian tradition, these philosophical worldviews stood in stark contrast to what is revealed in Scripture. To adopt these perspectives would be to affirm that there was always something that existed apart from God that compelled, constrained, or in some way limited his creative action. Theologically, neither Jews nor Christians could affirm this of the God of Scripture.[19]

One of the earliest explicit statements of *creatio ex nihilo* dates to the Second Temple period. This period was a time of great upheaval for the Jews, full of war and messianic hopefulness. In Second Maccabees, a mother encourages her seven sons, who are about to be martyred, with these words:

> I do not know how you came into being in my womb. It was not I who gave you life and breath, nor I who set in order the elements within each of you. Therefore the *Creator of the world, who shaped the beginning of humankind and devised the origin of all things*, will in his mercy *give life and breath back to you* again, since you now forget yourselves for the sake of his laws.[20]

Later in the same passage, she encourages her youngest son, saying,

14. Oliver, *Creation*, 36.

15. "For God desired that, so far as possible, all things should be good and nothing evil; wherefore, when He took over all that was visible, seeing that it was not in a state of rest but in a state of discordant and disorderly motion, He brought it into order out of disorder, deeming that the former state is in all ways better than the latter" Plato, *Timaeus* 30B.

16. Specifically, Aristotle argues that motion is "everlasting." For Aristotle, motion is "a sort of life." Oliver notes that motion (*kinesis*) is "a mysterious and broad category which encompasses not only local motion of bodies through space, but also the changes of, for example, growing, learning or thinking. . . . Motion is passage from potency to act, and therefore the means of actualization, or perfection, of creatures" (Oliver, "Trinity, Motion, and Creation Ex Nihilo," 136).

17. As per Plotinus, the "One" is the source of all things. The One is "perfect" and "has overflowed, and its exuberances has produced the new" (Plotinus, *Enneads* 5.2.1).

18. Wilken, *Christians as the Romans Saw Them*, 91.

19. Oliver, *Creation*, 35–38; Soskice, "Creation and the Glory of Creatures," 176, 181, 184.

20. 2 Macc 7:22–23, NRSV; italics added.

> My son, have pity on me. I carried you nine months in my womb, and nursed you for three years, and have reared you and brought you up to this point in your life, and have taken care of you. I beg you, my child, to look at the heaven and the earth and see everything that is in them, and recognize that *God did not make them out of things that existed. And in the same way the human race came into being.* Do not fear this butcher, but prove worthy of your brothers. Accept death, so that in God's mercy *I may get you back again* along with your brothers.[21]

Whether the mother had the doctrine of *creatio ex nihilo* in mind as she uttered these words is debatable. What is important here is that amid extreme suffering and tribulation, the God who created all things out of nothing and was capable of recreation was a source of hope and strength. This passage emphasizes the Creator's character and power rather than the created order's specifics. Unlike the contemporary Greek philosophies, this text asserts that God creates out of nothing.

Likewise, the authors of Scripture widely attest that God created all that is. However, they appear less concerned about *how* God created than *who* he is.[22] The story of salvation history opens by declaring, "In the beginning, God created the heavens and the earth. The earth was without form and void, and darkness was over the face of the deep. And the Spirit of God was hovering over the face of the waters" (Gen 1:1–3). Scholars have debated whether the formless, void world and its primordial waters were God's first creative acts or the materials God used to create. However, what is evident from Genesis is that as the sovereign Creator God, he is the cause of all created things. He has no rival, equal, or limitation. All that is comes into being by divine fiat, as the recurring "God said . . . and there was" makes clear. Levenson, who denies *creatio ex nihilo*, argues that the Genesis creation narrative is a "dramatic visualization of the uncompromised mastery of YHWH, God of Israel, over all else."[23] Contrasting other ancient Near Eastern cosmogonies, Genesis opens with no theogony or conflict. For instance, in the *Enūma eliš*, the Babylonian god Marduk must slay Tiamat to bring order to the cosmos. Once she is slain, he uses her body to form the heavens and the earth. Due to his triumph over Tiamat, Marduk is hailed king and "the most important among great gods."[24] In startling relief stands

21. 2 Macc 7:27–29, NRSV; italics added.

22. Gen 1–2; Exod 20:11; Prov 8:22–31; Pss 24:1–2; 74:12–7; 90:2; 93 102:25–27; 104; 121:2; 148:4–6; Job 38–39; Isa 40–55, especially 44:24; 45:5–7, 12; 48:13; John 1:1–3; Acts 4:24; Rom 4:16–17; 1 Cor 8:6; Eph 3:9; Col 1:15–17; Heb 11:3; Rev 4:11.

23. Levenson, *Creation and the Persistence of Evil*, 3.

24. Foster, "Epic of Creation," 371.

the Gen 1 creation story, which, says Levenson, is the story of "creation without opposition." Genesis begins where other cosmogonies end, with a sovereign God poised to create.[25]

The question becomes, what does the author of Genesis intend us to hear here? Conditioned by modern science (and certain translations), we may assume that the author of Genesis is primarily concerned with describing *how* God created the universe. That is, does Gen 1 primarily describe the *temporal* and *material* origins of the cosmos? Or does the author desire to communicate something about the created order in reference to its Creator?

The question of an entity's "beginning" can refer to one of several things. First, it can refer to an entity's temporal beginning, such as "when the play began." In this instance, the beginning is a moment within the already present flow of time. English translations such as the NRSV appear to imply temporal origins in Gen 1:1–2: "In the beginning *when* God created the heavens and the earth, the earth was formless and voice and darkness covered the deep."[26] As Oliver notes, the implication of this translation is that God's creative work is within time and utilizes primordial matter.[27]

However, an entity's beginning can also refer to the "root, principle or purpose" of something. That is, its metaphysical origins.[28] Drawing on Gen 1:1, John's Gospel opens by declaring, "In the beginning was the Word. . . . All things were made through him, and without him was not any thing made that was made" (John 1:1, 3). John's emphasis is not the temporal origins of the cosmos but its rationale and foundation. God's creative work encompassed all things, including time, and located them within the divine *Logos*. The *Logos* defines the metaphysical foundations of all that is.[29]

Creation passages in Scripture are less concerned with *how* God created, or even *what* he created, than with *who* created all that is. Scripture affirms that the Creator God, who is eternal, without rival, one, and all-powerful, graciously creates, sustains, and redeems out of his voluntary, loving, divine will. Indeed, early formulations of the doctrine drew predominantly not from Genesis but from the Psalms and Isaiah to describe the work of the Creator God, who is also creation's Redeemer.[30] As Oliver notes, *creatio ex nihilo* expresses a particular and utterly unique doctrine of creation in the

25. Levenson, *Creation and the Persistence of Evil*, 5–6, 122.

26. Emphasis added.

27. Oliver, *Creation*, 38.

28. Oliver, *Creation*, 39.

29. We see similar attestations elsewhere, see Pss 24:1–2; 90:2; Isa 44:24, Rom 11:36; 1 Cor 8:6; Col 1:16–17.

30. Soskice, "Why *Creatio Ex Nihilo*," 41.

ancient world as a unique expression of monotheism.[31] For our purposes here, three affirmations, and their significance for the nature of the Creator and creature, are principally important: (1) divine simplicity; (2) creation as an act of divine donation and participation; and (3) the difference between primary and secondary causation.

Divine simplicity, divine donation, participation, and the question of causation are significant for *creatio ex nihilo* because they define the distinction and relationship between the created and the Creator. God's simplicity speaks to his infinite, transcendent, and sovereign nature in contrast to creation's finite and contingent nature. All things exist because a self-sufficient God voluntarily brought them into being. Divine donation and participation point to God's ongoing providential work in sustaining the cosmos. Finally, primary and secondary causation recognizes that while God is the ultimate agent of action within creation, creation is not his puppet. Created entities are likewise causal agents, though of a different kind.

Divine Simplicity

The doctrine of divine simplicity affirms that whereas God is simple and constant, creatures are contingent and mutable. Augustine writes, "There is, accordingly, a good which is alone simple, and therefore alone unchangeable, and this is God. By this Good have all others been created, but not simple, and therefore not unchangeable."[32] By describing God as simple, Augustine asserts that there is no separation between who God is and what God has. Love, grace, goodness, and existence are not additions to his being. Therefore, God cannot lose these attributes, nor do they change over time. God simply is.[33]

In contrast, created entities are contingent, composed, and subject to change. In addition to a creature's physical structure, it has attributes. To illustrate this, Oliver uses the attributes of strength and knowledge. One can go to the gym and eat nutritious food to build physical strength. Likewise, one can read, go to school, or work with a mentor to grow knowledge. Strength and knowledge can also be lost through neglect, injury, illness, or

31. Oliver, *Creation*, 43.

32. Augustine of Hippo, *City of God*, 11.10.1, p. 210.

33. In discussing the simplicity of the Trinity, Augustine comments: "It is for this reason, then, that the nature of the Trinity is called simple, because it has not anything which it can lose, and because it is not one thing and its contents another" (Augustine of Hippo, *City of God*, 11.10.12, p. 211).

aging.[34] A creature is thus composed of its essential nature plus its attributes which change as they are gained and strengthened or weakened and lost.

Aquinas refines this picture using Aristotle's categories of substance and accident. A creature's substantial qualities define its essential nature, whereas its accidental qualities are added, mutable, and not required by the creature to be that particular kind of creature. For example, my pet's essential nature is that of a German Shepherd dog. Her DNA designates her as a dog rather than a fish, and a German Shepherd instead of a Pug or a wolf. She cannot grow or diminish in her dogness or her German Shepherdness. However, her name, age, weight, agility level, repertoire of commands, color of fur, and ongoing life are changeable qualities. These are accidental, not essential, to her nature. When we adopted her, we added the accidental quality of the name Ziva. Likewise, as she matures, we will train her to add the qualities of "obedience" and "housebroken" to her nature. Throughout her life, she will add and lose various accidental qualities to her nature. Even her existence is accidental. She exists by virtue of her causation and will someday cease to exist. All creatures are a mixture of essential and accidental qualities.

In contrast, there is nothing accidental to God. God's love, holiness, faithfulness, grace, and justice are not qualities in which he can grow or diminish. He is not God "plus" his love. He does not need to grow into the quality of grace. God *is* his love. His essential essence includes his holiness, faithfulness, and existence. "It is of God's essence to exist . . . God therefore exists by necessity and is totally *uncaused*."[35] God, Aquinas argues, is "subsisting being itself."[36] Everything that God *is*, including his existence, is essential to his nature.

As God is "subsisting being itself," everything else is contingent on him. Aquinas notes, "God's first effect in things is existence itself, which all other effects presuppose, and on which they are founded. And everything that exists in any way is necessarily from God."[37] God—not matter, time, or chance—is the beginning, the *Archē* of all that is. "And this shows that God, in creating things, does not need preexisting matter out of which to make things. For no efficient cause antecedently needs for its activity what its own activity produces."[38] As the *Archē* of all things, God creates out of nothing.

34. Oliver, *Creation*, 44.

35. Oliver, *Creation*, 46.

36. Aquinas, *Summa Theologica*, I q.4 a.2 resp. Elsewhere Aquinas affirms: "Therefore God has not an essence distinct from His existence . . . God exists *per se* necessarily. Therefore God is His own existence" (Aquinas, *Summa Contra Gentiles*, I.22, p. 53–54).

37. Aquinas, *Compendium of Theology*, §68.

38. Aquinas, *Compendium of Theology*, §69.

The emphasis here is on God's sovereign power. He has no restriction, as do creatures or the gods of the ancient Near East and Greek philosophy.

Created things, therefore, exist by participation in God's being. Existence is something creatures *have*, not something they *are*. Aquinas writes, "Therefore nothing the essence of which is not its existence, exists by its essence, but by participation of something, namely existence."[39] There is only a single existence—God's—and the created order exists because it participates in that existence. When God created, there was not suddenly God's existence, plus the existence of another entity called creation. Instead, "strictly speaking creation *in itself* is nothing because it is in continual receipt of its being from God."[40] There remains only one source of existence. Thus, Webster terms *creatio ex nihilo* a "metaphysic of privation." Creatures are devoid of any *intrinsic* "integrity or power or self-movement or self-subsistence" or worth. "To be *ex nihilo* is to be . . . *nihil*."[41] Creation is nothing outside of God's gracious, creative, and sustaining power.

Divine Donation and Participation

Precisely because the created order is nothing apart from its participation in God, creatures are of great significance and worth due to their dependence on the Creator. Recognizing creaturely dependence on God for ongoing existence emphasizes the radical asymmetry between God and the created order. It points to creation's "radically *gifted* nature. . . . Creation is . . . a pure act of gratuitous love precisely because God gains nothing by creating."[42] God is sovereign and self-sufficient. He does not need the cosmos, nor does it spontaneously emanate from his goodness. It is an intentional act of voluntary, intelligent, gratuitous love. "Creation is a work of wholly adequate love . . . In willing to create, God wills the realization of life which is not his own."[43] Through creating, God lovingly donates existence to the previously non-existent created order.

Additionally, God shapes his creatures through creation toward an ultimate goal or *telos* as defined by their essential nature. A human can only be a human—it cannot be a tree, rock, dog, or any other created thing. Nor can a human be a god. To be its most true self, the creature must strive "after its own particular good . . . by . . . imitating God, who is the universal

39. Aquinas, *Summa Contra Gentiles*, I.22, p. 53.

40. Oliver, *Creation*, 48.

41. Webster, "Love Is Also a Lover of Life," 166.

42. Oliver, *Creation*, 58.

43. Webster, "Love Is Also a Lover of Life," 168.

Good."[44] Creaturely perfection is defined by the measure by which the creature participates in the life of God. The goal is not to exceed our finitude but to celebrate our creaturely contingency on God by striving for his goodness in our lives.

However, as God made humans "real, potent, and free,"[45] we can decide the extent to which we share in God's life. The failure to participate in God's goodness makes goodness absent. As Oliver observes, the presence of evil and suffering in the scriptural narrative are "alien intrusions" to the created order where God's goodness is absent.[46] For instance, directly before the flood, in contrast to Noah's righteous and blameless character, the earth and all flesh were corrupt, and the earth was full of violence. Noah walked with God. The rest of the created order did not, and the absence of God's goodness proved catastrophic.[47]

Then how do created contingent beings participate in God? First, it is important to note that the immanent and transcendent worlds are differentiated. "God is not a 'better' version of humankind (such that humans are lesser gods, or God is a superhuman), nor is he of the same kind (whereas humans, dogs, and trees are all different kinds of created entities), God is uncreated. God is wholly other."[48] The relationship between God and the created order is a relation of *differentiated* sharing. Creatures share in the being of God as finite creatures. Aquinas describes this as analogical:

> Whatever is said of God and creatures, is said according to the relation of a creature to God as its principle and cause, wherein all perfections of things pre-exist excellently. . . . For in analogies the idea is not, as it is in univocals, one and the same, yet it is not totally diverse as in equivocals; but a term which is thus used in a multiple sense signifies various proportions to some one thing.[49]

By this, Aquinas means that whatever is of God's nature exists perfectly as part of who he is. He is excellent in himself. In contrast, creaturely goodness derives from participation in God's perfect goodness as finite creatures. The same quality applies differently to God and creatures. As Oliver explains, "When we call Benedict 'good' and God 'good', we are saying that Benedict's goodness is derived from God's goodness; the perfection of the good flows

44. Oliver, *Creation*, 82.

45. Oliver, *Creation*, 87.

46. Oliver, *Creation*, 84–88.

47. Gen 6:9–12.

48. Davis, "Sacramental Ontology," 28.

49. Aquinas, *Summa Theologica*, I q.13 a.15 resp.

from God to Benedict and is received by Benedict in a finite and particular form according to his human nature—namely, as the goodness of a man."[50] All that it means to be a creature, including its being, is received from God by the creature according to its particular mode of being.

Primary and Secondary Causation

If creation is a benevolent donation of being from the loving and sovereign God, and creatures exist only by their participation with God, what are the implications for causation? Here we must proceed cautiously. If we overemphasize God's omnipotent sovereignty, we may accidentally diminish or remove responsibility from finite creatures by assigning all causation to God's immanence. Likewise, the overemphasis on creaturely causation risks assuming a dualistic or closed universe in which God remains wholly transcendent, separated from an autonomous created order. Divine and creaturely causation need to be upheld.

As with participation, causation is *differentiated*. God's causal action is different from creaturely casual action. They are not univocal, as if creaturely causation is added to God's greater causation. Nor are they equivocal causes, competing with or canceling out one another. Oliver illustrates Aquinas's view of divine action using a football team. Behind any professional football team is a wealthy owner whose money makes the team possible. The owner enlists a coach who hires and trains the team. The players receive the coach's training and play the game. When the team wins the game, whose causal action secured the win? The immediate cause of the win is the coach and players. However, the hidden cause of the win is the owner. Without his involvement, there would be no team.

God is not a "cause among causes, but the basis of all causation."[51] Thus, through his power, God creates, enables, and sustains creaturely secondary causation through their participation in his primarily causal power. Further, just as creatures are neither univocal or equivocal, but analogical participants in the life of God, so their causal power is analogical; it is real and potent creaturely power that is wholly other than God's. As Webster notes, the "creature is a moved *mover*."[52]

50. Oliver, *Creation*, 69. Likewise, Webster writes that "by the work of divine love, finite things come to share in the universal good of being, but only in a finite manner, and only as they stand in relation to their creator God, the source of being" (Webster, "Love Is Also a Lover of Life," 164).

51. Oliver, *Creation*, 76.

52. Webster, "Love Is Also a Lover of Life," 171.

Creatio ex nihilo is a rich theological doctrine that theologians developed from Scripture to answer pressing questions of their day. Who is God? What is the nature of his creative work? What is his relationship to his creation? What is the purpose of his creation? When chaos and suffering come, is he sovereign over or subject to these forces? Like today's theologians, they resourced their theology with tools from the reigning philosophy of their day, judiciously appropriating what was congruent with Scripture and rejecting or correcting what was not.[53] However, as articulated thus far, *creatio ex nihilo* is not expressly trinitarian. How might we nuance the roles of the Trinity? It is now time to draw Smith's enchanted naturalism into the conversation. Smith is a Christian philosopher informed by the Reformed intellectual tradition and an experience of charismatic renewal. He sees the two traditions "as not only compatible but complementary in important ways."[54] Smith has authored several articles, as well as two books that explore the Pentecostal-charismatic contribution to theology and philosophy.[55]

Pneumatological Naturalism

Smith developed his approach over time in conversation with Radical Orthodoxy, the "enchanted" Pentecostal worldview, and science. In *Introducing Radical Orthodoxy*, Smith advances a "creational ontology." In this work, he approaches the conversation from a reformed perspective, seeking to construct a participatory ontology that rejects Platonism, which Smith terms a "persistent temptation" of the Christian perspective.[56] Smith's creational ontology makes three primary affirmations. First, it affirms the immanent involvement of the Creator in creation and, thus, the goodness of materiality. An affirmation of the goodness of materiality is "a mode of doxology, which indicates the worthiness of the Creator."[57] If the material world were not good, this would indicate a weakness or lack in its Creator. Second, to maintain the Creator/creature distinction, Smith affirms the transcendence of God. This affirmation underscores creation's contingent and non-self-sufficient nature. It is the nature of a creature to point to its Creator. Finally,

53. Boersma, *Heavenly Participation*, 5–6, 35.

54. Anderson, "Q&A with Jamie Smith."

55. Most notably see *Thinking in Tongues* and *Science and the Spirit* which he co-edited with Amos Yong.

56. Smith, *Introducing Radical Orthodoxy*, 219. Smith's own youth was marked by a Protestant fundamentalism and a docetic dualism that created a hierarchical bifurcation between the material and immaterial, privileging the immaterial and denigrating aspects of material or creaturely life. Smith, *Introducing Radical Orthodoxy*, 198.

57. Smith, *Introducing Radical Orthodoxy*, 219.

Smith's creational ontology affirms "the centrality of creation as an orienting hub that accounts for the unfolding that characterizes the differentiation and development of the material world." By this, Smith means that the material world is not a copy of some pristine Form or Ideal (as in Platonism), but rather, that "the invisible is seen *in* the visible," the created order carries an essential sacramentality. Creation is "the theater for the Creator's glory."[58] At this stage of development, Smith's participatory ontology is expressly christological, with the doctrines of creation, incarnation, and resurrection as central themes.

First, the doctrine of creation affirms the goodness of embodiment and finitude. Materiality is not something to be escaped or shed in pursuit of the immaterial. Second, the incarnation further affirms the goodness of materiality as "the transcendent inhabits the immanent without loss. . . . The 'putting on' of flesh was not a temporary cloak for an earthly pilgrimage but rather the assumption of materiality for eternity." Finally, Smith argues that the doctrine of resurrection affirms the goodness of eternal embodiment as "integral to human identity."[59] The doctrines of creation, incarnation, and resurrection affirm the goodness and sanctification of human and non-human matter. What God created as good, and was marred in the fall, he will make new in the eschaton. The Christian eschatological hope is not solely for a redeemed humanity. We hope for the renewal of *all things* in God's eternal kingdom.[60]

While Smith's creational ontology is pneumatologically suggestive, he did not develop the pneumatology of his ontological proposal. After a nudge from Amos Yong that his creational ontology needed a "pneumatological assist,"[61] Smith intertwined the voices of the Pentecostal enchanted worldview and science with his creational ontology to develop his enchanted naturalism. He begins by rejecting an entirely closed or open universe. The closed universe of pure naturalism assumes the natural world is autonomous and any intervention of the divine or spiritual world is at odds with the laws of nature. Conversely, the fundamentally open universe of "naïve supernaturalism" welcomes the miraculous intervention of God in the world. Smith notes that this position maintains an inherent "deistic hangover" or dualism that maintains God's intervention comes from outside, not within,

58. Smith, *Introducing Radical Orthodoxy*, 219–23.

59. Smith, *Introducing Radical Orthodoxy*, 225–27.

60. Rom 8:18–25; Rev 21:3–6.

61. Yong, "Radically Orthodox, Reformed, and Pentecostal," 233–50.

the created order.[62] In other words, the universe functions autonomously, except for when God contravenes the laws of nature and intervenes.

Smith seeks to find a middle ground in "enchanted naturalism." He argues that "*all* that *is* participates in the Creator . . . animated by the dynamic presence of the Spirit."[63] Creation is "suspended" in and "charged" by the Spirit's immanent presence,[64] "*primed* for the Spirit's manifestations."[65] However, not all created things participate "*in the same way* or *to the same degree*." Here, Smith differentiates between structural and directional participation. Structural participation coheres with the orderly function of natural laws, and directional participation is the special action of the miraculous.[66] Thus, the natural world has an inherent elastic rather than reified character.[67] While creation exists by its structural participation in the Spirit, not everything is *properly* ordered or directed to God. In the Fall, creaturely participation became disordered and de-intensified. Instead of a created world filled with the goodness of its creator, all of the earth was corrupted and filled with violence.[68] Throughout Scripture, corruption, violence, sin, and death feature as alien intrusions in God's good world. Thus, according to Paul, all of creation, not just humankind, yearns and groans for restoration in the new heavens and new earth.[69] Through redemption, creaturely participation in the divine is re-ordered and re-intensified, a sanctification process that will find its consummation in the eschaton, where *all things* will be made new.[70]

Smith's enchanted naturalism is helpful. It seeks to understand the created order in relationship with the Trinity and attempts to resolve the gap between science and Christian theology. Additionally, he engages many of the themes of *creatio ex nihilo* discussed above. However, he does so while bypassing the doctrine itself. As a result, his participatory ontology is less nuanced than it could be. First, while he affirms the Creator-creaturely distinction, he does not explicate the distinction. Second, he does not differentiate between primary and secondary causation. His discussion of structural

62. Smith, *Thinking in Tongues*, 87.

63. Smith, "Spirit, Religions, and the World as Sacrament," 256.

64. Smith, *Thinking in Tongues*, 40.

65. Smith, *Thinking in Tongues*, 101.

66. Smith, "Spirit, Religions, and the World as Sacrament," 256. Smith, *Thinking in Tongues*, 103.

67. Smith, "Is the Universe Open," 881.

68. Gen 6:11–12.

69. Rom 8:18–25;cf. Rev 21–22; 2 Pet 3:13; Isa 11:6–9.

70. Smith, "Spirit, Religions, and the World as Sacrament," 256.

and directional participation in the Spirit is similar to Aquinas's description of primary and secondary causation. However, Smith's discussion concerns God's causative power through the Spirit, vis-à-vis natural laws, not creaturely causation.

Conclusion—Archē—Logos—Dunamis

As this chapter draws to a close, it is time to weave the threads together. We do that first by revisiting Oliver's football analogy. While Oliver's illustration helps understand primary and secondary causation, it lumps Trinitarian causation into one category: primary causation. Smith's pneumatological naturalism did a better job of parsing the Son's and Spirit's roles but remained silent on matters of secondary causation. My goal is to bring the two together to develop a Trinitarian model of participation.

Returning to the football team, we start by casting God the Father as the team owner and thus its source or *Archē*. By the Father's will and pleasure, the created order comes into existence and continues to exist. He established the heavens and the earth, and by his command, all that inhabits the cosmos came into being. He has no rival, equal, need, or limitation. The created order continues to exist because that is what the Father desires. Likewise, the team exists at the will and the pleasure of its *Archē*. As their source, the *Archē* constitutes and sustains the team through his pleasure. As the owner, he sends not one but two coaches.

The first coach is the Son, the divine *Logos*. John asserts that the eternal *Logos* preexists creation, through him the Father made all things, and that "in him was life, and the life was the light of men."[71] Likewise, Paul asserts that the Son is "the image of the invisible God" and that the Father created all things, visible and invisible, through him. "He is before all things, and in him all things hold together." He is the beginning (*archē*) of all things, and in him, the "fullness of God was pleased to dwell."[72] Thus, while the created order is willed and sustained by the Father, its *Archē*, it is patterned on the *Logos*. The Son constitutes the logic of the created order that sustains the order of creation. As the coach, the divine *Logos* is the one who assembles the initial team, trains them, and ensures the championship win through his sustaining work. More than that, he is the architect of the sport and its first player. Thus, players who follow his pattern, and adhere to his training, are assured of the win.

71. John 1:1–4.

72. Col 1:15–20.

Finally, the *Archē* and *Logos* send another coach, the Holy Spirit (*Dunamis*). His job is to continue assembling, training, equipping, and empowering the team according to the Father's will and Son's work.[73] He applies the work for the *Archē* and *Logos* to the team and is thus its *Dunamis* or power. The *Dunamis* is akin to a specialty coach. He works with particular players,[74] correcting their errors (convicting of sin), instructing the players in proper gameplay, and enlivening and empowering their performance (gifting the charismatic fruit and gifts). He does this all for the glory of the Father and Son.[75]

However, like all metaphors and illustrations, at some point, they break down. So construed, we risk describing trinitarian participation in tritheistic terms. First, divine simplicity extends to God's triune nature. Augustine writes, "And this Trinity is one God; and none the less simple because a Trinity . . . we say it is simple, because it is what it has . . . because it has not anything which it can lose, and because it is not one thing and its contents another."[76] Second, as the *Archē*, *Logos*, and *Dunamis* of creation, the Godhead works together as the primary cause of all things. They are not three different causes but rather one cause. To come back to our football team metaphor, the Father, Son, and Spirit agree as one, without dissension or debate, that the assembly of the team was for one uniform purpose, to participate in its created purpose. Oliver rightly notes that "the primary cause—God—pours itself into every secondary cause by creating, sustaining, and applying it to action. This primary cause is universal and therefore most intimate and powerful because, without this primary cause, there would be no secondary causes in existence."[77] It is as the created order participates in the life of God that they can function as created beings in God's world.

At last, this brings us to the source of secondary causation—the players. Without the Godhead, there is no created order. Conversely, without the created order, there is no creation. God created all that is so that it could participate relationally in him. Aside from humans, the created order has no choice but to participate in the life and order of God. The sanctification of matter is bound up with its participation in God, which will ultimately find its fulfillment in the eschaton. As Peter asserts by quoting the prophet

73. John 14:27; 15:26–27; 16:7–17.

74. John 14:15–17; 15:26.

75. John 16:13–14.

76. Augustine, *City of God*, 11.10.1–2, pp. 210–11.

77. Oliver, *Creation*, 78.

Joel in Acts, at Pentecost, the Lord poured out his Spirit on "all flesh."[78] In the eschatological kingdom, the triune God will make all things new—including non-human created life.[79] Matter is sanctified through its ongoing participation in the life of God.

To humans, God gave a measure of choice. As per human existence, our creaturely finitude requires that we participate structurally in the life of God. Thus, even those who do not know God may reflect aspects of his character.[80] Likewise, Paul notes that the laws of God are etched into the fabric of creation.[81] However, we have a choice. While human sanctification is initiated, enacted, and will be perfected through the graciousness of God, each one of us plays a role in the process. We can choose to participate relationally in the life of God, submitting to his Lordship, and receiving the coaching and empowerment of the Spirit, or not. For to participate in the life of God is to participate in God's renewing work in creation.

Creatio ex nihilo is a rich and important doctrine. It celebrates the sovereign work of a sovereign and creative God in relationship to his creation. The philosophical tools of analytical theology explicate the Creator's identity and nature, define the act of creating as a divine donation, and establish the Creator/creature distinction. To this discussion, Pentecostal theology adds further depth by nuancing the roles of the members of the Trinity in creation and causation. When the Triune God created the world, he created all things. All created things have been corrupted by the realities of sin. The ongoing work of the Father, Son, and Spirit is to renew all things so that they participate to their fullness as creatures in the life of God. With its focus on God, *creatio ex nihilo* speaks not only to the origins of the created world but also points to its sanctified *telos* in the eternal kingdom of God.

Bibliography

Althouse, Peter. "Implications of the Kenosis of the Spirit for a Creational Eschatology." In *The Spirit Renews the Face of the Earth*, edited by Amos Yong, 155–72. Eugene, OR: Pickwick, 2009.

———. "'Left Behind'—Fact or Fiction: Ecumenical Dilemmas of Fundamentalist Millenarian Tensions within Pentecostalism." *Journal of Pentecostal Theology* 13 (2005) 187–207.

78. Acts 2:17, cf. Joel 2:28–32.

79. Rev 21:5.

80. Job 12:10; Dan 5:23; Acts 17:28; Heb 2:11.

81. Rom 1:19–20.

Anderson, Gary A. "*Creatio Ex Nihilo* and the Bible." In *Creation Ex Nihilo: Origins, Development, Contemporary Challenges*, edited by Gary A. Anderson and Markus Bockmuehl, 15–35. Notre Dame: University of Notre Dame Press, 2018.

Anderson, Myrna. "Q&A with Jamie Smith on Pentecostalism." *Calvin University: Calvin News*. September 17, 2010. https://calvin.edu/news-stories/qa-jamie-smith-pentecostalism.

Aquinas, Thomas. *Compendium of Theology*. Translated by J. Regan Richard. Oxford: Oxford University Press, 2009.

———. *Summa Contra Gentiles*. Translated by Fathers of the English Dominican Province. London: Burns Oates & Washbourne, 1924.

———. *Summa Theologica*. Translated by Fathers of the English Dominican Province. London: Burns Oates & Washbourne, 1921.

Augustine of Hippo. *The City of God*. Translated by Marcus Dods. Edinburgh: T&T Clark, 1913.

Badger, Steve, and Michael G. Tenneson. "Does the Spirit Create through Evolutionary Processes? Pentecostals and Biological Evolution." In *Science and the Spirit: A Pentecostal Engagement with the Sciences*, edited by James K. A. Smith, 92–116. Bloomington: Indiana University Press, 2010.

Boersma, Hans. *Heavenly Participation: The Weaving of a Sacramental Tapestry*. Grand Rapids: Eerdmans, 2011.

Chan, Simon. *Pentecostal Ecclesiology: An Essay on the Development of Doctrine*. Journal of Pentecostal Theology Supplement Series. Blandford Forum: Deo, 2011.

Chandler, Diane J. "Creation Care: A Call to Christian Educators and Church Leaders." *Christian Education Journal* 18 (2021) 112–28.

Clifton, Shane. "Preaching the 'Full Gospel' in the Context of Global Environmental Crises." In *The Spirit Renews the Face of the Earth: Pentecostal Forays in Science and Theology of Creation*, edited by Amos Yong, 117–34. Eugene, OR: Pickwick, 2009.

Davis, Melissa. "The Sacramental Ontology of the Church: Toward a Renewal Ecclesiology." *Pneuma* 43 (2021) 25–42.

Duffield, Guy P., and Nathaniel M. Van Cleave. *Foundations of Pentecostal Theology*. Los Angeles: L.I.F.E. Bible College, 1983.

Foster, Benjamin. "Epic of Creation." In *Before the Muses: An Anthology of Akkadian Literature*, 1:350–401. Bethesda, MD: CDL, 1996.

Griffiths, John D. "Spirit-Baptised Creation: Locating Pentecost in the Meta-Narrative of Creation and Its Implications for a Pentecostal Ecology." *Australasian Pentecostal Studies* 22 (2021) 46–60.

Lamp, Jeffrey S. "Ecotheology: A People of the Spirit for Earth." In *The Routledge Handbook of Pentecostal Theology*, edited by Wolfgang Vondey, 357–66. Abingdon: Routledge, 2020.

———. "Jesus as Sanctifier: Creation Care and the Five-Fold Gospel." In *Blood Cries Out: Pentecostals, Ecology and the Groan of Creation*, edited by A. J. Swoboda, 152–68. Eugene, OR: Pickwick, 2014.

———. "New Heavens and New Earth: Early Pentecostal Soteriology as a Foundation for Creation Care in the Present." *Pneuma: The Journal of the Society for Pentecostal Studies* 36 (2014) 64–80.

———. "Wisdom Pneumatology and the Creative Spirit: The Book of Wisdom in the Trinitarian Act of Creation." *Spiritus* 2 (2017) 39–56.

Levenson, Jon Douglas. *Creation and the Persistence of Evil: The Jewish Drama of Divine Omnipotence.* Princeton: Princeton University Press, 1994.

Macchia, Frank D. *Baptized in the Spirit: A Global Pentecostal Theology.* Zondervan: Grand Rapids, 2006.

Mays, James L. "'Maker of Heaven and Earth': Creation in the Psalms." In *God Who Creates: Essays in Honor of W. Sibley Towner*, edited by William P. Brown and S. Dean McBride Jr., 75–86. Grand Rapids: Eerdmans, 200.

Menzies, William W. *Bible Doctrines: A Pentecostal Perspective.* Springfield, MO: Logion, 1993.

Milton, Grace. "Salvation: Participating in the Story Where Earth and Heaven Meet." In *The Routledge Handbook of Pentecostal Theology*, edited by Wolfgang Vondey, 226–37. London: Routledge, 2020.

Oliver, Simon. *Creation: A Guide for the Perplexed.* London: T&T Clark, 2017.

———. "Trinity, Motion, and Creation Ex Nihilo." In *Creation and the God of Abraham*, edited by David B. Burrell et al., 133–51. Cambridge: Cambridge University Press, 2010.

Plato. *Timaeus and Critias.* Translated by Robin Waterfield. Oxford: Oxford University Press, 2008.

Plotinus. *The Enneads.* Edited by Lloyd P. Gerson. Translated by George Boys-Stones et al. Cambridge: Cambridge University Press, 2018.

Richie, Tony. *Essentials of Pentecostal Theology.* Eugene, OR: Resource, 2020.

Smith, James K. A. *Introducing Radical Orthodoxy: Mapping a Post-Secular Theology.* Grand Rapids: Baker Academic, 2004.

———. "Is the Universe Open for Surprise? Pentecostal Ontology and the Spirit of Naturalism." *Zygon* 43 (2008) 879–96.

———. "The Spirit, Religions, and the World as Sacrament: A Response to Amos Yong's Pneumatological Assist." *Journal of Pentecostal Theology* 15 (2007) 251–61.

———. *Thinking in Tongues: Pentecostal Contributions to Christian Philosophy.* Grand Rapids: Eerdmans, 2010.

Soskice, Janet M. "*Creatio Ex Nihilo*: Its Jewish and Christian Foundations." In *Creation and the God of Abraham*, edited by David B. Burrell et al., 24–39. Cambridge: Cambridge University Press, 2010.

———. "Creation and the Glory of Creatures." *Modern Theology* 29 (2013) 172–85.

———. "Why *Creatio Ex Nihilo* for Theology Today?" In *Creation Ex Nihilo: Origins, Development, Contemporary Challenges*, edited by Gary A. Anderson and Markus Bockmuehl, 37–54. Notre Dame: University of Notre Dame Press, 2018.

Studebaker, Steven M. "Creation Care as 'Keeping in Step with the Spirit.'" In *A Liberating Spirit: Pentecostals and Social Action in North America*, edited by Michael Wilkinson and Steven M. Studebaker, 248–64. Eugene, OR: Pickwick, 2010.

———. *From Pentecost to the Triune God: A Pentecostal Trinitarian Theology.* Grand Rapids: Eerdmans, 2012.

Swoboda, A. J. "Looking the Wrong Way: Salvation and the Spirit in Pentecostal Eco-Theology." In *A Liberating Spirit: Pentecostals and Social Action in North America*, edited by Michael Wilkinson and Steven M. Studebaker, 231–47. Eugene, OR: Pickwick, 2010.

Vondey, Wolfgang. *Pentecostal Theology: Living the Full Gospel.* Systematic Pentecostal and Charismatic Theology. New York: T&T Clark, 2018.

Warrington, Keith. *Pentecostal Theology: A Theology of Encounter.* New York: T&T Clark, 2008.

Webster, John. "'Love Is Also a Lover of Life': *Creatio Ex Nihilo* and Creaturely Goodness." *Modern Theology* 29 (2013) 156–71.

Willams, Andrew Ray. "Greening the Apocalypse: A Pentecostal Eco-Eschatological Exploration." *PentecoStudies* 17 (2018) 205–29.

Williams, J. Rodman. *Renewal Theology: Systematic Theology from a Charismatic Perspective (Three Volumes in One).* Grand Rapids: Zondervan, 1996.

Wilken, Robert Lewis. *The Christians as the Romans Saw Them.* 2nd ed. New Haven: Yale University Press, 2003.

Yong, Amos. "Radically Orthodox, Reformed, and Pentecostal: Rethinking the Intersection of Post/Modernity and the Religions in Conversation of James K. A. Smith." *Journal of Pentecostal Theology* 15 (2007) 233–50.

———. *Renewing Christian Theology: Systematics for a Global Christianity.* Waco, TX: Baylor University Press, 2014.

———. "*Ruach*, the Primordial Chaos, and the Breath of Life: Emergence Theory and the Creation Narratives in Pneumatological Perspective." In *The Work of the Spirit: Pneumatology and Pentecostalism*, edited by Michael Welker, 183–204. Grand Rapids: Eerdmans, 2006.

8

Spirit-Christological Anthropology

The Image of God and The Model of Faith

Christopher Woznicki[1]

Interest in christological anthropology is on the rise.[2] Some of this interest is expressed in the historical study of figures who advocated for christological anthropology. Myk Habets for example, points to Edward Irving as a theologian for whom "Jesus Christ supplies a knowledge of both God and humanity."[3] For Irving, "The Son is the perfect image of God in the sense of being a reflection-in-dependence."[4] I have argued that T. F. Torrance's view of the *imago Dei* is relational, dynamic, ecstatic, and christological: "Christ himself is the Word of grace that humans are designed to reflect."[5] And Marc Cortez has argued that, for Luther, the image of God is thought of "primarily in terms of our righteous relationship with God," however this righteousness is only understood through the lens of an explicitly christological understanding of justification.[6] Yet, interest in christological an-

1. Scripture quotations in this chapter are taken from the English Standard Version.

2. See for example: Williams, "Elements of a Christological Anthropology," 3–20; Mair, "Colin E. Gunton's Christological Anthropology," 63–81; King, "Reciprocating Self," 215–32; Peeler, "Eschatological Son," 161–76.

3. Habets, "Spirit Christology: Seeing in Stereo," 221.

4. Habets, "Spirit Christology: Seeing in Stereo," 221.

5. Woznicki, *T. F. Torrance's Christological Anthropology*, 76.

6. Cortez, *Christological Anthropology in Historical Perspective*, 97, 84.

thropology—and specifically a christological doctrine of the *imago Dei*—is not limited to historical analysis or even retrieval theology. Constructive accounts continue to be developed. This essay proposes one such version of an *imago Dei* doctrine. However, what sets the model proposed here apart from other christological models of the *imago Dei* is the place of the Holy Spirit in the doctrine. I argue for a Spirit-christological anthropology according to which Christ's relationship with the Holy Spirit reveals and models what it means to live as the image of God.

To argue for my Spirit-christological model of the image of God I begin with a brief examination of a proposal for a christological *imago Dei* put forth by Oliver Crisp—one of the founders of analytic theology. Then I amend Crisp's model, resulting in what I call the "Spirit-Christological Capacity Account of the *imago Dei*" (SC-CAID). Having set forth my view I then describe the underlying logic of Spirit Christology that grounds SC-CAID. To this end I develop a theology of Jesus's miraculous works that aligns with Chalcedonian orthodoxy. The model set forth in this section draws especially upon Thomas Morris's "Two-Minds Christology." I conclude by interacting with contemporary Pentecostal theology to set forth two features—both which will be of special interest to Pentecostal Christians—that speak to the virtue of my proposal: 1) it provides a way to articulate the Pentecostal emphasis on Christ as a model for living all of life; and 2) it enriches our understanding of the "functional model" of the image of God.[7]

A Spirit-Christological Doctrine of the *Imago Dei*

A christological doctrine of the image of God is one according to which christology warrants ultimate claims about the meaning of the *imago Dei*. Recently, Oliver Crisp has proposed what he calls "the christological doctrine."[8] According to his version of the doctrine, the image of God is possessed by one individual, namely Christ. All other human beings are made in the image of God to the extent that they image Christ.[9] Christ is the archetype of the image of God. All other humans are made in the image of God by being made in the image of Christ. To illustrate this concept, consider the relationship between the Star Wars characters Jango Fett, Boba

7. Throughout the essay, by "Pentecostal" I mean to refer to "Pentecostals proper, charismatic Christians, and pentecostal penumbra." See, Wariboko and Oliverio, "Society for Pentecostal Studies at 50 Years," 329.

8. Crisp, *Word Enfleshed*, 52.

9. Crisp, *Word Enfleshed*, 52.

Fett, and the clone army.[10] There is only one archetype—Jango Fett—the rest are facsimiles. Like Jango Fett in the *Clone Wars* scenario, Christ is the "original." Christ is the image of God. The rest of humanity is designed as facsimiles of the original. One would be right to ask, what makes Christ to be the original? The answer is not temporal, since the incarnate Christ comes into history subsequent to the first humans. This, however, is not necessarily problematic. According to one view, God's decree for the incarnation—and thus a christological image—is logically prior to God's decree regarding the creation of other human beings.[11] Thus, the original is logically prior to the facsimiles, though temporally posterior. This response, however, might not fully satisfy those who wonder in what specific sense Christ is the archetype given that this response merely explains how we can say Christ is the archetype of the image though being temporally subsequent to images of the image. What makes Christ the archetype?

Crisp explains that Christ being the image of God consists in the fact that God makes human nature capable of union with the divine.[12] Crisp further explains, "God ordained that human nature have certain properties and powers that would mean that the particular human nature God the Son assumes at the first moment of his incarnation conforms to, and is capable of being in personal union with a divine person."[13] Christ is the archetype whose human nature is the blueprint for all other human natures. In principle, any being with a human nature is created with the capacities and powers necessary for hypostatic union with the divine. To bear the image refers to the capacity to be in union with the divine. Christ is the original image in the sense that Christ's human nature is the prototype that subsequent models—i.e., all other human beings—are built to follow. Christ's human nature is designed to "fit" personal union with God. God ordained that this nature would in fact be personally united to God. The rest of humanity also has a human nature that is designed to "fit" personal union with God—following Christ's original design—though, the rest of humanity is not in fact personally, that is, hypostatically, united to God. Because Crisp's christological doctrine of the image

10. *The Clone Wars* originally aired 2008–2013 on *Cartoon Network*, now on *Disney+*.

11. This view is well established in the Christian tradition, and especially the Orthodox tradition. For example, note Cabasilas's comments: "It was not the old Adam who was the model for the new, but the new Adam for the old. For those who have known him first, the old Adam is the archetype because of our fallen nature. But for him who sees all things before they exist, the first Adam is the imitation of the second" (Cabasilas, *Life in Christ*, 190–91).

12. Crisp, *Word Enfleshed*, 63.

13. Crisp, *Word Enfleshed*, 63.

of God has to do with God making human nature capable of bearing union with the divine—with Christ being the archetype of such union—let us call Crisp's view the "Christological Capacity Account of the *imago Dei*."[14] For the sake of clarity let us define this account (C-CAID) as follows:

> C-CAID: To bear the image of God means to possess a nature that is capable of being personally united to the divine nature.

While C-CAID goes a long way toward explaining the biblical and patristic emphasis on Christ being *the image*, on its own it does not adequately address exegetical issues that arise regarding the Genesis account of the image, and specifically, the ancient Near Eastern context of those texts. C-CAID needs to be supplemented.

In contemporary biblical scholarship there is near consensus that the terms *selem* and *demut*—often translated as "image" and "likeness"—in Gen 1:27–28 ought to be read in light of the text's ancient Near Eastern context. Thus, these terms ought to be understood as having reference to the concept of idols.[15] Richard Middleton states it bluntly saying, "Any Old Testament scholar worth her salt will acknowledge that the semantic range of *selem* . . . includes idols."[16] Given that *selem* and *demut* are synonymous in this passage, we ought to understand the notion of being created as God's image as conceptually related to the function of idols in the ancient Near East. So what was the function of images or idols in the ancient Near East?

In Egypt, for example, the term "image" was used to refer to the king, who was considered to be the "image" of a God.[17] The king served as "a cultic intermediary who guaranteed the cosmic order, natural and social, on earth."[18] Although the concept of an image was used to designate kings as they stood in relation to the divine in the ancient Near East, the term for "image" primarily was used in a literal sense, designating three dimensional statues created for communicating presence.[19] If the statue was that of a king

14. Turner has argued against Crisp's formulation (see, Turner, "Identity, Incarnation, and the *Imago Dei*," 115–31) by arguing for an identity relation between a person and her concrete nature. For this reason, I have used the word "possess" in the following amended definition to describe how a being relates to a nature, as I believe that using this word does not commit one to a theory of a concrete human nature (per Crisp) and allows for one to hold to a theory of an abstract human nature. Crisp responds to Turner's objection in *God, Creation, and Salvation*, 107–21. Thus, if one is convinced of Crisp's reply, the word "possess" would still allow one to hold to a concrete human nature view.

15. McConville, *Being Human in God's World*, 17.

16. Middleton, *Liberating Image*, 25.

17. Middleton, *Liberating Image*, 108–9.

18. McConville, *Being Human in God's World*, 17.

19. Middleton, *Liberating Image*, 108–9.

it might be placed in some far off place designating that the king's authority still held sway in that location.[20] More often than not, however, the three dimensional object was a cultic statute—an idol—that symbolized the presence of a god. A deity's presence was marked by the image of that deity.[21]

John Walton provides a detailed description of how this concept played out in cultic rituals. In ancient Mesopotamia for example, a process was performed to transfer the presence of the god from the spiritual to the physical world, among these processes was the "mouth-washing ritual."[22] At the end of this ritual, "an incantation was pronounced indicating that hereafter the god would remain in his house . . . in this way the image mediated the worship from the people to the deity."[23] In light of this ritual, we can say that in ancient Mesopotamia the belief was that the three-dimensional cult statute not only represented the god, but it also manifested the god's presence. Similar rituals are noted in ancient Egyptian literature. Walton cites an Egyptian poem that describes a similar theology. Speaking of Ptah, a creator god and patron deity of craftsmen, the *Memphite Theology* states,

> He made their bodies according to their wishes.
> Thus the gods entered into their bodies.
> Of every wood, every stone, every clay,
> Every thing that grows upon him
> In which they came to be.[24]

Thus, idols were not just a physical representation of a god, the god's presence existed in the image. Walton summarizes the point explaining that "the image functioned in the cult as a mediator of the divine presence."[25]

Given the consensus around the relationship between *selem* and *demut* in Genesis and its ancient Near Eastern context, we should read Genesis's declaration that humans are made in the image of God in light of the concepts of divine presence in physical modes. As Marc Cortez puts it, "We should hear the declaration that God will make humans in the divine 'image' as an indication that he intends for them to be the means through which he will manifest his own presence in creation."[26]

20. Enns, *Evolution of Adam*, xv.

21. Walton, *Ancient Near Eastern Thought*, 114.

22. Walton, *Ancient Near Eastern Thought*, 114.

23. Walton, *Ancient Near Eastern Thought*, 115. For the mouth-washing ritual see: Berlejung, "Washing the Mouth," 62; and Walker and Dick, *Induction of the Cult Image*, 14.

24. Walton, *Ancient Near Eastern Thought*, 116–17.

25. Walton, *Ancient Near Eastern Thought*, 117.

26. Cortez, "Idols, Images, and a Spirit-ed Anthropology," 277.

How does God manifest his presence in creation? It is by means of the Holy Spirit.[27] There are various narrative threads that weave their way throughout the Christian Scriptures, one of the most prominent being that God seeks to have his presence fill the earth as the waters cover the sea. As one author puts it, the story of Scripture is one of sacred spaces where God's presence dwells.[28]

The story begins with God's presence—God's Spirit—hovering over the face of the waters (Gen 1:2) and moves on to an elaborate description of how God created the cosmos to serve as a cosmic temple. The garden of Eden was the first temple in which humanity experienced God's presence. As G. K. Beale explains, the Hebrew verbal form used for God's "walking back and forth" in the garden (Gen 3:8), is also used to describe God's presence in the tabernacle.[29] God's presence, however, was not to be limited to the garden of Eden. The garden-temple of Eden was to be expanded, with the goal of spreading God's presence throughout creation.[30] While there is a narrative thread according to which God seeks to be present to his creation—the thread follows through sacred spaces in the Old Testament, the tabernacle, the temple, and ultimately new creation—there is another sort of presence that is also emphasized through the story of Scripture. This sort of presence is God's presence—by means of God's Spirit—indwelling God's people. Numbers 11 illustrates this point. In this narrative, the LORD tells Moses to gather seventy elders so that God could put his Spirit on them as well. Gathered outside the tabernacle, the LORD comes down "and took some of the Spirit that was on him [Moses] and put it on the seventy elders. And as soon as the Spirit rested on them they prophesied" (Num 11:25). Joshua sees what happens—two other elders who were outside the camp receive the Spirit and prophesied—and complains to Moses that he ought to stop them. Moses's reply foreshadows God's intention for all of his people: "Would that all the LORD's people were prophets, that the LORD would put his Spirit on them" (Num 11:29)! This notion that God's Spirit would dwell within his people is reiterated in Joel 2:28—"I will pour out my Spirit on all people." This verse which states God's desire for his people is the basis for one of the most cited passages in the Pentecostal tradition, Acts 2:17–22. The passage illustrates God's eschatological end: that God would indwell all his people. Pentecost marks the beginning of this new age; "no longer would God's people be

27. God's presence is associated with the Spirit through much of Scripture. See Ps 51:11; 104:30; 139:7; Hag 2:5.

28. Hearson, *Go Now to Shiloh*, 133.

29. Beale, *Temple and the Church's Mission*, 66.

30. Beale, *Temple and the Church's Mission*, 85.

limited in their fellowship with God by a place or even by external communication," on the day of the Lord, God's own Spirit indwells his people.[31] The fact that God's presence dwelt within the temple, the tabernacle, and even the garden itself points to God's end, that God's Spirit would dwell within his people, both as a group (1 Cor 3:16; Eph 2:22) and as individuals (Rom 8:9; 1 Cor 6:9).

If the ancient Near Eastern context of Genesis reveals the belief that gods indwell images and if Genesis teaches that God creates humans as his image then we ought to read Genesis as saying that God has created humans to embody God's own presence. Thus, Cortez is right to say that "the image is inherently pneumatological since the Spirit is precisely the one who manifests divine presence in the world."[32] Given this point, how are we to think of the relationship between being made in God's image and being made to be the locus of God's Spirit in the world? I suggest that we adapt the "Christological Capacity Account of the *imago Dei.*"

Recall, C-CAID holds that to be made in the image of God is to possess a nature that is capable of being personally united to the divine. Not all who possess the image, however, will in fact be personally, i.e., hypostatically, united to the divine. In fact, only Christ's human nature is hypostatically united to the divine nature. Nevertheless, all those who possess such a nature are in fact capable of this sort of union. If we amend C-CAID to account for Genesis's teaching that to be an image of God necessarily includes being the physical locus of God's presence, via God's Spirit then what results is the "Spirit-Christological Capacity Account of the *imago Dei.*" For the sake of clarity let us define this account as follows:

> SC-CAID: To bear the image of God means to possess a nature that is capable of being personally united to the divine nature and being indwelt by God's Spirit.

If SC-CAID is correct and Christology warrants ultimate claims about what it means to be made in the image of God, then we would expect there to be a christological model that affirms the hypostatic union and affirms that Christ is indwelt by God's Spirit. So which christological model is commensurate with such an account? To answer that question we shall turn to Spirit Christologies.

31. Hearson, *Go Now to Shiloh*, 126.

32. Cortez, "Idols, Images, and a Spirit-ed Anthropology," 277.

Spirit Christology

We can distinguish between various types of Spirit Christologies. First, there are those that replace *Logos* Christology with Spirit Christology. Cornelis van der Kooi calls this approach the "substitute model."[33] Roger Haight, who falls into this category, provides a succinct example of what the substitutionists hold to. He explains, "By Spirit Christology I mean one that 'explains' how God is present and active in Jesus, and thus Jesus's divinity, by using the biblical symbol of God as Spirit, and not the symbol of Logos."[34] According to theologians like Haight, the concept of *Logos* is inadequate—and even a stumbling block—for modern articulations of who Christ is. Thus, it is preferable to speak of Christ's divinity in relation to the "Spirit of God." A second approach might be called the "mutual complementarity model." As the name implies, this view holds that to properly articulate who Christ is, one needs to appeal to both Logos and Spirit Christology.[35] Of these two models, only the latter is compatible with SC-CAID. Because of this we shall focus on the second model.

The mutual complementarity model follows a Chalcedonian Christology, where Christ is one divine person with two natures.[36] Chalcedon holds that the divine person is the Son. The Son subsists in the divine nature. The Son assumed a human nature, i.e., the hypostatic union. The Son now subsists in a human nature in addition to the divine nature which the Son had subsisted in from eternity.[37]

Besides affirming the above core elements of Chalcedonian Christology, the complementarity model makes claims about how the Holy Spirit relates to Christ. There are a variety of ways to articulate how this relationship works but in its most basic form, these articulations begin with the fact that Christ, i.e., *Messiah*, means "anointed one." Myk Habets, for example

33. Van der Kooi, "On the Identity of Jesus Christ," 198.

34. Haight, "Case for Spirit Christology," 257.

35. For contemporary examples see: McKirland, "Did Jesus Need the Spirit?,"43–61; McFarland, "Spirit and Incarnation," 143–58. For examples examining the model in the Reformed tradition see: Purves, "Interaction of Christology and Pneumatology," 81–90; Spence, "John Owen and Trinitarian Agency," 157–73; and Habets, "Surprising Third Article Theology," 195–211.

36. A person "is the owner, possessor, and master of a nature, a completion of existence, sustaining and determining the existence of a nature, the subject that lives, thinks, wills, and acts through nature with all of its abundant content, by which nature becomes self-existent and is not an accident of another entity" (Bavinck, *Sin and Salvation in Christ*, 306).

37. For an explanation of the minimal requirements of Chalcedonian commitments see, Coakley, "What Does Chalcedon Solve," 143–63.

recognizes six "messianic *kairoi*, or identity-disclosing episodes throughout the Life of Christ" in which the Spirit is revealed to be integral to Jesus's messianic identity.[38] These six events include: Jesus's miraculous conception by the Spirit,[39] Jesus's baptism in the Jordan and the wilderness temptation,[40] Jesus's messianic vocation,[41] the passion,[42] the resurrection,[43] and the exaltation which includes the ascension and Pentecost.[44] Each of these episodes reveal the fact that the critical turning points in Christ's ministry cannot be understood apart from the work of the Spirit.[45] Jesus is conceived by the Spirit (Luke 1:26–35), he is anointed by the Spirit (Luke 3:21–22), confirmed by the Spirit (Mark 1:10), driven by the Spirit to the wilderness to be tempted (Matt 4:1), offers himself on the cross as a sacrifice to God through the power of the Spirit (Heb 9:14), is resurrected by the Spirit (Rom 8:11), and sends the Spirit to his people (John 16:7). Jesus's messianic identity cannot be understood apart from the Spirit's involvement in these critical moments. However, Christ's messianic vocation extends beyond these critical moments. His messianic—that is, Spirit anointed—vocation is expressed in his ministry among the crowds and religious leaders. The Gospels present Jesus as being empowered by the Spirit to minister. One of the greatest contributions of specifically Pentecostal Christology is how it puts the four-fold identity of Christ as savior, healer, baptizer in the Spirit, and coming king at the forefront of its Christology.[46] These four aspects of who Christ is cannot be thought of apart from the Holy Spirit.[47] More than any other tradition, however, Pentecostalism reminds us that Christ is savior and healer in virtue of his relationship to the Spirit.[48]

Pentecostal Christology is on good grounds in ascribing Christ's power for ministry to the Spirit. The Gospel of Luke, for example, presents this power as being rooted in the Spirit's anointing. Immediately after he presents himself as a Spirit anointed preacher and minister (Luke 4:16–21),

38. Habets, "Spirit Christology," 209.

39. Habets, *Anointed Son*, 123–31.

40. Habets, *Anointed Son*, 131–44.

41. Habets, *Anointed Son*, 144–60.

42. Habets, *Anointed Son*, 160–70.

43. Habets, *Anointed Son*, 170–76.

44. Habets, *Anointed Son*, 176–86.

45. For a historical example of this argument from the Reformed tradition see Owen, "Work of the Holy Spirit," 2.5.

46. Atkinson, "Christology," 216.

47. Stephenson, "Fivefold Gospel and Spirit Christology," 200–220.

48. Richie, *Essentials of Pentecostal Theology*, 74–78.

he exercises this vocation by driving out an impure Spirit (Luke 4:31–36) and healing many (Luke 4:38–44).

That Jesus is empowered for ministry by the Spirit, however, is not limited to Luke. Matthew teaches that Jesus drives out demons by the power of the Spirit (Matt 4:28) and John writes that Jesus performed "signs" in virtue of his messianic anointing (John 20:31). Peter's sermon to Cornelius and the gentiles in Acts presents perhaps the most succinct statement describing the Spirit's empowerment of Jesus's messianic vocation. Peter preaches, "God anointed Jesus of Nazareth with the Holy Spirit and with power. He went about doing good and healing all who were oppressed by the devil, for God was with him" (Acts 10:38). Given the teaching of Scripture, Habets is right to say that "Jesus is who he is because of the Spirit," his ministry and vocation cannot be understood apart from pneumatology.[49]

Jesus's Miraculous Works

It's clear that on the model described above that Jesus's miraculous works are done in the power of the Holy Spirit. But what is the person of the Son's role in these works?

Consider, for example, various episodes in the Gospels where we are told that Jesus "knew" people's thoughts. Matthew, for example, writes, "Knowing their thoughts, Jesus said, 'Why do you entertain evil thoughts in your heart?'" (Matt 9:4). Speaking of the Pharisees and teachers of the law who were looking for a reason to accuse him, Luke says that "Jesus knew what they were thinking" and describes how Jesus does the very thing that would provoke these leaders (Luke 6:8). Of course, these episodes need not be chalked up to a miraculous source of knowledge—though most of Christian tradition has done so. Jesus could merely "know" such things because he is aware of the psychology of his accusers. We could ascribe this to Jesus's highly developed emotional intelligence. Other episodes, however, cannot be explained by Jesus's emotionally intelligent awareness of other people's mental states. In the beginning of John, the author narrates a story where Jesus sees Nathanael approaching him. Upon seeing him, Jesus says "Here truly is an Israelite in whom there is no deceit." Shocked, Nathanael exclaims, "How do you know me?" Jesus responds saying that "I saw you while you were still under the fig tree before Philip called you." Nathanael's response, "Rabbi, you are the Son of God; you are the king of Israel," indicates that he believes something supernatural has occurred. Moreover, Jesus's reply to Nathanael—"You believe because I told you I saw you under

49. Habets, "Spirit Christology," 211.

the fig tree. You will see greater things than that"—demonstrates that Jesus equates his "seeing" of Nathanael with "great things"—an echo of the phrase used in John to describe miraculous works empowered by the Spirit.[50]

Some Pentecostals would point to the similarity between these episodes and "words of knowledge."[51] This term refers to insight, illumination, or knowledge that comes immediately and spontaneously from the Holy Spirit apart from natural means.[52] Pentecostals believe, and in fact expect, that the Spirit continues to provide words of knowledge to ordinary believers.[53] The Spirit can provide revelation that brings strength, encouragement, or comfort to believers.[54] Or the Spirit can empower evangelism by directing believers to specific places providing specific information about the subjects of evangelism.[55] No contemporary Pentecostal—to my knowledge—would attribute the word of knowledge directly to the divine person of the Son, rather, they would attribute the revelation to the person of the Spirit.[56]

Shall we attribute Jesus's supernatural knowledge to the Spirit as well? One Reformed-Baptist-charismatic pastor-theologian says yes; we should think of Jesus's knowledge in these instances as part of the revelatory ministry of the Holy Spirit.[57] Sam Storms writes, "To live a fully human life, God the Son voluntarily suspended the exercise of certain divine attributes (such as omniscience). He in no sense ceased to be fully God, but he chose not to make use of those attributes that would have proved inconsistent with a genuine human life of weakness and finitude."[58] Regrettably, Storms decides that discussion of the relationship between the incarnate Christ and his dependence on the Spirit "cannot detain us here."[59] Thankfully, the subject *can* detain us in this essay!

One way to flesh out the relationship between the incarnate Christ and the Holy Spirit is the sort of kenoticism advocated for by Clark Pinnock. He writes that "in becoming dependent, the Son surrendered the independent

50. John 14:12.

51. 1 Cor 12:8–10.

52. Storms, *Understanding Spiritual Gifts*, 154.

53. See for example, Deere, *Surprised by the Voice of God*, 179; and Luhrmann, *When God Talks Back*, 39–71.

54. Fee, *Paul, the Spirit, and the People of God*, 170–72.

55. Tyra, *Holy Spirit in Mission*, 86–88.

56. This does not mean a denial of the principle that the external works of the Trinity are undivided, merely that such a work is appropriated to the person of the Holy Spirit.

57. Storms, *Understanding Spiritual Gifts*, 150.

58. Storms, *Understanding Spiritual Gifts*, 150.

59. Storms, *Understanding Spiritual Gifts*, 150.

use of his divine attributes in the incarnation. The Word became flesh and exercised power through the Spirit, not on his own. The Son's self-emptying meant that Jesus was compelled to rely on the Spirit."[60] Pinnock believes that if the Son did not empty himself of using divine attributes he would not be living a fully human life. Thus, the Son does not make use of divine attributes, Christ depends on the Spirit for things like supernatural knowledge.

Pinnock's proposal falls under the category of Functional Kenotic Christology (FKC). Accordingly, FKC "affirms that in becoming incarnate, the second person of the Trinity did not abdicate any of his responsibilities or attributes, such as power and knowledge for the period he was incarnate" but the Son does not put them into use.[61] Some advocates of FKC argue that the Son *never* uses his divine attributes. Others, however, believe that the Son "*occasionally* uses his divine attributes, but that *predominately* the Son lives his life as we do—not in his deity but in his humanity—dependent upon the Spirit, and through whom the Spirit acts."[62]

While FKC rightfully notes Christ's dependence upon the Spirit for the miraculous, FKC is not without its problems. What should we say, for example, about the *extra calvinisticum*? Does the Son, who does not exercise the attribute of omnipotence, give up his role in sustaining the universe? Some would say yes.[63] But by my lights, such a claim comes at a steep price. Moreover, other concerns remain.[64] There is, however, another way to articulate how Christ performs miracles—like words of knowledge—without appealing to kenosis.

Two-Minds Christology and the Holy Spirit

Consider Thomas Morris's "Two-Minds Christology." According to this view, we can think of Christ possessing the eternal mind of God, as the Son—with omniscience being an attribute that is possessed and exercised—and a human mind "that came into existence and grew and developed as the boy Jesus grew and developed."[65] The distinction between the divine mind and the human mind is used to explain why the incarnate Christ can be said

60. Pinnock, *Flame of Love*, 88.

61. Crisp, *Divinity and Humanity*, 140.

62. Wellum, *God the Son Incarnate*, 381–82. He cites Hawthorne as an example of the former view and DeWeese as an example of the later. See, Hawthorne, *Presence and the Power*, 208–19 and DeWeese, "One Person, Two Natures," 67.

63. Issler, *Living into the Life of Jesus*, 125n31.

64. See Wellum who levels four critiques in *God the Son Incarnate*, 405–9 and 416.

65. Morris, *Logic of God Incarnate*, 103.

not to know certain things despite being an omniscient divine person, e.g. the timing of Day of the Lord (Mark 13:32) or how to set the time on a VCR. Morris speaks of there being an asymmetric accessing relation between the two minds.[66] So when it comes to Jesus, "The divine mind had full and direct access to the earthly human experience resulting from the incarnation, but the earthly consciousness did not have such full and direct access to the content of the overarching omniscience proper to the Logos, but only such access on occasion, as the mind allowed it to have."[67]

Taking Morris's Two-Minds Christology on board, how might we describe instances where Jesus has supernaturally revealed information? Consider the following just-so-story describing the events of John 1:43–50 (Jesus calls Philip and Nathanael):

> Jesus is praying about the disciples whom he will call. In prayer, the divine mind grants access to the human mind of Christ. The divine mind—because of its omniscience—knows that Nathanael is sitting under a fig tree. Having been granted access to the information contained by the divine mind, the human mind of Christ now knows where Nathanael was sitting. When Jesus encounters Nathanael he shares this divinely revealed information with him.

The source of this information is the person of the Son. This just-so-story, however, is not an example of a "word of knowledge," neither does it emphasize the features of Spirit Christology according to which the Spirit is the source of Jesus's miraculous works. Let's consider another just-so-story describing the events of John 1:43–50:

> Jesus is praying about the disciples whom he will call. The divine mind—because of its omniscience—knows that Nathanael is sitting under a fig tree. The Son could grant the human mind of Christ access to this information. However, the Son does not exercise this prerogative. Instead, the divine mind reveals a "word of knowledge" by the Spirit to the human mind of Jesus. The Spirit reveals to Jesus's human mind that Nathanael was sitting under the fig tree. When Jesus encounters Nathanael he shares this word of knowledge, revealed by the Holy Spirit with him.

66. This would be like the relationship between the minds of the comic book characters Eddie Brock and Venom. Venom has full access to Eddie Brock's mind, but Eddie Brock only has access to Venom's mind as Venom gives access to him. The accessing relationship is asymmetrical.

67. Morris, *Logic of God Incarnate*, 103.

This latter scenario has the benefit of matching up with how Christians receive words of knowledge; they aren't directly informed by the Son, rather they are directly informed by the Spirit. The story I just detailed can be used to explain how Christ's other miracles are performed as well. Jesus doesn't cast out spirits by the power of the Son—though he could—rather he casts them out by the power of the Spirit. Jesus doesn't heal the blind by the power of the Son—though he could—rather he heals the blind by the power of the Spirit. The pneumatological version of Spirit Christology I'm proposing affirms the asymmetric access relationship when it comes to knowledge and power but unlike Morris's Two-Minds view, it denies that the divine side of the relationship grants access to the human side. Rather, access is denied and power and knowledge are given by the Holy Spirit. Thus, in the same way that Christians perform supernatural works, Jesus's supernatural works are performed through the Holy Spirit.

A Spirit-Christological Doctrine of the Image of God

Let us take stock. So far I've proposed a Spirit Christology that affirms the core components of Chalcedonian Christology and affirms that Christ's ministry is empowered by the Holy Spirit. According to my view, the Son does not give up divine attributes like omniscience or omnipotence and the Son continues to exercise those attributes. In his messianic ministry, Christ's human nature is neither omniscient nor omnipotent, it is empowered by the Spirit. I also proposed that a christological doctrine of the image of God is one according to which christology warrants ultimate claims about the meaning of the *imago Dei*. If we follow the approach of christological anthropology and my christological proposal is correct, then how we articulate the doctrine of the image will need to correspond to the model I've proposed. One way to articulate the meaning of the *imago Dei* that fits my suggested Spirit Christology is SC-CAID. Recall that according to this view, to bear the image of God means to possess a nature that is capable of being personally united to the divine nature and being indwelt by God's Spirit. SC-CAID has the benefit of being a christological doctrine of the image of God. It is sensitive to the ANE context of Genesis. It also reflects a Spirit Christology that affirms Chalcedon and does not suffer from some criticisms that could be leveled at functional kenotic Christologies. I take these three features to be virtues of my position. SC-CAID, however, possesses at least two other virtues, which, by my lights, will be especially attractive to Pentecostals.

Christ Our Model

Describing his ecclesiological vision, the Newfrontiers founder, Terry Virgo, begins by focusing on Jesus. Jesus, he writes, is full of both compassion and power. Noting that even though it's a slight exaggeration, Virgo writes that "every time we meet Jesus in the gospels, He is either healing someone or just returning from healing or just going to heal."[68] That Virgo focuses on Jesus to describe the church's task is significant. Jesus spent most of his ministry doing works empowered by the Spirit. Christians, according to Virgo, are called to follow Christ as their model of compassionate, Spirit-empowered ministry. Another charismatic minister, Charles Carrin, makes a similar point regarding Jesus's paradigmatic Spirit-empowered ministry. He writes,

> In every capacity, Jesus intended the Church—like Himself—to operate in the power of the Holy Spirit. If we try to preach the Gospel of the Kingdom without the anointing, we will experience failure in many vital areas. If Jesus depended on the Holy Spirit, how can we succeed with less?[69]

Finally, Bill Johnson—who remains controversial even among Pentecostals—denies functional kenosis and affirms that Jesus's Spirit-empowered ministry is our model. He explains,

> If Jesus did miracles of healing, deliverance, multiplying food and raising the dead as God, I am still impressed—but it is not something I can duplicate. I am a spectator, which I am very happy about if that is my divine assignment. But when I realize that He did what He did as a man yielded to God, then I am compelled to follow, discovering that is my real assignment![70]

The belief that Jesus's Spirit-empowered life and ministry is paradigmatic for believers, however, isn't limited to popular preachers and ministers; it's part and parcel of Pentecostal theology. Tony Richie explains that "the ultimate example of Spirit-filled life and ministry is Jesus Christ himself."[71] Pentecostals are people who take Jesus as their model for all of life, modeling their life after the relationship between Jesus and the Holy Spirit should not be surprising. They "believe the Spirit's anointing of Jesus is both precedent and pattern for the Spirit's anointing of believers today."[72]

68. Virgo, *Spirit-Filled Church*, 49.
69. Carrin, "Theology of Anointing," 172.
70. Johnson, *Experience the Impossible*, 36.
71. Richie, *Essentials of Pentecostal Theology*, 74.
72. Richie, *Essentials of Pentecostal Theology*, 80.

SC-CAID follows the Pentecostal emphasis on making Jesus's Spirit-filled life paradigmatic. Like Christ, all humans are created with the capacity for Spirit indwelling. However, Christ also models what it looks like to live the Spirit-indwelt life.[73] A Spirit-indwelt life can look like leaning upon the Spirit for sanctification and empowerment. All humans are made in accordance with the image of God, who is Christ. But those who are actually indwelt and empowered by the Spirit embody that image in a different way. As Wolfgang Vondey explains, there is not a difference in quantity of the *imago Dei*, "but in the quality of its embodiment, that is in the way the divine image is grasped, mirrored, and communicated by a human person."[74] This is not to suggest that someone who exercises the gifts of the Spirit more often or in more spectacular ways qualitatively lives out the image in a superior way to someone who does not actively exercise the gifts. Such a view could result in ableism. Rather, the quality in which one reflects the image of God is judged against the standard Christ himself sets forth: Being indwelt by the Spirit (as opposed to not being indwelt by the Spirit) and intimacy with the Spirit.

An Expanded Functional Account

Most biblical scholars favor understandings of the *imago Dei* in which the concept refers to a particular vocation given to humanity. Typically, this vocation has to do with the ancient Near Eastern practice of kings setting up images of themselves as reminders of their rule. On this view, humans are imagined to be like statues or icons representing God and his rule.[75] This cultural background leads us to believe that the term denotes a particular role, thus it is a functional view of the image of God. This point does not necessarily mean that SC-CAID, which as a capacity account might be considered "structural" view of the image of God, is misguided however. The best definitions of the imago Dei recognize the multifaceted nature of the image. We can still define the *imago Dei* in the terms of SC-CAID while affirming that in virtue of the image, humanity is granted a particular function.

Most functional views talk about dominion in terms of stewarding creation and mediating God's blessings to the earth.[76] Other's talk about the

73. My proposal shares some similarities with Christa McKirland's proposal in *God's Provision, Humanity's Need.* A key difference, however, is that McKirland approaches the topic from a needs-based anthropology. See, especially, McKirland, *God's Provision, Humanity's Need*, 157–79.

74. Vondey, *Pentecostal Theology*, 181.

75. Wenham, *Genesis 1–15*, 5–10; Walton, *Lost World of Adam and Eve*, 56–57; McDowell, "In the Image of God," 42.

76. Farris, *Introduction to Theological Anthropology*, 81.

function in priestly terms.[77] And still others talk about the vocation in more nuanced terms, for example, the vocation of discerning order within creation, instituting order where order has not fully developed, and rectifying disorder in creation, all for the purpose of glorifying God.[78] The call to rectify disorder may consist, in part, of defeating certain sorts of evil, namely "the powers." These powers play a corrupting role in creation. They create disorder in the social structures of creation, including, morality, religious practices, administration of justice, the ordering of the state, politics, class, ethnicity, race, gender, and the use of resources.[79] Rectifying this type of disorder will also occur in the personal lives of individuals who suffer at the hands of the demonic. As the paradigm of the *imago Dei* we see Jesus carrying out the function of bringing order to where the powers have brought disorder. Jesus casts out demons by the power of the Spirit. Pentecostals highlight the fact that Jesus is the deliverer; he delivers people from evil and the demonic.[80] In virtue of having the same Spirit as Jesus—and Jesus's victory over the powers upon the cross—believers can effectively engage in spiritual warfare.[81]

The Pentecostal ethos emphasizes the importance of confronting the demonic. As Pentecostals engage in spiritual warfare, whether in deliverance ministry or in missional efforts, they follow Jesus's Spirit-filled example of fulfilling the vocation that goes along with being images of God.[82]

Conclusion

To be the image of God is to possess a nature which is capable of union with the divine nature and is capable of being indwelt by the Holy Spirit. Christ, is the archetype of the image of God. He is a divine person who has hypostatically united the divine nature to human nature. In his humanity he is indwelt—and empowered—by the Spirit. The rest of humanity is made according to the prototype. All human beings are made in the image of God. When a human is united to God through Christ and is indwelt by the Holy Spirit, they express the image as best they can. Greater intimacy with God through union with Christ and greater intimacy and dependence upon the

77. Beale, "Adam as the First Priest," 9–24.

78. Woznicki, *T. F. Torrance's Christological Anthropology*, 125.

79. Berkhoff, *Christ and the Powers*, 22; Dumsday, "Origen on Demonic Ignorance," 463–79; Vondey, *Pentecostal Theology*, 168.

80. Atkinson, "Christology," 218.

81. Onyinah, "Spiritual Warfare," 118.

82. Kraft, *Christianity with Power*; Wimber and Springer, *Power Evangelism*; George, "Overview of Spiritual Mapping," 29–47.

Spirit leads to a qualitatively superior manner of living as images of God. We would expect as much in a Pentecostal doctrine of the image of God.[83]

Bibliography

Atkinson, William P. "Christology: Jesus and Others; Jesus and God." In *The Routledge Handbook of Pentecostal Theology*, edited by Wolfgang Vondey, 216–25. London: Routledge, 2020.

Bavinck, Herman. *Reformed Dogmatics Volume 3: Sin and Salvation in Christ.* Grand Rapids: Baker Academic, 2006.

Beale, G. K. "Adam as the First Priest in Eden as the Garden Temple." *Southern Baptist Journal of Theology* 22 (2018) 9–24.

———. *The Temple and the Church's Mission: A Biblical Theology of the Dwelling Place of God.* Downers Grove, IL: IVP Academic, 2004.

Berkhoff, Hendrikus. *Christ and the Powers.* Scottdale, PA: Herald, 1977.

Berlejung, A. "Washing the Mouth: the Consecration of Divine Images in Mesopotamia." In *The Image and the Book*, edited by K. Van der Toorn, 45–72. Lueven: Leuven University Press, 1997.

Cabasilas, Nicholas. *The Life in Christ.* Translated by C. J. De Catanzaro. Crestwood: St. Vladimir's Seminary Press, 1974.

Carrin, Charles. "Theology of Anointing." In *Word, Spirit, Power*, edited by R. T. Kendall et al., 172. Bloomington, IN: Chosen, 2012.

Coakley, Sarah. "What Does Chalcedon Solve and What Does It Not?" In *The Incarnation: An Interdisciplinary Symposium on the Incarnation of the Son of God*, edited by Stephen T. Davis et al., 143–63. Oxford: Oxford University Press, 2002.

Cortez, Marc. *Christological Anthropology in Historical Perspective: Ancient and Contemporary Approaches to Theological Anthropology.* Grand Rapids: Zondervan, 2016.

———. "Idols, Images, and a Spirit-ed Anthropology." In *Third Article Theology: A Pneumatological Dogmatics*, edited by Myk Habets, 267–83. Minneapolis: Fortress, 2016.

Crisp, Oliver. *Divinity and Humanity.* Cambridge: Cambridge University Press, 2007.

———. *God, Creation, and Salvation.* London: T&T Clark, 2020.

———. *The Word Enfleshed: Exploring the Person and Work of Christ.* Grand Rapids: Baker Academic, 2016.

Deere, Jack. *Surprised by the Voice of God.* Grand Rapids: Zondervan, 1996.

DeWeese, Garrett. "One Person, Two Natures: Two Metaphysical Models of the Incarnation." In *Jesus in Trinitarian Perspective*, edited by Fred Sanders and Klaus Issler, 114–55. Nashville: B&H Academic, 2007.

Dumsday, Travis. "Origen on Demonic Ignorance and Why It Might Still Matter for the Theology of World Religions." *Philosophia Christi* 20 (2018) 463–79.

Enns, Peter. *The Evolution of Adam: What the Bible Does and Doesn't Say About Human Origins.* Grand Rapids: Brazos, 2012.

83. I would like to thank J. T. Turner and Andrew Hollingsworth for their valuable feedback on earlier versions of this chapter.

Farris, Joshua. *An Introduction to Theological Anthropology: Humans, Both Creaturely and Divine*. Grand Rapids: Baker Academic, 2020.

Fee, Gordon. *Paul, the Spirit, and the People of God*. Grand Rapids: Baker Academic, 1996.

Habets, Myk. *The Anointed Son: A Trinitarian Spirit Christology*. Eugene, OR: Pickwick, 2010.

———. "Spirit Christology: Seeing in Stereo." *Journal of Pentecostal Theology* 11 (2003) 199–234.

———. "Spirit Christology: The Future of Christology?" In *Third Article Theology: A Pneumatological Dogmatics*, edited by Myk Habets, 207–33. Minneapolis: Fortress, 2016.

———. "Surprising Third Article Theology of Jonathan Edwards." In *The Ecumenical Edwards: Jonathan Edwards and the Theologians*, 36–57. London: Routledge, 1991.

Haight, Roger. "The Case for Spirit Christology." *Theological Studies* 53 (1992) 257–87.

Hawthorne, Gerald F. *The Presence and the Power: The Significance of the Holy Spirit in the Life and Ministry of Jesus*. Eugene, OR: Wipf & Stock, 2003.

Hearson, N. Blake. *Go Now to Shiloh: A Biblical Theology of Sacred Space*. Nashville: B&H Academic, 2020.

Issler, Klaus. *Living into the Life of Jesus: The Formation of Christian Character*. Downers Grove, IL: InterVarsity, 2012.

Johnson, Bill. *Experience the Impossible*. Bloomington: Chosen, 2014.

King, Pamela Ebstyne. "The Reciprocating Self: Trinitarian and Christological Anthropologies of Being and Becoming." *Journal of Psychology and Christianity* 35 (2016) 215–32.

Kraft, Charles H. *Christianity With Power: Your Worldview and Your Experience of the Supernatural*. Eugene, OR: Wipf & Stock, 2005.

Luhrmann, T. M. *When God Talks Back: Understanding the American Evangelical Relationship With God*. New York: Vintage, 2012.

Mair, Elaina R. "Colin E. Gunton's Christological Anthropology: Humanity's Relationships in the Image of Christ." *Perichoresis* 19 (2021) 63–81.

McConville, J. Gordon. *Being Human in God's World: An Old Testament Theology of Humanity*. Grand Rapids: Baker Academic, 2016.

McDowell, Catherine. "In the Image of God He Created Them: How Genesis 1:26–27 Defines the Divine-Human Relationship and Why It Matters." In *The Image of God in the Garden of Eden*, 29–46. Winona Lake, IN: Eisenbrauns, 2015.

McFarland, Ian. "Spirit and Incarnation: Towards a Pneumatic Chalcedonianism." *International Journal of Systematic Theology* 16 (2014) 143–58.

McKirland, Christa L. "Did Jesus Need the Spirit? An Appeal for Pneumatic Christology to Inform Christological Anthropology." *Perichoresis* 19 (2021) 43–61.

———. *God's Provision, Humanity's Need: The Gift of our Dependence*. Grand Rapids: Baker, 2022.

Middleton, Richard J. *The Liberating Image: The Imago Dei in Genesis 1*. Grand Rapids: Brazos, 2005.

Morris, Thomas V. *The Logic of God Incarnate*. Eugene, OR: Wipf & Stock, 2001.

Onyinah, Opoku. "Spiritual Warfare: The Cosmic Conflict Between Good and Evil." In *The Routledge Handbook of Pentecostal Theology*, edited by Wolfgang Vondey, 321–30. London: Routledge, 2020.

Otis, George Jr. "Overview of Spiritual Mapping." In *Breaking Spiritual Strongholds in Your City*, edited by Peter Wagner, 33–50. Shippensburg, PA: Destiny Image, 2015.

Owen, John. "The Work of the Holy Spirit in and on the Human Nature of Christ." In *Pneumatologia*, 113–26. London: CCEL, 1674.

Peeler, Amy. "The Eschatological Son: Christological Anthropology in Hebrews." In *Anthropology and New Testament Theology*, edited by Jason Matson and Benjamin Reynolds, 161–76. London: Bloomsbury, 2018.

Pinnock, Clark H. *Flame of Love: A Theology of the Holy Spirit*. Downers Grove, IL: IVP Academic, 1996.

Purves, Jim. "The Interaction of Christology and Pneumatology in the Soteriology of Edward Irving." *Pneuma* 14 (1992) 81–90.

Richie, Tony. *Essentials of Pentecostal Theology: An Eternal and Unchanging Lord Powerfully Present and Active by the Holy Spirit*. Eugene, OR: Wipf & Stock, 2020.

Spence, Alan. "John Owen and Trinitarian Agency." *Scottish Journal of Theology* 42 (1990) 157–73.

Stephenson, Christopher A. "The Fivefold Gospel and Spirit Christology." In *Pentecostal Theology and Ecumenical Theology*, edited by Peter Hocken et al., 200–221. Leiden: Brill, 2019.

Storms, Sam. *Understanding Spiritual Gifts*. Grand Rapids: Zondervan, 2020.

Turner, James T. "Identity, Incarnation, and the Imago Dei." *International Journal for Philosophy of Religion* 88 (2020) 115–31.

Tyra, Gary. *The Holy Spirit in Mission: Prophetic Speech and Action in Christian Witness*. Downers Grove, IL: IVP Academic, 2011.

Van der Kooi, Cornelis. "On the Identity of Jesus Christ: Spirit Christology and Logos Christology in Converse." In *Third Article Theology: A Pneumatological Dogmatics*, edited by Myk Habets, 193–207. Minneapolis: Fortress, 2016.

Virgo, Terry. *The Spirit-Filled Church: Finding Your Place in God's Purpose*. Grand Rapids: Monarch, 2011.

Vondey, Wolfgang. *Pentecostal Theology: Living the Full Gospel*. London: Bloomsbury, 2017.

Walker, Christopher, and Michael Dick. "Induction of the Cult Image in Ancient Mesopotamia: The Mesopotamian Mis Pi Ritual." In *Born in Heaven, Made on Earth: The Making of the Cult Image in the Ancient Near East*, edited by Michael Dick, 55–121. Winnona Lake, IN: Eisenbrauns, 1999.

Walton, John. *Ancient Near Eastern Thought and the Old Testament*. Grand Rapids: Baker Academic, 2006.

———. *The Lost World of Adam and Eve*. Downers Grove, IL: IVP Academic, 2015.

Wariboko, Nimi, and L. William Oliverio Jr. "The Society for Pentecostal Studies at 50 Years: Ways Forward for Global Pentecostalism." *Pneuma* 42 (2020) 327–33.

Wellum, Stephen J. *God the Son Incarnate: The Doctrine of Christ*. Wheaton, IL: Crossway, 2016.

Wenham, Gordon. *Genesis 1–15*. Word Biblical Commentary Series. Grand Rapids: Zondervan, 1987.

Williams, Rowan. "The Elements of a Christological Anthropology." *Perichoresis* 19 (2021) 3–20.

Wimber, John, and Kevin Springer. *Power Evangelism*. Rev. ed. Minneapolis: Chosen, 2009.

Woznicki, Christopher G. *T. F. Torrance's Christological Anthropology: Discerning Humanity in Christ*. London: Routledge, 2022.

9

The Necessary Ambiguity of Charismatic Experience

Experience with God Is Irreducible to Mere Experience of God

Kimberley Kroll

The language used to elucidate and articulate any "charismatic experience" of God post-regeneration will, if tagging the experience properly, remain necessarily ambiguous. In contrast to the doctrinal distinctiveness and commitments of Pentecostalism, charismatic Christians are only loosely united to one another given their commitment to the phenomenological nature of experiencing God via the Spirit of God. But, can one actually communicate a pneumatological experience of God such that we can create a model for how it is that one *can* or *should* expect to experience God? In this chapter, I argue that attempting to identify, categorize, and articulate any charismatic experience of the Spirit indwelt human creature will remain necessarily ambiguous and ultimately incommunicable.[1] That is, charismat-

1. Though I am using this term generally, I am speaking specifically of human creatures that are "in Christ." It is to refer to any experience that a human creature "in Christ" identifies as a personal experience of God. An experience that is in some way revelatory of God and that human creature's relation to God. This means that the experience is not usually considered universally prescriptive. I am not necessarily talking about "particular" experiences but any experience that a redeemed human creature identifies as an experience of God. There are only two boundaries I set for what I am

ic experience of the Spirit indwelt creature is not merely experience *of* God, lending itself to propositional statements. Instead, it is experience *with* God having a particular uniqueness and quality that is irreducible to its parts.

First, any experience of God requires that the Spirit of God work within the complex mereology of the human creature as an individual subject with prior experiences, configurations of thought, and memory, etc. which is unique to *that* human creature. That is, any experience of omniscient God with or by the Spirit-indwelt creature is one in which God can make use of all the conscious, unconscious, and embodied bits of the human creature to rightly communicate with the redeemed human creature. Second, and more importantly, the Spirit-indwelt human creature experience of God always involve an unconstrained and non-qualifiable agent—the Spirit of God. The unique union that instantiates between the Holy Spirit and the human person on conversion makes experiences of God post-conversion, not merely experiences *of* or *about* God as other, but experiences *with* God as the Spirit of God is united to the human creature and the human creature to the Son via the indwelling Holy Spirit. Third, because any experience of God is necessarily revelatory of God,[2] it is by nature gestalt. All this means is that the human creature's perception of a given experience of the Spirit's acts and manifestation within her life, and her understanding and articulation of such experiences, will always be via interpretation of that experience with that interpretation itself being bound up in and restrained by her uniqueness as a singular subject and the particularized way in which God communicates with her. The human creature may be able to articulate a "reason" for that experience, or "meaning" to be drawn from it, however being able to articulate the experience itself or how one gleans such a "reason" or "meaning" remains incommunicable.

---

labeling pneumatic experience. (1) It is post-conversion. I am talking only about people who have placed their faith in Christ, have become new creatures, and are indwelt by the Spirit of God. (2) My assumption is that any experience of God is revelatory of God in a particular way. This does not mean that a human does not learn about themselves, or a situation (these are necessary consequences of God revealing himself), but the pneumatic experience (and content if I can say that) is of God. I am talking about the experiencing of God and not the consequences of experiencing God. It is this experience of God being with God that I think is non-communicable.

2. I am using the term revelation very generally. All I mean is that any true experience of God and with God's Spirit will illumine the mind and heart of the human creature such that they know God more intimately and deeply. I am not talking about some sort of hidden knowledge of God, but what one might call a purer, truer, more intimate, and deeper knowledge of God (all of which should be sifted and confirmed in the clearest creaturely revelation—the Word of God). After such an experience, one might think I thought I understood the nature of God's justice but now I see it more fully.

The Difficulty of Locating a Charismatic Theology and Its Pneumatological Doctrine

To begin, there exists no consensus regarding what a charismatic theology itself is. There is only one clear distinction which can and needs to be made regarding what charismatic theology is not—Pentecostalism.[3] Sadly, when one attempts to locate any identifiers of a uniquely charismatic theology, one can only find literature that presents charismatic doctrine as a sub-set of Pentecostalism, with charismatic doctrine being merely one wave in an on-going Pentecostal narrative; yet, this can be quite misleading.[4] It is particularly misleading because the self-identified charismatic Christian does not need to find herself within a particular denomination, whether that be Anglicanism, Pentecostalism, Presbyterianism, Catholicism, etc.[5] She can be found in *any* denomination. What is common to the self-identified charismatic is some sort of experience or various experiences of the Holy Spirit which are novel to her. This experience does not entail a separation from her community of believers she is currently tethered to, but a further binding and uniting of her to them in a profound way; often she begins to intercede for them to also experience the Holy Spirit in a novel and intimate way. Thus, in most cases the experience of the Holy Spirit does not disrupt her theological commitments, but instead deepens said commitments giving them new life and power.[6]

Given the Pentecostal narrative, it is easy for one to be misled into believing that charismatics have a single theological history and (Pentecostal)

3. I think this is a common misunderstanding because the addition of the adjective "charismatic" to one of any denomination is understood as having is conception primarily in the Pentecostal movement and clear distinctions between the two have not been clearly understood "on the ground." For example, see Bartos, "Three Waves," 20–42.

4. More appropriately, one might want to root a charismatic theology historically in so-called mystical theology, pre-dating it to Pentecostal theology, loosening it from a particular modern denomination. However, I could see this also leading to misunderstanding regarding what one is theologically committed to and thus my minimal distinction.

5. See Medved, "Doctrine of Baptism," 171–86. Medved discusses the range of understanding and practice regarding Spirit baptism within a variety of churches and denominations where charismatics are found.

6. Now, this does not mean that one might come to know that some sort of first order theological doctrine she has been committed to is false. If this occurred, and the denomination held to some sort of classically heretical doctrine (e.g., Oneness Pentecostalism which is merely a modern form of modalism) then she would not need to change denominations. I am just trying to make the point that charismatic Christians need not fit into a particular denomination.

tradition in which they locate themselves and their doctrinal commitments though this is not the case. Thus, there is great ambiguity regarding what one is attempting to communicate about one's theological commitments when one identifies as a charismatic Christian.[7] In some sense, the additional adjective "charismatic" does not do any work to restrain the understanding of the noun it modifies to a particular theological system; instead, it widens the scope. However, one might argue it widens the theological scope in one unique way—pneumatologically. That is, charismatic Christians are open to and expect free movement of the Spirit of God, which is novel and tangibly experienced by individual human creatures or communally by the creature of the Word, i.e., the church; the Spirit remains untethered by any restraints let alone the restraint of a particular denomination's praxis. How these sorts of manifestations of the Holy Spirit and their consequent experiences are identified as such remains in the wind.

The Difficulty of Pneumatological Language

Because I understand pneumatology as the only theological loci in which charismatic Christians find commonality and my focus will be on a particular aspect of pneumatological doctrine, the doctrine of indwelling, I will only mention language commonly associated with and in relation to the person and work of the Holy Spirit and the redeemed human creature.[8] I only mention indwelling because all charismatics will understand their own experiences of God as *in relation* to the Spirit who indwells them, and thus as experiences that occur *with* God and not only *about* God. Complicating this matter is that, because charismatic Christians remain within their theological traditions, charismatic Christians do not necessarily find consensus regarding their trinitarian commitments. This means that charismatic theology is often associated, primarily, with *experience* of the Spirit and not the Holy Spirit as single hypostasis of the Godhead. I point this out merely to highlight that even the shared pneumatological commitment of charismatics is minimal because how the individual charismatic understands, relates, and constrains her pneumatological doctrine in relation to other theological doctrine can vary drastically. Further, the difficulty of finding and making

7. One is not merely a charismatic Christian. One is, for example, a charismatic Presbyterian. The adjective "charismatic" requires another qualifier or to be itself qualifying a noun to denote a more specific subject.

8. My only objective here is to further muddy the waters. The study of pneumatology has its own unique complications. See Kroll and Leidenhag, "On the Revelation of the Holy Spirit," 71–96.

use of particular theological language regarding experiences of redeemed creatures is not confined to articulating a uniquely charismatic pneumatology, but is found in any concentrated systematic study of pneumatology in general. However, I believe the sole unifying factor of charismatic theology is its commitment to the phenomenal nature of experiencing the Spirit of God and this makes it particularly difficult to define and articulate a uniquely "charismatic" pneumatology.

First, all theological language found within the Scriptures is in some way analogical. If this makes the reader uncomfortable, one might narrow the scope of theological language under consideration to language associated with the Spirit of God *in relation* to creation—not language like the Spirit *is* Paraclete, though I think this too is language that cannot attain to the ontological status of the Godhead in Godself, but language that helps us to work out what it means *for us* that the Spirit is Paraclete. The term Paraclete itself already implies being in relation to something other than Godself. For instance, as Paraclete, the Spirit acts in particular ways *towards* the creature who has been reconciled to Christ. The author of John's Gospel informs us the Spirit abides in us, and the author of Ephesians that the Spirit fills us. The acts of *abiding in* and *filling up* are terms that are not ordinarily associated with persons in relation to other persons unless they are being used analogically, though we have no clear grasp of how to understand them. Normally, these sorts of terms refer merely to the relation between objects. For example, a cat sits in a box, or the cup is filled with water. Yet in the Scriptures, these terms are used to identify the way in which the third person of the personal Godhead uniquely relates to and within redeemed human creatures and thus how the human creature experiences God.

Second, one may say, "Well, the Spirit does not have physical form, so maybe these sorts of spatial relations are the literal representation of the relation of the Spirit of God to redeemed human creatures." Still, this seems a naïve assumption. The Spirit of God cannot be partially distributed as if God himself is mere liquid or power. Neither does God take up space in an ordinary way, being either here or there. God can somehow be omnipresent and located "in" space as we see in the incarnate Christ. Even more perplexing, as God remains omnipresent and incarnate in Christ, we know it is the fullness of the Godhead somehow dwelling in the incarnate Christ and not more or less of the Godhead and yet the Son himself is not confined to a specific location lacking the attribute of omnipresence. What we can glean from this is God either is in a particular relation to a particular created thing or not, and God is fully "located" in a particular space via a particular relation (i.e., incarnation, the holy of holies, indwelling, etc.) or God is not.[9] However, it seems, all of this sort of language is used to elucidate particular relations. All I seek to do here is show that even the pneumatic language in the Scriptures requires careful consideration and interpretation given the sort of being God is and the sorts of beings creatures are. Uncreated Being and created beings relate asymmetrically,[10] and this is evident even in the reading of the Scriptures. It seems the biblical authors are employing language to articulate the uniqueness of God's relations to his redeemed creatures via the Spirit of God indwelling in contrast to God's relations to the creation at large; even under the guidance and inspiration of the Spirit, the biblical authors are constrained by the vocabulary at hand in their lived context to describe particular experiences of the Spirit and their significance for the life of a Christian.[11]

Third, various pneumatological language is used to tag singular experiences of the human creature in relation to God. This language is not consistent, nor would one expect it to be if the Spirit is free to engage the human creature and act out and for the will of God.[12] What I mean here is terms are used to identify experiences of God, but these experiences are always God-in-relation to a unique human creature (or creatures as community which still is understood to be a united single creature) within a particular context, at a particular time, and to a particular end, communicating some sort of truth. This may be reason for the gospel writers use of a multiplicity of narratives and parables. There is no inconsistency or contradiction in Christ's character, however, as Christ encounters singular subjects, being in a particular relation at a particular time to a particular creature, he acts in

9. Inman, "Omnipresence and the Location of the Immaterial," 168–206. See Inman for a defence of the fundamental location of God's omnipresence.

10. Webster, "*Non Ex Aequo*," 115–26.

11. For clarity's sake, inspiration of the biblical authors is a very specific "experience" of God/work of the Spirit in relation to human creatures. We have no biblical content regarding *what it was like* for the authors to be-in-inspiring-relation to the Spirit of God. This experience is not explicitly described. We occasionally are given insight into the human response to the experience (which is almost always a sense of rebuke and insight into the nature of God). I think this can most clearly be seen in many of the prophetic texts (and patterned in the minor prophets). The most we get in the biblical witness regarding the experience of being in-inspiring-relation to the Spirit of God is in 2 Peter: "For no prophecy was ever produced by the will of man, but men spoke from God, as *they were carried along by the Holy Spirit*." The verb φέρω (to carry, bear, lead) is used four times within verses 17–21, each being slightly nuanced regarding God's revelation of himself to people. It is very unclear as to what is mean by this.

12. One can see the minimal trinitarian commitment, the charismatic needs to hold, i.e., the Spirit is God and as such is free to do what the Spirit wills to do. There is no consensus among charismatics as to *how* this happens.

a manner singular to the subject so that the subject might perceive Christ's revelation of himself as the Son of God. Even if Christ interacted with two human creatures in the same exact way, the experience of each individual would be unique due to the individual being a subject; the interpretation would be unique, and the language employed to communicate that experience would be unique. This is the case even when one attempts to describe the same encounter and possibly the same consequential truth derived from a given experience. The truth or message remains singular, but the reception and communication of it most likely will vary. This is not *merely* because each is an individual but because the experience in itself cannot be adequately communicated to another as there is an infinite and inexpressible God participating in the encounter. That is, there is always, when an indwelt human creature is experiencing God, a divine factor who is not merely a part of an experience but somehow *present in the whole of it.*

The Difficulty of the Object Under Investigation

Pneumatic Experience as Irreducible Gestalt Experience: What is the scope of pneumatic experience being discussed? First, our object of study is in some sense specific in that the experiences under investigation are only available to a particular group of creatures—human creatures redeemed through Christ, having received the gift of God himself in the Holy Spirit upon the Son's ascension. This assumes, that the experience of the Spirit is by one who has been adopted into the family of God and is in indwelling relation with the Holy Spirit. Thus, all experiences post-conversion are uniquely indwelt experiences and these are the particular sorts of experiences examined here. In such cases, the relation between the Holy Spirit and the human creature, and the experience of the Holy Spirit as other is not one of a merely omnipresent God external to the creature, but somehow one in which the Holy Spirit is internal to the creature in a unique way, i.e., somehow the experience is singular though two persons—Creator and creature—are involved. The former, being the One who is being revealed, the One revealing, and the One receiving/applying that revelation in tandem with the human creature. Second, I am not looking, at least in this work, to identify types of pneumatic experiences. Instead, we will look at the phenomena involved in pneumatic experience, particularly: (1) its gestalt nature, specifically regarding novelty and violation; (2) the presence and participation of the Spirit of God; and (3) the "qualia" of pneumatic experience. Upon concluding, it will become clear that actual pneumatic experience and its communication, if properly tagged, will maintain a sense of ambiguity and require humility both in attempts to communicate that experience and its reception. And thus, identifying a clearly charismatic theology, given its sole consensus being openness and expectation of pneumatic experience, will remain unattainable.

All human pneumatic experience is gestalt in nature. No pneumatic experience can be understood in, nor communicated to another through the abstraction of its part from the whole (and this is all humans have to work with). In Luke's Gospel, Jesus heals ten lepers (Luke 17:11–19).[13] According to the text, all approach together, cry out for pity together, are healed together, and are sent to the priest together. And yet, only one returns. Why? It seems that the experience of the one must have been unlike the nine. It seems the one either experienced something different, or understood the experience differently than the other nine. What we do know is that something about the experience beckoned the leper to respond in a particular way. When reflecting upon this situation, the human tendency is to begin to break down the experience into parts to see what one might find to be unique in the experience of the one in contrast to the other nine, i.e., what must be "added" to the experience of the one leper such that he responds as he did? Yet, this is unhelpful because "we do not perceptually analyse individual constituents and every detail of sensory signal to later on merge them into a unified representation, but rather we perceive the constituents holistically as a 'gestalt' in its own right."[14] That is, even if some unique "additive" could be identified in the one leper's experience (e.g., some prior experience/ knowledge relevant to the situation and incorporated into it), it would not have been perceived as such nor necessarily function as such in the experience of the one leper. And here, we have the simple complication of the gestalt nature of all experience.

Gestalt psychologists attempt to understand the complexities of human experience through how information is received, grouped, and related in simple momentary experiences, such as seeing a red ball on the lawn, as well as in more complex experiences, such as hearing music or conversing with another human being.[15] Primarily exploring the phenomena of the experience, gestalt psychologists identify different ways in which humans

13. The healing of the lepers is not a case of a uniquely indwelt experience of God as the lepers are coming into contact with the Son. However, I chose this because it sets out the first layer of complexity, i.e., experiencing God yet without the further complication of being in indwelling relation. The indwelling relation complexities will be explained in the following section.

14. Trujillo and Holler, "Interactionally Embedded Gestalt Principles," 1137.

15. For an overview of the history and development of Gestalt Theory, see Smith, "Gestalt Theory," 11–81.

experience information through: (1) the binding and segregation of particular elements involved in the experience, and how this binding and segregation are tied to one's already in place structures of comprehension; (2) the loci of attention; (3) a desire for identifying meaning; and (4) the act of prediction while participating in the phenomena.[16] Now, if one begins to investigate experience through this lens, even seeing a red ball becomes a complicated case. In the case of the leper, multiple gestalts (e.g., seeing Christ, hearing Christ, leaving, being healed, etc.) and continuous gestalts (i.e., there is an unfolding of experiences that are bound to and present in the whole [e.g., spiritual healing] contra a singular presentation, being one among many, etc.) are occurring and then organized by an internal hierarchical structure "informed by learned, statistical associations or similarity in perceptual features" of the experience.[17] In addition, what the one experiencing is attentive to during the experience as well as one's expectations for the experience further distinguishes the uniqueness of experiences and the difficulty that comes with interpreting and articulating the whole.

Moreover, and most important for the focus of this investigation, certain novel gestalt experiences involve what is considered a "violation of expectation" and "ostension."[18] I am making an assumption here but, I think, most experiences of God (in the case of the leper seen in the Gospel, in the person of Jesus as incarnate God *and* in the redeemed Spirit indwelt creatures post Christ's ascension) *can* only be identified as true experiences of God if the experience entails: (1) novelty (i.e., a violation of expectation);[19] and (2) an awareness of some sort of communicative relevance. That is, the experience is in some way new to the human creature and has a unique "texture" to it which requires the one experiencing it to reflect back not merely on communicative parts, but also the way in which it felt to experience it as creature.[20] There is no hierarchical part/whole structure in the experience

16. Gestalt Theory focuses primarily on sensory experience, and initially studies were concentrated in visual experience. However, studies in Gestalt Theory have progressed to more complex states of affairs, experiences, and phenomena. Here, I am merely focusing on an assumed given of Gestalt Theory. The Law of Pragnanz states that when humans are presented with complex stimuli (or phenomena), they interpret these in the simplest manner using: proximity, similarity, closure, symmetry, trend of motion, continuity, past experience.

17. Trujillo and Holler, "Interactionally Embedded Gestalt Principles," 1142–43.

18. Trujillo and Holler, "Interactionally Embedded Gestalt Principles," 1147.

19. I do not mean that the one who has an experience of God will then always have absolutely unique experiences of God. It is the texture of the experience that is new, i.e., there is something unique in the way in which the experience is experienced that implies it is an experience not merely of God and with God.

20. It is worth noting that I am not making any attempts to discern how to identify

itself; it is a single and, dare I say, direct mode of awareness and the communication of knowledge of God through acquaintance with Godself. Here, experience of God is understood as unbound in its intimacy as God gives himself to be experienced by and communicated to the creature in a uniquely subjective way. And yet, for the human creature to then communicate this experience to another requires that the experience be somehow related to or restrained by the structures the creature already has in place for the sake of comprehension (within oneself), and further downstream for the communication to and comprehension of others. Immediately the gestalt pneumatic experience moves from something direct and via acquaintance, to something bound within the creature's finite categories of understanding communicated through mere analogy even if some bits of the experience can be communicated propositionally; knowledge by acquaintance, in its relation to God, is irreducible.

Pneumatic experience is irreducible even to the phenomenon itself. All pneumatic experience is primarily a movement of God toward the redeemed creature. This is not inspiration as experienced by the biblical authors, nor is it illumination as this would restrict all pneumatic experience to the confounds of the biblical text. Instead, I understand all pneumatic experience post Christ's ascension (1) to be revelatory of God via the indwelling Holy Spirit; (2) to require the attention of or a response from the human creature; and (3) to increase conformity to, intimacy with, and participation in the Godhead. There are three primary components to pneumatic experience that are non-quantifiable and, regarding the latter two, non-communicable: God himself, qualia, and knowledge by acquaintance. God is able to directly and perfectly reveal himself to any human creature as he sees fit, and he is able to preserve a right revelation of himself even within the limitations of a finite creature. However, qualia are unique to the human subject and knowledge by acquaintance is not publicly accessible; they are bound within the phenomenal experience of the subject—the single human creature.

First, pneumatic experience involves the third person of the Trinity. The Spirit, in relation to the redeemed creature, is simultaneously engaged in the experience as the creature experiences Godself while the Spirit witnesses to himself. The Spirit is at work as (at least) the internal principle and

a "true" experience of the Holy Spirit nor am I attempting to say something about the purpose of said experiences. I am assuming there are true experiences of the Holy Spirit and trying to evaluate if someone is able to then communicate said experiences in a way that does not move towards doctrinal division but maintains the freedom of the Spirit and the diversity of human creatures. What I am highlighting in this paper is the ambiguity of language that will be used in an attempt to communicate that experience given it has a incommunicable nature.

possibly an external principle within the experience. As internal principle, the Spirit in some way facilitates the experience and imparts some sort of revelatory content regarding God himself (external principle)[21] through the mediation of the human creature itself. And yet, the Spirit of God is immeasurable and uncontainable. God cannot be a mere *part* of the pneumatic experience; the Spirit of God is somehow *the whole of the experience*: facilitating, maintaining, uniting the experience while also being that which the experience consists of—a revelation of God himself. Thus, the Spirit of God cannot be quantified, nor clearly identified as a part of the whole because in some sense *he just is the experience*. Commonly, one talks about revelation and knowledge of God as being mediated through his effects. Part of the perplexing aspect of the Spirit of God in indwelling relation with the human creature is that somehow it is via the redeemed human creature that the effects of God are manifested. That is, the Spirit of God mediates revelation of God through its effects on, in, and by way of the human creature. The human creature is the means by which the effects of God are mediated. The pneumatic experience of God consists of the Spirit of God, the revelatory content, the means of mediation of the revelatory content, and its effects all occurring in a single human creature. And it is this sort of experience that is rightly named a pneumatic experience—a direct experience of the Spirit of God mediated through the human creature itself and yet also for the sake of and having the effect that the human creature come to know God anew.

Second, pneumatic experience as all human experience involves qualia (phenomenal aspects of our mental lives, which are unique to each subject). Qualia are *what it is like* for me to experience something. For example, *what it is like* for me to smell a rose is unique to me; or, more relevant to this discussion, both *what it is like* to love God, and *what it is like* for God to love me is unique to me. I cannot describe the experience of being loved by God without using analogy because I cannot actually explain what the experience itself feels like.[22] For simplicity, think about the experience of smelling a rose. No matter how well I understand a rose and olfaction (metaphysically, scientifically, phenomenally, etc.), I can never communicate to you a key component as to my experience of smelling a rose and that is *what it*

21. I assume all revelatory content consists of God and is for the sake of union with God. To maintain Creator/creature distinction, I will say that true knowledge and content of God is external to the redeemed human creature. However, the uniqueness of the indwelling relation of the Spirit of God with the human creature also makes it somehow internal.

22. This is heightened when talking about God, but not as much as one might suppose because the object experienced is not the central loci, but the experience of experiencing.

feels like to smell and experience smelling a rose. My expression will never directly tag the experience itself; my interpretation and expression of such an experience, at best, is communicated through analogy. A key aspect of pneumatic experience is this what it is like, often posed by another human creature in the form of a question: *how do you know it was the Spirit of God and not something else?* The information being requested is incommunicable.[23] One might just say, "there was a particular texture (qualia) to the experience such that I know what I experienced was of God and occurred with God."

Third, pneumatic experience is not primarily for the sake of obtaining propositional knowledge, but *knowledge of acquaintance.* The highest end of humans is not to know things about God, but to know God himself for the sake of being united to him. This sort of knowledge requires encounter, exposure, and experience of the object of knowledge—God. However, the intimate nature of this sort of knowledge is incommunicable. One can confirm the truth of the propositional statement "God is kind," but one cannot fully know "God is kind" without personally experiencing God's kindness via a pneumatic experience. Remember all experiences of the Christian are indwelt pneumatic experiences and any true knowledge or deepening of one's knowledge of God is from God and thus requires encounter, exposure, and experience of him (all of which are his accommodation to the creature.) However, *what it feels like* (qualia) to have the God of the cosmos bestow kindness in a tangible way is something that is incommunicable among creatures—a creature only comes to increasingly grasp and participate in the kindness of God as one actually experiences it. One normally will attempt to describe the phenomenology of the experience and then, out of necessity) turn to analogy or metaphor hoping that figurative language might just allow for a bridge to be built. However, description and analogy fall short because this sort of intimate knowledge can only be known through actually experiencing and being acquainted with the object of knowledge. This is not some secret gnostic knowledge, but knowledge of God himself that God freely determines when and with whom to share.

23. Obviously, there are times that people wrongly think they are experiencing God. I do think that we can in some (even many cases) know when it is not God. For example, it clearly conflicts with the biblical text, manipulates, oppresses, etc. However, I also believe that we never have evidential proof that it is God. This is what makes "experiences" of God tricky if they are understood as doing something more than revealing something about the nature of God and increasing intimacy between the one experiencing God and God. All of this to say, this chapter is assuming that one can have a personal experience of God in which God reveals something about his nature. And if this is the case, this is what we can say about that phenomenon of experiencing God while in indwelling relation to the Spirit.

Conclusion

What one can see is that if the single thread that marries charismatic Christians together is a commitment to the fact that there is a phenomenological nature of experiencing God via the Spirit of God, it is a thin thread. A charismatic Christian might believe that: (1) one can experience God phenomenologically; (2) through the indwelling relation of the Spirit of God; and (3) increase in knowledge of God via this personal acquaintance with him. However, attempting to articulate this experience such that one can figure out a charismatic theology of pneumatic experience will fail—the pneumatic *experience simpliciter* will always be irreducible to its parts and ambiguous in its articulation. As noted above, pneumatic experiences are not mere gestalt experiences, but gestalt experiences that often involve novelty or violation. An experience of God, though occurring within the context and limitation of the human creature, necessarily intervenes, reorders, overwrites, or deepens in profound ways some prior system of thought. It is a "new thing," a novel experience—an experience of the inexhaustible God. And, these experiences have a participant—God in the third person of the Holy Spirit—who is not merely a part of the said experience but somehow participates in the whole and is the whole of what is experiencing and coming to a knowledge of. Finally, we have the human creature experiencing the Holy Spirit, somehow internally, being the one through whom God is mediating himself via his effects in the human creature itself, while deepening and complexifying a knowledge of God by acquaintance via the human creature's qualia. Such an experience may be described but, in the description, which requires breaking the whole into parts and working within particular theological doctrine, categories, etc. available to the particular human creature, the experience itself is no longer able to maintain its unique pneumatic components; the thing that one attempts to articulate the pneumatic experience itself—not merely *of* God but *with* God—loses its integrity. In the communication of pneumatic experience, there is an attempt to norm that which cannot be normed—the freedom, complexity, and diversity of the Spirit of God in relating to the creature, revealing himself within the creature and through the mediation the creature itself.

Bibliography

Bartos, Emil. "Three Waves of Spiritual Renewal of the Pentecostal-Charismatic Movement." *Res* (2015) 20–42.

Inman, Ross D. "Omnipresence and the Location of the Immaterial." In *Oxford Studies in Philosophy of Religion Volume 8*, edited by Jonathan L. Kvanvig, 168–206. Oxford: Oxford University Press, 2017.

Kroll, Kimberley, and Joanna Leidenhag. "On the Revelation of the Holy Spirit and the Problem of Thirdness." In *The Third Person of the Trinity*, edited by Oliver D. Crisp and Fred Sanders, 71–96. Grand Rapids: Zondervan Academic, 2020.

Medved, Goran. "The Doctrine of Baptism in the Spirit in the Charismatic Movement." *Kairos* 9 (2015) 171–86.

Smith, Barry. "Gestalt Theory: An Essay in Philosophy." In *Foundations of Gestalt Theory*, 11–81. Munich and Vienna: Philosophia Verlag, 1988.

Trujillo, James, and Judith Holler. "Interactionally Embedded Gestalt Principles of Multimodal Human Communication." *Perspectives on Psychological Science* 18 (2023) 1136–59.

Webster, John. "*Non Ex Aequo*: God's Relation to Creatures." In *God Without Measure: Working Papers in Christian Theology. Volume 1: God and the Works of God*, 115–26. Bloomsbury T&T Clark, 2016.

10

Charisma or Hierarchy?

Troubling a Disjunction Through Fictive Kinship

CHRISTA L. MCKIRLAND AND MATTHEW MCKIRLAND

What is the relationship between leadership and authority in the church? Further, how is this relationship conditioned by the Spirit, who is the ultimate authority and giver of all gifts, including leadership? Church leaders are often understood as having authority over others they lead, even if this is only true in practice and non-existent in aspiration or theory. Coming from a Baptist charismatic perspective, however, we find this inconsistency problematic. Also, as Baptists, examining the New Testament is an illuminating starting point for thinking of how the Spirit has intended for us to relate to one another. This is especially relevant as it relates to the current debate over the kinds of authority relations that may have characterized the churches of the New Testament.[1]

Broadly, this debate can be glossed into two theories—the "egalitarian" (also known as "charismatic") and "hierarchical." These terms refer to how the first disciples of Jesus related to one another before, during, and after his ascension and the giving of the Holy Spirit. On the egalitarian view, the *charismata* were determinative for functioning, and the gift of the Spirit determined a person's function in the assembly. "Institutionalization"

1. This is not because Baptists are the only ones who look to the New Testament for ecclesial principles, however, this is (in theory) a Baptist prerogative.

of leadership was seen as a later development.[2] A major weakness of the egalitarian view is the understanding that leadership was not present in the early church. It clearly was. What is in question here is the nature of that leadership. According to the hierarchical view, institutionalized leadership was present in the earliest forms of the Christian community and included interpersonal authority. The goal of this essay is to interrogate the weaknesses of the hierarchical understanding of leadership as interpersonal authority while also recognizing its strengths, then to expand upon the strengths of the egalitarian theory, while not rejecting the presence and value of leadership altogether.

To do this, we will begin with a summary of the multifaceted ways of understanding authority, then turn to the world of biblical studies and the debates that have surrounded the use of authority in the New Testament with special focus on the work of John H. Elliott and Andrew D. Clarke. After briefly sketching the egalitarian and hierarchical views and their conceptions of authority in the early Christian communities, we will focus our critique on the hierarchical theory before providing a mediating view that is eschatologically conditioned. As there is still much debate about how early Christians practically related to each other, we believe a theological understanding of human *telos* can provide another way to conceive of authority in the ancient church with implications for the here and now.

What Is Authority?

Scholars often trace their conceptions of authority based on ancient usages, and there is considerable overlap with the common usage of this word today and its ancient context. Today, we often think of authority as the person "in charge," and able to command obedience. This would have been a natural understanding of this term in the heavily hierarchical context of the ancient world as well. However, while "authority" is a common enough word and often involves commanding obedience, there are many kinds of authority that were present then as well as now. These different kinds of authority are helpfully parsed out by analytic philosopher, Richard De George. In his book *The Nature and Limits of Authority*, there are two major families of

2. "Egalitarian" and "hierarchical" are the broad terms used for the power/status relations within the early church, not more narrowly on gendered relations, which have used these terms in more recent decades. Pulling from Berger and Luckman, Margaret Y. MacDonald defines institutionalization as "whenever there is a reciprocal typification of habitualized actions by types of actors. Put differently, any such typification is an institution." MacDonald, *Pauline Churches*, 11, quoting Berger and Luckmann, *Social Construction of Reality*.

authority: executive and nonexecutive authority. Executive authority is the power to command obedience or to perform an act on or for someone else. These kinds of authorities are political (government), professional (employer/employee), and familial (parent/child).[3] As complex as defining authority has been and will be, defining power and right is even more complex. For our purposes, we will understand power as "an ability to do something" and a right as a "title to do certain acts."[4]

However, there is also nonexecutive authority, which does not include authority over others. Often, we talk about a person being an authority because they have more knowledge or expertise in a certain domain than we do. This is called epistemic authority, and it is always subject to being questioned. Importantly, epistemic authority involves belief, and "the appropriate means to change belief are rational persuasion, argument, and demonstration. The notion of forcing belief or demanding belief involves a misconception of the nature of belief."[5] While the expected response to epistemic authority may be belief, this is ideally because the epistemic authority is legitimate, not because it is manipulative. Thus, De George goes on to explain how to test the legitimacy of epistemic authority and gives four conditions that this form of authority would need to meet.

First, for epistemic authority to be legitimate, the person must have knowledge—including practical know-how—and that knowledge must be testable. This is because their knowledge is always open to challenge because it is fallible (knowledge criterion). Second, a person must have good reason to believe that the one with perceived epistemic authority has knowledge of that field or domain (induction criterion). Third, the one with epistemic authority must be part of the relevant field of the knowledge they are presumably an authority on (relevance criterion). And finally, but importantly, is the trustworthiness criterion. This has to do with the person's character. The person listening to the claims of the perceived epistemic authority "must have good reason for believing" that this person is telling the truth or, at least, that this authority believes what they are saying when they make the claims they are making. So, while those with epistemic authority have power, this power is meant to be testable, and within the church, should even be temporary (1 Cor 3:1–15; Heb 5:12–14; 8:11). And even then, it is not a power over others as that is not the kind of authority that epistemic authority is. As theologian Letty Russell explains, "Because authority only

3. Given space constraints, this summation is necessarily brief and unnuanced. See De George, *Nature and Limits of Authority*.

4. De George, *Nature and Limits of Authority*, 62, 17.

5. De George, *Nature and Limits Authority*, 57.

works when the relationship of assent is accepted by less powerful parties, disbelief becomes a powerful tool for standing against the powers."[6]

The one other form of nonexecutive authority De George recognizes is exemplary authority. With epistemic authority, the response is belief or change of mind. With exemplary authority, the response is imitation, though belief that the imitation will enable one to perform that task, or cultivate that virtue, is likely present. At the same time, if the exemplar is lacking in competence or authenticity, this exemplary authority will be questioned and likely not yield the authority response of imitation. Finally, the same criteria of legitimation (knowledge, induction, relevance and trustworthiness) apply, except now regarding what the person is exemplifying.

Thus, there are ways of understanding authority that do not involve the power to command obedience and these types of nonexecutive authorities may be what many leaders in today's churches claim are active in their communities. Unfortunately, we have one word, "authority," that is unnuanced and often assumed to mean an executive, imperative authority, when in fact, it is nonexecutive, epistemic authority or exemplary authority that is most operative in "non-hierarchical" churches today.[7] However, before we can talk about today's church, looking at the early church and how the gospel first affected the interpersonal relations of disciples of Jesus, is our foundational starting point.[8]

Authority Between Christians in the Early Church: Two Primary Theories

In 1892, Rudolf Sohm published a seven-hundred-page tome on church polity. In his view, "Charisma (describing the free guidance of the Holy Spirit)

6. Russell, *Household of Freedom*, 81. By "powers" she means those oppressive structures, often patriarchal in nature, that are fixated on power over and not power with. While Russell does not distinguish between executive and nonexecutive authorities in the way we are here, her point resonates most closely with leveraging unbelief as a mode of resistance to nonexecutive authorities. Arguably, this can also be done to executive authorities, but because they are not contingent on belief in order to be enforced, unbelief is most efficacious in the realm of resisting nonexecutive epistemic authority.

7. By "non-hierarchical," we mean churches that do not have a pope, bishops, or priests. However, these churches often are hierarchical in practice because of the conflations of executive and nonexecutive kinds of authority.

8. We believe this not because we can reenact the first-century context but because there seem to be principles in play in those early communities that can be recontextualized in our contexts today. We will seek to distill those principles by the article's end.

was opposed to any idea of church office."[9] As such, there were no recognized leaders, and the only authority was the Spirit, which could be temporarily given to a Christ-follower to teach, lead, or prophesy. His views were influential on biblical scholars to build their own egalitarian views such as Elizabeth Schüssler Fiorenza, John Dominic Crossan, Gerd Theissen, Klaus Schafer, and Annette Merz.[10] While less clear on what is meant by equality (as the basis for egalitarian views), the best definition among these thinkers is given by Crossan as "an absolute equality of people that denies the validity of any discrimination between them and negates the necessity of hierarchy among them."[11] As an outworking of this way of conceiving of relationships between disciples of Christ, this view is often called the "charismatic" view because the gifts of the Spirit determined function.[12] Consequently, when turning to church order, the earliest Christian communities are understood as a "community of equals" wherein patriarchal structures, hierarchy, and social inequity were critiqued and eliminated. Schüssler Fiorenza, in particular, argues that Jesus intended this egalitarian way of being to pervade the early discipleship community, but that Paul reverts these intentions, especially in his later letters.[13] She argues that Jesus inaugurated a community of equals that Paul later undermines by introducing hierarchies (permanent offices) and reifying patriarchal cultural norms.

This interpretation is dubbed the "idealistic fallacy" by its critics, whereby "statements by Jesus and his followers are inferred to be affirmations

9. Van Zyl, "Evolution of Church Leadership," 590. Ridderbos, *Ontwerp van zijn theologie.*

10. While less clear if they would be deemed "egalitarian" in the same way, Clarke notes that nineteenth-century ecclesiologists also argued that "the earliest churches were devoid of established structures of leadership," and he recognizes Dunn, Schweitzer, Campenhausen, and Sohm together in this. See, Clarke, *Pauline Theology of Church Leadership*, 15.

11. Crossan, *Essential Jesus*, 73. However, Elliott also concedes that there should be "an elimination of discrimination" but this does not mean that difference is eradicated, Elliott, "Jesus Movement," 181.

12. Clarke, *Serve the Community*, 2144. This language is most often used by Dunn who is sometimes classified as being in the egalitarian camp by Elliott and Clarke, but who may not share the same assumptions as those taking this view. This seems evident in their willingness to concede that leadership was indeed present in the early church, even if it was of a charismatic sort. For the prevalence of positive uses of leadership language see Dunn, *Jesus and the Spirit*.

13. Part of the argument has also been that not all thirteen NT letters ascribed to Paul are actually Pauline and instead span two generations of the early church (at which point, Paul would have been dead). The later, non-Pauline, letters thus describe a more institutionalized church as this developed over time. We are less concerned with Pauline authorship and more concerned with the content of those letters, and whether they are all written by Paul in the same generation or not does not change our argument.

of social and economic equality. This alleged *idea* of equality, in turn, is then credited as an indication of *actual* social and economic relations."[14] Such critique is mounted by John H. Elliott and Andrew D. Clarke who argue that Jesus and Paul are not endorsing "a restructuring of the family along egalitarian lines, but rather a redefinition of the identity of the family of Jesus and the basis for membership—not blood or marriage but obedience to the will of God."[15] Elliott and Clarke thus seek to establish the process of institutionalization occurring since the beginning of the church instead of being a later development. They also seek to establish the grounds on which leadership was established—which were based more on social standing than charismata.[16] Given both of these claims, reconstructing the historical realities of the family, or household, and social statuses are the focal point of these critics' counterarguments.

Chiefly, the Graeco-Roman household structure of *paterfamilias* bears a lot of weight in the hierarchical argument, as the household was a microcosm for authority structures at every level of Graeco-Roman existence. The gospel comes to people in these highly hierarchical environments. However instead of reading Jesus as dismantling these structures, these scholars argue that he works within them and in some cases, inverts them. For instance, Jesus's reversals of high and low rankings and first and last positions assume the realities of these social orders in order to be radical in and of themselves.[17] When turning to church order and authority, Clarke concludes that leadership as hierarchy was present in these earliest communities and not a later development away from the egalitarian ideal set forth by Jesus.[18] Similarly, Elliott cannot conceive of "how equality is imagined to prevail in groups where some are leaders but others are not."[19] Implicit in that admission, for Elliott, is that leadership entails hierarchy, and hierarchy entails executive authority of some over others. This implication extends from the *paterfamilias* in which the father of the family had absolute executive

14. Elliott, "Jesus Was Not an Egalitarian," 89, emphasis mine. Cf. Holmberg, *Paul and Power*.

15. Elliott, "Jesus Was Not an Egalitarian," 82; Cf. Clarke, *Serve the Community*; Clarke, *Pauline Theology of Church Leadership*. A more sociological approach that takes a similar line of argument is found in MacDonald, *Pauline Churches*.

16. Pulling from Berger and Luckman, MacDonald defines institutionalization as "whenever there is a reciprocal typification of habitualized actions by types of actors. Put differently, any such typification is an institution." MacDonald, *Pauline Churches*, 11, quoting Berger and Luckmann, *Social Construction of Reality*.

17. Elliott, "Jesus Was Not an Egalitarian," 81.

18. Clarke, *Pauline Theology*, 16.

19. Elliott, "Jesus Movement," 180. See also, Elliott "Jesus Was Not an Egalitarian," 87.

authority over the household. Ultimately, for these scholars, hierarchy was present from the time of Jesus through to the late Pauline Letters and was not something Jesus or the apostles sought to eradicate, but to relativize.[20] For both Clarke and Elliott, inclusiveness and unity are the thrust of the household metaphor, not equality.[21]

Strengths and Weaknesses of the Two Theories

A major strength of the egalitarian theory is that it seeks to name the radical nature of what Jesus inaugurates—an eschatological community that is led by the Spirit. Unfortunately, in so doing, it does not adequately recognize *how* Jesus inaugurates this new reality. Herein lies the major strength of the hierarchical theory, especially modelled through Elliott and Clarke, in that the radical nature of what Jesus is doing is creating both a new family *and* a new way to belong to this family. Jesus offers a new way of relating to God as Abba, to one another as siblings, and thus to a generous way of life to those beyond just the blood family.[22] For Elliott and Clarke, texts such as Gal 3:28 are about the inclusiveness of the family of God, not the equality of social and economic statuses of members within the family of God.[23] While we believe this text is about inclusiveness we believe it is also about equality, which we will argue for as a corrective to this weakness in the hierarchical view.

In sum, the egalitarian view's strength is how radically it paints the effects of the gospel via the Spirit at work in the early church. Its weakness is in not sufficiently reckoning with the social-historical context which was highly hierarchical and was the context in which the church was birthed. The hierarchical view's strength is how it reckons with the social-historical context as it seems to have related to the effects of the gospel via the Spirit at work in the early church. Its weakness is not reckoning enough with the theological ideology that was being applied in these social-historical contexts since the Spirit was birthing the church as a reschematized *paterfamilias* household.

The argument for a reschematized *paterfamilias* household that was about both inclusion *and* equality can be made both theologically and

20. Both assume, for the sake of being comprehensive in their argument, that Paul wrote the thirteen Epistles attributed to him.

21. Elliott, "Jesus Movement," 180.

22. Elliott, "Jesus Movement," 176.

23. Elliott, "Jesus Movement," 178.

historically.[24] We will make this case via four primary reasons: the quantity and quality of sibling language, the significance of equal indwelling by the Holy Spirit, the eschatological *telos* of the entire New Testament, and how leadership as authority over others would have been reshaped considering those three reasons.[25]

Quantity and Quality of Sibling Language

Given the focus on God as Father and Jesus as the firstborn son by nature, all of those in the family of God are adopted siblings by grace (Rom 8:15–23, 29; Eph 1:5). However, neither Clarke nor Elliott engage sufficiently with the sibling bond, which was the relationship with the lowest status differential in the ancient world.[26] At the same time, both mention the sibling language, and Clarke even acknowledges that this is "Paul's favourite term of address toward his correspondents."[27] Clarke engages with the idea of brotherly love communicated by this metaphor, in that "brother language conveys mutual dependence, support and love, notwithstanding the status differentiations within the family context."[28] Similarly, Elliott resists the equality that sibling language might convey since the idea that "all believers are 'brothers' eliminates the rabbi-student distinction, but says nothing about equality since brothers can be quite unequal in terms of position or privilege (as

24. We will argue for this in brief, however, see especially Hellerman, *Ancient Church as Family*.

25. Elliott, "Jesus Movement," 185. Elliott does mention eschatological readings of Gal 3:28 but does not apply that lens to his own interpretation, saying, "If, as seems likely, it refers to something to be effected at the final consummation, this 'eschatological equality' has no relevance for assessing the actual concrete structure of the house churches" ("Jesus Movement," 190).

26. Sandnes, "Equality Within Patriarchal Structures," 150–65.

27. Clarke, *Pauline Theology*, 93. For frequency of "brothers" language see 93, 139.

28. Clarke, *Pauline Theology*, 93. Cf. Clarke, "Equality or Mutuality?," 151–64. For instance, he questions how brother language can indicate equality when Paul uses this language but also has an apostolic authority over the communities he founded. We concede that Paul does have a unique authority as an apostle distinct from how post-apostolic disciples were meant to relate to one another. Using our categories, Paul did have an executive authority given by God and for a critical function of establishing the early church and writing Scripture. By making prescriptive Paul's dual roles as apostle and brother is to conflate apostolic leadership (which does include authority over others) with new covenant believer leadership (which does not). Finally, we do not believe that apostolic authority remains operative today as the church has been established and the Scriptures have been written. For much more extensive defense of this view, see Barclay, *By What Authority?*, 129; Ramm, *Christian View of Science and Scripture*, 55; Plummer, "Apostle," 84; Dunn, *Jesus and the Spirit*.

affected by age, birth mother, strength, etc.)."[29] However, in all of the sibling language used in the New Testament between Christian siblings, such status distinctions are not enacted or implied.[30] Instead, this new relational status impinges on the way status operated in these early communities. The new ways of relating were grounded in Jesus's status as the firstborn son, and thus having the right to share his inheritance with others. Jesus's unique sonship as the "firstborn among many brothers" (Rom 8:29; cf. Col 1:15, 18; Heb 12:23; Rev 1:5) is the only distinction given as it relates to sibling terminology.

What Clarke and Elliott do not address is how the sibling bond is even more equalized in light of the new *paterfamilias* and expansive family. Such is the case because, first, within the family of God, siblings are not vying for the paternal estate because the *paterfamilias* will never die, and second, Jesus is the firstborn and is already graciously sharing his inheritance with his siblings.[31] Thus, the reasons why friction or rivalry might exist between older and younger siblings is eliminated. Consequently, scholars specializing in ancient kinship bonds, such as Joseph Hellerman, have critiqued Clarke saying, "The use of sibling terms for leaders and congregants alike in Christian writings 'leveled the playing field' in such a way as to suggest that the social model of the Roman family could only be adopted with significant modification by Paul and his followers."[32] In Hellerman's own work, he notes that in Greek associations, kinship language was rare and that in Roman associations kinship language was more common but "only among social equals."[33] To speak in brotherly language of slaves, for instance, "is almost wholly unattested even in Roman associations."[34] The weight of Jesus's and Paul's use of sibling language is thus not sufficiently engaged in this debate as the household language is prioritized in these scholars' readings at the expense of the sibling language.

29. Elliott, "Jesus Was Not an Egalitarian," 82.

30. While some scholars argue that equality is not communicated in the sibling language, we will argue this below. Further, we do not feel these scholars engage sufficiently with texts such as Matt 23:8.

31. Heim, "In Him and Through Him," 129–49.

32. Hellerman, "Review of Serve the Community," 736.

33. Hellerman, *Ancient Church as Family*, 22. And even when this sibling language does appear, it must be read in its context. A brotherhood of silversmiths is not pulling from the same metaphysical framework as the siblinghood of God's expanding family. Hellerman goes on to address the contextual nature of kinship terminology in these associations and that there is not a one-to-one correspondence in the Christian community. Hellerman, *Ancient Church as Family*, 23–25.

34. Hellerman, *Ancient Church as Family*, 23.

Hellerman goes on to critique Clarke, noting too heavy a sociological dependence on voluntary associations in order to understand the relational dynamics of the early church. Instead, "the relative scarcity of kinship terminology in extant sources documenting the associations shows that the Christians' self-awareness of their communities as surrogate families was unparalleled among the voluntary associations."[35] For Clarke and Elliot, it seems the voluntary associations and household structure inform how they understand Paul's use of sibling language. However, Paul's (and Jesus's) use of sibling language seems rather to inform how we are to understand the household as it pertains to being members of God's new family. While it is true that God is the Father of the Christian community, and Paul sometimes refers to himself as a father or mother of those churches he has founded, when it comes to the interpersonal relationships of non-apostolic followers of Jesus, the sibling bond is normative. Further, even as an apostle, Paul predominantly uses sibling language to refer to himself in relationship with other followers of Jesus.[36] As the kinship relation within ancient times with the lowest status differential, the frequency of its use in the New Testament, and the infrequency of its use in the surrounding Graeco-Roman culture even in voluntary associations, the sibling metaphor is the best metaphor for conceiving of the equalizing relations between members of the early church. As such, Christian siblinghood has even more scandalous implications than Clarke and Elliott acknowledge, and these implications undermine the assumption that hierarchy was meant to be normative among members of the body of Christ. Leadership was determined by the Spirit, and at most it would include an epistemic and exemplary, nonexecutive authority that is always testable by the rest of the siblings. This leadership could be a *charismata* but it could also be based on the fruit of the Spirit in that brother or sister's life. In either case, it was demonstrable and reviewable and did not include authority over others in an executive sense of the word.

Significance of Equal Indwelling Spirit

Another significant under-emphasis in Elliott and Clarke's writing regards the Holy Spirit. At one point, Elliott admits, "The only way in which it is

35. Hellerman, "Review of Serve the Community," 736.

36. Cf. 2 Cor 2:13; Phil 2:25; Phlm 7, 20; Rom 16:23; 1 Cor 16:12; 2 Cor 2:13; 2 Cor 8:22; 1 Thess 3:2. Referring to himself as a mother implicitly, especially the pain of birthing these churches, nursing them, and the care he gives them: 1 Thess 2:7; Gal 4:19; 1 Cor 3:1–2. And as a father of the Corinthians and Thessalonians: 1 Cor 4:15, 1 Thess 2:11; and in his relationship to Timothy, Phil 2:2; 1 Tim 1:2; 2 Tim 1:2; and his relationship to Onesimus, Phlm 10.

conceivable for interpreters of the New Testament to speak of equality in the early church is in respect to equal access to the grace, forgiveness, and mercy of God effected by the life, death, and resurrection of Jesus."[37] He may mean Holy Spirit by the "equal access to grace," phrase, but this does little justice to the way Paul and others talk about what this personal indwelling presence now means for disciples of Jesus or the *charismata* that the Spirit distributes (1 Cor 12:11; Heb 2:4). Similarly, Clarke rarely mentions the Holy Spirit, but when he does, he recognizes that

> Paul does, however, argue for one aspect of equality within the community. In 1 Cor. 12.7 he presents the case that the Spirit equips *all* within the community for the sake of *all* the community. The charismatic community of the body is precisely one in which tasks are variously distributed to all by the Spirit and grace of God. All have a function or ministry, yet these ministries differ from each other in their nature and significance.[38]

Related to the first weakness for hierarchicalists about underestimating the siblinghood relationship, the shared Spirit is what enables the sibling relationship to be instantiated and enacted because of the Spirit enabling the adoption of children into God's family (Rom 8:15–17; cf. Gal 4:5–7). Thus, "adoption is the telos of humanity, meaning that it is the proper end to which humans were created" and why eschatology must condition the nature of these relationships.[39]

Eschatological Telos

A third weakness of the hierarchical theory is theological as it pertains to accommodation and inauguration. Jesus, and later Paul, work within and accommodate the fallen structures and finite limitations of being in relationship with humans in human society. Yet, within this work are the seeds of a new reality—an inaugurated eschatology, that grows over time. The kingdom of heaven is often small, seemingly mundane, and yet powerfully at work. Contra the egalitarian view, instead of stressing the primacy

37. Elliott, "Jesus Was Not an Egalitarian," 89.

38. Clarke, *Pauline Theology*, 135; emphasis his. And again, "The portrayal that power is something that is a resource that derives from God, from the Holy Spirit, or from Jesus—and is not, therefore, a resource that is exclusively accessible to him [Paul]; others have access to the power of God available in the gospel" (127–28).

39. Heim, "In Him and Through Him," 134. "Although those who live by the Spirit have received the Spirit of adoption, Christ is 'firstborn' among the many adopted brothers and sister" (Cf. Rom 8:15–23, 29; Eph 1:5).

of a full-grown egalitarian church context wherein only charismatic gifting determined function, the primacy is on the work of the Spirit cooperating with human beings in human societies. This cooperation occurs in their household structures within which certain roles and expectations would have come more naturally to humans of that time, space, and culture. Yet, consistent with the egalitarian view, distinctions in roles does not mean status distinctions were meant to exist between members of God's family. So, when Elliott notes, "Within the Jesus movement, children did not in fact become leaders in the movement, though they were favored by Jesus. Slaves were not in fact liberated and made equal to masters. Women were not put on a social parity with men. The disparity between poor and rich did not cease to exist among those in Jesus [*sic*] group" we can concede this historical fact without conceding that this was and is God's intention.[40] Instead, these disparities may be evidence of accommodation as each of these, being a child, a slave, a woman, or poor, is either a reality of human development (i.e. being a child) or a result of human sinfulness (i.e. oppressing people based on status) and not disparities that are permanent or endorsed.

For instance, the existence of slavery in that context is clearly an exploitative practice that demeaned the humanity of those in these roles. Just because Paul is not actively deconstructing the slave economy, does not mean that he endorses it. Instead, using the best analogue of their time, siblinghood—both Jesus and Paul leverage this relational category for how disciples are meant to relate to one another. For instance, in the Letter to Philemon, we see Paul urging a new way for the slave owner, Philemon, to relate to his slave, Onesimus, and he uses brother language to recondition how Philemon now relates to Onesimus.[41] Sandnes supports this new way of relating in that "Paul argues that Onesimus has become the brother of his master. This means that Philemon no longer has any claim on sovereignty in dealing with Onesimus. . . . Paul presents the issue in front of the 'tribunal' of the whole congregation."[42] While Philemon is still the master

40. Elliott, "Jesus Was Not an Egalitarian," 85.

41. We recognize this relationship has come under scrutiny in recent work by biblical scholars such as Esau McCauley. However, even if the historicity of this relationship is questionable, the theological point still stands.

42. Sandnes, "Equality Within Patriarchal Structures," 159. Per our categories above, the only executive authority that seems held by the non-apostolic followers of Christ (including us today) is the power to discipline a member of the congregation. However, even this authority would be because church discipline has been pursued (Matt 18) and the entire community has agreed (due to discernment of the mind of Christ) that this brother or sister is to be expelled. Thus, the executive authority is still grounded in the Spirit of Christ, which is then discerned communally by the entire body. It is still fallible, as the community can get this decision wrong and it is local in

and Onesimus the slave (accommodation), they are also now brothers, and the brotherhood relationship is the lens through which the master–slave relationship is viewed (inauguration), not the other way around. In fact, Paul considers everyone a slave, including himself (Rom 1:1; 6:16–18)! Yet, Elliott's objection to the egalitarian theory, especially as it relates to spiritual unity and inclusion of all in Christ is that this did not restructure social reality.[43] However, this lack of social restructuring is first, to be expected, because God accommodates human cultural expressions, and second, not entirely true, because of an inaugurated eschatology wherein God is empowering movement beyond the fallen cultural context.

While we have already seen this social restructuring in the relational status of disciples to God and one another as siblings in Philemon and Onesimus, to see the inaugurated eschatology more fully, a further illustration comes out of Galatians. In Gal 3:28, being included in Christ is not merely about inclusion in union with God, but it also has practical implications—the Jews and gentiles are meant to eat together. Sharing table fellowship was an outworking of seeing each other as equal in value and in spiritual status, even while remaining Jew and gentile, slave and free, male and female. As Scott Bartchy notes, "Being welcomed at a table for the purpose of eating food with another person had become a ceremony richly symbolic of friendship, intimacy and unity" and that, in Jesus's case, he used "table fellowship as a divine tool for undermining boundaries and hierarchies."[44] Based on their arguments, it is unclear if Elliott and Clarke might envision this meal with the slaves still serving the masters, and the women eating after the men, and the largest portions going to the homeowners—however, that would seem to undermine the unity *in Christ* that Elliott and Clarke have admitted is being established, as well as the way of relating that siblings would have shared.[45] One wonders how true unity can persist where true equality does not.

Though Galatians occurs in a Pauline context, Elliott also notes that "Jesus knew the economic and social disparities of his time and urged conduct that would relativize but not eliminate such disparities. Suffering and want caused by inequity were to be alleviated by generosity, almsgiving, and compassion toward one's fellow human beings, but Jesus engaged in

---

that it only pertains to that specific congregation. We seem to see this kind of authority in play here with Philemon and Onesimus.

43. Elliott, "Jesus Movement," 185.

44. Bartchy, "Table Fellowship," 796–97.

45. They never state this explicitly, but their insistence on hierarchy maintenance suggests this would be the implication.

no program to eradicate altogether the causes of such disparities."[46] However, this reads Jesus's task *too* historically. The impact of Jesus's life is not simply in what he did during his years while physically present, but also in what he was inaugurating. Suffering and inequity *are* part of what Christ came to eradicate. The crux of the issue lies, between these two theories, on *when* such eradication will occur. The eschatological orientation of Jesus's and Paul's ministries invites followers of Jesus to pursue the eradication of unjust disparities in the here and now due to being one body by the Spirit. This eschatological orientation thus enables today's Christ-follower to ask, "Can certain inequities be eradicated, and how can the church be a place where they cease to exist?"

Re-Schematizing Authority and Thus Leadership

This leads us to our fourth point, which puts us in agreement with some of Elliott and Clarke's conclusions. There does indeed seem to be leadership in the earliest churches, with distinctions in rôles and functions. However, they assume that such leadership entails hierarchy, with some in authority over others. Yet, considering the three other concerns, we want to question that assumption. For instance, the use of "office" for permanent leadership positions is often assumed but not substantiated in their writing. However, the distinction between an office and a function is not at all clear.[47] Further, that an office then necessitates a hierarchy is also not clear, as well as what hierarchy means for Elliott and Clarke. While Elliott critiques those who hold the egalitarian view for not being clear on what is meant by "equality" and "egalitarian," likewise, how "hierarchy" is used by Elliott and Clarke is unclear. For instance, Clarke, in reference to Paul and Philemon, claims that "Paul is explicitly not claiming hierarchical superiority over Philemon; equally, he desires that no distinction is drawn between brothers and sisters in terms of status."[48] If there is not superiority or inferiority or distinction in status between these two brothers in Christ, what then is the meaning of

46. Elliott, "Jesus Was Not an Egalitarian," 85.

47. Van Zyl, "Evolution of Church Leadership in the New Testament," 587. In a helpful, unpublished dissertation, Kowalksi defines office as "the community-given status of the individual, typically with an accompanying title. 'Office' therefore is the recognition and codification by the community of an original function." Kowalski, "Reward, Discipline, and Installation." Further, the Greek word for "office" only occurs in Acts 2 in the selection of a replacement disciple and before the giving of the Holy Spirit.

48. Clarke, *Serve the Community of the Church*, 1712.

"hierarchy"? Clarke goes on to say that there are "responsibilities which go with Philemon's status" but that does not require hierarchy.[49]

For Elliott, hierarchy and egalitarianism are mutually exclusive, but he still does not give his definition of hierarchy.[50] In critiquing an egalitarian reading of Gal 3:28, he states that equality and the presence of leaders are mutually exclusive.[51] In light of this, one wonders if hierarchy has a different meaning for these scholars. For instance, in Elliott's 2002 article, he uses the language "stratified in structure."[52] Stratification is to arrange, layer, or classify. Such language does not require a distinction in value, though it can recognize difference in economic and social positions. To our minds, this would be the most charitable definition of hierarchy.[53] The question then becomes, did economic and social distinctions give some members of the community more value and privileges in the spiritual family?

For Clarke, he assumes that hierarchy, however he defines it, was present in the early church but does not clearly explain how hierarchy relates to authority, leadership, or status. At points, he seems to be pushing against an egalitarianism that would see all people as able to lead, which he seems to conflate with having authority over others. For instance, he positively endorses Alastair Campbell's argument regarding Acts 14:23, in "that the 'appointing' of elders by Barnabas and Saul was a process not of selecting leaders from the whole pool of believers in a locality, but of recognizing and blessing those whose social status in the Christian community was already recognized."[54] This statement raises two questions. First, on what basis was social status weighed in the early Christian community, and second, how

49. Clarke, *Serve the Community of the Church*, 1717.

50. Elliott, "Jesus Movement," 188.

51. Elliott, "Jesus Movement," 180.

52. Elliott, "Jesus Movement," 175.

53. At one point, Clarke indicates what he does not mean by hierarchy when he says, "One, now obsolete, meaning of 'hierarchy' is 'rule/dominion.' This may be a returning element in contemporary usage, where the word, when applied to rankings of individuals rather than things, often conveys negative connotations of subordination and, therefore, domination." However, since this is the most common way to use this word, clarification is need. Clarke, *Pauline Theology*, 81. He pulls this definition from the 2000 Oxford Dictionary.

54. Clarke, *Pauline Theology*, 86–87. Another clue to what Clarke means by egalitarian is in his methodology section wherein he quotes R. P. Caroll favorably, "Some forms of postmodern approach to biblical readings would insist on an egalitarian relationship between competing interpretations whereby everybody's point of view must be respected and acknowledged as equal to everybody else's point of view," Clarke, *Pauline Theology*, 30. If "egalitarian" means every person's voice has the exact same weight, then we would agree that this is not what Paul had in view. We will return to this in our modified view below.

did this relate to a hierarchy in the early church? Perhaps Campbell is being hyperbolic in his characterization of the egalitarian view ("selecting leaders from the whole pool of believers in a locality"), but the egalitarian view can easily lead to this conclusion. Instead, we believe the egalitarian view should be more nuanced by advocating for a non-hierarchical way of relating to one another that would have also colored the leadership/led relationship.

Returning to the question of social status, as encultured beings, it only makes sense that church members were bringing their full selves with their related statuses into the Christian gathering. However, how these would have been evaluated and enacted remains unclear from the scholarship on a hierarchical perspective. For instance, while Clarke demonstrates at length that leaders in the early church did not have an authoritarian type of leadership, at points he conflates being a head of household with then making that person the default overseer of that gathered body:

> Paul's conception of the Christian leader is one who is the head of a household, and master of domestic slaves, and whose house-church in all probability includes other slaves. Accordingly, the message of servanthood as it appears in the Pauline corpus is not a thorough-going servanthood that inverts the normal hierarchy of the home; the head of the household remains the leader. Rather, the context of humility, vulnerability and service set a context for the exercising of authority, rather than its removal.[55]

Clarke also sees being head of a household as making that person the de facto overseer who was also "responsible for all teaching."[56] This conclusion rests on his interpretation of 1 Tim 3 and 5 in that Paul sets out the qualifications for overseers, which includes managing a house well. Good household management assumes having a household to manage. However, this conclusion is unconvincing for three reasons. First, it is not clear if the list of qualifications for elder/overseer are exclusive.[57] For instance,

55. Clarke, *Pauline Theology*, 102. In *Serve the Community of the Church*, 164, Clarke endorses Lane's observation that "those who acted as patrons were in some sense also involved in governance of the community. A position of authority emerged out of the benefits that individuals of relatively higher wealth and social status could confer upon the community." Cf. Lane, "Social Perspectives in Roman Christianity," 211–12.

56. Clarke, *Pauline Theology*, 154.

57. Which Clarke does, at one point, admit: "The phrasing is unclear as to whether this statement is intended to sustain the view that those who have no wife, no household, or no children are thereby disqualified, or whether the kind of skills evidenced by the married head of household are merely a helpful analogy—but it is the skills, not the analogous circumstances, that are essential" (Clarke, *Pauline Theology*, 51). Thus, the consistent association of householder and elder/overseer seems overblown.

could a single person or someone without children serve as an elder or overseer? Instead, this seems to be a list of character qualifications, and being able to manage a household could help establish a potential leader's *bona fides*. If this was a rigid list, Jesus himself, as well as Paul, would not have been able to serve in these capacities. That seems to undermine the purpose of elders/overseers who are meant to help the body to mature, especially through the function of teaching and being imitable. Second, given the function of teaching, there were likely many household heads who were not gifted or even suited to teach. Being the *paterfamilias* and owning the home does not entail competence in teaching. Could a person host a church gathering and not be the elder/overseer of it? That seems possible, though not necessarily according to Clarke. Also, the Spirit is the one who gifts. So, what does the person gifted to teach do if they are not a head of household? This leads to the final, and most disconcerting aspect of this argument. This preference for those with social status as head of household establishes a hierarchy of "haves and have-nots" who are able to teach and be overseers/elders in the community.[58] However, if such a preference was given to those with a certain socioeconomic status this would establish a precedent that runs contrary to the teachings of Jesus and the New Testament. For example, such an economic hierarchy as it relates to church members walking in their gifts seems contrary to many other exhortations in the New Testament that do not delimit who the Spirit will empower to teach, and also sets up a status-based hierarchy of value differentiation that could eliminate even mature and otherwise qualified believers from being overseers in the church simply because they did not own homes (Eph 4; 1 Cor 12; etc.).[59]

Considering these weaknesses in the hierarchical theory, we cannot accept this way of framing the interpersonal relations of the early church members. However, Clarke and Elliott's critiques of the egalitarian reconstruction of the history of the early church have legitimacy. We therefore turn to our own modified egalitarian theory as one way forward between these two approaches.

58. The final sentence of Clarke's book ends with a summative statement that leadership did indeed exist (with which we agree) but that it was "often determined by social status rather than other 'charismatic' qualities" (Clarke, *Serve the Community of the Church*, 252).

59. For another possible argument in favor of this reading, see Joe Hellerman's proposal for how Paul and Silas seek to keep the playing field equal when it came to their status of citizenship in the Philippian community. Hellerman, "Vindicating God's Servants," 85–102.

Modified Egalitarian Theory: Eschaton as Conditioning Criterion

We can maintain that the early church still had social and economic inequities when they gathered together. However, because of the sharing in the one Spirit, these inequities are reprioritized under the siblinghood of the gathered saints. While Paul and other apostles would have had an executive authority, they wielded it sparingly, and further, the need for this kind of executive authority has now ceased.[60] Those leaders within the early community (and there were, indeed, leaders) possessed a nonexecutive authority. They had the epistemic authority of teaching, which was always testable, and the exemplary authority of being imitable, which could also be called out if they were not living up to the standards of Christ (cf. 1 Tim 5:19–20). As such, the community had a critical role to play in both testing these nonexecutive authorities as well as aspiring to become competent and imitable themselves, as all are called to maturity and Christlikeness. Such is possible because of the indwelling of the Holy Spirit, which is both the executive authority in the believer's life and also an internal power to enable each believer's imitation of Jesus (often mediated by imitating other, more mature, followers of Jesus). We believe this understanding of nonexecutive authority remains operative in the church today. The same Spirit is at work in the disciples of Jesus and the same criteria of legitimacy for testing epistemic and exemplary authority remain.

Consequently, there are those within the family of God who have more maturity, and consequently, more nonexecutive authority (better termed, "weight" or "influence" given modern assumptions about authority as predominately executive). Being a head of household would have *potentially* increased the person's epistemic or exemplary authority, thereby making them a more natural fit in certain roles in the early church, such as overseeing the community's needs. However, it is also clear from the qualifications of elders and overseers that the qualifications were primarily about exemplary authority in that they were worthy of imitation. What is egalitarian about this picture is the potential for *anyone* in the body of Christ to gain influence based on their maturity in Christ and to lead out of their own gifting regardless of their social status. Thus, everyone in the Christian community has equal value due to being indwelt by the Holy Spirit and being a sibling. However, depending on the sibling's maturity, the weight of that sibling's voice may differ from person to person. At the same time, *no one* is above being reviewed and tested by those in the community.

60. Clarke, *Pauline Theology*, 93.

If, by hierarchy, we mean that individuals have different weight of influence, roles, and functions with some leading and some being led, this does not then entail having executive authority over one another. What makes present-day hierarchies in the church problematic is they tend to set up the inferiority of some (the laity) and superiority of others (the clergy). In other words, they undermine the dignity of every member of Christ's body who is a gifted sibling. However, as we have seen, nonexecutive authority is not an authority over others but pertains to epistemic and characterological domains, and they are permeable. Kathy Ehrensperger, who endorses the hierarchical view, comes closest to this modified approach we are endorsing when she says, "As long as they [hierarchies] remain flexible and open to the members of the group in question hierarchies need not necessarily lead to domination and oppression. Thus, hierarchical relationships as such need not be detrimental to a movement that emphasizes the equality of all its members."[61] However, the difficulty for us today is also sociological. First, we do not tend to have leadership structures that are transparent, reviewable, and permeable and consequently, language of "leadership" and "hierarchy" typically connote someone in charge, and other, less important people, perpetually subordinate to them. Given the dignity of each member of the body of Christ, these pervasive understandings need to be challenged and corrected.

Conclusion

While the idealistic fallacy is to be avoided due to its standing on shaky historical footing, an idealistic mandate is to be embraced due to the seeds of what was planted in the first-century church. Followers of Christ are people of new creation because of the indwelling Holy Spirit. Thus, the problem with opponents of the idealistic fallacy (hierarchicalists) is not that they question the egalitarian historical reconstruction. The problem is that they concede too much to the "already" of economic and social disparity instead of being conditioned by the "not yet" of fully eliminated disparity and inequity. As a dignifier of people and cultures, the Spirit did not implode the structures that were already in place but worked within them—often (as we have seen) quite radically. At the same time, we agree with proponents of the hierarchical view in their recognition of those exercising leadership in the early church, though with the caveat that becoming a leader was permeable as all were intended to grow in epistemic and exemplary authority. We might summarize our view by saying every sibling has a voice in

61. Ehrensperger, "Striving for Office."

the Christian community; each sibling's voice may have a different weight, but every sibling can (and should) mature, which will increase the weight of their voice in the community, while each voice is reviewable, no matter the weight. However, the goal is not to have more influence, but that influence is incidental to each believer striving after the One whom we chiefly imitate, and who welcomes the world into his family.

Bibliography

Barclay, William. *By What Authority?* Valley Forge, PA: Judson, 1975.

Bartchy, Scott. "Table Fellowship." In *Dictionary of Jesus and the Gospels*, edited by J. B. Green and S. McKnight, 796. Downers Grove, IL: InterVarsity, 1992.

Berger, Peter L., and Thomas Luckmann. *The Social Construction of Reality*. Garden City, NY: Doubleday, 1966.

Clarke, Andrew D. "Equality or Mutuality? Paul's Use of 'Brother' Language." In *The New Testament In Its First Century Setting: Essays On Context and Background In Honour of B. W. Winter on His 65th Birthday*, edited by P. J. Williams et al., 151–64. Grand Rapids: Eerdmans, 2004.

———. *A Pauline Theology of Church Leadership*. Repr. ed. London: T&T Clark, 2013.

———. *Serve the Community of the Church: Christians as Leaders and Ministers*. Grand Rapids: Eerdmans, 2000.

Crossan, John. *The Essential Jesus: Original Sayings and Earliest Images*. San Francisco: Harper, 1994.

De George, Richard T. *The Nature and Limits of Authority*. Lawrence: University Press of Kansas, 1985.

Dunn, James D. G. *Jesus and the Spirit: A Study of the Religious and Charismatic Experience of Jesus and the First Christians as Reflected in the New Testament*. Grand Rapids: Eerdmans, 1997.

Ehrensperger, Kathy. "Striving for Office and the Exercise of Power in the 'House of God': Reading 1 Timothy 3:1–16 in the Light of 1 Corinthians 4:1." In *The Bible in Church, Academy, and Culture: Essays in Honour of the Reverend Dr. John Tudno Williams*, edited by Alan P. F. Sell, 104–23. Eugene, OR: Pickwick, 2011.

Elliott, John H. "The Jesus Movement Was Not Egalitarian but Family Oriented." *Biblical Interpretation* 11 (2003) 173–210.

———. "Jesus Was Not an Egalitarian. A Critique of an Anachronistic and Idealist Theory." *Biblical Theology Bulletin* 32 (2002) 75–91.

Heim, Erin. "In Him and Through Him from the Foundation of the World: Adoption and Christocentric Anthropology." *In Christ and the Created Order: Perspectives from Theology, Philosophy, and Science*, edited by Andrew B. Torrance and Thomas H. McCall, 2:129–50. Grand Rapids: Zondervan, 2018.

Hellerman, Joseph H. *The Ancient Church as Family*. Minneapolis: Fortress, 2001.

———. "Review of Serve the Community of the Church: Christians as Leaders and Ministers. By Andrew D. Clarke." *Journal of the Evangelical Theological Society* 44 (2001) 736–37.

———. "Vindicating God's Servants in Philippi and in Philippians: The Influence of Paul's Ministry in Philipi Upon the Composition of Philippians 2:6-11." *Bulletin for Biblical Research* 20 (2010) 85–102.

Holmberg, Bengt. *Paul and Power: The Structure of Authority in the Primitive Church as Reflected in the Pauline Epistles.* Philadelphia: Augsburg Fortress, 1980.

Kowalski, Waldemar. "The Reward, Discipline, and Installation of Church Leaders: An Examination of 1 Timothy 5:17–22." PhD thesis, University of Gloucestershire, 2005.

Lane, W. L. "Social Perspectives in Roman Christianity during the Formative Years from Nero to Nerva: Romans, Hebrews, *1 Clement*." In *Judaism and Christianity in First-Century Rome*, edited by K. P. Donfried and P. Richardson, 196–244. Grand Rapids: Eerdmans, 1998.

MacDonald, Margaret Y. *The Pauline Churches.* Cambridge: Cambridge University Press, 1988.

Plummer, A. "Apostle." In *Dictionary of the Apostolic Church*, edited by James Hastings, 82–84. Edinburgh: T&T Clark, 1918.

Ramm, Bernard. *The Christian View of Science and Scripture.* Milton Keynes, UK: Paternoster, 1955.

Ridderbos, Paulus H. *Ontwerp van zijn theologie.* 3rd ed. Kampen: Kok, 1973.

Russell, Letty. *Household of Freedom: Authority in Feminist Theology.* Philadelphia: Westminster, 1987.

Sandnes, Karl Olav. "Equality Within Patriarchal Structures: Some New Testament Perspectives on the Christian Fellowship as a Brother- or Sisterhood and a Family." In *Constructing Early Christian Families: Family as Social Reality and Metaphor*, edited by Halvor Moxnes, 150–65. London: Routledge, 1997.

Van Zyl, Hermie C. "The Evolution of Church Leadership in the New Testament—a New Consensus?" *Neotestamentica* 32 (1998) 585–604.

11

Mary Come and Console Your Daughters

An Approximation to Feminicide and Mariological Discourses in Latin America

JULIANY GONZALEZ NIEVES[1]

On October 8, 2016, sixteen-year-old Lucía Pérez was kidnapped, drugged, gang-raped, and sodomized with a wooden pole by three men in Argentina. The assault was so brutal that she went into cardiac arrest, and later died due to internal injuries.[2] The horrific crime sparked protests across Latin America in what was called *Miércoles Negro* or Black Wednesday—a day in which thousands mourned Lucía's death and demanded justice.[3] Their cries echo until this day, and in them you will hear the voices of all the murdered women and girls who preceded and followed Lucía in that fatal destiny. Like seven-year-old Indigenous Colombian Yuliana Samboní, who was kidnapped, raped, and killed by thirty-eight-year-old architect Rafael Uribe Noguera; or the at least 4,599 women killed in the region in 2023, victims of misogynous violence.[4]

1. Scripture quotations in this chapter are taken from the New International Version.

2. Gordon, "NiUnaMenos."

3. BBC, "Lucia Perez Case."

4. D'Angelo and Spagnoletti, *Femi(ni)cidios*.

The pervasiveness of this kind of violence in one of the most Christianized regions in the world demands theological attention. In this chapter, I explore traditional depictions of Mary, examining their relevance within the frameworks of *marianismo* and the *Tres Marías Syndrome*. I then consider the potential correlation of these narratives in the shaping of a theo-socioethical imagination that, in turn, has contributed to the persistence of gender-based violence. Given the impossibility of assessing the entirety of the region, the chapter focuses on México and Puerto Rico as representative countries.

The structure of the chapter is fourfold. The first section provides a concise overview of the historical context within which Mariology was introduced to Latin America and the Caribbean, and its early pivotal role in reshaping conceptions of gender and womanhood in the region. The second section explores traditional depictions of Mary, examining their relevance within the frameworks of *marianismo* and the *Tres Marías Syndrome*, and how these theo-socioethical narratives have been correlated to gender-based violence. Thirdly, the chapter considers three theological and missiological imperatives for Christian communities in Latin America and the Caribbean in light of this reality. The chapter concludes with an imprecatory psalm by Puerto Rican reggaetón icon Ivy Queen.

It is worth noting what this chapter does not do. It does not argue that Mariology inescapably entails the sociological subordination of women. It also does not argue for a causal relationship between Mariology and gender-based violence.

My methodology is both interdisciplinary and intersectional, integrating history, social sciences, and the humanities, and conscious of how our embodied existence is impacted by the multiple identities we inhabit. I write in a Protestant Latin American and Caribbean feminist theological key that aims toward an analytic intuition. This does not come without its challenges. For one, I am someone *de facto* trained to approach theology using the resources of continental philosophy. Secondly, scholars within the feminist tradition have raised concerns, and not without reason, about analytic theology's understanding of "objectivity," its seeming "view from nowhere approach," the apparent correspondence between how God is described in Perfect Being Theology and the disembodied ideal observer, and material power dynamics.[5] Yet, as Coakley has noted, "Clarity, incisiveness, coherence, and philosophical persuasiveness are not in themselves the

5. See Griffioen, "Nowhere Men and Divine *I*'s."

feminist problem."[6] Furthermore, constructive responses to these critiques have been already provided by Coakley, Griffioen, and others.

Of particular importance to this chapter is how an analytic approach provides a limit to the thesis that everything is construction. This limit helps us move beyond what could become a closed loop of hermeneutics, allowing us to make claims about human moral deliberation in relation to reality. When considering theological and missiological imperatives in light of femicide and its potential correlation to theo-sociocultural discourses, this approach prevents us from falling into a cycle of simply endlessly substituting one hermeneutical lens for another.

While the contributions of Roman Catholic scholar-practitioners are of paramount importance to my theological work, I also write as someone rooted in the autochthonous Pentecostal tradition of the Puerto Rican archipelago, which will shape my particular theological analysis of Mariology in these regions.

Defining Femicide

Violence against women has a long history as a sociopolitical and cultural global phenomenon. Its manifestations are multiple and varied. *Femicide* is its pinnacle. The term was coined in the North by Diana Radford and Jill Russell in 1992 to refer to "the misogynous killing of women by men."[7] Radford would expand and rephrase this definition in 2001 as "the killing of females by males *because* they are female."[8] However, it is documented that in the 1980s, activists and women's groups in the Dominican Republic had already coined the Spanish term *feminicidio* to describe the particular experience of Latin American women with gender-based violence.[9] The term was then introduced into academia in 1997 by Mexican anthropologist Marcela Lagarde. *Feminicidio* names a horrifying reality—"the murders of women and girls founded on a gender power structure . . . rooted in social, political, economic, and cultural inequalities." This violence is not the exclusive domain of private individual agents but a shared sphere cultivated at structural and systemic levels.[10]

It was *las muertas de Juárez*, the dead women of Juárez, who became the paradigmatic case for the public discussion, when in 2001, eight bodies

6. Coakley, "Feminism and Analytic Philosophy," 516–17.
7. Radford and Russell, *Femicide*, 3.
8. Russell, "Introduction," 3.
9. Fregoso and Bejarano, "Introduction," 5.
10. Fregoso and Bejarano, "Introduction," 5.

were discovered in a cotton field. Only seven were identified.[11] Through the marks on what was left of their mutilated bodies, Laura, Claudia, Esmeralda, Mayra, Merlín, María, and María de los Ángeles, pointed the international press to the reign of death and impunity that had been ruling over Juárez, collecting women's and girls' bones since 1993. And while the border city continues to be an epicenter—for many *the* epicenter—of *feminicidio* in Latin America and the Caribbean, the trail of bodies and disappearances indict the entire geographical region. So much so that in 2017, the United Nations named it the deadliest for women outside of a war zone.[12] That same year, the Center for the Study of Global Christianity at Gordon-Conwell Theological Seminary released data that identified Latin America as the world region with the most number of Christians.[13] Although the crisis of feminicidal violence in any location calls for theological attention, its occurrence in one of the most Christianized regions in the world makes the demand inescapable.

Although there are a number of publications that have approximated the topic of *feminicidio* in the region from a theological perspective, these are few and sparse.[14] The work has been spearheaded by journalists, activists, and scholars in the field of the social sciences. They have approached the discussion from multiple lenses, including economics, politics, law, and anthropology, but not religion—at least not in a prominent manner. Given the region's religious context, this lack is consequential not only from theological and missiological points of view but also from a sociological one. This chapter responds to that shortage and seeks to contribute to an interdisciplinary dialogue by bridging the social sciences and theology.

11. EFE, "Inauguran un memorial."

12. Unidas Naciones, "Latinoamérica es la región más peligrosa."

13. Gina Zurlo notes that "Latin America has been a majority-Christian continent for over 500 years due to European colonization and the importation of Catholicism" and the religious makeup of the region has changed little between 1970 and 2020. See Zurlo, "Demographic Profile of Christianity."

14. See Luévano, *Woman-Killing in Juárez*, 317; Pineda-Madrid, *Suffering and Salvation*, 348. Both authors are in the Roman Catholic tradition. I have not yet found a book-length treatment on the topic by a Protestant theologian or religious scholar in English or Spanish. However, Nancy Elizabeth Bedford addressed the topic in her chapter "De Cara al Feminicidio."

Encountering Mary: From Mary the Conqueror to Mary the Mother Liberator

Theology is a human endeavor that is neither formulated nor received in a vacuum. It takes place within history and its many layers, which in turn mediate its impact. The figure of Mary was introduced to the Caribbean and Latin American regions through the *Conquista* and its reign of the cross and the sword. In that context, conquistadors frequently attributed the success of their colonial military enterprise to the Virgin.[15] This triumph encompassed not only the plundering and pillaging of the land but also the violent subjugation of the Amerindian population, and, with it, the disparagement of the Amerindian woman.[16] In his book *De María Conquistadora a María Liberadora*, Jesuit scholar Antonio González correlates this new diminished status of the Indigenous woman with "a macho exploitation" of Marian devotion that promoted a culturally bound and racially coded discourse on womanhood and femininity. Following the thought of Vilma Moreira da Silva, he writes,

> We must remember that in some sectors of the West, there was a macho exploitation of the cult of the Virgin Mary, by reducing the Marian model to the 'ideal of femininity' in the sense of exalting some of the virtues that are said to be 'proper to women,' such as modesty, acceptance, passivity, resignation, submission, humility, etc., culturally and alienatingly reducing the global dimension of the feminine being.[17]

Although González does not elaborate further on this particular point, a more comprehensive understanding of this correlation is offered by Vieira Powers. She observes that while the Spanish invasion is frequently interpreted within the context of cultural and political clashes, it also precipitated a collision in terms of gender, resulting in a profound transformation of Indigenous gender parallelism and complementarity. Mariology was instrumental in this dramatic shift. She writes,

> The Catholic cult of Mary . . . played an essential role in educating young native women about the rules of sexual conduct and about appropriate Christian gender roles. While the goddesses of the Aztec and Inca pantheons were powerful, often sexually charged women, Mary was quiet and submissive

15. See Gebara and Bingemer, *Mary*, 129–30; Hall, *Mary, Mother and Warrior*, 45–80; and Remensnyder, *La Conquistadora*.

16. See Socolow, *Women of Colonial Latin America*, 34–55.

17. González Dorado, *De María Conquistadora*, 44.

> . . . Mary's perpetual virginity and obedience were held up as the ideal for which earthly women should strive in their relations with men.[18]

These teachings, which, among other aspects, contradicted Amerindian perspectives on virginity, eventually steered certain elite Indigenous families to embrace the Iberian notion of women's purity as a paramount virtue linked to familial honor. The ideological shift materialized in multiple ways, including the adoption of women's enclosure practices. Contrastingly, these ideas were seemingly less conspicuous among non-elite Amerindians and those residing in rural areas. But considering the early displays of Marian devotion within these communities, Viera Powers notes that it is reasonable to infer that *marianismo* also played a role in shaping their gender dynamics.[19]

The Iberian Marian ideal occupied a paradoxical social matrix in which women were considered "weak, malleable, [and] susceptible to the temptations of the devil" yet "spiritually superior to men," their "natural" guardians.[20] The importation of this socio-ethical and theological discourse combined with Spanish society's leniency towards men's indiscretions, created an uneven moral standard. As a result, Indigenous women bore the heaviest responsibility for safeguarding sexual purity—and, by extension, personal and familial honor. Furthermore, it should not be forgotten that the transformation in conceptions of gender and gender relations in colonial Latin America unfolded against a backdrop of violence, marked by ideological battles regarding the nature of the *Indian* and claims about their alleged cultural and rational inferiority. The latter, in turn, intersected with Iberian notions of racial purity, honor, the emerging sociopolitical reality, and the prevailing dominance of Iberian men, forming a lens through which Amerindian women were devalued due to their triple identity as women, *Indians*, and *heathens*.[21] Although this devaluation was not uniform and evolved over time, it was frequently employed to legitimize their exploitation, which often included sexual abuse. Inevitably, many Amerindian women found themselves excluded from the paradigm of the Marian feminine ideal.

Women who did not conform to Iberian notions of modesty and femininity, often found themselves ensnared in a web of stigmatization, being associated with prostitution and sexual deviancy. However, some women were not beyond social and religious redemption. There was an alternative

18. Powers, *Women in the Crucible*, 55.
19. Powers, *Women in the Crucible*, 56.
20. Powers, *Women in the Crucible*, 124.
21. See Dussel, *History of the Church*, 334, and Pagán, *Violent Evangelism*, 111, 222.

archetype, that of Mary Magdalene, the redeemed *puta*. And there was also a place: enclosure institutions, which were established in some regions to "rehabilitate" and "[prevent] women from being 'out of control,'" meaning outside the purview of male authority.[22]

Black women brought to the region through the transatlantic slave trade experienced the exclusion to an even greater degree. As historian Susan Socolow notes, Blackness in the Iberian social imaginary was associated with ontological immorality. This misconstrued view rendered Black women and women of African descent beyond any notion of purity, including virginity, a foundational Mariological tenet. Socolow explains,

> By the social and moral definitions of the Iberian world, women of color because of their racial "stain" had no claim to honor. "Virtuous" sexual conduct was seen as being outside the ken of slaves, and the moral code that privileged virginity in women did not extend to any black or *mulata* woman. . . . Slave owners themselves controlled the sexuality of slave women by restricting their freedom and enjoying unimpeded access to their bodies. Because they were legally the property of their masters, slave women had even less power to resist the sexual advances of their masters than did Indian women.[23]

Indigenous and Black women were then trapped in a paradoxical situation where violence against them was justified in part through a socio-theological discourse that placed patriarchal and racialized Mariological interpretations at its core. This discourse promoted an archetype of the ideal feminine that served the economic and political interests of the Spanish crown by commodifying those who were excluded by it. In other words, the exclusion of Indigenous and Black women, the latter to a more significant degree, from the ideal feminine and ultimately womanhood—or at least "proper" womanhood—rendered them as objects of production, service, and exploitation for empire building in the project of colonization.

In spite of the violence that characterized *la Virgen*'s introduction to the continental regions, she was eventually reclaimed by oppressed communities in their struggle for liberation. Examples of the latter are *la Virgen de Guadalupe*, Copacabana, and *Nuestra Señora de la Concepción Aparecida*. In the words of González, María "La Conquistadora" became María "La Madre Liberadora," "the Mother of the Oppressed, who were not left motherless."[24] This reclamation, however, did not free Mary from the gaze of

22. Dussel, *History of the Church*, 124–25.

23. Socolow, *Women of Colonial Latin America*, 144.

24. González Dorado, *De María Conquistadora*, 22.

patriarchy and pigmentocracy. And it certainly did not free Latin American and Caribbean women from the social impact which certain Mariological discourses would continue to have on notions of femininity, womanhood, motherhood, gender roles, and sexuality.

The Bodies We Inhabit and the Narratives We Inherit

Marianismo

In the early 1970s, Evelyn Stevens coined the term *marianismo* to name the societal expectations imposed on women's behavior in Latin America. In her view, *marianismo* functions as the complementary counterpart to *machismo*—a sociocultural anti-value in which the heterosexual man is deemed as superior and dialectically opposed to all that is considered feminine.[25] While Stevens draws a distinction between the religious practice of Marian devotion and the social phenomenon she describes, she underscores their correlation. According to her analysis, the former has played a pivotal role by offering "a central figure and a convenient set of assumptions upon which practitioners of *marianismo* have built a secular framework of beliefs and practices pertaining to the position of women in society."[26]

Within this framework, the idealized "true" or "good woman" is predicated on her perceived spiritual and moral superiority, which elevates her to a quasi-divine status. This spiritual strength finds its greatest form of embodiment in self-abnegation and submissiveness. The latter often understood as an unwavering compliance owed not only to fathers and husbands but also to sons and brothers. These virtues find a poignant emblematic representation in traditional portrayals of Mary as the handmaid of the Lord that render her words, "I am the Lord's servant. . . . May it be done to me according to your word," as an act of passivity and feminine acquiescence before a (g)od who is perceived as a male authority figure.[27]

Within this ideological discourse, men then frequently become extensions of the divinity, their authority elevated beyond reproach or scrutiny. Simultaneously, however, a deeply ingrained societal belief endures, encapsulated in the phrase "boys will be boys." So, in *marianismo*, feminine

25. I appreciate González Dorado's definition of machismo as "un antivalor cultural latinoamericano," a Latin American cultural antivalue, in which the man is deemed as superior and dialectically opposed to the woman, and, by extension, to the homosexual. See González Dorado, *De María Conquistadora*, 6. Stevens uses the term to refer to "el culto a la virilidad," the cult to virility. See Stevens, "El marianismo," 17.

26. González Dorado, *María Conquistadora*, 18.

27. Johnson, *Truly Our Sister*, 28.

submissiveness paradoxically rests upon the infantilization of men, the shared belief that men require coddling and their transgressions warrant forgiveness, for they are akin to children, "not to blame for being the way they are."[28] It is this combination of power and lack of accountability that serves as the fertile soil where gender-based violence thrives and feminicidal acts flourish.

Another notable characteristic observed by Stevens among Latin American women is a profound sadness. She attributes this to the alleged inherent and distinct tendency of men toward sin, referred to as *la pecaminosidad masculina*. In popular Latin American Roman Catholicism, this innate inclination is thought to consign men to an extended stay in purgatory, a fate that even the most fervent prayers offered by women relatives cannot substantially alleviate.[29]

As a result, the Latin American woman assumes an intercessory role, one that, though limited, mirrors that of the *Mediatrix*. Through lives marked by piety, self-sacrifice, and constant prayer, women become a conduit for the redemption of men's souls. This role extends beyond the spiritual realm into the social sphere, with women frequently acting as mediators within the household—particularly between the male head of the family and other members occupying lower positions within the domestic hierarchy. This function becomes crucial in times of conflict.

Women's sadness finds some of its most visible liturgies in the context of mourning, especially following the death of a father, husband, or son.[30] While mourning customs have evolved over time, some communities continue to uphold expectations regarding women's attire and demeanor for a designated period of time. Any deviation from these prescribed norms can elicit social judgment and even lead to questions about a woman's moral character and virtue. Thus, women are obliged to demonstrate respect to these departed men beyond the realm of the living—restricting their own joy and suppressing its outward expression.

For Stevens, then, "the image of the Latin American woman is almost indistinguishable from the classic religious figure of the *Mater Dolorosa*," also known as the Mother of Sorrows.[31] This Mariological archetype is primarily associated with Simeon's prophetic words to Mary in Luke 2:35—"a sword will pierce your own soul"—words that are often interpreted as ultimately finding fulfillment at the foot of the cross. Mary is the mother who

28. Stevens, "El marianismo," 20.
29. Stevens, "El marianismo," 21.
30. Stevens, "El marianismo," 21.
31. Stevens, "El marianismo," 21.

suffers the most indescribable sorrow of seeing her son being tortured to death, his body broken in a public spectacle of injustice, sponsored by the Roman state and Jewish religious leaders.

Latin America and the Caribbean is full of *Mater Dolorosas*. On one hand, we have the mothers of the victims of *feminicidio*, carrying the unbearable grief of their daughters' horrifying deaths. A profound suffering that is exacerbated by the widespread impunity that allows perpetrators to evade accountability, often due to the complicity or leniency of the state and other institutions. To compound their pain, these grieving mothers are frequently expected—particularly within communities of faith—to extend forgiveness to their daughters' murderers and to endure their suffering in silence.

In *Woman-Killing in Juárez*, Rafael Luévano vividly documents the profound suffering endured by Paula Bonilla Flores, whose seventeen-year-old daughter, Sagrario, was abducted and murdered on her way home from work by a man she had previously rejected, along with his accomplices. Paula's grief is made even heavier by the pressure she faces from friends urging her to forgive the perpetrators, based on the belief that God will ultimately pardon them.[32]

Beyond this expectation, Paula has also been subjected to the judgment of certain community members who believe she has transgressed her role by making her quest for justice a public matter. These individuals consider Paula and other mothers of *feminicidio* victims as *escandalosas* for not bearing their suffering "with a dignified silence."[33] But for Paula, this public pursuit of justice represents the only avenue available, even if it means bearing the label of *inapropiada*.

On the other hand, and on the other side of this reign of death, we also encounter the mothers of the perpetrators, grappling with their own burden of guilt, shame, and pain. These women often find themselves scrutinized by public opinion, blamed for their sons' actions as though their perceived failures in motherhood led to such horrific crimes. For in a society that bestows power to men while excusing their transgressions, blame can only be attributed to women.

The Tres Marías Syndrome

Within Chicano and Mexican cultures, *marianismo* has provided the foundation upon which the *Tres Marías Syndrome* has been constructed.

32. Luévano, *Woman-Killing in Juárez*, 55.

33. Luévano, *Woman-Killing in Juárez*, 55.

Following Alicia Gaspar de Alba's definition, this is a theo-socioethical patriarchal discourse that conceptualizes women's role and sexuality through the lens of three biblical archetypes—the virgin, the mother, and the whore. These archetypes find symbolic representation in the figures of the Virgin Mary, who perpetually maintained her virginity; Mary, the mother of James and Joseph (Mark 15:40); and Mary Magdalene, the whore.[34]

La Virgen María is exalted as the ultimate ideal for all women, the embodiment of meekness and obedience toward a masculine (g)od. Her virtue is defined by submission—not only to the divine but also to the social order that mirrors this hierarchy. In a patriarchal society, where male authority is perceived as divinely sanctioned, women are expected to exist under continuous male guardianship—first their fathers, then their husbands, and, in the absence of the latter, their sons. So, the archetype of *la Virgen* is the woman who remains ignorant of her own sexuality, dresses modestly, does not call attention to herself, and does not leave her parents' home unless there is a wedding ring on her finger and a husband by her side. Parallel to *la Virgen María* is Mary, the mother, envisioned as the archetype of a woman whose *raison d'etre* is her husband and children. She is the one whose sexuality is reduced to the act of procreation, rendering her as "a virtually celibate ideal even in motherhood."[35]

At the bottom of the hierarchy, we encounter Mary Magdalene, residing in the shadows. She is the one "who has sex for pleasure, takes birth control, corrupts men, [and] shames her family," thereby transgressing the *mythos* of what a woman should be. She is the one "who deserves what she gets."[36] It is this kind of narrative that is exemplified in the ways femicide cases are discussed at all levels, from the communal to the judiciary. "She had to do something to make him angry. That is why he killed her." "What was she wearing?" "What was she doing outside of the house at that time of the night?" "If she had been at her house doing what women are supposed to do, she would be alive today."

While in the popular biblical-theological imagination, Mary Magdalene is the redeemed whore, there is no redemption for her in this mythos. Rather, she is understood as the foremother of an even more complicated figure in the Mexican/Chicana culture, La Malinche, also referred to by some as the "Mexican Eve" and "La Chingada," the fucked one.[37] As Alicia Gaspar de Alba notes, the *Tres Marías Syndrome* provides a socio-ethical

34. Gaspar de Alba, "Poor Brown Female," 81.

35. Johnson, *Truly Our Sister*, 33.

36. Gaspar de Alba, "Poor Brown Female," 82.

37. Gaspar de Alba, "Poor Brown Female," 81. Also see Cereijido, "La Malinche."

discourse not only on how to be a good woman but also a way for "women's sexuality to be scrutinized, proscribed, protected, or punished at all times."[38]

Theological Discourses Pierce Bodies

These theological discourses are not abstract. Their judgments materialize in girls' and women's bodies, and the socioeconomic and political arrangements that normalize violence against them. Furthermore, they are inescapably mediated by the material conditions of the region, characterized by political corruption, widespread poverty, high unemployment rates—especially concerning job opportunities for men—displacement, and the exacerbated impact of natural disasters. These contingencies are particularly dire within Black, Indigenous, and rural communities due to racism and other forms of historic systemic injustice and marginalization. The amalgamation of these realities translates into higher vulnerability for Black and Indigenous women, as well as *campesinas*.

Mercedes Olivera notes that, in Mexico, these very conditions have "forced women to join the labor market under conditions of great inequality and vulnerability."[39] Due to limited educational and professional training opportunities, their employment options are often limited to jobs within the service industry, transnational factories—infamously known as *maquiladoras*—and the informal economy. The mass integration of women into the labor force not only signifies a departure from but also constitutes a transgression of theo-socioethical discourses that traditionally confine women's roles and bodies to the domestic sphere while exclusively reserving the public sphere for men.

As a result, women working outside the home have faced criticism not only from their communities but also from the government. The government, for instance, blames them for juvenile delinquency, citing their alleged neglect of maternal responsibilities.[40]

Additionally, the newfound acquisitive power of these women, coupled with the potential for self-determination it affords, has triggered what can be described as a crisis in men's self-perception.[41] This crisis has resulted in some men choosing to either abandon or divorce their partners. Simultaneously, others have sought to reassert their dominance through acts of violent retaliation. Rafael Luévano explains this phenomenon as part of "the

38. Gaspar de Alba, "Poor Brown Female," 82–83.

39. Olivera, "Violencia Feminicida," 53.

40. Olivera, "Violencia Feminicida," 54.

41. Olivera, "Violencia Feminicida," 54.

backlash discourse," a narrative that contends that "women have violated traditional gender roles in both the workplace and the home; men, in response to the collapse of their patriarchal constructs and control over women, retaliate violently."[42] In all of these scenarios—be it abandonment, divorce, or violence—women are held responsible for provoking the actions of men by rejecting their divinely appointed roles and attempting to usurp men's positions. Consequently, the violent acts perpetrated by men against these nonconforming women "[acquire] a punitive aspect, and the aggressor takes on a moralizing profile as a safeguard of social morality, because in that shared imaginary women's destiny is to be contained, censored, disciplined and reduced by the violent gesture."[43]

Gender-based violence and *feminicidio* in Latin America and the Caribbean can only be explained when the "simultaneity and cross-fertilization of various forms of violence linked to various forms of social oppression" are considered.[44] Among these forms of violence is the ideological manipulation of Christian theology—in this case, Mariology—in the service of the sociological subordination of women. This complex situation gives rise to an urgent challenge for Christian communities in the region: the need to confront both the discursive structures that sustain these harmful narratives and the tangible material oppressions stemming from them. The central question that emerges is: How?

Before addressing that question, I offer a word of invitation to Latin American and Spanish-speaking Caribbean Pentecostals. It may be tempting to dismiss discussions on Mariology as irrelevant. At first glance, we might even fail to see the influence of *marianismo* and the *Tres Marías Syndrome* within our own communities. Yet, while Pentecostalism—through its emphasis on the Holy Spirit's empowerment of both women and men—has historically created more opportunities for women's participation in the ecclesial public sphere, gender dynamics and expectations in some conservative Pentecostal churches seem to mirror these same narratives.

For instance, girls' and women's attire is often regulated in ways that indict the female body for men's sin. Similarly, discourses that invoke Jezebel and Eve as a symbol of dangerous femininity often parallel the way Mary Magdalene is framed within the *Tres Marías Syndrome*. Furthermore, in many cases the public power of Pentecostal women coexists with a different reality in the domestic space, in which they are encouraged to fit the archetypes of the virgin and the mother.

42. Luévano, *Woman-Killing in Juárez*, 45.

43. Segato, "Territory, Sovereignty, and Crimes,"76.

44. Lagarde y de los Ríos, "Preface," xix.

At the same time, because of Pentecostalism's emphasis on the Holy Spirit's empowerment of both women and men, along with its affirmation in word and deed of the priesthood of all believers, I believe we are uniquely positioned to meaningfully contribute theologically and missionally to this discussion.

Theological and Missiological Imperatives

So, how can we confront both the discursive structures that sustain these harmful narratives and the tangible material oppressions stemming from them? A first theological imperative is to challenge and move away from theological discourses that exclusively portray human nature as male, thus marginalizing women. The contributions of Brazilian theologians Ivone Gebara and María Clara Bingemer in this area carry profound significance. They observe that anthropological conceptions within theological work, particularly in Mariology, have predominantly drawn from Platonic origins, even though this connection has not been systematically articulated.[45] Within this entrenched anthropological framework, men are tethered to the lofty realms of reason and logic, elevating them closer to the zenith of perfection, while women are relegated to a secondary status, often pejoratively linked with the emotional domain. Recognizing the dangerous implications of this ideological framework, Gebara and Bingemer advocate for an alternative anthropological perspective—one that is human-centered instead of male-centered, unifying rather than dualistic, realist instead of idealist, and pluri-dimensional instead of one-dimensional. Within this reimagined perspective, there is a deliberate absence of privilege granted to the male expression of humanity over the female, and there are no efforts aimed at diminishing one gender to elevate the other.[46] Moreover, this framework adopts a more holistic approach to the material-spiritual reality of the human, striving to eschew oppositional binaries. These guiding principles offer immense value to Christian communities as they reevaluate the views on humanity operating within and beyond their confines. This critical examination represents a pivotal initial step towards dismantling the oppressive frameworks that serve the liturgies and cultures of death in our world.

A second theological imperative involves a commitment to a theology that not only speaks but actively fosters the empowerment of women—and, along with them, men—to cultivate an environment where all creation can

45. Gebara and Bingemer, *Mary*, 1.

46. Gebara and Bingemer, *Mary*, 4.

flourish.[47] This is what Argentinean theologian Nancy Bedford calls *feminismo teológico*. Its central concern is to ensure that "the gospel of Jesus is truly good news for women—and consequently also for men, liberated from the burden of a presumed superiority for which they were not created."[48] This vision understands that the gospel holds relevance beyond the afterlife and encompasses the well-being of all creation in the present.

This perspective should permeate our theology, ecclesiology, and missiology. Pentecostal popular theology is particularly well-positioned to achieve the first part—a theology that empowers women—especially given its pneumatology and ecclesiology. However, its tendency toward eschatologies of escapism presents a challenge to the idea of a gospel that nurtures abundant life in the here and now.

Finally, our third imperative centers the challenging recognition that we are all complicit in gender-based violence and femicide through our passivity, which often reeks of apathy. Within theological and spiritual traditions, this apathy is frequently identified as *acedia*, counted among the cardinal sins.[49] Fundamentally, *acedia* can be defined as "the failure to love."[50] This failure becomes evident in the form of indifference, which hinders any action aimed at transforming the conditions that perpetuate realities of injustice and death. A valuable resource for Christian communities seeking concrete steps to respond to gender-based violence is *Creada a su imagen: Una pastoral integral para la mujer* by Pentecostal theologian Agustina Luvis Núñez. In it, she provides pedagogical materials, liturgies for times of crisis, prayers, and suggestions regarding the use of inclusive language.

The church, as the company of those who have been threatened with resurrection, ought to be "a social space of contrast . . . a community that does not rehearse the dominant or minuscule oppressions of the world."[51] Rather, she understands herself as called to "[reproduce] the Spirited practices of Jesus, [mirroring] the life of a society made righteous and just."[52] It is the community that should be known by love, showing that another world is possible. And in that world, Latin American and Caribbean women live.

47. Bedford, *La porfía*, 14; translation mine.
48. Bedford, *La porfia*, 15; translation mine.
49. Luévano, *Woman-Killing in Juárez*, 87.
50. Luévano, *Woman-Killing in Juárez*, 88.
51. Martínez Olivieri, *Visible Witness*, 192.
52. Martínez Olivieri, *Visible Witness*, 193.

Conclusion

In this chapter, I have provided a concise overview of the historical context in which Mariology was introduced to Latin America and the Caribbean, highlighting its pivotal role in reshaping conceptions of gender and womanhood in the region. I then explored traditional depictions of Mary, examining their relevance within the frameworks of *marianismo* and the *Tres Marías Syndrome*, and how these theo-socioethical narratives have been correlated to gender-based violence. Finally, I briefly outlined three theological and missiological imperatives for Christian communities in Latin America and the Caribbean, emphasizing the necessity of engaging these realities with theological depth and ethical urgency.

Writing this chapter was, in many ways, a birthing in the midst of many deaths. It was written as I traveled between the continental USA and Puerto Rico. It experienced the stress of Felix Verdejo's trial, accused of the vile assassination of Keishla Rodríguez Ortíz and her unborn child. It grieved the femicide of Angerilis Marrero García, who was pregnant, as well as the horrifying rape and murder of two-year-old April Thais Ortíz Quiñones at the hands of her biological father. And it also accompanied me as I visited the second oldest church in the Western Hemisphere, the *Catedral de San Juan Bautista*, to light candles for them and their mothers before the *Virgen de la Divina Providencia.*

Throughout this time, the iconic song "Muchos quieren tumbarme" by Marta Ivelisse Pesante, popularly known by her stage name Ivy Queen, gave me the words to pray.

> Ay Dios
> Cuida de las yales de todo el mundo
> No permitas que caigan en el dolor
> El matrato físico y la depresión
> Y la muerte
>
> Solo tú
> Sabes lo que habrá en el juicio final
> Para todo aquel hombre que quiera abusar
> Después que vive de ella, la ha de trastornar
> Dale fue(r)te.

As we cry for our dead, we also pray for the protection of the living, and ground our work in the promise *de un Dios que viene a hacer justicia.*

This chapter is dedicated to Keishla Rodríguez Ortíz and her unborn baby, Andrea Ruiz Costas, Alexa Negrón Luciano, Angerilis Marrero García and her unborn baby, Blanca Arellano, and two-year-old April Thais Ortíz Quiñones. Que la justicia corra como río.

Bibliography

EFE. "Inauguran un memorial para las víctimas de Juárez sin el apoyo de sus familiares." *20 Minutos*, August 11, 2011. https://www.20minutos.es/noticia/1212600/0/mexico-memorial/ciudad-juarez/victimas/.

BBC. "Lucia Perez Case: Latin America Protests Against Gender Violence." *BBC*, October 20, 2016. http://www.bbc.com/news/world-latin-america-37712931.

Bedford, Nancy E. "De cara al feminicidio: un camino crítico de Resistencia no-violenta para la antropología teológica." In *Teología feminista a tres voces*, 317–48. Santiago, Chile: Ediciones Universidad Alberto Hurtado, 2016.

———. *La porfía de la resurrección: Ensayos desde el feminism teológico latinoamericano*. Barcelona: Ediciones Kairós, 2008.

Cereijido, Antonia. "La Malinche: The Sory of Mexico's Eve." Latino USA, July 3, 2015. https://www.latinousa.org/2015/07/03/la-malinche-the-story-of-mexicos-eve/.

Coakley, Sarah. "Feminism and Analytic Philosophy of Religion: Prospects for Rapprochement?" In *The Oxford Handbook of Philosophy of Religion*, 494–525. Oxford: Oxford University Press, 2004.

D'Angelo, Eugenia, and Paula Spagnoletti. *Femi(ni)cidios bajo la lupa en América Latina y el Caribe: Entre las que sobreviven y las que ya no están: Datos y relatos de la violencia machista—Informe Anual 2023*. Le Puy-en-Velay, France: MundoSur, 2024.

Dussel, Enrique. *A History of the Church in Latin America: Colonialism to Liberation*. Grand Rapids: Eerdmans, 1981.

Fregoso, Rosa-Linda, and Cynthia Bejarano. "Introduction: A Cartography of Femicide in the Américas." In *Terrorizing Women: Femicide in the Américas*. Durham, NC: Duke University Press, 2010.

Gaspar de Alba, Alicia. "Poor Brown Female: The Miller's Compensation for 'Free' Trade." In *Making a Killing: Femicide, Free Trade and La Frontera*, edited by Alicia Gaspar de Alba, with Georgina Guzmán, 63–93. Austin: University of Texas Press, 2010.

Gebara, Ivone, and Maria Clara Bingemer. *Mary: Mother of God, Mother of the Poor*. Eugene, OR: Wipf & Stock, 1989.

González Dorado, Antonio. *De María Conquistadora a María Liberadora: Mariología popular Latinoamericana*. Editorial Sal Terrae, 1988.

———. "El marianismo: la otra cara del machismo en América Latina." *Diálogos: Artes, Letras, Ciencias humanas* 10 (1974) 17–24.

Gordon, Sarah. "NiUnaMenos: How a Schoolgirl's Brutal Rape and Murder United the Women of Argentina." *The Telegraph*, October 21, 2016. https://www.telegraph.co.uk/women/life/niunamenos-how-a-schoolgirls-brutal-gang-rape-and-murder-united/.

Griffioen, Amber L. "Nowhere Men and Divine *I*'s: Feminist Epistemology, Perfect Being Theism, and the God's-Eye View." *Journal of Analytic Theology* 9 (2021) 1–25.

Hall, Linda B. *Mary, Mother and Warrior: The Virgin in Spain and the Americas*. Austin: University of Texas, 2004.

Johnson, Elizabeth A. *Truly Our Sister: A Theology of Mary in the Communion of Saints*. New York: Continuum, 2004.

Lagarde y de los Ríos, Marcela. "Preface: Feminist Keys for Understanding Femicide: Theoretical, Political, and Legal Construction." In *Terrorizing Women: Femicide in the Américas*, xi-xxv. Durham, NC: Duke University Press, 2010.

Luévano, Rafael. *Woman-Killing in Juárez: Theodicy at the Border*. Maryknoll, NY: Orbis, 2012.

Martínez Olivieri, Jules A. *A Visible Witness: Christology, Liberation, and Participation*. Minneapolis: Fortress, 2016.

Mauro, J. P. "Africa Overtakes Latin America for the Highest Chrisitian Population." *Aleteia*, July 24, 2018. https://aleteia.org/2018/07/24/africa-overtakes-latin-america-for-the-highest-christian-population/.

Núñez, Agustina Luvis. *Creada a su imagen: Una pastoral integral para la mujer*. Nashville: Abingdon, 2012.

Olivera, Mercedes. "Violencia Feminicida: Violence against Women and Mexico's Structural Crisis." In *Terrorizing Women: Femicide in the Américas*, 49–58. Durham, NC: Duke University Press, 2010.

Pagán, Luis Rivera. *A Violent Evangelism: The Political and Religious Conquest of the Americas*. Louisville, KY: Westminster John Knox, 1992.

Pineda-Madrid, Nancy. *Suffering and Salvation in Ciudad Juárez*. Minneapolis: Fortress, 2011.

Powers, Karen Vieira. *Women in the Crucible of Conquest: The Gendered Genesis of Spanish American Society, 1500–1600*. Albuquerque: University of New Mexico Press, 2005.

Radford, Jill, and Diana E. H. Russell, eds. *Femicide: The Politics of Woman Killing*. Toronto: Mawell Macmillan Canada, 1992.

Remensnyder, Amy G. *La Conquistadora: The Virgin Mary at War and Peace in the Old and New Worlds*. Oxford: Oxford: University Press, 2014.

Russell, Diana E. H. "Introduction: The Politics of Femicide." In *Femicide in Global Perspective*, 3–11. New York: Teachers College Press, 2001.

Segato, Rita Laura. "Territory, Sovereignty, and Crimes of the Second State: The Writing on the Body of Murdered Women." In *Terrorizing Women: Femicide in the Américas*, 70–92. Duke University Press, 2010.

Socolow, Susan Migen. *The Women of Colonial Latin America*. Cambridge University Press, 2000.

Stevens, Evelyn, and Martí Soler. "El marianismo: la otra cara del machismo en América Latina." *Diálogos: Artes, Letras, Ciencias humanas* 10 (1974) 17–24.

Unidas Naciones. "Latinoamérica es la región más peligrosa del mundo para las mujeres." November 25, 2017. https://www.un.org/sustainabledevelopment/es/2017/11/latinoamerica-es-la-region-mas-peligrosa-del-mundo-para-las-mujeres/.

Zurlo, Gina A. "A Demographic Profile of Christianity in Latin America and the Caribbean." In *Christianity in Latin America and the Caribbean*, edited by Kenneth R. Ross et al., 3–16. Edinburgh: University of Edinburgh Press, 2022.

Practices and Spirituality

12

Waiting on the Spirit

A Charismatic, Analytic Theology of Liturgy

Joshua Cockayne[1]

Waiting on the Spirit

"Come Holy Spirit Come." After the minister utters these words, a sense of anticipation fills the room. Palms are turned upwards, eyes scrunched into their sockets, and an eerie hush descends on an otherwise energetic gathering. The soft hum of keyboard pads masks the faint sounds of sirens and the slow trudge of traffic passing by outside. For just a moment, the attention of those gathered is fixated on the possibility that something unexpected might happen. The tension is palpable as the room waits, expectant to know what God will do in the midst of this community. Perhaps someone will be healed from an illness? Maybe someone will come to faith for the first time? A word or a picture might be shared to bring encouragement and comfort to those gathered. As they wait, the congregation are united in this sense of anticipation.[2]

1. Scripture quotations in this chapter are taken from the New Revised Standard Version.

2. This example is a description of the author's own experience in the charismatic tradition within the Church of England in the United Kingdom. By "charismatic" I

This chapter seeks to reflect on this liturgical act of "waiting on the Spirit" and to offer an account of charismatic worship, drawing from work in the philosophy and psychology of joint action. While there is an increasing amount of work on the theology of charismatic liturgy and worship,[3] the uniqueness of the approach taken in this chapter is that the main dialogue partners come from the analytic philosophical tradition, hence, it is a work of "analytic theology."[4] It might be surprising to some that the analytic tradition has something to contribute to this conversation. But over the last ten years, there has been an increasing engagement with liturgy in the analytic tradition.[5] Despite this engagement, many of the key proponents of the so called "liturgical turn"[6] in analytic theology, are writing from the perspective of mainstream high-church traditions, such as the Eastern Orthodox tradition, and the American Episcopal Church.[7] This chapter seeks to contribute to the ongoing conversation in analytic theology and liturgy and to broaden the focus to include charismatic, low-church traditions.[8]

The chapter will proceed by arguing for four theses which aim to provide a philosophically informed theology of waiting on the Spirit:

1. Waiting on the Spirit is a liturgical act.
2. Waiting on the Spirit is a scripted, spontaneous liturgical act.
3. Waiting on the spirit is a scripted, spontaneous joint liturgical act.
4. Waiting on the spirit is a scripted, spontaneous joint liturgical act of quiescence.

Each thesis is intended to build on the previous, offering a proposal for thinking about the nature of this simple act of waiting on the Spirit, which

---

mean a form of liturgy that can be practiced by both mainstream (non-Pentecostal) denominations (e.g., Anglican, Roman Catholic, Methodist) and Pentecostal denominations (e.g., New Frontiers, Four Square Churches, etc.) See the introduction of this volume for a fuller discussion of the charismatic tradition.

3. See Chan, *Liturgical Theology;* Smith, *Thinking in Tongues.*

4. See Wood, *Analytic Theology.*

5. See Wolterstorff, *God We Worship;* Wolterstorff, *Acting Liturgically*; Cuneo, *Ritualized Faith*, and my summary of the literature, Cockayne, "Analytic Theology and Liturgy." Also see the recent volume bringing together voices across different traditions, Simmons et al., *Philosophies of Liturgy.*

6. A phrased coined by James K. A. Smith in his review of Cuneo's work. See Smith, "Review of Terence Cuneo."

7. I.e., Wolterstorff considers the American Book of Common Prayer, and Cuneo focuses on the Eastern Orthodox liturgy.

8. Two notable exceptions come from essays by Leidenhag, "For We All Share"; and Shin, "Feasts of Resistance."

is practiced each week in churches around the world. My contention is that the act of "waiting on the Spirit" is typically a highly scripted and planned liturgical act, which is not unlike liturgical acts in more formal traditions. I will also argue that understanding waiting on the Spirit in these terms can help us to see something of its value, namely, that it allows for a joint act of responsiveness to God. This joint responsivity could not be achieved by acts of pure spontaneity, or so I will argue. Lastly, I offer a reflection on the nature of this joint act, namely, that it is an act of quiescence, in which a community plan to cease acting in worship to create space for the work of the Holy Spirit.

Waiting on the Spirit Is a Liturgical Act

The first claim is that waiting on the spirit should be thought of as a liturgical act. Now, the notion of "charismatic liturgy" may seem to some an oxymoron; the charismatic tradition is the antithesis of formal, "liturgical traditions," it might be held. But by "liturgy," I do not mean to denote a particular tradition. Liturgy (in the sense that I intended it here) is simply a pattern of practices or rituals used in the context of gathered worship in the church.[9]

All churches, regardless of tradition, use some form of liturgy. The very fact that we know what to anticipate (broadly speaking) when showing up to worship indicates that there are practices in place; people sit to listen to preaching and don't sing spontaneously over the top of the sermon, people know what time to show up for the beginning of worship (even if the time of the ending is sometimes more mysterious in charismatic traditions!). This is not just an academic technicality. It is a central contention of this chapter that charismatic liturgical traditions have more in common with formal traditions than they sometimes suppose. The first step to seeing these commonalities is to acknowledge that, when they gather to worship together, participants in charismatic worship are participating in the same

9. There is a broader sense of liturgy that is used in the literature, such as in the work of Smith, *Desiring the Kingdom*. I here follow the distinction offered by Charles Price and Louis Weil between "extensive" and "intensive" liturgies (Price and Weil, *Liturgy for Living*, 15). Intensive liturgy refers to the practices of gathered worship, and extensive to the practices which happen outside of this context. As they describe, "To engage in either intensive or extensive liturgy drives one to seek out the other. From the extensive liturgy of a Christian's life in the world, one comes to the intensive liturgy for assurance, pardon, and renewal. From the intensive liturgy, one 'goes forth into the world to love and serve the Lord.'" (Price and Weil, *Liturgy for Living*, 15). I explore this distinction in greater detail in chs. 6 and 7 of Cockayne, *Explorations in Analytic Ecclesiology*. It is intensive liturgy which is the subject of this chapter.

kind of thing as in many more formal or traditional settings. And to do this, we must admit that charismatic traditions also have a liturgy.

One good way of reflecting on the liturgical content of a tradition is to reflect on the features which are commonly present in acts of worship. In many formal traditions it is more obvious what to reflect on because the content of a service is written down. That is, their liturgical scripts include some combination of the following: gathering prayer, confession, hymns, readings sermon, intercession, peace, Eucharist, dismissal. In the charismatic tradition, many of the features above may be practiced in common with formal traditions. But one unique feature of charismatic liturgies is the place of "waiting on the Spirit," in which space is left for the congregation to respond to the work of the Holy Spirit and to exercise spiritual gifts of various kinds.[10] Although waiting on the Spirit could happen at any point in the service, there are also expected times within the order of the whole service where this occurs (i.e., towards the end of the service, or towards the end of the first section of sung worship, and/or immediately after the sermon).[11] The fact that this act is anticipated and repeated each gathering, even if it is seemingly unstructured, speaks to its liturgical nature.[12]

Waiting on the Spirit Is a Scripted Spontaneous Liturgical Act

Given this acknowledgment of waiting on the Spirit as a liturgical act, let's now consider how it might relate more broadly to the nature of liturgy. To do so, we will consider the discussion of liturgy in the work of Evelyn Underhill, the twentieth-century Anglo-Catholic theologian. In her book *Worship*, Underhill begins by establishing that worship primarily concerns and orientation towards God, rather than a set of practices. "Worship," Underhill describes, "at every level, always means God and priority of God."[13] Moreover, worship is shaped by our understanding of human teleology. Underhill writes that "there is a sense in which we think of the whole life of the Universe, seen and unseen, conscious and unconscious, as an act of worship, glorifying its Origin, Sustainer, and End."[14] In this wider sense, there is

10. See Leidenhag, "For We All Share" for a more detailed exploration of charismatic gifts.

11. With thanks to Joanna Leidenhag for this suggestion.

12. Leidenhag also makes the claim that waiting on the Spirit is a liturgical action in her essay.

13. Underhill, *Worship*, 6.

14. Underhill, *Worship*, 3.

very little about creation which does not relate to the question of worship; worship of the creator provides a way of understanding what it is to stand in the creator/ creature relationship.

Against this backdrop of seeing the fundamental nature of worship for human creatureliness, Underhill goes on to spell out the place of liturgy. She argues that worship "must have embodiment, concrete expression," for human beings are "embodied spirit; even though all that is involved in this mysterious relationship be veiled from us. [They live] under conditions of time and place. . . . [Their] worship begins as a spontaneous reaction to this stimulus; and this reaction always takes the form of something which must be *done*."[15] This need for embodied *action* isn't therefore intrinsic to the nature of worship, for Underhill, it is an implication of the kind of creatures that human beings are. Worship needs a concrete, embodied expression because human beings cannot engage with the divine outside of their embodiment.[16] But human beings are also "amphibious creatures,"[17] occupying both the world of spirit and sense. Liturgy reflects this; it is an embodied and sensible way of participating in an act of spirit which transcends the particular forms and rituals being used.

This reflection on the need for liturgy provides a context to offer some overarching principles for practicing liturgy which will help inform our understanding of charismatic traditions. Underhill presents these principles by way of a presentation of a set of tensions which exist in all liturgies. For instance, she argues, Christian worship is both personal and corporate; liturgy must be the expression of personal devotion to God, but that same person must always exist within a corporate context. All liturgy possesses, "a marked social quality," Underhill writes, which makes "it possible for [people] to do things together . . . . Personal and social action must cooperate all the time."[18] This tension must be upheld in the worshiping life of the church—liturgy which is only an opportunity for individual devotion is a failure to grapple with the theological foundations of worship in the Christian tradition. Likewise, liturgy which never goes beyond the corporate to individual devotion and adoration is lacking in important ways.

15. Underhill, *Worship*, 13; emphasis added.

16. Underhill provides a helpful theological framework for much of the recent literature on embodiment and liturgy. I explore some of this literature in more detail in ch. 1 of Cockayne and Salter, *Liturgical Jointness*. See, for example, Brown and Strawn, *Physical Nature of Christian Life*; Strawn and Brown, *Enhancing Christian Life*; Doyle, *Embodied Liturgy*; Taylor, *Body of Praise*.

17. Underhill, *Worship*, 23.

18. Underhill, *Worship*, 22.

Similarly, Underhill thinks, there exists a tension which exists between what she calls "habit" and "attention" in liturgy. She writes that

> habit and attention must therefore co-operate in the life of worship; and it is a function of cultus to maintain this vital partnership. Habit alone easily deteriorates into mechanical repetition, the besetting sin of the liturgical mind. Attention alone means, in the end, intolerable strain. Each partner has his weak point. Habit tends to routine and spiritual red-tape; the vice of the institutionalist. Attention is apt to care for nothing but the experience of the moment, and ignore the need of a stable practice, independent of personal fluctuations; the vice of the individualist. Habit is a ritualist. Attention is a pietist. But it is the beautiful combination of order and spontaneity, docility and freedom, living humbly—and therefore fully and freely—within the agreed pattern of the cultus and not in defiance of it, which is the mark of a genuine spiritual maturity and indeed the fine flower of a worshipping life.[19]

As with the tension between the personal and the corporate, the tension between habit and attention reflects the amphibious nature of human beings. Liturgy must provide a context for engagement with the transcendent divine, but it must also reckon with the embodied, and ritual nature of human beings. This awareness of the importance of spontaneity for avoiding vain repetition is no doubt familiar to those in the charismatic tradition. But equally important is the emphasis on what structure can bring; namely, a context in which meaningful spontaneity can occur, and in which a community can be sustained into spiritual maturity.

It's important to see that this tension between habit and attention (or between spontaneity and scriptedness) are present in every tradition to different degrees. Nicholas Wolterstorff reflects on this tension in the context of the very formal liturgical act of reciting creeds together (a common feature of most traditional liturgies):

> Together following the script is not sufficient for together enacting the liturgy. If one person, for example, says the creed very slowly and another says it very quickly, they are not saying the creed *together* . . . . Normally the acting together that occurs in liturgical enactments is achieved by a blend of following the script and mutual responsiveness. When it comes to the people

19. Underhill, *Worship*, 27–28.

> singing together in harmony, prescription necessarily falls short; mutual responsiveness is unavoidable.[20]

Even in this highly scripted formal act of reciting a piece of text together, there are aspects of both habit and attention which need to be present; the script may provide a strong emphasis on habit, but without paying attention to who is doing what, it would not be possible to read a liturgical script *together*.

The place of spontaneity and attention in charismatic liturgy seems more obviously present than in the formal act of reciting a creed. As we saw in the opening example, charismatic liturgy typically allows for many spaces in which participants can act spontaneously and without a script. Indeed, it is arguably a feature so pervasive of such liturgies that it warrants little more discussion. The less often explored question, I think, is to ask what place *habit* or *scriptedness* plays in charismatic liturgy.

The philosopher Bruce Ellis Benson observes that there is a commonly held misconception that traditional, formal liturgical contexts are less spontaneous than informal, contemporary contexts. As Benson goes on to argue,

> In general, members of so-called nonliturgical churches value spontaneity, a feeling of being fresh and authentic, since those praying, for example, are speaking from their hearts. Conversely "liturgical" churches find the depth and richness of their prayers which have been painstakingly written, to be preferable. But these assumptions are somewhat misleading. . . . Those in the evangelical tradition know how "spontaneous" prayers can become predictable ("Lord, we just . . . "). Less formal churches often rely on a rather small set of worship songs that are rotated rather frequently.[21]

For Benson, what presents as "spontaneity" in informal contexts is often a fairly repetitive set of norms, such as a small set of worship songs, or a learnt vocabulary of prayer. The air of spontaneity which these liturgical norms present presumably arises from the fact that these liturgical acts are not written in books or hymn sheets. But to state that a script is not formally written down is not the same as saying there is no script; even in very informal settings, there are norms and expectations which frame the liturgical shape of a context. In the charismatic tradition, these norms are often shaped by the repetition of certain practices (e.g., services typical have a familiar shape, such as "music-sermon-ministry-music"). Even the act of

20. Wolterstorff, *Acting Liturgically*, 64; emphasis in the original.

21. Benson, *Liturgy as a Way of Life*, 140.

waiting on the Spirit, which we began this chapter by focusing on, which may feel like a spontaneous liturgical act, has elements of scriptedness to it. As the theologian Simon Chan describes,

> Many Christians of a charismatic bent . . . are not satisfied with just freedom for a variety of forms. What they want to see is freedom within the service for someone to give a word of prophecy or a "message in tongues." A fixed form of worship, it is argued, tends to stifle the Spirit's "surprising works." . . . When one has been in charismatic churches long enough, one notices that prophecies and tongues occur at predictable moments. Some form of "planned spontaneous happenings" is at work in these churches, even if it is not explicitly recognized. A message in tongues in the middle of the sermon would be ruled out of order in most chiasmatic churches. There is an unwritten structure within which such "spontaneous" expressions are allowed to take place.[22]

As Chan highlights, despite the many *surprises* of charismatic worship, there are clear norms and expectations which make it possible to respond to the Holy Spirit in ministry. This description of "planned spontaneous happenings" is a helpful way of understanding the liturgical act of waiting on the Spirit. The point isn't that the charismatic tradition is less spontaneous than it thinks (even if that is the undertone of both Benson's and Chan's comments) but that noticing the scripted nature of charismatic liturgy can help us to notice valuable features of its practice which may sometimes be ignored.

A common comparison—between liturgy and jazz—can help press the point about the of seeing spontaneity in the context of structure. In the music world, sometimes jazz is thought of as exemplifying spontaneity, to the extent that it is easily mistaken for having a lack of structure of form (especially to those who don't take the time to understand jazz properly). But, as Benson shows, improvisation in jazz is only possible within the context of community and tradition; "to improvise is always to speak to others, with other (even when one improvises alone), and in the name of others . . . when I play a tune, I am never simply improvising on that tune alone. I am improvising on the tradition formed by the improvisations upon that tune."[23] Similarly, Benson thinks, jazz is not without a script or certain rules of correctness—but, rather, our improvisations must take place against the backdrop of this script. "Not only are many 'improvisations' often

22. Chan, *Liturgical Theology*, 127.

23. Benson, *Liturgy as a Way of Life*, 92.

significantly 'scripted,' but spontaneity is only possible when one is well prepared. . . . It takes a great deal of work to be spontaneous."[24]

This provides a helpful way of thinking about liturgy. Like jazz, the spontaneity which exists within charismatic liturgy can only be made sense of within a context and a community. In other words, because there is a script present. As Joanna Leidenhag explores in depth, this comparison with jazz can provide a helpful framing for charismatic liturgies. She writes that

> the skills of musical and spiritual improvisation are similar in that they can only be learnt through participation and imitation. One must learn to really listen, before one can learn to play. Jazz does not have scores, but transcriptions which guide but do not determine a performance. . . . For charismatic gifts, the pedagogical emphasis on improvisation is essential since it allows participants to anticipate and respond to the Spirit's presence and prompting as experienced through charismatic gifts. . . . Sometimes this leading of the Spirit might occur in a pre-set time within the liturgical script, comparable to an improvised pre-planned solo section within jazz. At other times, the prompting of the Spirit may take, guide or even interrupt a section of the liturgical script that was not previously set aside for charismatic gifts. In either setting, explicit interest is often on novelty and what God is doing differently today through the enactment of charismatic gifts, understood to occur in the context of faithfulness to the core narrative and eternal identity of God.[25]

The parallel between jazz and charismatic liturgy and the ways in which this expresses the tension between habit attention help us to see something important. That is, that charismatic liturgy in general, and the act of waiting on the spirit in particular, are (contrary to first impression) highly structured liturgical acts which create space for attentiveness to the Holy Spirit.

Waiting on the Spirit Is a Scripted Spontaneous Joint Liturgical Act

Moving from thinking of waiting on the Spirit as an act of planned spontaneity, I now propose a third thesis, that waiting on the spirit is a scripted spontaneous *joint* liturgical act. In seeing both the scripted and spontaneous nature of charismatic liturgy we can also see the importance the other

24. Benson, *Liturgy as a Way of Life*, 41.
25. Leidenhag, "For We All Share," 74–75.

liturgical tension outlined by Underhill, namely, the personal/corporate tension. If charismatic liturgy is thought of as a kind of formless spontaneity, then it is difficult to see how it could be performed in a collective setting at all.

At its worst, charismatic liturgy is merely a collection of individuals privately engaging with God, in which the liturgy provides the context for worship, but makes little difference to its substance. At its best, charismatic liturgy is a corporate act, in which a community jointly attend to the work of the Spirit, for the sake of the community. There is an important theological point to stress here. Consider Paul's words in 1 Corinthians:

> Those who speak in a tongue build up themselves, but those who prophesy build up the church. Now I would like all of to speak in tongues, but even more to prophesy. One who prophesies is greater than one who speaks in tongues, unless someone interprets, so that the church may be built up. (14: 4–5)

As Leidenhag summarizes it, "Paul's overarching argument in 1 Corinthians is that charismatic gifts are given to up—build the Christian community, unifying it into the Body of Christ."[26] Given this communal emphasis of charismatic gifts, charismatic liturgy must find ways of expressing the corporate as well as the personal dimensions to liturgy. And it is difficult to see, without some established form, how a community might engage in a liturgical task *together*. It is rather like expecting a jazz quartet to show up and play a beautifully improvised piece without first knowing what key they were playing in, or without an understanding how to play their instruments.

As some philosophers have explored at length, when acts are performed together (rather than in synchrony, such as two people happening to move in the same way at the same time) intentions move from being individual intentions (e.g., I play my instrument) to become "we intentions" (e.g., we intend to perform the jazz quartet).[27] This shared intentionality allows for the possibility of joint or collaborative activities to take place. In the context of liturgy, we might think, one important role that both structure and spontaneity play is that they allow participants to act jointly. Scripts and structures provide liturgical norms and expectations, whereas spontaneity and attention allow for a responsiveness to the situation and to one another. To return to Wolterstorff's example of reciting the creeds—the difference between reciting a creed synchronously and collectively is that in the latter case participants pay attention, not just to the words of the script but to

26. Leidenhag, "For We All Share," 70.

27. See Searle, *Making the Social World;* Bratman, "Shared Agency."

the other members of the congregation. In doing so, the participant is able to mesh her intentions to the other participants so that they can recite the creed *together.*[28]

One of the crucial aspects of shared intentionality in the wider literature is the role of attention in jointly acting. The psychologist Michael Tomasello and his colleagues have argued at length that the roots of shared intentionality lie in the capacity to jointly attend with another person.[29] Put simply, joint attention is a situation in which persons attend to a mutual object together, such as the way in which a young child will navigate the world by triangulating their attention to objects of their environment with their caregiver. This link between joint attention and shared intentionality is vital for the development of joint actions.

Return again to the example of jazz. After their unexpected and joyous receipt of the 2023 Mercury Music Prize, the British jazz group Ezra Collective rather aptly performed a version of their track "Victory Dance." Despite having played the track earlier in the ceremony, the piece of music performed after being awarded the prize was vastly different—the solos were sprawling and took unexpected turns, the tempo felt faster, and the performance had an air of celebration. Yet, the track was recognizably the same. The music never felt out of control, the melody never got lost. How are the Ezra Collective able to perform in this recognizable, yet highly spontaneous manner? Surely, the answer is not simply because they are all talented individual musicians playing their own instruments with skill. But we must also be able to say something about how their engagement with one another over time means that their individual actions are able to form part of a wider "We." In other words, their performance is more than the sum of its individual parts—it is the way their intentions are meshed together to perform a collective that makes them able to perform with such proficiency. This is precisely what psychologists and philosophers seek to understand when they talk about shared intentionality.

Moreover, in describing the ways in which they are able to perform together, we can refer directly to the importance of joint attention. In a recent interview, the group were asked about the importance of improvisation in their live music. The bassist TJ Koleoso replied, "That's why we make so much eye contact. . . . We try not to be too rigid, it keeps the excitement there. And yeh when someone plays something cool, we're gunna react and

28. See Cockayne and Salter, *Liturgical Jointness*, for an extensive discussion of joint attention, shared intentionality, and liturgy.

29. Tomasello et al., "Understanding and Sharing Intentions."

its always different everytime, so yeh, that's why we're smiling."[30] What Koleoso reflects on here—the importance of eye contact in jazz performance—helpfully highlights the importance of joint attention in spontaneous joint acts. The example of eye contact is one example, but we might use many different methods to attend to the presence of others: language, gestures, facial expressions. These all help us to attend to other people and to pay attention to what they are paying attention to.

Thus, in thinking about joint scripted spontaneous acts of liturgy many of the same features are present. Formal liturgy (think about the example of reading the creeds) operates in ways more like playing in an orchestra. While the score dictates the majority of the content of the music, the musicians still need to be attentive to one another to play well together (a moving orchestral performance is surely more than everyone playing their instruments well). Both script and spontaneity are present but play different roles. But in charismatic liturgy, as with jazz, while the script is still present (the joint action has to be performed against the context of the tradition, liturgical norms and expectations, etc.), there is a permission to deviate from the script in response to one another and to the perceived promptings of the Holy Spirit.

The important skill (in both jazz and liturgy) is in deviating in such a way that the melody is still discernible and that all participants can follow what is happening. It is here that joint attention becomes all the more important. Just as the Ezra Collective require an understanding of one another to improvise faithfully, in liturgy we must know who has permission to riff from the central melody, who can take the service in a new direction, what is required to ensure the right song still gets performed, and what it would be like to fail to enact the liturgy faithfully. These are questions which push beyond *liturgical* towards discussions of *polity*. They might lie beyond the scope of this chapter, but they are nevertheless important questions to ponder further, especially for those who seek to lead others in acts of charismatic liturgy.

Waiting on the Spirit Is a Scripted Spontaneous Joint Liturgical Act of Quiescence

I have so far claimed that waiting on the Spirit is a scripted spontaneous joint liturgical act. Finally, given these claims we might ask: What kind of joint liturgical act is waiting on the Spirit? To offer an answer to this

30. Ezra Collective, "KCRW: Live from HQ."

question I propose that recent philosophical and theological discussions of "quiescence" might provide a helpful answer.

Eleonore Stump, in exploring the role of the will in the theology of salvation, proposes an innovative account of what she calls "quiescence," in which the will is neither actively resisting, nor accepting God's will. She offers the following to illustrate what this means:

> Consider, for example, a person who is suffering a dangerous allergic reaction to a bee sting and who fears death, but who nonetheless vigorously refuses his doctor's attempt to inject him with the urgently needed antidote to the allergen because he has an almost ungovernable fear of needles. Such a person might not be able to bring himself to will that the doctor give him the much-needed injection. That is, if the doctor were to ask him whether he is willing to accept the injection, he might not be able to bring himself to say "yes." But he might nonetheless be able to stop actively refusing the injection, knowing that, if he ceases to refuse it, the doctor will press it on him. If he does this, then his will becomes quiescent with regard to the injection, neither accepting it nor refusing it, but simply turned off in relation to the injection.[31]

For Stump, this concept of quiescence provides a helpful way of seeing how God could provide the means of salvation without overriding a person's freedom of will. Stump's use of quiescence in soteriology is not without its critics,[32] but, while sidestepping these issues, we can see that this concept has significant potential in the application to liturgy. Consider the following example which I have offered elsewhere in the discussion of liturgical silence:

> In ceasing to act in liturgy, in the moments before a service begins, or in the brief pauses after the reading of Scripture we might come to a state of quiescence. That is, in these moments, we cease to perform some action which is attempting to engage with God through petition or praise, and we cease trying to merge our actions with our fellow members in the body of Christ. But neither are we resisting God's will in uniting his Church. And in so doing, much like the quiescent bee-stung patient analogy, we allow the Spirit to move in us and through us in ways that are not possible through our own efforts. In other words, in the moments before a service starts, or in short time

31. Stump, *Wandering in Darkness*, 167.

32. See Kittle, "Grace and Free Will."

> of reflection after a reading, there is space for an individual to cease acting altogether and to be still.[33]

The above example attempts to think about the place of silence in liturgy more generally, but the application to charismatic liturgy seems apparent.

Liturgy, in the charismatic tradition, is active, requiring high levels of engagement from its participants. Even the seemingly passive act of listening to a sermon is often accompanied by verbal affirmation (shouts of "Amen!") or encouraging mumbles. Charismatic liturgy often prides itself on avoiding participation by rote or mindless repetition by expecting a significant amount of joint intentionality from all (rather than a handful of authorized ministers or leaders). Most participants are *doing* something most of the time in acts of charismatic liturgy. It is all the more important, then, to see the place of quiescence in the charismatic liturgical tradition. If what is valued is not merely the agency of human participants, but also the work of the Holy Spirit in the midst of the community, then we must see the place not just of liturgical action, but also of liturgical *inaction.* Waiting on the spirit, I propose, is precisely this. It is a moment of highly scripted cessation of action. In waiting on the Spirit, the participants are not attempting to jointly praise, or jointly respond, or jointly petition. Their aim is for a joint cessation of action, in which the Holy Spirit can work in and through the gathered community.

This is not to say that the liturgical act of waiting on the spirit is always *quiescent.* Surely, this is an act which is sometimes misused and manipulated to push a certain agenda or idea (e.g., "I have a word from the Lord to all give your money to my personal fund!"). It is also often difficult to genuinely respond with quiescence in liturgy; all too often the tendency is to revert very quickly back to acting and doing. To think of waiting on the Spirit in these terms is a proposal for what charismatic liturgy might be in an ideal form. For it is in learning to cease to act that we are most able to allow God to work in and through our humble and imperfect liturgical forms.

Conclusion

I have argued for four theses in understanding waiting on the Spirit in the charismatic tradition:

1. Waiting on the Spirit is a liturgical act.

33. Cockayne, "Corporate Liturgical Silence," 262–63.

2. Waiting on the Spirit is scripted spontaneous liturgical act.
3. Waiting on the Spirit is a scripted spontaneous joint liturgical act.
4. Waiting on the Spirit is a scripted spontaneous joint liturgical act of quiescence.

These are intended not as a final word on the topic of charismatic liturgy in analytic theology. Rather, my hope is to show what a fertile area for further theological and philosophical thinking the charismatic tradition provides, especially in the context of its liturgies. Just as we have seen a recent development in thinking liturgically about formal traditions, my hope is that a similar development might flow from the charismatic traditions.

Bibliography

Benson, Bruce. *Liturgy as a Way of Life*. Ada, MI: Baker Academic, 2013.

Bratman, Michael. "Shared Agency.'" In *Philosophy of the Social Sciences*, edited by Chrysostomos Mantzavinos, 41–60. Cambridge: Cambridge University Press, 2009.

Brown, Warren S., and Brad D. Strawn. *The Physical Nature of Christian Life: Neuroscience, Psychology, and the Church*. Cambridge: Cambridge University Press, 2022.

Chan, Simon. *Liturgical Theology: The Church as Worshiping Community*. Downers Grove, IL: InterVarsity, 2006.

Cockayne, Joshua. "Analytic Theology and Liturgy." In *T&T Clark Handbook of Analytic Theology*, edited by James M. Arcadi and James T. Turner Jr., 477–88. London: Bloomsbury, 2022.

———. "Corporate Liturgical Silence." In *Philosophies of Liturgy: Explorations of Embodied Religious Practice*, edited by J. A Simmons et al., 263–76. London: Bloomsbury, 2023.

———. *Explorations in Analytic Theology: That They May Be One*. Oxford: Oxford University Press, 2023.

Cockayne, Joshua, and Gideon Salter. *Liturgical Jointness: Theological and Psychological Perspectives on Liturgy, Joint Attention and the Value of Gathered Worship*. Waco, TX: Baylor University Press, forthcoming.

Cuneo, Terence. *Ritualized Faith*. Oxford: Oxford University Press, 2016.

Doyle, C. A. *Embodied Liturgy: Virtual Reality and Liturgical Theology in Conversation*. New York: Church, 2021.

Ezra Collective. "KCRW: Live from HQ." May 18, 2023. https://www.youtube.com/watch?v=7tJRifi-orY.

Kittle, Simon. "Grace and Free Will on Quiescence and Avoiding Semi-Pelagianism." *European Journal for Philosophy of Religion* 14 (2022) 70–95.

Leidenhag, Joanna. "For We All Worship in One Spirit." *Theologica* 4 (2020) 64–87.

Price, Charles P., and Louis Weil. *Liturgy for Living*. New York: Church, 1979.

Searle, John. *Making the Social World*. Oxford: Oxford University Press, 2010.

Shin, Sarah. "Feast as Resistance: Eucharist and Table Fellowship as Ecclesial Resistance to Evil." *TheoLogica: An International Journal for Philosophy of Religion and Philosophical Theology* 4 (2020) 30–52.

Simmons, J. A., et al., eds. *Philosophies of Liturgy: Explorations of Embodied Religious Practie*. London: Bloomsbury, 2023.

Smith, James K. A. *Desiring the Kingdom*. Ada, MI: Baker Academic, 2009.

———. "Review of Terence Cuneo, *Ritualized Faith*." *Scottish Journal of Theology* 71 (2018) 118–19.

———. *Thinking in Tongues: Pentecostal Contributions to Christian Philosophy. Vol. 1*. Grand Rapids: Eerdmans, 2010.

Strawn, B. D., and W. S. Brown. *Enhancing Christian Life: How Extended Cognition Augments Religious Community*. Downers Grove, IL: InterVarsity, 2020.

Stump, Eleonore. *Wandering in Darkness: Narrative and the Problem of Suffering*. Oxford: Oxford University Press, 2010.

Taylor, W. David O. *A Body of Praise: Understanding the Role of Our Physical Bodies in Worship*. Ada, MI: Baker, 2023.

Tomasello, Michael, et al. "Understanding and Sharing Intentions: The Origins of Cultural Cognition." *Behavioral and Brain Sciences* 28 (2005) 675–91.

Underhill, Evelyn. *Worship*. London: Mayflower, 1936.

Wolterstorff, Nicholas. *Acting Liturgically*. Oxford: Oxford University Press, 2018.

———. *The God We Worship*. Grand Rapids: Eerdmans, 2015.

Wood, William. *Analytic Theology and the Academic Study of Religion*. Oxford: Oxford University Press, 2021.

13

A Radical Theology of the Eucharist for Pentecostals

Steven Nemes[1]

The goal of the present essay is to propose and defend a radical theology of the Eucharist for Pentecostals. It would be well to begin the discussion with an explanation of what is meant by these terms before proceeding to the substance of the argument.

The theology to be proposed in the following pages is "radical" in two senses. On the one hand, it pushes the understanding of the Eucharist beyond the bounds of ordinary evangelical and Pentecostal theologizing. The proposal of the present essay is "radical" in this first sense because it arises out of a confrontation with the profound, unavoidable fallibility of human knowing. In this matter, it shares with other Pentecostal figures such as James K. A. Smith and J. Aaron Simmons a commitment to the phenomenological tradition of the twentieth-century philosophy.[2] It is also "radical" in this first sense to the extent that it calls for a greater sacramentality in the Pentecostal understanding of the Lord's Supper than one usually encounters. On the other hand, it does all this with a mind to being faithful to the

1. Scripture quotations in this chapter are taken from the English Standard Version.

2. See Smith, *Thinking in Tongues*. Consider also the interview with Simmons, "Pentecostal and Postmodern."

fundamental biblical-spiritual roots (*radices*) of the Pentecostal *ethos*: the lived experience of redemption through faith in Jesus Christ as a gift of God in the Holy Spirit. It is consequently "radical" in the second sense because it is not afraid to contest, in a typically Pentecostal manner, the inherited presuppositions of the catholic tradition. It is also thus "radical" to the extent that it strives to be true to Scripture and to the freedom of God.

The concern of the present essay is also that of presenting a theology of the Eucharist for Pentecostals. These terms (Eucharist, Pentecostals) have been carefully chosen despite how strange it may seem to see them both together. Veli-Matti Kärkkäinen writes that it is "safe to say" that the understanding of the Eucharist of the majority of Pentecostals is more or less Zwinglian in nature.[3] This means that the doctrine of the Real Presence of Jesus's body and blood in the bread and wine of the meal is rejected. The latter are rather understood as symbols of the former. This Zwinglian view is also the perspective taken in the present essay. Some Pentecostals with an appreciation of the historical catholic tradition of Christian theology show a sympathy toward the doctrine of the Real Presence, such as Simon Chan.[4] But it will be argued below that such a symbolic interpretation of the Eucharist as Huldrych Zwingli offers is preferable for Pentecostals for making sense of the meaning of the sacrament, especially given the Pentecostal emphasis on the role of experience as a source of theological knowledge, but also in light of the interpretation of the early church sources. It must also be mentioned here that there is nothing about this Zwinglian conception of things or even the Pentecostal spirit itself which demands an allergy to the language and patterns of worship of the pre- and non-Pentecostal Christian traditions. Zwingli for example defines a "sacrament" in his treatise titled *On the Lord's Supper* as "a sign of a holy thing."[5] He is in this matter following the definition of "sacrament" proposed by Augustine in *City of God* as a "sacred sign" (*sacrum signum*).[6] He also complains that it is fundamentally a misunderstanding of the term "sacrament" to imagine that it implies the inhabitation of some kind of divine or magical power in an inanimate object.[7] There is consequently nothing essentially un-Zwinglian or un-Pentecostal about being "sacramental" or using terms such as "Eucharist." To understand the bread and wine of the eucharistic meal as symbols of Jesus's body and blood is precisely to think of them as "sacraments" in this proper sense.

3. Kärkkäinen, "Pentecostal View," 122.

4. See Chan, *Liturgical Theology*, 144–45.

5. Zwingli, "Treatise on the Lord's Supper," 188.

6. Augustine, *City of God* 10.5:123.

7. Zwingli, "Treatise on the Lord's Supper," 188.

As for the term "Eucharist" itself, it brings to light the understanding of the memorial of the Lord's passion, death, and resurrection as an opportunity for joyous thanksgiving (*eucharistia*). This will form part of the argument to be given below for the more frequent celebration of the Eucharist in Pentecostal churches as a way of encountering Jesus in joy of the Holy Spirit (cf. Rom 14:17).

The argumentation of the present essay will consequently take the following order. It begins with a consideration of the relationship between sacraments and metaphysics (§1). The Real Presence tradition presents a "metaphysical" understanding of the sacrament of the Eucharist *par excellence* insofar as it fundamentally distinguishes between the world of experience and a non-manifest dimension of reality in which lie the true and deepest realities of things. But one can find arguments in the phenomenological tradition that such distinctions must be rejected insofar as they compromise the possibility of knowledge and lead to fallacious modes of reasoning. This sort of argumentation is consonant with the Pentecostal emphasis on lived experience with God and on the manifest work of God in the Spirit. The "metaphysical" understanding of the sacrament should therefore be rejected. The work of the Holy Spirit is not invisible but shows itself in experience.

The discussion then proceeds to a consideration of the interpretation of the Eucharist in early church sources (§2). This section raises the question of the relation between such a Pentecostal theology of the Eucharist and the understanding of the sacrament in the history of Christian theology. The common assumption is that the discourse about the sacraments of the ancient writers should be interpreted in a metaphysical manner, yet this is an entirely unwarranted assumption with some arguments to be made against it. The *Didache* is arguably implicit and Tertullian explicit that the bread and wine of the eucharistic meal are figures or images for Jesus's body and blood. Likewise, Justin Martyr, Irenaeus, and Tertullian say things about the Eucharist which suggest that their discourse about the sacraments should rather be interpreted phenomenologically or symbolically. This means that a memorialist or Zwinglian conception of the Eucharist would place Pentecostal theology closer to the early roots of the church than the metaphysical doctrine of later generations.

The final section will raise the question of the relationship between Christian belief and eucharistic communion (§3). How should Pentecostals understand the celebration of the Eucharist vis-à-vis the nature of Christian faith? The Eucharist can be understood as an exercise in Christian belief, but it is possible to distinguish two senses of "belief." On the one hand, there is belief-that. This is a way of relating to a proposition. On the other hand, there is belief-in. This is a way of entrusting oneself and one's life over to another person. The argument is given that the true essence of Christian belief as the gift of the Holy Spirit is to be understood as belief-in Jesus. Yet it is possible for two or more persons to share belief-in Jesus even despite considerable differences among them in matters of theological beliefs-that. The Eucharist itself can be understood as an invitation to express one's belief-in Jesus "sacramentally" through the consumption of the bread and wine as symbols of His person and sacrifice. This reinterpretation of the essence of Christian belief as belief-in Jesus, together with the symbolic interpretation of the Eucharist, consequently provides a way for seeing the Eucharist as a means provided by Jesus for accomplishing Christian unity.

Sacrament and Metaphysics

The doctrine of the Real Presence maintains that the body and blood of Jesus are really present in the bread and wine of the eucharistic meal.[8] Bernard Prusak defines the word "real" in this doctrine as follows: "The word 'real' emphasizes that Christ's presence is 'more than [by] sign,' but it does not eliminate the fact that it is a presence in and through what looks like bread and wine."[9] To say that Christ is really present is consequently to say that he is present in a further way than by means of a symbol. But there is an obvious rejoinder to this point of view. Guy Duffield and Nathaniel Van Cleave argue against the doctrine of transubstantiation as an iteration of the Real Presence tradition on the grounds that it is "contradicted by experience, for testing does not show that the elements physically change when blessed by a priest."[10] This appears to be a version of the argument given by Zwingli: "How can they say the bread is flesh when we do not perceive it to be so? If the body were there miraculously, the bread would not be bread, but we should perceive it to be flesh."[11] Brett Salkeld likewise notes that some versions of this argument had been given by Berengarius at the turn

8. The present essay will not consider in any detail the idea of a real "spiritual" presence of Christ during the Eucharist. This doctrine seems to be committed to the idea that Christ is somehow invisibly present in the celebration of the eucharistic meal even as it refuses to identify Christ with the bread and wine themselves. See Vermigli, *Oxford Treatise*. The opinion of this author is that the scriptural data sooner emphasizes the symbolic significance of the bread and wine and the nature of the meal as the church's act of expressing its faith, so that the preoccupation with a "spiritual" presence seems unmotivated or beside the point.

9. Prusak, "Explaining Eucharistic 'Real Presence,'" 254.

10. Duffield and Van Cleave, *Foundations of Pentecostal Theology*, 439.

11. Zwingli, "Treatise on the Lord's Supper," 196.

of the millennium as well.[12] The most obvious objection to make against the doctrine of the Real Presence is therefore that it is contradicted by the facts of experience.

This line of argument was not unknown to the proponents of the Real Presence doctrine throughout history. The response they gave effectively consists in denying that experience gives the whole of reality. The sacramental transformation takes place in a further dimension of being, lying beyond the manifest world of experience. Cyril of Jerusalem therefore writes, "Do not then think of the elements as bare bread and wine; they are, according to the Lord's declaration, the Body and Blood of Christ. Though sense suggests the contrary, let faith be your stay" (*Mystagogical Lectures* 4.6). And he later writes that "the bread which is seen [*ho phainomenos artos*] is not bread, though it is bread to the taste, but the Body of Christ" (4.9). Lanfranc of Bec similarly argues against Berengarius that the true catholic position maintains that

> the earthly substances, which on the table of the Lord are divinely sanctified by the priestly ministry, are ineffably, incomprehensibly, miraculously converted by the workings of heavenly power into the essence of the Lord's body. The species and whatever other certain qualities of the earthly substances themselves, however, are preserved, so that those who see it may not be horrified at the sight of flesh and blood, and believers may have a greater reward for faith at the sight. It is, nonetheless, the body of the Lord himself existing in heaven at the right side of the Father, immortal, inviolate, whole, uncontaminated, and unharmed.[13]

He therefore insists that "it is his true flesh which we eat, and his true blood which we drink" despite all appearances to the contrary (23 442D). And Thomas Aquinas would write succinctly that "the presence of Christ's true body and blood in this sacrament cannot be detected by sense, nor understanding, but by faith alone, which rests upon Divine authority."[14]

The Real Presence tradition consequently responds to the argument from experience by distinguishing between appearance and being as two "spheres" or domains of reality without essential correlation to each other. There is a manifest sphere, which consists in what is given and accessible in perception by means of the natural endowments and powers of human

12. Salkeld, *Transubstantiation*, 64.

13. Lanfranc of Bec and Guitmund of Aversa, *On the Body and Blood of the Lord* 18 430B-C.

14. *Summa Theologiae* III, q. 75, art. 1, taken from http://aquinas.cc/.

beings. In addition, there is a non-manifest, experientially inaccessible sphere in which the deepest reality of things resides. There is the world of experience and then there is world of trans-experiential reality. The transformation of the bread and wine into the body and blood of Jesus takes place in this latter, non-manifest sphere. And one can say that this is a "metaphysical" interpretation of the sacrament insofar as it appeals to realities which are not experienced, the non-reality of which would make no difference to the content of experience, and which can only be "grasped" by being posited by the intellect.

This distinction of appearance and being into separate and non-correlated spheres of reality is highly problematic from a philosophical point of view. Thinkers in the phenomenological tradition argue that it leads to skepticism and an "egocentric predicament."[15] The argument can be succinctly stated as follows. Aristotle defined truth as speaking or thinking about a thing as it is: "to say of what is that it is, or of what is not that it is not, is true" (*Metaphysics* 1011b25).[16] "Truth" is therefore a relation of adequacy obtaining between what one thinks or says about a thing and that thing itself. One can further say that "knowledge" is a matter of consciously truthful thought or speech about a thing. To know is to be aware that a thing is as precisely as one thinks or speaks about it. But things belong to the sphere of being, and it is impossible to become aware of a relation in the absence of one of the related items. One cannot see that one cat is fatter than another unless both cats are presented in some way or another, whether "in the flesh" or by means of an accurate photograph. Neither can one see that $x > 100$ unless the value of x is specified. From this it follows that knowledge as the awareness of the truth of one's opinion about a thing is not possible unless one can be presented with the thing itself in experience. Awareness is experience. But to deny that appearance and being are essentially correlated with one another, as the Real Presence tradition does, is to deny one's access to the thing itself. Every judgment one forms honestly is founded upon an appearance, i.e. on the way things seem to one at some point in time. And it is impossible to step outside oneself and to escape the subjective theater of one's consciousness in order to determine whether these appearances correspond to anything real. Hence it follows that one cannot become aware of the truth of one's opinions about things. As Sokolowski writes, "We do not

15. Sokolowski, *Introduction to Phenomenology*, 9–16; Schindler, *Catholicity of Reason*, 6.

16. Aristotle, *Metaphysics*, 65.

know how to show that our contact with the 'real world' is not an illusion, not a mere subjective projection."[17]

This conclusion was granted by some figures in the history of the Real Presence tradition. Thomas argues that the conversion of the substance of the bread and wine into the body and blood of Jesus is possible in principle as a result of the divine omnipotence (*ST* III, q. 75, art. 4). This implies that the distinction of appearance and being into separate spheres of reality without essential correlation follows as a matter of principle. And Gary Macy cites the following passage from the fourteenth-century theologian Robert Holcot:

> It must be said that God is able to do more than the intellect can understand and therefore it is not inappropriate to agree that God could change the entire world and to make it exist under the species of a single mouse . . . Concerning the certitude of experience, I believe that there is no certitude about an individual created thing as it presently exists, since it is able to become false through (this sort of) change, and it would be hidden from me whether it were true or false.[18]

Holcot accepts this conclusion because he is committed to the doctrine of the Real Presence as a matter of principle. The Fourth Lateran Council in 1215 CE had used the term "transubstantiation" to consecrate the generic belief in the Real Presence as a matter of catholic faith.[19] But Pentecostal theology is not beholden to such ideas about the infallibility of the ecclesial hierarchy or the authority of church tradition. It consequently should have no problem in rejecting the onto-epistemological presuppositions of the Real Presence tradition together with its "metaphysical" interpretation of the Eucharist.

It is true that the argument given here was phenomenological in nature. Phenomenology is concerned with "human experience and the way things present themselves to us in and through such experience."[20] Pentecostalism is a theology closely founded in experience. Pentecostals hold that there is a dynamic of manifestation that accompanies the work of the Holy Spirit. This work accomplishes effects that are manifest both internally in one's inner life as well as externally in the world. George Floyd Taylor writes,

17. Sokolowski, *Introduction to Phenomenology*, 10.

18. As cited in Macy, "Medieval Inheritance," 29.

19. Salkeld, *Transubstantiation*, 36.

20. Sokolowski, *Introduction to Phenomenology*, 2.

> We know that when the Spirit strives with a man, there is an uneasiness in his soul, and a troubled look on his face. . . . Sanctification brings the invisible manifestation of joy (Luke 24:50–52), and the visible manifestation of fruit unto holiness (Rom. 6:22). . . . A person who receives an anointing of the Spirit has an internal manifestation of an insight into God's dealings with His children (Ps. 23:5, 6), and an external manifestation of boldness and liberty (Acts 4:29–31).[21]

Taylor thus speaks about a manifest work of the Holy Spirit with an interior and exterior aspect. This is indeed a fundamentally Pentecostal theological point: the operation of the Holy Spirit should be manifest in some clear way. And this distinction between the "interior" and "exterior" domains of manifestation would later come to be the foundational contribution of Michel Henry to the phenomenological tradition of philosophy in the twentieth century.[22] As he writes, "Any visible appearance is paired with an invisible reality."[23] It would therefore seem consonant with this Pentecostal emphasis upon the manifest quality of the work of the Holy Spirit to deny the doctrine of the Real Presence. There could be no inner transformation of the bread and wine without an outward change in their appearance. As Zwingli himself said, "Since, however, we see and perceive bread, it is evident that we are ascribing to God a miracle which he himself neither wills nor approves: for he does not work miracles which cannot be perceived."[24]

Early Church Sources

If Pentecostals do deny the Real Presence doctrine of the Eucharist, would this not put them out of continuity with the early church? Many persons are of the opinion that the Real Presence tradition represents the unanimous testimony of the church regarding the understanding of the Eucharist from the earliest days.[25] The Pentecostal desire to turn back to the roots of the church and its experience of Christ in the Holy Spirit would seem to run into a problem if it has to reject the early church's eucharistic doctrine. But this opinion about unanimity is in fact exaggerated. For the sake of space, the discussion here will not focus so much on the New Testament as upon the earliest post-apostolic sources. (The discussion will return to Scripture

21. Cited in Jacobson, *Reader in Pentecostal Theology*, 62.
22. See Henry, *Seeing the Invisible*. See also Nemes, "Life-Idealism of Michel Henry."
23. Henry, *I Am the Truth*, 258.
24. Zwingli, "Treatise on the Lord's Supper," 196.
25. Fitzmyer, *First Corinthians*, 439; cf. Kreeft, "Why?," 145.

in the final section.) A close reading of these earliest sources suggests that the bread and the wine were taken to be symbols or images of Jesus's body and blood rather than really becoming them.

The Didache contains no notion of the Real Presence at all.[26] None of the eucharistic prayers prescribed in the text make mention of or invoke a transformation of the elements into Jesus's body and blood. The Eucharist itself is rather presented as a thanksgiving meal. The bread and the wine of the meal only provide opportunities to offer prayers to God thanking him for the accomplishment of salvation in Jesus and asking him to bring about the eschatological unity of his church (Didache 9–10). And Tertullian explicitly interprets Jesus's statement during the Last Supper as figurative: "The bread which was taken and distributed to His disciples He made His body, saying, 'This is my body,' that is, a figure of my body" (*Against Marcion* 4.40).[27] The meaning of his word "figure" is evident in context. He earlier writes that "scorpions" and "serpents" are used as "figures" in Scripture for evil spirits (4.24), he compares "figures" with "allegories" (4.25), he mentions that Christ "figuratively" (*figurate*) enjoins the Pharisees to wash the inside of their vessels but "really" or "obviously" (*manifeste*) to perform works of mercy (4.27), and so on. The Didache is therefore arguably implicit and Tertullian certainly explicit that the relation between the bread and wine of the eucharistic meal and the real body and blood of Jesus is a symbolic relation of imaging or representation.

Still other sources arguably propose a symbolic interpretation of the Eucharist, even if their words are commonly taken otherwise.[28] Justin Martyr (*First Apology* 66), Irenaeus (*Against Heresies* 4.18, 5; 5.2, 3), and Tertullian (*On the Resurrection of the Flesh* 8) all write in one way or another that the substance and flesh and blood of believers are "nourished," "increased," and "fed" in the celebration of the Eucharist by the flesh and blood of Jesus. This appears at first glance to be an assertion of cannibalism: the eating of a human body. And yet the Real Presence tradition insists that it proposes no such thing. Ludwig Ott consequently writes, "The absence of any heretical counter-proposition often resulted in a certain carelessness of expression to which must be added the lack of a developed terminology to distinguish the sacramental mode of existence of Christ's body."[29] But it is possible to understand the situation otherwise. Justin, Irenaeus, and Tertullian need not be speaking clumsily or inaccurately; they are after all perfectly capable of

26. See Holmes, *Apostolic Fathers*.

27. My own translation. Latin text taken from Tertullian, *Adversus Marcionem*.

28. Contrary to Rordorf, *Eucharist of the Early Christians* and many others.

29. Ott, *Fundamentals of Catholic Dogma*, 378.

explaining themselves clearly about other matters. Moreover, Justin Martyr explicitly denies in *Second Apology* 12 and *Dialogue with Trypho* 10 that Christians have anything to do with eating flesh. It would seem better to say that these early authors are referring to the bread and wine as the body and blood of Jesus because they are the symbols or images of these. Consider how one can refer to a portrait as one's grandfather or to an actor on the stage as Hamlet. Augustine writes thus that the sacred rites "generally take their names from the mysteries they represent" (*Letter* 98).[30] The one thing "is" the other because it represents or images it. They thus are referring to the bread and wine and asserting that they "nourish" the body in a normal, natural way.

These authors speak about the bread and the wine in this way because they are concerned to emphasize that the salvation accomplished by God in Jesus includes the body as well as the soul. This implies also that the Father of Jesus is the same God as the one who created the material world. They appeal to the use of bread and wine in the ritual of the Eucharist established by Jesus himself to support this point. Justin thus compares the Eucharist to the fact that Jesus was made flesh for salvation through the word of God (*First Apology* 66). Note that he does not say that the word of God was made flesh but rather that Jesus was made flesh by the word of God. His point is not to propose the incarnation as a metaphor for the eucharistic change, but rather to emphasize the doctrine that Jesus had true humanity. Tertullian also writes against Marcion that Jesus does not despise "the bread by which He represents His own proper body, thus requiring in His very sacraments the beggarly elements of the Creator" (*Against Marcion* 1.14). And Ignatius of Antioch notes that the heretics who deny the reality of Jesus's flesh and suffering excuse themselves from the Eucharist because "they refuse to acknowledge that the Eucharist is the flesh of our savior Jesus Christ" (*Epistle to the Smyrnaeans* 6.2). Here he is offering no different an argument than Tertullian would do more than a century later against Marcion: "The bread which was taken and distributed to His disciples He made His body, saying, 'This is my body,' that is, a figure of my body. But there would not have been a figure if there were not a true body. An empty thing, which is to say a phantom, could not have a figure" (*Against Marcion* 4.40). Jesus must have had a true body if he proposed the bread as the figure or image of his body. The early church fathers thus appealed to the symbolism of the Eucharist to mount an *argumentum ad eucharistiam* against creation- and body-denying heresies.

30. Augustine, *Letters* 137.

Many people who believe in a unanimous testimony to the Real Presence from the earliest days seem to assume that ancient discourse about the sacraments must be interpreted metaphysically. The language of "being" and "becoming" used by these ancient authors to describe the relation between the bread and the wine and the body and blood of Jesus is taken as obviously referring to a non-manifest change in their real being. They also seem to take for granted that early Christian discourse about the sacraments was a matter of making dogmatic pronouncements as if *ex cathedra*. One never finds an author remarking that, say, the docetic opponents of Ignatius or Irenaeus should never have been convinced by the bald assertions of eucharistic realism taken for granted by their catholic interlocutors. This assumption may well hold true in the case of figures, such as Cyril of Jerusalem mentioned earlier, who are explicitly doing catechetical work. But these assumptions are entirely unfounded as regards the earliest polemical sources, wholly apart from the problems of skepticism raised by the metaphysical understanding of the sacraments mentioned earlier. It is possible and arguably better to understand them, not as making dogmatic declarations, but rather as arguing in a phenomenological manner from the symbolic content of the ritual itself.

Irenaeus, for example, plainly does this in his polemics against various "gnostic" heresies. He maintains that in the Eucharist food items are offered to God with thanksgiving according to the example of Jesus during the Last Supper (*Against Heresies* 4.17, 5).[31] On this basis he argues that the heretics who deny that the Father of Jesus is the creator of the material world make him out to be "covetous of another's property and desirous of what is not His own" when they offer the Eucharist. He also maintains that those who teach that the things of the material world came about as a result of some primordial ignorance, passion, and sin are insulting God by offering them to him in their eucharistic celebrations (4.18, 4). He is thus not making dogmatic pronouncements about what the true church teaches, but rather arguing against the theologies of the heretics on the basis of the symbolic content of a ritual shared by both parties. These arguments take the Eucharist as a symbolic ritual intended to communicate certain theological truths by means of its images. This is the same hermeneutic Irenaeus applies to the sacrifices of the Old Testament as well (4.14, 3). He maintains that the ritual is turned into a farce when one denies, as the heretics do, that the Father of Jesus is the Creator of the material world. The same applies also to what he says at 4.18, 5, when he claims that the body and blood of Christ "nourish" the bodies of those participating in the Eucharist. The denial of the salvation

31 All Irenaeus quotations are from Roberts et al., *Ante-Nicene Fathers, Volume 1.*

of the flesh makes no sense if in the Eucharist itself the bodies of believers are nourished with food. The involvement of body and spirit alike in the ritual is what consistently announces "the fellowship and union of flesh and spirit." Both must be saved if both are involved in the ritual interaction with God that is the Eucharist. And the bread becomes "earthly and heavenly" because it is "no longer common bread" but rather bread eaten in relation to God. The change on the part of the bread is one of signification or meaning rather than being ontological.

More would naturally need to be said on this point, and there is no room here for a comprehensive treatment of the understanding of the Eucharist in the earliest church. This discussion is taken up elsewhere.[32] But the comments provided here should suffice as a preliminary justification of the thesis that the symbolic interpretation of the Eucharist need not be taken as a late or modern invention, and its acceptance by Pentecostals would not put them out of sync with the early church. It is a faulty assumption of the Real Presence tradition that the discourse of the earliest Christians simply has to be interpreted metaphysically and dogmatically. Entirely apart from the problem of skepticism, reading them in this way turns their words into an affirmation of cannibalism. One therefore has to suppose like Ott that they did not know how best to express themselves. But their language is perfectly intelligible when interpreted symbolically. They refer to the bread and wine as the body and blood of Jesus because they are the symbols of these, and they appeal to the symbolic content of the ritual of the Eucharist to prove to heretics who celebrated the same ritual as they that Jesus had a true human nature and that the body therefore also participates in salvation.

Symbol and Communion

Some people, like Herbert McCabe, are of the opinion that a symbolic interpretation of the Eucharist devalues it or in some way makes it less meaningful.[33] But this is a confusion. To attribute symbolic value to a thing is to make it more valuable than it could be otherwise, as Eric Perl writes.[34] A thing is not functioning as a symbol unless one sees "through" it to something else. A ring is not a symbol when one spins on its side on the surface of a table, but it is a symbol when one sees with shock that one's spouse has taken it off in the heat of an argument. It functions as a symbol then because the mind is led through it to something else beyond it. It is not just that a

32. See Nemes, *Eating Christ's Flesh*.

33. McCabe, "Eucharist as Language."

34. Perl, *Theophany*, 108.

piece of jewelry has been removed from a finger but that one's spouse has rejected, if only for a moment, the very identity of spouse. Neither is a flag functioning as a symbol when one sees it blowing in the wind, but it does function as a symbol when one takes offense at its burning. This is because it is no longer just a matter of a piece of fabric being set on fire but rather of a statement being made against the nation as a whole. The value and meaning of the symbol are thus a function of the thing which it symbolizes. And the Eucharist is all the more valuable because the bread and wine are proposed as symbols or images of the body and blood of Jesus. One might therefore question the contrast proposed by Kärkkäinen between Calvin's "representational" conception of the Eucharist to Zwingli's "memorial" view.[35] To treat the bread and wine as symbols with Zwingli is precisely not to see mere bread and wine any longer but rather the very person and work of Jesus being offered through them.

Jesus taught that whoever does not eat his flesh and drink his blood does not have life in him or her (John 6:53–58). And on the night in which he was betrayed, he took bread and wine, gave thanks for them, and distributed them to his disciples to be consumed calling them his body and blood (1 Cor 11:23–25). The question is therefore how to understand the relation between these teachings. The Real Presence tradition arguably cannot answer this question in a satisfactory way insofar as it insists that Christ's body and blood are not locally present in the bread and wine.[36] Eating is a local process; a thing cannot be eaten if it is not there in the mouth where the eating is happening. That is why one cannot eat one's cake and have it in the hands too. So long as it is in one's hands, it's not in one's mouth and therefore not being eaten. The eating of Christ's flesh consequently cannot be literal even on the Real Presence view. It must rather be spiritual. But in that case there is no necessity in adopting a Real Presence interpretation of these texts. The Pentecostal theologian should instead follow Zwingli in saying that "eating Christ's flesh" is a matter of finding spiritual joy, nourishment, and edification in the person and sacrifice of Jesus and that this eating takes place "sacramentally" when it is enacted through the consumption of the symbols of the bread and wine in the eucharistic meal: "To eat the body of Christ sacramentally is to eat the body of Christ with the heart and the mind in conjunction with the sacrament. . . . You do inwardly that which you represent outwardly, your soul being strengthened by the faith which you attest in the tokens."[37] Believers appropriate Christ to themselves

35. Kärkkäinen, *Hope and Community*, 395.

36. Cf. Thomas Aquinas, *Summa Theologica* III, q. 76, art. 5.

37. Zwingli, "Exposition of the Faith," 258–59.

by consuming the symbols he offers to them in the bread and the wine, just as a woman accepts a man by accepting the ring which he offers her with a promise to be faithful to her as a husband. The bread and the wine are not "really" Jesus any more than the ring "really" is the proposing man, but the one person is really appropriated by the other through the acceptance of the symbol by which he offers himself to that other.

The acceptance of Christ in the heart is the work of the Holy Spirit. The Spirit glorifies Christ (John 16:14), and he is also called the Spirit of Christ (Rom 8:9). Another way of referring to this acceptance is "faith" or "belief." As Jesus says in the bread of life discourse: "This is the work of God, that you believe in Him whom He has sent" (John 6:29). But this only serves to raise a question about the nature of this belief that constitutes a person as a Christian. It is in fact possible to distinguish between two senses of belief. "Belief-that" is a matter of adopting a certain attitude toward a proposition. One can believe-that God exists or believe-that Jesus was raised from the dead. Even the demons believe-that God is one (Jas 2:19). "Belief-in" is a matter of committing to a person and entrusting oneself and one's life to him or her. Children thus believe-in their parents, best friends also believe-in one another, and sick persons believe-in the doctors to whom they appeal for treatment. The question is therefore which sense of "belief" is fundamental for understanding the identity of a Christian.[38]

Christian theology in the catholic tradition has mostly privileged belief-that. For example, the *Quicunque Vult* or "Athanasian Creed" affirms that whoever wishes to be saved must before all else hold to the catholic faith.[39] This catholic faith is then elaborated in the "Creed" as a series of statements about the consubstantiality of Father, Son, and Holy Spirit, as well as about the hypostatic union of the two natures in Christ. But there is a significant case to be made for rejecting belief-that as fundamentally definitive of Christian identity. Phenomenological reflection reveals that beliefs-that formed on the basis of the appearance of things in the world are inevitably fallible and subject to revision in principle. Two arguments can be given for this conclusion.

On the one hand, every experience is multiply interpretable. One is always in a position of choosing between two possible interpretations of what appears: "This is an *X*," or "This is not really but only presently resembles an *X*." A person in a crowd may be a friend or may be a stranger. An item in the dark may be a coiled rope or a snake. It is true that the initial impression one has about a thing can subsequently come to be confirmed

38. See Nemes, "Against Infallibility"; and Nemes, "Theology Without Anathemas."

39. Schaff, *Creeds of Christendom*, 2:66.

or disconfirmed by later appearances. But then one is once more put in the situation of choosing between two possible interpretations of what appears: "This is in fact an *X*," or "This is not really but has only persistently appeared until now to be an *X*." The ambiguity of a single appearance becomes the inescapable, multiple interpretability of a series of appearances. On the other hand, the access to things in the world is never direct but always mediated by the exercise of one's powers of perception and interpretation. One does not simply see things directly but only such as one's power of sight permits. Neither does not simply understand things directly but only such as one's prior notions and preconceptions allow. And it is obviously impossible to step outside oneself to determine the adequacy of the access to things one is afforded by means of one's powers of perception and thought. This means that experience itself does not permit one to say with utmost confidence: "This is an *X*," but rather only: "This seems to me, given the way I am now, to be an *X*." But to relativize one's statements about what things are to the way one happens to be is to admit that things can still be otherwise; it is to admit the possibility that one's judgment is false. It therefore follows that any beliefs-that formed on the basis of the way things appear to one given one's faculties and powers of experience is fallible and subject to revision in principle.

The fallibility of belief-that implies that the decision to privilege belief-that as the condition of the identity of a Christian has disastrous consequences. Everything one believes-that as a Christian is founded upon the appearance of things in the world. One believes, for example, on the basis of what seems to one to be taught in Scripture or through the testimony of others. But one can never be sure that one believes-that correctly. From this it would follow that one could never be sure that one is a Christian. This leads to a situation of persistent salvation-anxiety; one's relation to Jesus would be always and inescapably uncertain. It is consequently preferable to privilege belief-in. What makes one to be a Christian is not first and foremost one's beliefs-that but rather the fact that one believes-in Jesus. This happens when one commits to him and entrusts oneself and one's life to him. This does not raise questions of salvation-anxiety because can one know whether one does this or not. The condition of one's own heart in this respect is not so hidden as the inner nature of the things that appear in the world.

It is true that belief-in is not totally separable from belief-that. To believe-in another is at minimum to believe-that one's life will be made manifestly better or at least preserved from becoming worse through the action of this other. But it is clearly possible for persons even of radically divergent beliefs-that nevertheless to share one and the same object of belief-in. Philosophers who disagree with one another about the ontological constitution of human beings nevertheless can believe-in the same doctors, firefighters, and policemen when the appropriate situation arises. And children can believe-in their parents even apart from any clear or sophisticated understanding of philosophical anthropology altogether. Christians of various kinds are certainly distinguished among themselves with respect to their beliefs-that. Pentecostals for example have beliefs-that regarding the work of the Holy Spirit which other Christians may not share. But there is a deeper level of unity beneath the diversity of their opinions. This is their shared belief-in Jesus.

The celebration of the Eucharist involves the re-presentation of the person and work of Jesus through the use of bread and wine as symbols or images of his body and blood. There is no need for the presence of a rightly ordained priest or member of an official ecclesial hierarchy to serve as the signal or assurance that the ontological transformation of the elements has taken place as Lateran IV taught.[40] As Simon Chan writes, "Pentecost was the event that signalled the breaking down of the age-old racial divisions and the creation of a new spiritual order in which Jews and Gentiles, men and women, slaves and free participate as complete equals."[41] It would seem contrary to the equalizing work of Pentecost to reintroduce hierarchical distinctions among Christ's disciples, who in fact are to think of themselves as equally brothers and students of the Messiah (cf. Matt 23:8–10). In any case, anyone in principle can make use of food in a symbolic manner, and Jesus himself commanded that this re-presentation and ritual re-appropriation of himself be done: "Do this in remembrance of me" (Luke 22:19). The Eucharist is therefore an invitation to exercise faith in the sense of claiming Christ to oneself, together with other Christians sharing in the priesthood of all believers, in joyous remembrance of his sacrifice, irrespective of where and when this celebration takes place. Just as one accepts another into one's life by accepting his gift as a symbol of his offer of friendship, so also one claims Jesus for oneself anew by receiving the symbols of his body and blood in the bread and wine. The symbols of course do not function in this way apart from the ascription of such a meaning to them on the part of those celebrating the meal. This is in keeping with what Kärkkäinen, following Harold Hunter, calls the "cognitive/symbolic" function of the sacrament.[42] But they become a "point of encounter" between Jesus and believers in the Holy Spirit when this meaning is ascribed to them.[43] Pentecostals admit-

40. Denzinger, *Sources of Catholic Dogma*, 168.

41. Chan, *Pentecostal Theology*, 52.

42. Kärkkäinen, "Pentecostal View," 121.

43. Cf. Kärkkäinen, "Pentecostal View," 123.

tedly do not normally celebrate the Eucharist as often as Christians in other traditions.[44] Yet the power and significance of the symbolism of the meal nevertheless provide a reason to celebrate the meal all the more frequently.

Christians may of course disagree among themselves about any number of beliefs-that. They may even find these differences in belief-that so significant that they feel uneasy sharing the meal of the Eucharist together. But belief-that is fallible. No one can point to his or her beliefs-that as a basis for justification before God. No one is made any worthier of the goodness of Jesus because of his or her beliefs-that. One may even say that the radical fallibility of belief-that makes belief-in Jesus all the more important. The biblical conception of things teaches that Jesus alone is the hope of salvation for human beings (Acts 4:12). One must therefore throw oneself into the arms of Jesus even despite one's preferred theological opinions rather than making idols out of them. One may say with Peter, "On the contrary, we believe that we will be saved through the grace of the Lord Jesus, just as they will" (Acts 15:11). And this means that eucharistic communion around a common belief-in Jesus is both possible and desirable even where Christians do not share the same beliefs-that. Here yet another parallel with Zwingli can be noted. He wrote that a *sacramentum* is an "oath of allegiance."[45] Allegiance is a way of believing-in. Differences in belief-that can be set aside in an act of radical "suspension" (to use the phenomenological phrase) and their shared belief-in Jesus affirmed by partaking of the bread and wine together. In this way they can be formed into one body as the eucharistic meal becomes a "sharing" (*koinōnia*) in the body and blood of Jesus (cf. 1 Cor 10:16–17) through the symbols of the bread and wine.

This essay has proposed a radical theology of the Eucharist for Pentecostals. First, in keeping with the Pentecostal emphasis upon the manifest work of the Holy Spirit in experience, as well as with the phenomenological argument for the necessary correlation between appearance and being, it rejects the doctrine of the Real Presence of Christ's body and blood in the bread and wine of the eucharistic meal as having no basis in experience and implying skepticism. Second, against the common assumption that the Real Presence tradition represents the unanimous testimony of the church from the earliest days, the case can be made that the earliest church sources ought to be interpreted as proposing a symbolic understanding of the Eucharist. In this case, such a theology of the Eucharist for Pentecostals would put them closer to the theology of the early church than the Real Presence alternative. Finally,

44. Kärkkäinen, "Pentecostal View," 122.

45. Zwingli, "Exposition of the Faith," 264–65.

the radical theology of the Eucharist sees the meal as a celebration of Christ's sacrificial death and a joyful declaration of belief-in him, something for which particular beliefs-that area not necessary and which thus makes it possible even for Christians of divergent theological perspectives to celebrate together.

Bibliography

Aquinas, Thomas. *Summa Theologica.* Translated by Fathers of the English Dominican Province. Denver, CO: New Advent, 2017.

Aristotle. *Metaphysics.* Translated by C. D. C. Reeve. Indianapolis: Hackett, 2016.

Augustine. *City of God.* Translated by Gerald G. Walsh and Grace Monahan. Washington, DC: The Catholic University of America Press, 1952.

———. *Letters, Volume II (83–130).* Translated by Sister Wilfrid Parsons. Washington, DC: The Catholic University of America Press, 1953.

Chan, Simon. *Liturgical Theology: The Church as Worshiping Community.* Downers Grove, IL: IVP Academic, 2006.

———. *Pentecostal Theology and the Christian Spiritual Tradition.* New York: Sheffield Academic, 2003.

Cyril of Jerusalem. *Works.* 2 vols. Translated by Leo P. McCauley and Anthony A. Stephenson. Washington, DC: The Catholic University of America Press, 1970.

Denzinger, Heinrich. *The Sources of Catholic Dogma.* Translated by Roy J. Deferarri. Fitzwilliam, NH: Loreto, 1955.

Duffield, Guy P., and Nathaniel M. Van Cleave. *Foundations of Pentecostal Theology.* Los Angeles: Foursquare Media, 2016.

Fitzmyer, Joseph A. *First Corinthians: A New Translation with Introduction and Commentary.* New Haven: Yale University Press, 2008.

Henry, Michel. *I Am the Truth: Toward a Philosophy of Christianity.* Translated by Susan Emanuel. Stanford: Stanford University Pres, 2003.

———. *Seeing the Invisible: On Kandinsky.* Translated by Scott Davidson. New York: Continuum, 2009.

Holmes, Michael W. *The Apostolic Fathers: Greek Texts and English Translations.* 3rd ed. Grand Rapids: Baker Academic, 2007.

Jacobson, Douglas, ed. *A Reader in Pentecostal Theology: Voices from the First Generation.* Bloomington: Indiana University Press, 2006.

Justin Martyr. *The First Apology, The Second Apology, Dialogue with Trypho, Exhortation to the Greeks, Discourse to the Greeks, The Monarchy or Rule of God.* Translated by Thomas B. Falls. Washington, DC: The Catholic University of America Press, 1948.

Kärkkäinen, Veli-Matti. *Hope and Community.* Grand Rapids: Eerdmans, 2017.

———. "The Pentecostal View." In *The Lord's Supper: Five Views,* edited by Gordon T. Smith, 117–35. Downers Grove, IL: IVP Academic.

Kreeft, Peter. "Why?" In *Faith and Reason: Philosophers Explain Their Turn to Catholicism,* edited by Brian Besong and Jonathan Fuqua, 125–50. San Francisco: Ignatius, 2019.

Lanfranc of Bec and Guitmund of Aversa. *On the Body and Blood of the Lord and On the Truth of the Body and Blood of Christ in the Eucharist.* Translated by Mark G. Vaillancourt. Washington, DC: The Catholic University of America Press, 2009.

Macy, Gary. "The Medieval Inheritance." In *A Companion to the Eucharist in the Reformation*, edited by Lee Palmer Wendel, 15–38. Boston: Brill, 2014.

McCabe, Herbert. "The Eucharist as Language." *Modern Theology* 15 (1999) 131–41.

Nemes, Steven. "Against Infallibility." *Criswell Theological Review* 19 (2021) 27–50.

———. *Eating Christ's Flesh: A Case for Memorialism*. Eugene, OR: Cascade, 2023.

———. "The Life-Idealism of Michel Henry." *Journal of French and Francophone Philosophy* 29 (2021) 87–108.

———. "Theology without Anathemas." *Journal of Analytic Theology* 9 (2021) 180–200.

Ott, Ludwig. *Fundamentals of Catholic Dogma*. Translated by Patrick Lynch. Fort Collins: Roman Catholic, 1954.

Perl, Eric D. *Theophany: The Neoplatonic Philosophy of Dionysius the Areopagite*. Albany: State University of New York Press, 2007.

Prusak, Bernard P. "Explaining Eucharistic 'Real Presence': Moving Beyond a Medieval Conundrum." *Theological Studies* 75 (2014) 213–59.

Roberts, Alexander, et al., eds. *Ante-Nicene Fathers*. Volume 1. Buffalo, NY: Christian Literature, 1885.

Rordorf, Willy. *The Eucharist of the Early Christians*. Translated by Matthew J. O'Connell. New York: Pueblo, 1978.

Salkeld, Brett. *Transubstantiation: Theology, History, and Church Unity*. Grand Rapids: Baker Academic, 2019.

Schaff, Philip. *Creeds of Christendom with a History and Critical Notes. Volume II: The Greek and Latin Creeds, with Translations*. Harper & Brothers, 1877.

Schindler, D. C. *The Catholicity of Reason*. Grand Rapids: Eerdmans, 2013.

Smith, James K. A. *Thinking in Tongues: Pentecostal Contributions to Christian Philosophy*. Grand Rapids: Eerdmans, 2010.

Sokolowski, Robert. *Introduction to Phenomenology*. New York: Cambridge University Press, 2000.

Tertullian. *Adversus Marcionem*. Translated by Ernest Evans. New York: Oxford University Press, 1972.

———. *De Resurrectione Carnis*. Translated by Ernest Evans. SPCK, 1960.

Vermigli, Peter Martyr. *The Oxford Treatise and Disputation on the Eucharist*. Translated by Joseph C. McClelland. Moscow, ID: The Davenant, 2018.

Zwingli, Ulrich. "A Short Exposition of the Faith." In *A Global Sourcebook in Protestant Political Thought: 1517–1660*, edited by Matthew Rowley and Marietta van der Tol, 171–74. London: Routledge, 2024.

———. "Treatise on the Lord's Supper." In *Zwingli and Bullinger*, edited by G. W. Bromiley, 185–238. Louisville, KY: Westminster John Knox, 2007.

14

"But I Don't Know What That Means!?"

Glossolalia and Analytic Philosophy of Language

Joanna Leidenhag[1]

Introduction

In the context of academic philosophy seminars, few scenarios cause more trepidation than when a senior figure in the field, oh-so-innocently declares to their younger interlocutor, "But I don't know what that means!?" I don't know the provenance of this expression of critique so distinctive to the parlance of analytic philosophy, but I have sometimes wondered if it arose due to the analytic tradition's preoccupation with philosophy of language and a core assumption that transparency of meaning positively correlates with intellectual rigor.

The focus on language is unsurprising given the origins of analytic philosophy, which date back to Gottlob Frege's and Bertrand Russell's application of mathematic logic to language, such that meaning was seen as a function of syntax and logical inference. This initiated the so-called "linguistic turn" in Anglo-American philosophy, which took philosophy of language to be foundational for other philosophical topics such as

1. Scripture quotations in this chapter are taken from the New International Version.

mathematics, truth, mind, substance and time. The subsequent movement of ordinary language philosophy took the analytic tradition in a new direction, but maintained a commitment to the transparency of language as the primary way that philosophers dissolve philosophical conundrums.

Around the same time as the emergence of the strange new language of analytic logic, the origins of Pentecostalism were also heralded by the widespread use of the glossolalia, or the gift of speaking in unknown tongues, present at the Welsh Revival (1904), mission in India (1905), and the Azusa Street Revival in Los Angeles (1906).[2] A good, general definition of glossolalia is that it is a "usually, but not exclusively, religious phenomenon of making sounds that constitute, or resemble, a language not known to the subject."[3] It is often assumed that glossolalia necessarily involves a loss of control akin to spirit possession or a trance state, but it is neither depicted as such in the New Testament, nor is glossolalia always practiced in this uncontrolled way within Pentecostal and charismatic communities today.[4] In 1 Corinthians in particular, Paul clearly expects his readers to be able to follow his guidelines of their own volition, which means he presupposes that even their chaotic glossolalic practice does not entail a loss of control of their mental or vocal faculties. Contemporary Pentecostal and charismatic theologians have tended to see glossolalia in a sacramental, rather than ecstatic light, by drawing parallels to spiritual practices within other Christian traditions, such as Quaker silence, the Jesus Prayer in Eastern Orthodoxy, or liturgical and contemplative practices in Roman Catholic and Anglican traditions.

In classical Pentecostalism (and neo-Pentecostalism within mainstream denominations), speaking in tongues came to have special function as a sign, or as "physical evidence" of a second, post-conversion experience, known as baptism in the Spirit.[5] The so-called Third Wave movement, associated with John Wimber and the Association of Vineyard Churches, denied this two-stage process separating water baptism from Spirit baptism, and saw glossolalia as one gift among many, shifting the focus instead to gifts of

2. Cartledge, *Gift of Spirit in Tongues*, 3. Of course, Pentecostalism should not be reduced to this one phenomenon. As Frank Macchia writes, "Pentecostalism is not a 'tongues movement,' but a movement that supports the gospel of Jesus Christ in salvation, sanctification, empowerment for global witness, healing, and eschatological hope" (Macchia, "Groans Too Deep for Words," 164).

3. Spittler, "Glossolalia," 670.

4. For example, see the interview with a church leader recorded in Cartledge, *Practical Theology*, 137–46. For more sociological data see, Stanley et al., "Some Characteristics of Charismatic Experience," and Kavan, "Glossolalia and Altered States."

5. Cartledge, "Introduction," 4, 10.

healing and prophecy. This de-emphasizing of the gift of tongues, as one gift among many that are regularly experienced within the church, represents a more charismatic theology of glossolalia. Unlike Pentecostalism, charismatic Christianity is not confined to any particular denomination or historical tradition. Therefore, we should not think of glossolalia as restricted to Pentecostal communities, since it is an experience found across almost the full range of Christian denominations.[6]

Given this ongoing debate between Pentecostal and charismatic understandings of glossolalia, it is unsurprising that a great deal of theological work on this topic has focused on the question of what the sign of glossolalia means in general, or what it means for the individual at the point of initial reception.[7] For example, we might ask: Is glossolalia evidence for a person's salvation or a particular vocation or anointing, or evidence for the existence of God? There has also been a significant amount of neurobiological and psychological research into glossolalia, which focuses on non-communicative effects, such as correlations between glossolalia, trance states and mental health.[8] These are not the questions that concern this paper. Instead, this essay focuses on the question of whether and how glossolalic speech can be a meaningful act of communication.

While the pursuit of ordinary and transparent language through methods such as conceptual analysis presents many advantages and opportunities to theology, the topic of glossolalia seems to present a uniquely difficult challenge. As James K. A. Smith summarizes, even after the rise of analytic theology, the "valorisation of 'ordinary language philosophy', has had little room for considering a strange, quite extraordinary, phenomenon such as glossolalia."[9] In fact, few topics seem more antithetical to analytic methods, such as conceptual analysis, than glossolalia. Furthermore, because philosophy of language lies at the origin and heart of analytic philosophy and the gift of tongues has been historically central to Pentecostal identity, this topic is more than just one topic among others that are worth pursuing—it cuts

6. The exception to this is a subsection of Reformed churches, which believe in cessationism and so actively discourage the use charismatic gifts.

7. This question is not alien to the biblical text since Paul makes some complex (and apparently contradictory) statements on glossolalia as a sign to unbelievers (1 Cor 14:20–22). See, Peppiatt, *Women and Worship*, 114–25.

8. For a helpful overview of a century of such research see, Kay, "Mind, Behaviour and Glossolalia." Kay concludes, "Recent research has overturned most of the findings of earlier research: glossolaliacs are not in trance-like states when they are speaking in tongues; they do not show signs of psychopathology; they are not especially susceptible to hypnosis; they are not neurotic; evidence for social learning of glossolalia is weak; glossolalics are not especially dependent on authority figures."(204–5).

9. Smith, "Tongues as 'Resistance Discourse,'" 81.

to the heart of the question of whether analytic Pentecostal and charismatic theology is possible.

Let me assuage a potential worry. I do not think it is the case that if analytic philosophy of language cannot make sense of the meaningfulness of glossolalia that we should thereby conclude that glossolalia is meaningless. Instead, this would indicate a shortcoming in the current scope of philosophical analysis. One of hope for this paper, and the larger project that it is a part of, is that by considering Christian practices and beliefs from the majority world, and which the large majority of Christians today adhere to, analytic theology may expand its scope. This latter goal can only be achieved if the tools and theories of philosophy are mutable and receptive to the lived experiences it seeks to understand. Happily, in this paper I shall argue that analytic philosophy offers a range of viable answers to the question of how to understand the meaningfulness of glossolalic communication.

The structure of this chapter is as follows: Section one summarizes the account of glossolalia in the New Testament and makes a distinction between two different types of glossolalia, which I call "xenolalia" and "private prayer glossolalia." Section two focuses on xenolalia, whereby the believer is divinely inspired to speak in another language, whether human or heavenly, which is otherwise unknown to them. In such cases, the inspired speech is seen to have semantic content and syntactical form, but this content or form is entirely unknown to the speaker themselves, unless a separate gift of interpretation is also received. I argue that this phenomenon is best made sense of by expanding Tyler Burge's anti-individualist version of externalism. Section three examines private prayer glossolalia, which consists in utterances that are not typically, or not necessarily, taken to contain either semantic or syntactical content. I argue that these utterances can still be taken as forms of meaningful, and indeed beneficial, speech according to either expressionism or speech-act theory. Speech-act theory is preferred in this case because it explains the wide range of uses of private prayer glossolalia and the ways in which this spiritual practice can go wrong.

Two Types of Glossolalia in the New Testament

The practice of glossolalia in Pentecostal and charismatic Christianity finds precedent and justification in the New Testament witness to this phenomenon in at least three texts: as part of Jesus's post-resurrection commissioning of the disciples in the longer ending of Mark (16:17), as the result of the outpouring of the Spirit at the day of Pentecost (Acts 2:1–13), and in Paul's description of the worship of the early Christian community in Corinth (1 Cor 12–14). This section considers these passages and argues for a distinction between xenolalia and private prayer glossolalia. This distinction is important because each type of glossolalia raises different philosophical questions, which are then considered separately in the two subsequent sections of this chapter.

The earliest and longest New Testament text to explicitly discuss glossolalia is 1 Cor 12–14. Paul takes it for granted that his readers know what glossolalia is and experience this phenomenon frequently. It is, therefore, likely that many of Paul's churches, not just the Corinthian congregation practiced glossolalia. It is generally agreed by scholars that this particular text was written for the purpose of correcting a Corinthian abuse of this gift, which makes it difficult to reconstruct a full Pauline theology of glossolalia from this one text.[10] In 1 Cor 12–14, Paul is concerned that in times of gathered worship all the charismatic gifts be practiced "in a fitting and orderly way," so that each speaker can be understood (1 Cor 14:40; cf. 14:26–33). Paul is particularly concerned that unbelievers or visitors in the church should understand what is being said and come to the Lord, which is why he expresses a preference for prophecy (1 Cor 14:21–24). It is for the same reason that Paul clearly instructs the Corinthian church that when glossolalic utterances are addressed to the whole congregation, rather than addressed directly to God, these utterances should be accompanied by interpretation, whether from another person or from the glossolalic speaker themselves (1 Cor 14:28).

Even among his admonitions, Paul's description of glossolalia is overall positive. Paul is clear that speaking in tongues is a genuine gift of God, or Spirit-inspired utterance, for the benefit of the church (1 Cor 12:7–11, 28; 14:2). Paul himself claims to speak in glossolalia more frequently than the congregation in Corinth (1 Cor 14:18), so it is unlikely he wants them to use this gift less. Indeed, he explicitly instructs them not to forbid the use of glossolalia (1 Cor 14:39). Nor does Paul want to restrict the use of this gift to a particular segment of the congregation, for he says, "I wish for all of you to speak in tongues" (1 Cor 14:5).[11]

Paul sees two separate functions or kinds of glossolalia. On the one hand, there is glossolalia that is addressed to the whole congregation, to

10. Fee, "Toward a Pauline Theology," 26.

11. This includes affirming the role of women to speak in tongues and prophecy. As Peppiatt has shown, the most consistent and plausible way to read 1 Cor 14:34–35 is that Paul is quoting, as a rhetorical argument aimed at correcting, his opponents, who seek to silence women within the Corinthian church. Peppiatt, *Women and Worship*, 130–31.

which the whole congregation should stop and listen, and for which they should pray for an interpretation. He compares this type of tongues to both foreign languages and music (such as the bugle's call for battle; 1 Cor 14:7–8, 11). Paul argues that this gift has to be widely understood in order for it to achieve its purpose of edifying the whole community. On the other hand, Paul also discusses glossolalia that is addressed only to God (1 Cor 14:2; 14:18; 14:28; Rom 8:26). This type of glossolalia should not disrupt or demand the attention of the wider congregation. There is no need to pray for an interpretation of this second type of glossolalia, since the purpose of this tongue is to edify the individual speaker (1 Cor 14:4, 17).

The dramatic description of "tongues of fire" in Acts 2 is heard immediately as earthly languages unknown to the speaker, but easily understandable to listeners without an additional gift of interpretation. Despite this notable difference, John Christian-Eurell argues that Acts "follows the Pauline scheme quite closely," and as the later text, the author of Luke–Acts may well have been aware of Paul's discussion in 1 Corinthians.[12] In Acts 2, when glossolalia is not understood by the crowd, the disciples are perceived as mad or drunk and the speech functions as a judgment upon the unbeliever (cf. 1 Cor 20–25). When glossolalia is interpreted and understood, as when Peter gives his explanatory sermon, it functions the same as prophecy and builds up the church.

Two subsequent mentions of glossolalia in Acts have a notably different context but follow the same Pauline schema of being used as evidence of conversion in a way that builds up the church.[13] In Acts 10:46, a whole crowd of gentiles at the house of Cornelius starts speaking in tongues and praising God during Peter's sermon. This is taken as evidence that the Spirit is at work in the gentile community and the Jewish believers agree that these gentiles should be baptized. In Acts 19:1–6, believers start speaking in tongues immediately after being baptized and the laying on of hands by Paul, again giving evidence of the Spirit's activity within them and their belonging to the new Christian community. It's worth noting that there is no mention of the need for or the giving of an interpretation in these two passages, which might mean that, although occurring in the context of a communal gathering, this outbreaking of glossolalic speech depicts the second kind described above, namely that of private prayer to God.[14]

12. Christian-Eurell, "Nature of Pauline Glossolalia," 185.

13. Christian-Eurell, "Nature of Pauline Glossolalia," 186–87.

14. It is also worth noting that there are two other passages where the Spirit is said to have been received, but there is no mention of speaking in tongues (Acts 8:17 and 9:17–18). This would imply that glossolalia is not a necessary (but may be a sufficient) condition for the belief that someone (or some group) is indwelt by the Holy Spirit.

To sum up so far, glossolalia is a multiplicitous and multifunctional practice within the early church and around the world today. For the purposes of this essay, I have categorized glossolalia into two kinds. The first category, which I'll refer to henceforth as xenolalia, is when, although the speaker does not understand their own speech, nor do they as an individual mean anything by it, their utterances constitute recognizable and meaningful speech in another language. At present it does not matter so much whether this language is a human or angelic language. The important point is that the speech could, in principle, be translated or interpreted by someone suitably proficient in both languages. The philosophical challenge of xenolalia, which I will discuss in the next section, is to give an account of how meaning is generated when the speaker themselves has little or no intentionality behind their utterances.

The second category of glossolalia is as a private prayer language between the individual and God, which I will call private prayer glossolalia. There are two key differences between private prayer glossolalia and xenolalia. First, private prayer glossolalia does not need to be interpreted, and perhaps cannot be translated. As such, it is not necessarily a "language" in the formal sense since we have no reason to suppose there are intersubjectively agreed systems of grammar or conventions of vocabulary, even between the individual and God. Second, unlike xenolalia, the speaker of private prayer glossolalia takes this utterance to be meaningful communication to God and, importantly, may themselves know at least roughly what they intend to communicate. Here, the philosophical challenge is to give an account of how such non-semantic utterances convey meaning.[15]

Meaning Without Speaker Intent: Expanding Anti-Individualism for Xenolalia

In instances of xenolalia, although the speaker remains at least partially in control of their faculties, they do not know the meaning of their utterance, nor do they intend to communicate anything by it. And yet, their utterance constitutes recognizable and meaningful speech in another language. How can words spoken without psychological intension be interpretable into natural language sentences with meaning? One of the main disputes in

15. It might interest readers to note that Smith makes a similar distinction between two kinds of glossolalia but reverses which kind includes intentional meaning of which the speaker is psychological aware. Smith regards xenolalia as "a clear case of communicative speech" with the speaker intention of witnessing to the gospel, and private prayer glossolalia as "tongues-speech which does not properly communicate *meaning*, but which he describes as an ecstatic sign." Smith, "Tongues as 'Resistance Discourse,'" 91–92.

philosophy of language in regard to meaning is between internalists, who locate meaning entirely within psychological states, and externalists, who argue that psychological states only partly determine meaning.

The most famous twentieth-century externalist in analytic philosophy of language is Hilary Putnam. Putnam casts his own view against the backdrop of internalism, which he called, the traditional theory of meaning. The traditional theory of meaning held two core tenets:

1. "Knowing the meaning of a term *T* is just a matter of being in a certain psychological state (in the sense of 'psychological state,' in which states of memory and psychological dispositions are 'psychological states'; no one thought that knowing the meaning of a word was a continuous state of consciousness, of course).
2. The meaning (in the sense of 'intension') determines its extension (in the sense that sameness of intension entails sameness of extension)."[16]

Putnam elaborates that (1) claims that the psychological state of the speaker fully determines—provides the necessary and sufficient conditions for—the meaning (intension) of the terms they speak. In according with (2), a sameness in psychological states also determine the identification of the objects that the term refers to (extensional meaning). So, on the traditional internalist theory of meaning, if two speakers utter the word "water," and they both associate this word with the same set of descriptors (e.g. wetness, transparent, thirst-quenching, etc.), then the term "water" for these two speakers will mean the same thing and identify the same physical substance in the world.[17]

The traditional internalist theory of meaning seems incompatible with xenolalia. By definition, xenolalic speech is meaningful in the absence of the appropriately determining psychological state, since the speaker themselves does not know, nor do they claim to know, what their utterance means. They do not have any sense of the necessary or sufficient conditions for their utterance, nor do they know what objects their utterances identify. As Paul puts it, "For if I pray in a tongue, my spirit prays, but my mind is unfruitful" (1 Cor 14:14). If internalism about language is true, then, it seems xenolalic speech is literally meaningless.

16. Putnam, "Meaning of 'Meaning,'" 7.

17. Putnam rejects this picture through his famous Twin Earth thought experiment, whereby two people have identical psychological states but mean two different things because of differences in their physical environment. Putnam is an externalist because meaning is partly determined by the external physical environment in which speakers find themselves.

One way out of this conclusion for the Pentecostal internalist might be to place stronger emphasis on the role of the interpretation as the sole generator of meaning. This solution loosens the connection between the glossolalic utterance and the interpretation such that the utterance may function as a necessary trigger for the interpreter's speech but is not straightforwardly an interpretation of that speech. This makes the interpreters speech identical to a stand-alone prophecy. David Hilborn suggests this model when he draws on Relevance Theory developed by Dan Sperber and Deirdre Wilson to argue that the (mislabelled) "interpretation" fulfils the informative intention of communicating information and the prior glossolalia serves a different purpose, namely the communicative intention of informing the listener that the subsequent "interpretation" is a "word from God."[18]

This is a plausible solution, but there are two potential concerns. First, this solution cannot be applied to cases of xenolalia where the language is another earthly language, understandable without further divinely inspired interpretation or subsequent prophecy, as in the case of Acts 2.[19] Second, although closely related, Paul makes a clear distinction between glossolalia and prophecy in 1 Cor 12–14, suggesting that collapsing these two gifts together distorts the texts and phenomena we are trying to explain. Although I am attracted to Hilborn's model, these are sufficient reasons to seek alternative models that avoid these concerns.

An alternative solution might appeal to God's psychological states and intentions as the locus of meaning, instead of the human speakers. On this model, the glossolalic speaker is parroting the Holy Spirit. Philosophers from Locke to Wittgenstein considered whether a parrot's mimetic speech is meaningful. For Locke, parrots don't mean what they say because their words are not accompanied by, do not represent, ideas in their own minds. Wittgenstein disagreed with this and argued that the parrot's speech is not meaningful because the parrot does not know how to use the human words it mimics; that is, the parrot will may repeat the phrase "Polly wants a cracker," but not to signal hunger. Could we say that xenolalia is a kind of parroting speech? Yes, I think we could. It is not that the speech itself carries no meaning to hearers, but that—like the parrot—the xenolalic speaker themselves

18. Hilborn, "Glossolalia as Communication," 133.

19. A possible response to this is that the xenolalia depicted in Acts 2 was ostensive to Peter's subsequent sermon. This makes the claim that "each one heard their own language being spoken" (Acts 2:6) a distinct miracle of *hearing*, rather than one of speaking. Hilborn is unlikely to be too troubled by this objection because his model is primarily motivated by the worry (taken from Samarin) that "experimental evidence for modern-day xenolalia, and thus for the thoroughgoing 'translation' of tongues, is at best very weak, and at worst non-existent." Hilborn, "Glossolalia as Communication," 114–15; Samarin, *Tongues of Men and Angels*, 73.

does not have specific ideas in mind that are being communicated by their utterance, nor do they know how to use the phonemes to communicate specific content. In both the case of the parrot and the case of xenolalia, we have interpretable speech although the meaning is not determined by the individual human speaker. Does this mean that xenolalia is, like Locke's and Wittgenstein's judgment regarding parrots, meaningless? Not if we expand the search for a solution to this problem to externalist accounts.

In the case of xenolalia, *someone*, namely the Holy Spirit, *means* something by the utterance. In fact, this is something of an advantage because, it generates an error theory. As with the parrot, xenolalic speech is meaningful if it is passing on a message from another agent who understands and intends the meaning, but not if it is coming from the parrot themselves. Likewise, xenolalia that does not come from the Holy Spirit, but is made-up by the speaker, is not meaningful. Publicly accessible ways to discern the difference between valid and invalid xenolalic utterances is not something this model provides in itself—additional work is needed for this, which is beyond the scope of this paper.[20]

By introducing an analogy to parroting we have moved beyond internalism to something closer to Tyler Burge's anti-individualism, which is a form of externalism. According to Burge, ordinary speakers do not determine the meaning of the terms they use on their own because ordinary speakers do not always know the necessary and sufficient conditions for using the term correctly. Instead, Burge argues that it is the practice of experts within the relevant linguistic community who determine meaning. Thus, when an ordinary speaker uses a work in a non-standard way, they can typically be interpreted as making a mistake rather than deliberately giving the term a novel meaning.

Applying Burge's anti-individualism to xenolalia has a number of advantages. First, Burge gives significant attention to speaker incompetence, which goes some of the way towards the more extreme case of xenolalia where the human speaker is wholly incompetent.[21] Second, as in the analogy to the parrot, xenolalic practice has a clear linguistic expert whom determines the meaning of the unknown utterance; namely, the Holy Spirit. Third, Burge's anti-individualism acknowledges the role of the wider linguistic community

20. An additional factor distinguishing xenolalia from parroting is the xenolalia is not typically described by Pentecostal and charismatic practitioners as a two-step process of prior listening and subsequent speaking but a single event of inspired speech. The xenolalic speaker hears the utterance for the first time as it comes out of their own mouth but experiences these words as coming from a source that is beyond themselves.

21. Burge does not, of course, think of speakers as *wholly* incompetent, as in this stronger xenolalic case.

in providing the normative context in which the utterance is interpreted as meaningful. If the xenolalic utterance is a human language (unknown to the speaker), then the norms of the native linguistic community will partially determine the meaning of the utterance. If the xenolalic utterance is an angelic language, then it is still the case that the conventions and expectations of the gathered church community, the norms of the Christian tradition to which they belong, and the role of experts all play an important role in marking this utterance as either meaningful or fraudulent, and in accepting or rejecting the subsequent interpretation. Fourth, Burge has also described his anti-individualism as meaning that the relations between the speaker's psychology and the wider environment are "constitutively necessary for the states and events to be the specific kinds of states or events that they are."[22] This idea can be transposed into a theological register to make the more specific claim that a relationship of indwelling of the Holy Spirit within the mind of the speaker is necessary for xenolalic utterances to be a meaningful linguistic event.

This section has outlined the philosophical challenge generated by xenolalia and provided some initial reasons why the best way to understand how xenolalic utterances can be deemed meaningful is to expand Burge's anti-individualism. As with all versions of externalism, the main attraction of externalism over internalism in this context is the deflationary role that externalist proposals give to the psychological state of the speaker—even though no philosophical theory of externalism entirely excludes the role of the speaker's psychological states in determining meaning as is needed in the case for xenolalia. The advantage of Burge's anti-individualist version of externalism in particular is the role that he gives to social relations, which can be employed in this Pentecostal and charismatic context to explain the necessity of the speaker's psychological relationship to the Holy Spirit and the interpretative role of the gathered church community in determining the meaning of the xenolalic utterance.

Expressivist and Speech-Act Theory Accounts of Private Prayer Glossolalia

The second form of glossolalia we see described in Scripture and practiced widely in Pentecostal and charismatic churches is private prayer glossolalia. This is the form of glossolalia that Paul describes as a means of communication from the individual believer to God, that is not required to have an interpretation to make it accessible to other people.

22. Burge, *Foundations of Mind*, 3.

There are some notable similarities between private prayer glossolalia and theories in early analytic philosophy regarding senseless or meaningless language. In Wittgenstein's *Tractus*, ordinary language sentences that cannot be constructed by logical operations on atomic sentences, such as those containing ethical, psychological or religious terms, are deemed senseless. Similarly, for A. J. Ayer, statements that cannot be verified empirically even in principle are meaningless; incapable of being either true or false. Famously and inconsistently, of course, this includes all religious, ethical and metaphysical statements. The early Wittgenstein and Ayer did not think, however, that senseless or meaningless statements have no function whatsoever. Rather they argued that, even though the words were not strictly speaking vehicles for representation or knowledge, such statements could convey emotive force or an expressive quality, in a manner similar to music or laughter.

One possible account of private prayer glossolalia is that it is purely expressive of mental states (e.g., desires, emotions, trust, pro and con attitudes, commitments).[23] The motivation to consider this possibility need not be because such forms of glossolalia are unverifiable, but because expressivism seems to fit parts of the biblical and contemporary description of this kind of glossolalia fairly well, which could not be said of the first category of xenolalia discussed above. In particular, this would make sense of why private prayer glossolalia is discussed by Paul as legitimately edifying to the individual, but not to the community.

Expressivism highlights that human language commonly serves more purposes than simply a vehicle for literal descriptions of reality. In addition to semantic content, language also contains (what Frege called) various kinds of "force." The force of speech is the quality by which a statement counts as either a command, a question, a warning, a promise, an apology, etc. The idea that philosophy should attend to the messy ways we *use* language in ordinary life, rather than search for an ideal language with transparent inferential structures, was one of the major transformations in Wittgenstein's thought and the origin of what is now called Ordinary Language Philosophy. As Wittgenstein writes in *Philosophical Investigations*, "For a *large* class of cases of the employment of the word 'meaning'—though not for all—this word can be explained in this way: the meaning of a word is its use in the language."[24] Therefore, to understand what glossolalia means we also need to look and see how it is used. To answer this question, we

23. Several influential scientific studies of glossolalia have broadly come to this conclusion. See, Pattison, "Behavorial Science Research"; Samarin, *Tongues of Men and Angels*; Williams, *Tongues of the Spirit*.

24. Wittgenstein, *Philosophical Investigations*, §43, p. 25e.

turn to the work of Wittgenstein's student, J. L. Austin, and his posthumous publication *How to Do Things with Words*.

Austin's *How to Do Things with Words* is often seen as the origin of what is called speech-act theory, which conceives of speech not only as informative, but also as the performance of an action. Austin distinguished between three aspects of speech, all of which contribute to meaning: locution, illocution, and perlocution. The locution is what is said or done, it is the words, sounds or gestures used in the act of communication. This is different, Austin argued, from the illocutionary force of speech, which is the act that is performed by the locution. Illocutionary force is not a feature of what is said, but of how what is said is meant. For example, when Arnold Schwarzenegger, in the titular role of *The Terminator*, says "I'll be back," he could be interpreted as making a factual assertion, based on his knowledge of the future as a time traveling being, a prediction, a promise, a threat, or a warning. The Terminator's speech can act in different ways. Furthermore, a speech-act does not have to be verbal. If I bow before you, I might be expressing deference, ridicule, or merely indigestion. These examples not only show that locutions (i.e., the words or gesture) can be distinguished from the illocutionary force or meaning, but that locutions underdetermine illocutions—the same locution can have different possible illocutionary meanings. The reverse is also true; roughly the same illocution may be achieved by multiple possible locutions.

This distinction and underdetermination between locutionary content and illocutionary force is why speech-act theory is a promising way to understand private prayer glossolalia. Glossolalia can have a wide range of seemingly meaningless locutions that still have the illocutionary force of either praising, thanking, repenting, or petitioning God.[25] What determines which illocution is achieved does not depend on the precise phonemes uttered, but on the intention of the speaker. The locutionary utterance still plays an indispensable role. The illocutionary act of praising or thanking God would not be achieved, in this instance, without the glossolalic utterance, although the act could, of course, be achieved by a range of different utterances, words, or actions. Such extreme, mutual underdetermination is clearly not the case for xenolalia, where the speaker is speaking a language with more established and extensive rules and conventions.

Glossolalic speech-acts can also achieve an additional perlocutionary act. A perlocution is the resulting act or effect in the world that results from the combination of locutionary content and illocutionary force. For

25. This list is taken from Nicholas Wolterstorff's analysis of Anglican liturgies through the lens of speech-act theory. Wolterstorff, *Acting Liturgically*, 87.

example, I might say "It's cold in here" (locution) and mean it as a request for you to shut a window (illocution), in response to which you stand up and do so (perlocution). I will not give thorough consideration to the perlocutions achieved by glossolalia here, but simply say that, without interpretation, they will approximately mirror discussions of the general "sign" of glossolalia (e.g., a catalyst for conversion, unifying the community, empowerment, "othering" outsiders).[26]

Speech-act theory is not only beneficial because of the gap between the content and the force of speech accurately reflects what is going on with private prayer glossolalia, but also because it allows us to establish normative criteria for the successful practice of private prayer glossolalia and predict when this form of glossolalia might go wrong within Christian communities. In *How to Do Things With Words*, Austin gives considerable attention to conditions that must be met for a locution to achieve their illocutionary aim or, as he put it, for speech-acts to be performed "felicitously." From this we can ask what the conditions are for glossolalia to be performed felicitously, and so achieve their illocutionary and perlocutionary aims.

Austin saw two possible ways in which a speech-act can fail, both of which are relevant for private prayer glossolalia: "misfire" and "abuse." A misfire is when an act of speech is made, but no speech-act is performed. This might be because the speaker does not have the authority to perform the action, such as if I declare two people married without having a licence giving me the power to marry people. Another reason that a speech-act might misfire is if there is no uptake from the addressee(s), such as when I offer you a bet, but you refuse to accept it—then no bet has been made. In addition to misfires, Austin argued that speech-acts can be abused. This is when a speech-act is achieved, but under false pretences, such as if I make a promise or threat that I have no intention of honouring. For Austin, "sincerity is a paradigm condition for the felicity of speech acts."[27]

These failures are clearly possible for glossolalia and they help us understand the normative conditions for felicitous glossolalic speech-acts. It would be misleading to say that the glossolalic speaker needs authority, but they do need to be indwelt by the Holy Spirit. Without this, even if an identical utterance is made, it does not succeed as an instance of glossolalia. Since God is both the addressee and the empowering agent of glossolalic speech, it is not possible for the misfire to be due to a failure of uptake by God. It is reasonable to assume that for all instances of inspired glossolalia are

26. When xenolalia is accompanied by an interpretation then, in addition to these possible perlocutions, perlocutions specific to the information content conveyed in the interpretation may also result (e.g., a call to repentance).

27. Green, "Speech Acts."

taken up, or accepted, by God. However, not all instances of inspired glossolalia are accepted by the community of believers, and there is sociological evidence that "glossolalia requires a social context that is supportive of the practice and that provides meaning for its use."[28]

Glossolalia can also be abused, whenever the speaker performs the locutionary utterance without really intending on praising God or repenting of their sins. Instead, the speaker may intend to draw attention to themselves, persuade their community to give them spiritual authority, or just to fit in a context where glossolalia is a mark of belonging. There is the further question of whether these acts of glossolalia are necessarily also misfires, or whether it is possible to perform an inspired glossolalic utterance without sincerely performing the illocutionary act of praise, thanksgiving, repentance or petition. In such cases, the human's intentions would be misaligned with the Holy Spirit's intentions, but the Holy Spirit would nevertheless use the speech of this sinful human to further God's kingdom and build up the church.

Conclusion

This paper has made an initial enquiry into how analytic philosophy of language can help make sense of glossolalia as a meaningful form of communication with others and with God, despite the lack of either meaning within the psychological state of the believer or the lack of semantic content within the spoken utterance, both of which are normally take as necessary, if not sufficient, determiners of meaning.

Using the New Testament references to glossolalia as my initial guide, I suggested that there are two types of glossolalia, each of which poses distinct challenges for traditional models in philosophy of language and require different philosophical treatment. To make sense of how xenolalic speech can convey meaning and be interpreted into natural or angelic languages, when the speaker themselves does not know what they are saying, I argued that Burge's anti-individualist externalism offered the best hope for a solution that does not collapse the interpretation of xenolalia into a stand-alone gift of prophecy. However, developing a model of how xenolalic speech is meaningful would require Burge's work to be significantly expanded beyond current proposals.

To make sense of private prayer glossolalia, where the speaker themselves does have psychological awareness of their meaning but the utterance does not require interpretation because it does not contain semantic

28. Poloma, "Glossolalia, Liminality, and Empowered Kingdom Building," 172.

content, I examined expressivism and speech-act theory. Although expressivism captures part of the psychological purpose of glossolalia, speech-act theory was better at accounting for a wider variety of utterances, intentions, and effects. Furthermore, unlike expressivism, speech-act theory accounts for the wide range of benefits glossolalia can bring to churches, as well as generates rules or guidelines for successful and appropriate uses of glossolalia, thereby also explaining ways in which glossolalia can go wrong. In conclusion, we can see that rather than being the Pentecostal crags upon which the ambitions of analytic theology are dashed, analytic philosophy of language provides a range of helpful accounts of meaning that can be applied to the diversity of Christian glossolalic practices.

Bibliography

Burge, Tyler. *Foundations of Mind*. Oxford: Oxford University Press.

Cartledge, Mark J. *The Gift of Spirit in Tongues*. Cambridge: Grove, 2005.

———. "Introduction." In *Speaking in Tongues: Multi-Disciplinary Perspectives*, edited by Mark J. Cartledge, xix–xxiv. Carlisle: Paternoster, 2006.

———. *Practical Theology: Charismatic and Empirical Perspectives*. Carlisle: Paternoster, 2003.

Christian-Eurell, John. "The Nature of Pauline Glossolalia and Its Early Reception." *Scottish Journal of Theology* 72 (2019) 182–90.

Fee, Gordon D. "Toward a Pauline Theology of Glossolalia." *Crux* 31 (1995) 24–37.

Green, Mitchell. "Speech Acts." *The Stanford Encyclopedia of Philosophy*, fall 2021 ed. Edited by Edward N. Zalta. https://plato.stanford.edu/archives/fall2021/entries/speech-acts/.

Hilborn, David. "Glossolalia as Communication—A Linguistic-Pragmatic Perspective." In *Speaking in Tongues: Multi-Disciplinary Perspectives*, edited by Mark J. Cartledge, 111–46. Carlisle: Paternoster, 2006.

Kavan, Heather. "Glossolalia and Altered States of Consciousness in Two New Zealand Religious Movements." *Journal of Contemporary Religion* 19 (2004) 171–84.

Kay, William K. "The Mind, Behaviour and Glossolalia: A Psychological Perspective." In *Speaking in Tongues: Multi-Disciplinary Perspectives*, edited by Mark J. Cartledge, 174–204. Carlisle: Paternoster, 2006.

Macchia, Frank. "Groans Too Deep for Words: Towards a Theology of Tongues as Initial Evidence." *Asian Journal of Pentecostal Studies* 1 (1998) 149–73.

Pattison, E. M. "Behavorial Science Research on the Nature of Glossolalia." *Journal of the American Scientific Affiliation* 20 (1966) 73–86.

Peppiatt, Lucy. *Women and Worship at Corinth: Paul's Rhetorical Arguments in 1 Corinthians*. Eugene, OR: Cascade, 2015.

Poloma, Margaret M. "Glossolalia, Liminality, and Empowered Kingdom Building—A Sociological Perspective." *Speaking in Tongues: Multi-Disciplinary Perspectives*, edited by Mark J. Cartledge, 147–73. Carlisle: Paternoster, 2006.

Putnam, Hilary. "The Meaning of 'Meaning.'" In *The Twin Earth Chronicles: Twenty Years of Reflection on Hilary Putnam's the 'Meaning of Meaning'*, edited by Andrew Pessin and Sanford Goldberg, 3–52. London: Routledge, 1996.

Samarin, W. J. *Tongues of Men and Angels.* London: Macmillan, 1972.

Smith, James K. A. "Tongues as 'Resistance Discourse: A Philosophical Analysis." In *Speaking in Tongues: Multi-Disciplinary Perspectives*, edited by Mark J. Cartledge, 81–110. Carlisle: Paternoster, 2006.

Spittler, Russell P. "Glossolalia." In *The New Dictionary of Pentecostal and Charismatic Movements*, edited by S. M. Burgess and E. M. van Der Maas. Grand Rapids: Zondervan, 2003.

Stanley, Gordon, et al. "Some Characteristics of Charismatic Experience: Glossolalia in Australia." *Journal of the Scientific Study of Religion* 17 (1978) 269–78.

Williams, C. G. *Tongues of the Spirit: A Study of Pentecostal Glossolalia and Related Phenomena.* Cardiff: University of Wales, 1981.

Wittgenstein, Ludwig. *Philosophical Investigations.* Translated by G. E. M Anscombe et al. Rev. 4th ed. by P. M. S. Hacker and Joachim Schulte. Oxford: Basil Blackwell, 2009.

Wolterstorff, Nicholas. *Acting Liturgically: Philosophical Reflections on Religious Practice.* Oxford: Oxford University Press, 2018.

15

Who Gets to Name and Claim?

Authority and Invoking the Spirit

Christopher Whyte

As I set out to write this chapter, reports emerged from Asbury University of what many involved deemed "revival." Spontaneous, student led worship services ran continuously for two weeks attracting students from more than twenty other campuses and international engagement.[1] Professor Tom McCall of Asbury Theological Seminary shared that the revival developed out of a scheduled chapel event. At the close of the service, students remained in the auditorium to continue in worship and prayer, "expressing repentance and contrition for sin and interceding for healing, wholeness, peace, and justice."[2] Attempting to reassure the larger faith community that a genuine move of God was occurring, McCall attested that the gathering was free of "pressure," "hype," "manipulation," and "emotional fervor."[3] Instead, McCall saw in the gathering peace, calm, joy, serenity, and a powerful but gentle move of the Spirit. He spoke hopefully of coming fruit arising from that move of God.[4]

1. Ferguson, "Nonstop Worship Service," para. 1–3.
2. McCall, "Asbury Professor," para. 1–3.
3. McCall, "Asbury Professor," para. 8–25.
4. McCall, "Asbury Professor," para. 8–25.

However, the event did not unanimously inspire hopeful response and claims to the Spirit. For example, theologian Robert Monson responded online to reports of the event:

> I enter this conversation as a Black man and as a theologian and as I have researched many revival settings that have taken place on American soil, I confess that I enter the chat jaded. While I am a huge believer in the moves of God, I stop short at largely white audiences being able to authoritatively name something. . . . When we all take a glimpse into what is happening at Asbury and what has happened in previous moves of God, who gets to know?[5]

For Monson, it wasn't just about epistemic uncertainty regarding who gets to attest to God's action, but also the fact that past "revivals" failed to forestall ethical *failures*: the rise of white supremacy, oppression within the church, and sanctioning of injustice and unjust actors by Christians.[6] That second aspect of Monson's critique brings up a larger issue. It is not only about who should speak of God's action in the world but also about whether we rightly discern when God is moving.

These responses, marking opposite poles, speak to the challenge I engage in this chapter. Specifically, I ask: "Who gets to name and claim the Spirit?" While naming and claiming has been used by charismatics to describe a process of calling an outcome into being,[7] I am somewhat provocatively reappropriating the term here to discuss the identification and invocation of the Spirit. More fully, I have in mind the ways in which "naming and claiming" the Spirit is a means of asserting authority for justifying certain spaces, persons, or expressions. I engage this topic as a Pentecostal-charismatic (henceforth P-C) Christian from what is broadly the white evangelical tradition. And, to be clear, I am committed both to desiring the Spirit's presence in like manner to McCall *and* confronting the types of failures Monson identifies. I am not attempting to explore whether God moves, but instead what types of postures and practices should define how the church should respond when it thinks God might be moving.

Therefore, in this brief chapter, I will attempt to excavate the implications of naming and claiming the Spirit and provide one methodology for approaching instances when it seems the Spirit might be working profoundly

5. Monson, "What to Black America Is Your Revival?" para. 3–4.

6. Monson, "What to Black America Is Your Revival?" para. 3–4.

7. Here I have in mind the practice, in some circles, to name and claim desired outcomes or blessings expecting that they will be given by God. Piper, "Can I 'Name It and Claim It?'" para. 1–2.

or uniquely. I am not claiming to have the authoritative or only approach to this thorny issue. Instead, I am minimally offering a methodology that holds the disparate views of McCall and Monson in tension.[8]

Naming and Claiming: A Theological Conundrum

In his seminal *Pentecostalism: Origins and Developments Worldwide*, Walter Hollenweger notes that since the early 1900s Pentecostals have wrestled with problematic high-profile claims to the power of the Holy Spirit. As an example, he points to healing evangelists all too often corrupted by manipulative practices serving personal wealth and influence.[9] And this seems to indicate that, since faith healing has so often been a ruse or a ministry merely serving the bottom line of the minister, that "miracles" should be mistrusted. However, Hollenweger also argues that the answer simply be this type of dismissal, because authentic healing is a vital component of the church's ministry. As an example, he recounts the healing ministry of an Anglican hospital chaplain in Europe. That vicar conducts brief eucharistic services for members of his parish awaiting operations. Sometimes, after the service, the operation succeeds, and all are thankful. Sometimes the patient dies during the procedure or just after, and the family of the departed are thankful to have been cared for by a minister. Sometimes, however, the patient is found to have been healed after the Eucharist yet before the operation, which is "the most interesting case but also the most difficult to explain."[10] And it is those difficult to explain outcomes that are at the heart of this chapter. While there is something deeply unsettling about those who profit off the vulnerable and desperate, about those who fabricate moves of God, there is something profoundly hopeful about unexpected outcomes that may well evidence the Spirit's direct help. Should those who claim to wield the Spirit, but are shown to be charlatans, cause P-C Christians to be reticent to invoke the Spirit? Or is the benefit of a miraculous healing so great that its very possibility justifies a degree of risk in naming and claiming?

To further unpack what I mean here, when I speak of the "naming" of the Spirit, I define that naming as the explicit demarcating of the Spirit's action, direction, or resourcing power. In short, I define "naming the Spirit" as statements made to communicate that the Holy Spirit is identifiably

8. Thanks are owed to Sarah Shin for her invaluable feedback on early drafts of this chapter.

9. Hollenweger, *Pentecostalism*, 229–30.

10. Hollenweger, *Pentecostalism*, 235.

active or present. Someone might say, "The Spirit led me here," "The Spirit filled me with peace," or "The Spirit healed my ailment." I define "claiming" the Spirit as requests for the identifiable help and presence of the Spirit. I also utilize that term in a double sense as an attestation that the Spirit has authorized or affirmed agents, expressions, or actions vis-à-vis identifiable presence and help.

For a scriptural example of what I mean by "naming the Spirit," I would point to Acts 2, when Peter clarifies that *glossolalia* is not incoherent drunken speech but instead the promised gift of the Spirit prophesied in Joel.[11] For a scriptural example of what I mean by "claiming the Spirit" *à la* request for help, I would identify Acts 8, when Peter and John realize a group of converts had not yet received the Spirit and therefore pray for the Spirit to be given to the new Christians, which is then said to occur.[12] For an example of "claiming the Spirit" *à la* divine affirmation, I would cite Jesus's reading of Isa 61 in which he declares, "The Spirit of the Lord is on me, because he has anointed me."[13] For an example of both, I would point to Acts 4, wherein the fellowship of believers identify Ps 2 as a prophetic unction spoken by the power of the Holy Spirit. They then ask for the Lord to grant them boldness and are subsequently filled with the Holy Spirit as it releases bold speech.[14] With these terms established, we can now turn to address the challenge of appropriate naming and claiming.[15]

The Complexity Inherent in Naming and Claiming

While I have offered functional definitions, the naming and claiming of the Spirit is a notoriously complex matter within the history of P-C Christianity. The problem of bad actors considered at the beginning of this chapter speaks to the real consequences of inappropriate naming and claiming for the vulnerable. However, that danger does not seem to excuse the avoidance of such ministry when one considers, as Hollenweger points out, that the

11. Acts 2:14–21. Scripture quotations in this chapter are taken from the New International Version unless otherwise indicated.

12. Acts 8:14–17.

13. Luke 4:18.

14. Acts 4:24–31.

15. I will, here, concede that individuals do not always explicate the Holy Spirit in the manner I have in mind. Persons might instead refer to God, or Lord, or other titles for a variety of reasons. That said, as I specifically will be engaging pneumatology and canonical texts referencing the Spirit, I will prioritize the Spirit in this discussion. There may be applications to language less explicitly spiritual, but that is beyond the bounds of this chapter.

text of the great commission in Matthew includes an admonition to minister supernaturally alongside proclamations of the gospel.[16] Further, there is a challenge in having this conversation within the context of P-C Christianity. This is because, broad strokes, the community has been notoriously reticent to engage pneumatology. Again, from Hollenweger, P-C Christians are "strong on experience of the Spirit, on pneuma*praxis*, but they are weak on the interpretation of these experiences."[17]

This interpretation issue is strongly felt in P-C Christian assessments of tongues. Hollenweger asserts that Pentecostals validly claim the Spirit's presence therein but wield this experience as the basis for a dogmatic insistence that tongues are the sign of Spirit-baptism distinct from salvation.[18] Gordon Fee identifies something similar. He observes that early Pentecostals, from a presumption that Scripture was Spirit-inspired, imposed their subjective named and claimed experiences on scriptural accounts of the Spirit as means to validate their conclusions. They not only identified tongues in the Bible, they attempted to exegetically justify a view that tongues are a necessary work by drawing *prima facie* conclusions from personal encounters.[19] Fee articulates that while he, like Hollenweger, believes Pentecostals were right to name the Spirit as present in tongues, they went too far in claiming biblical support for tongues as a necessary work of grace.[20] Experientially driven naming and claiming too easily results in the development of new theologies unseating tradition or denominational claims. I recognize that these assessments might prove controversial for some Christian communities. For some, it is heretical to call tongues anything less than a necessary work. For others, it is too much to claim tongues at all. The presentation of Fee's and Hollenweger's analysis here is not intended to validate or invalidate tongues but instead to identify how commonly experience licenses exegetical conclusions stronger than available evidence. A community might be right for the wrong reasons, and this is enough cause to reconsider methodology.

Fee highlights another interpretive issue linked to tongues in the P-C Christian belief that any "experience . . . so empowering, so thoroughly life-changing, both in terms of personal obedience to God and readiness and empowerment for witness . . . *must* be God."[21] Naming and claiming, it seems, is easily sanctioned according to the power of perceived benefits.

16. Hollenweger, *Pentecostalism*, 228–29.

17. Hollenweger, *Pentecostalism*, 218.

18. Hollenweger, *Pentecostalism*, 222–23.

19. Fee, "Baptism," 88.

20. Fee, "Baptism," 89.

21. Fee, "Baptism," 88.

In such a case, the Spirit is subjectively discerned according to perceived edification. The observations presented by Fee and Hollenweger implicitly highlight a normative hermeneutic for many P-C Christians who name and claim. If an experience inspires obedience to God, witness to God, and service to God then there is good reason to name that experience as the Spirit's presence and claim that experience in future need. Further, in the event the experience is personally beneficial, individuals tend to develop new theologies to resolve contradictions between felt experience and tradition or denominational beliefs.

Weaponized Naming and Claiming: William Seymour and Charles Parham

These interpretative features of naming and claiming were present at the very advent of P-C Christianity. Consider the example of William Seymour, the leader of the Azusa Street Revival. Seymour has been deemed "one of the leading figures of early Pentecostalism."[22] The son of freed slaves, Seymour was raised in Louisiana amid racial violence and segregation. Convinced of a call by God's Spirit to be a messenger of God's will, he traveled extensively, seeking a place for ministry free of "the stifling oppression of southern racism along with its reign of terror."[23] In Houston, Seymour met Charles Parham, a Bible teacher and Pentecostal revivalist who allowed Seymour to attend classes, though only if Seymour was segregated to the hallway or adjacent space. While Seymour was captivated by teachings on the availability of tongues, he was troubled by Parham's racist attitudes and controversial theological stances. And so, he accepted a pastorate in Los Angeles that demanded a move away from Parham's ministry.[24] After initial difficulties (he was expelled from the church after preaching that all true Christians should ultimately speak in tongues), Seymour began a prayer meeting. What was first a prayer gathering at a small cottage on South Union Street quickly grew and was moved to the Asberry home on Bonnie Brae Street in a predominately African American neighborhood.[25] After again outgrowing its setting, Seymour found a new location in Los Angeles at Azusa Street.

22. Strong, *They Walked in the Spirit*, 33.

23. Espinosa, *William Seymour*, 47–48.

24. Parham was an ardent white supremacist and segregationist. He was also a nonconformist who was more willing than his white supremacist counterparts to engage non-white Christians so long as they were segregated and subjugated. Espinosa, *William Seymour*, 51–53.

25. Espinosa, *William J. Seymour*, 53.

Congregants at that location testified they experienced a powerful move of the Spirit uniting their diverse community.[26]

In light of the burgeoning revival, and its rapid growth demanding an increase in ministerial responsibilities, Seymour reached out to Parham to request credentials under the Apostolic Faith Movement. Parham balked at this request until Seymour offered to host a unified Los Angeles revival and Parham saw this as an opportunity to assert leadership over the Azusa revival. Parham sent credentials to Seymour and months later traveled to California to observe the events first-hand.[27] Parham immediately rejected the gathering as counterfeit, which included desegregated worship practices that he found repulsive, and accused Seymour of falsely presenting African American cultural practices as the Holy Spirit's work. And in making that point, Parham openly employed racist, demeaning language.[28]

Parham's response can easily cause unease for various reasons. Those reticent to agree that Seymour accurately named or claimed a manifestation of the Spirit at Azusa could just as easily be uncomfortable about sharing that position with a noted racist. That unwelcome association might inspire pause regarding arriving at the same theological conclusions. Others might observe that Parham's attack mirrors the P-C exegetical move discussed earlier in reverse. Where P-C Christians use positive experience to license exegesis, Parham was so appalled by racial mixing that he concluded that Azusa's worship must be devoid of the Spirit.[29] This move is, at the core, a negative naming and claiming based on a racialized aesthetic which presumes African American culture and practice are ill-suited to true spirituality.[30] This corrupted hermeneutic ontologically subordinates non-white communities and presumes the Spirit would never engage subordinate

26. Anderson, "William Seymour," 188.

27. Espinosa, *William J. Seymour*, 53–54.

28. Anderson, "William Seymour," 188.

29. Parham's language explicitly cites Black spirituality as proof of apostasy. He observes, "In these fanatical meetings . . . two thirds of the so called baptisms are only a worked up animal spiritism with chattering and jabbering and no language at all. The so called Heavenly Choir [singing in the spirit] was only a modification of the Negro chanting of the Southland, and was not the result of the Pentecostal baptism." Charles Parham in Espinosa, *William J. Seymour*, 380–87, 384–85.

30. I employ aesthetic here in the Kantian sense. While an exhaustive treatment of this subject is beyond the scope of this chapter, David Lloyd convincingly argues that Kantian aesthetics presuppose an anthropological spectrum on which the white, human, formal subject and the non-white, savage, pathological subject are poles. This racial aesthetic spectrum presumes the white subject to be superior and better suited for virtue than the non-white subject. Lloyd, *Under Representation*, 7–8. For more on this topic, see also Carter, *Race*.

spaces. Much of Parham's theology is built on this hermeneutic. He claims that non-whites were created on the sixth day of creation while whites are the morally, spiritually supreme race created on the eighth day.[31] He separates all humanity into ontological hierarchies in which some are created for the highest expressions of spirituality and others were ill-suited to even the most minimal expressions of conversion.[32] This ontic hierarchy informed claims: 1) no overtly African spirituality would be met by God with an outpouring of his Spirit; and 2) that no African Americans could fully experience or appreciate such a blessing in the first place.

After reflecting on all the examples presented thus far, it could be argued that the way forward is to lean on uncertainty rather than strong, emphatic attestations. Claiming, it seems, raises the stakes and don't seem to guarantee ethical outcomes. Claims to the Spirit can theologically sanction new ground-breaking worship *à la* Seymour, entrench injustice *à la* Parham, or mask corruption *à la* certain "healing" evangelism. And it is not just how these claims are utilized but the fundamental diversity that marks how even P-C Christians respond to claimed moves of the Spirit. There is no clearly established method for defining with certainty if the Spirit actually moved. Here, one might be inclined to make an appeal to the integrity of those doing the naming and claiming. One could say that appropriate character is a prerequisite to discerning the Spirit's presence (for instance by saying Seymour did in fact have the necessary authority Spirit but Parham and healing evangelists did not). However, Scripture itself can undercut this move.

There are multiple examples in the Protestant canonical texts of individuals who rightly name the Spirit while simultaneously displaying bad character or distorted relationship to God. Balaam prophesies while not a member of God's people.[33] Samson, just after experiencing the rushing Spirit of the Lord, goes to "take" a woman who looks pleasing to him and eats from a lion's carcass.[34] The Spirit of God causes Saul's servants to prophesy while on a mission to capture David.[35] Saul takes on their failed mission, is similarly disrupted by the Spirit, strips naked, and prophesies.[36] These accounts further muddy the waters of identifying the Spirit, for while they are all moments when Scripture names the Spirit, none represent righteous

31. Espinosa, *William Seymour*, 44–45.

32. Green, "Spirit That Makes Us," 400–401.

33. Num 24:2.

34. Judg 14:6–8, NASB.

35. 1 Sam 19:18–20.

36. 1 Sam 19:23–24.

action. Not one is an actor we would regard as virtuous. It would be unwise to validate all of Samson's actions by virtue of the Spirit's presence. Saul is hardly a biblical example of godly or faithful action.

The complexity that is inherent in canonical naming of the Spirit inspires further caution about what actions, positions, or character can serve to arbitrate the Spirit's presence. Who does get to know? Certain actions and attitudes may honor to the Spirit's presence, but we should be reticent to say they mediate or justify that presence. While bad character might corrupt discernment, this does not mean that one has to be righteous to recognize the Spirit is moving.

However, these issues do not seem to justify abdication of naming or claiming. Consider the fact that Peter specifically names and claims the Spirit when announcing the inauguration of the church.[37] Without naming, there is no witness to the church's inception at Pentecost and no invitation to the diaspora to repent and join the body of Christ. Therefore, despite the fact that naming and claiming, historically, has been a fraught pursuit, it is also fundamental to the church's story. In light of the Spirit's confrontation of the diaspora at Pentecost towards repentance,[38] a contemporary community that avoids naming and claiming might fail to recognize and/or obey the Spirit's guidance toward greater faithfulness to Christ.

So how does one move forward? Who gets to name and claim? In the space that remains, I will provide evidence that the naming and claiming of the Spirit are central themes in the New Testament accounts of life in the church. Thus, the issues inherent in naming and claiming cannot be resolved by avoidance, but instead must be confronted while attending to common and frequent naming and claiming within the redeemed community. Humility demands that Christians take great care in these tasks. Rather than providing strict definitions of when and how the Spirit can rightly be named and claimed, I will instead offer a set of postures the church might well adopt to ensure it expresses appropriate care when naming and claiming the Spirit.

A Pauline Pneumatology

D. A. Carson's exegesis of 1 Cor 12–14, a text that defines the work of the Spirit in the church, observes that Paul does not begin by distinguishing between true and false manifestations of the Spirit. Instead, Paul points out that "to be able confess that the Jesus of the incarnation, cross, and

37. Acts 2:14–41.

38. Acts 2:37.

resurrection is truly the Lord . . . attests the powerful, transforming work of the Holy Spirit."[39] Fee, in agreement with this conclusion, highlights that "one who is indwelt by the Spirit . . . is led to the ultimate Christian confession."[40] These exegetes expand the horizon of naming and claiming by indicating that faithful confession of Christ as Lord implicitly names the Spirit and claims the Spirit's help. From Fee, it is "easy for God's people to think of the power and gifts as the real evidence of the Spirit's presence. Not so for Paul. The ultimate criterion of the Spirit's activity is the exaltation of Jesus as Lord, which in turn expresses itself in loving concern for others."[41] In this way, confession of Christ's Lordship is always reliant on the Spirit, and thus naming and claiming are central and repeated features of Christian community even when Christians do not recognize this link.

Carson points out another consideration for the church's naming and claiming. He argues that in 1 Cor 12, Paul unifies natural and supernatural giftings under the one umbrella of spiritual gifts. As he puts it, "Gifts, service, and work alike . . . all . . . manifest the Spirit; they show the Spirit."[42] Fee agrees here, stating, "*All things* done in the church are ultimately effected by the powerful working of God."[43] God resources the common good, Carson argues, rather than self-aggrandizement.[44] Thus, the text of 1 Corinthians indicates:

1. The Spirit is necessary to the faithful confession of Christ
2. The gifts of the Spirit encompass all supernatural manifestations and seemingly natural abilities that resource the common good.

 If (1) and (2) then:

3. Any community that confesses Christ and works together for the common good would be well served to explicitly name and claim the Spirit's presence in every member of the church.

This type of naming and claiming might undermine the work of bad actors as healing evangelists. Those individuals might operate in the power of the Spirit when praying for healing, but the accumulation of opulent wealth and the manipulation of the vulnerable are clearly not the "common good." Thus, their naming and claiming actions are entangled with manipulation

39. Carson, *Showing the Spirit*, 32–33.
40. Fee, *Corinthians*, 644.
41. Fee, *Corinthians*, 645.
42. Carson, *Showing the Spirit*, 41.
43. Fee, *Corinthians*, 650.
44. Carson, *Showing the Spirit*, 42.

dishonoring the Spirit's presence and should be confronted. Further, regular naming and claiming while submitting to each other in love,[45] resists the idea that a lone individual can claim unique, special, or authoritative gifting. The Spirit benefits all for the benefit of all.

This, though, does not help the issues inherent to Parham's critique of Seymour. Parham did not accuse Seymour of misrepresenting the Spirit's help in confessing Christ, in the ministries of the church, or in the gifts of the Spirit. Parham rejected Seymour's ministry as misrepresenting the Spirit by means of being animalistic, fanatical, and spiritualistic.[46] Here, some readers might be inclined to agree that those designators run counter to faithful Christian worship. However, Parham's later reflections provide more insight into what informed his terms. Years after the revival, he commented that Azusa made him "sick . . . to see white people imitating unintelligent, crude negroism of the Southland, and laying it on the Holy Ghost."[47] Thus, Parham equated animalism, fanaticism, and spiritualism to African and African American Christianity. His racial aesthetic could not accept African or African American spirituality as Spirit-ed or Christian. So it's not so much that the worship was unrighteous, but that Parham was repulsed by the fact that the worship was too Black and he found terms to justify his disgust.

This is good cause to reconceptualize what constitutes disorderly worship that dishonors the Spirit, *à la* 1 Cor 14:40. Assertions of disorder may be more informed by cultural or ethnic proclivities than one realizes. Just as Parham rejected Seymour based on his biases, claims to revival may cite subjective order while failing to recognize the dishonoring fruit arising from that order. As indicated by Monson, historic claims to revival have too often resulted in the mistreatment of marginalized communities. In this way, while persons or groups might think they are safeguarding a culture that honors the Spirit, whether through constraint or claim to appropriate revival, historically this type of move has been far too often an accommodation of racist, sexist, or classist impulses.

This goes to the heart of my concerns regarding naming and claiming. When the Spirit is said to be the source or author of something that is simultaneously enticing to some and revolting to others, calls can be raised for either theological affirmation or rejection. How can the church know which is appropriate? When is the Spirit overturning our revulsions that impede the common good? When is the Spirit responding to the deep cries of our

45. Eph 5:21.

46. Espinosa, *William J. Seymour*, 96–97.

47. Anderson, *Vision of the Disinherited*, 190.

hearts by inaugurating the fulfillment of our hopes? Who has the authority to say which is the case? For some, Azusa was a miraculous outpouring of the Spirit marked by healings, powerful worship, and interracial unity. It was marveled that "the color line that divided America . . . was washed away by the blood of Jesus."[48] For others, Azusa was the machination of false prophets preying on the misguided. It was "foolishness, fanaticism, and the work of the devil."[49] For Parham, it was an affront to his white supremacist theological anthropology. While many today would affirm racial unity in the church and reject Parham's brand of white supremacy, not all have embraced Azusa. In other words, there are many who might reject racism but question whether the Spirit actually moved in the Apostolic Faith community at Azusa. Rightly identifying and rejecting the personal biases that corrupt interpretations of the Spirit does not automatically instill confidence in naming and claiming. So, how can the church today identify when it is rightly arbitrating possible manifestations of the Spirit and when personal biases have corrupted interpretation?

Returning to Carson and Fee, I think that this is a particularly difficult task. If supernatural gifts and natural skillsets, the cultivation of the common good, and the confession of Christ as Lord are all attributed to the Spirit's presence, the Spirit seems simultaneously everywhere at once while being incredibly difficult to pin down. Recalling Jesus, "The wind blows where it pleases . . . you cannot tell where it comes from or where it is going. So it is with everyone born of the Spirit."[50] While this might inspire apophatic reticence to pin down the Spirit, doing so can deny the Spirit's voice in communities and persons that only the Spirit would speak through. If the Spirit was moving at Azusa, failing to acknowledge that movement only reinscribes white supremacist oppression and impedes multi-racial community. I think, therefore, that the church must always take special care to discern if the Spirit might be speaking through the "least" of their moment. Here, I will appeal to Gordon Fee again to flesh out this claim.

As Fee engages the body metaphor of 1 Cor 12, he provides a compelling and nuanced reading of the various forces that informed disunity within the early church. The full breadth of that discussion is beyond this chapter, but after emphasizing the importance of not demeaning or subordinating any Christian[51] he offers a helpful conclusion:

48. Espinosa, *William J. Seymour*, 58.

49. Espinosa, *William J. Seymour*, 66.

50. John 3:8.

51. Fee, *Corinthians*, 678–81.

> Paul's concern is for diversity, on the one hand, and for mutual concern in the body, on the other. According to the analogies themselves, that means (1) that there must be a greater acceptance of a variety of gifts in the church. The singular focus on one gift, be it tongues, prophecy, or healing in charismatic churches or strictly cerebral gifts in others, destroys the diversity God intended for the body. But it also means (2) that, in terms of people, we must stop negating others as less important than ourselves. That is to destroy unity.[52]

Here, I think there is much that applies to Parham's treatment of Seymour. Parham clearly negated Seymour's role in the body for aesthetic reasons presented as spiritual concerns. He clearly felt not only that Black spirituality was deficient, but more fully that it was counterfeit because it was Black. His pneumatological rejection, therefore, runs counter to Paul's treatment of gifts and persons in the church. Rather than considering how the least honored in society might be the most indispensable bearers of the Spirit, Parham's white supremacist pneumatology destroys unity, devalues diversity, and fails to express mutual concern.

Seymour, in contrast, saw the Spirit's work in Azusa in a far different light. As he put it, "We are not fighting men or churches, but seeking to displace dead forms and creeds and wild fanaticisms with living, practical Christianity. 'Love, Faith, Unity' are our watchwords, and 'Victory through the Atoning Blood' our battle cry."[53] For Seymour, the events at Azusa arose because the Spirit powerfully resourced faithful Christian practice, love, and unity. One can hear in these reflections a view to "the common good." Parham interpreted the event as an unjustifiable transgression. He made that claim according to the *a priori* assumption that Black spirituality was inviable and that whites evoking Black spirituality was an abomination. This hardly prioritizes unity in diversity. Seymour, in contrast, saw the socially transgressive space as the divine establishment of authentic Christian community in the midst of segregating ideologies.

Here, we have not come any closer to determining whether Seymour rightly named and claimed the Spirit. However, we can say that Seymour's reasons for affirming the presence of the Spirit ring far truer to Pauline logic than Parham's reasons for rejecting the same. Further, we can say that Seymour, and Azusa's congregants, willingly prioritized the culturally negated of their day, which is a posture more aligned with the logics of 1 Cor 12. This does not inherently imply that Seymour was wholesale right in all his

52. Fee, *Corinthians*, 682.

53. Espinosa, *William J. Seymour*, 164.

interpretations. As evidenced in my very brief survey of Old Testament examples, even bad actors might rightly name the Spirit. It does, though, indicate that Seymour is more faithfully aligned to Pauline guidance for discerning where the Spirit is at work. Methodologically, the church should posture itself to discern the Spirit together while paying special attention to those society least expects to be in positions of honor.

Here, I think several methodological postures for naming and claiming have come into focus:

1. The work of Spirit simply *is* central to the life and confession of the church.
2. Manifestations of the Spirit Christ and serve the common good of the Body of Christ.
3. All are likely recipients of these manifestations, and especially the marginalized.

As 1–3 has failed to prevent bad actors from fabricating the work of the Spirit or from acting unethically after claiming to receive the Spirit:

4. The church must submit its interpretations to the shared discernment.

And:

5. Shared discernment processes must uphold as indispensable those culturally deemed dispensable.

Christians may never fully know whether they have heard or heeded the Spirit rightly this side of the eschaton, but they can know if they have sought the Spirit's help or guidance within a posture that worshipfully honors Christ, is committed to the common good, and attends to those marginalized in society.

As evidence that what I am presenting aligns with the Pauline logics discussed thus far, Fee notes that in 1 Cor 13, Paul establishes the ethical context for the expression of the gifts of the Spirit. That context is one of love that builds up the church and deprioritizes self-interest.[54] As Fee frames it, "Love is the primary motivation behind everything . . . an eager desire for expressions of the Spirit that will build up the community is *how* love acts in this context."[55] In other words, communities seeking to name and claim the Spirit should prioritize love above all else, while simultaneously desiring the manifestations of the Spirit that make that love possible and never losing

54. Fee, *Corinthians*, 692.

55. Fee, *Corinthians*, 695.

sight of the fact that those manifestations should build up other members of the body.[56] Fee points out that, for Paul, love abandons rivalry, is not self-centered, is not self-aggrandizing, does not humiliate others, seeks the good of others first, and is not easily provoked to anger. In short, the *agape* of God is the standard for the ethic of God's people.[57] This type of love exposes and rejects aesthetic presuppositions that prioritize what is familiar or similar at the expense of the other.

Therefore, in addition to the five postures I have identified above, churches could adopt a Pauline ethic of loving support for one another. Considering that testimonies from Asbury were broadcast on such a scale that visitors from across the world were drawn to participate, communities should not constrain their understanding of love to purely local ideals. One community's naming and claiming may have implications for the life of a neighboring community or communities. A wise church might take special care to heed the Spirit's work in those that society or culture demotes, both within and without their ecclesial context, and seek to lovingly support the same. Thereby, churches might resist aesthetic tendencies that subordinate others based on preexisting hierarchies of value. And here, I am ultimately unconcerned about arbitrating whether the Spirit moved at Asbury (though I remain hopeful this was the case). I am fundamentally concerned about how we attend to voices like Monson's who questions the methods by which we name and claim the Spirit.

Azusan scholarship itself wrestles with this challenge. As Keri Day points out, while most leadership points to Seymour as the leader of the Azusa Street Revival, Seymour was not the only leader worthy of recognition at Azusa Street. While it is important to recognize his role, she argues, one should also recognize that a community of "black women domestics helped to lead and guide" at Azusa.[58] She argues these women were influential because, when one recognizes that "slave religious practices" informed Seymour's Christianity, one must also note that it was "black women leaders who preserved and maintained these practices that Seymour would perform."[59] While Azusa's leaders, and later scholars, may have not recognized this, in the language of this chapter, it is important to name the Spirit in the women who faithfully preserved the practices through which many claimed to experience the Spirit's work. Careful naming and claiming, like

56. Fee, *Corinthians*, 709.

57. Fee, *Corinthians*, 703–8.

58. Day, *Azusa Reimagined*, 100–101.

59. Day, *Azusa Reimagined*, 87.

these observations by Day, takes pains not to overlook those who are necessary to a sufficiently complex, nuanced naming of the Spirit.

Conclusion

The methodology I have presented simply cannot imbue infallible accuracy when naming and claiming the Spirit. To be fair, I have avoided landing on a hard and fast determination on this matter. I remain agnostic that this is consistently possible. Instead, I have presented postures committed to seeking the Spirit's help while confronting actions and attitudes that dishonor that same Spirit. When naming or claiming the Spirit requires a rejection of one or more of the postures I have identified, communities can display care and wisdom by stopping to prayerfully seek the Spirit's help in reestablishing greater faithfulness to Christ's intentions. This ethical framework, as I have presented it, should not be read as universal. I expect that it must be modified to better engage particular denominational proclivities. As an example, if a member church of an Anglican diocese experiences something like an Azusa event, the leadership of that diocese might need to adapt my recommendations to preexisting denominational structures installed to guide discernment processes. My goal is not to overly prescribe, but instead to point to a priority for love, worship, and obedience while mitigating destructive behaviors and attitudes. Considering what has been discussed from 1 Corinthians, the Spirit guides the church in the right confession of Christ as Lord and builds up that church through the collective release of resources to the whole body. The redeemed-community is thus helped to honor Christ together. Recognition of this help inspires naming and claiming of the Spirit in every gift, skill, and work that builds up the common good and honors Christ. Churches should do so explicitly and frequently so as to undercut the exclusivity of those bad actors claiming special rights to wield the Spirit. The church should listen to those members of the body that society and culture might demean or dismiss. We name and claim the Spirit as a body deeply interdependent, in which none are dispensable, trusting that the Spirit again and again founds new faithfulness to Jesus by working through any and all.

Bibliography

Anderson, Allan. "William Seymour." In *Handbook of Pentecostal Christianity*, edited by Adam Steward, 186–89. Dekalb: Northern Illinois University Press, 2012.

Anderson, Robert Mapes. *Vision of the Disinherited: The Making of American Pentecostalism*. Oxford: Oxford University Press, 1979.

Carson, Donald A. *Showing the Spirit: A Theological Exposition of 1 Corinthians* 12–14. Grand Rapids: Baker, 1987.

Carter, J. Kameron. Race: *A Theological Account*. Oxford: Oxford University Press, 2008.

Day, Kerri. *Azusa Reimagined: A Radical Vision of Religious and Democratic Belonging*. Redwood, CA: Stanford University Press, 2022.

Espinosa, Gastón. *William J. Seymour and the Origins of Global Pentecostalism: A Biography and Documentary History*. Durham, NC: Duke University Press, 2014.

Fee, Gordon D. "Baptism in the Holy Spirit: The Issue of Separability and Subsequence." *Pneuma* 7 (1985) 87–99.

———. *The First Epistle to the Corinthians (Revised Edition)*. Grand Rapids: Eerdmans, 2014.

Ferguson, Amber. "Nonstop Worship Service at Kentucky College Set to End After Attracting Thousands." *Washington Post*, February 2023. https://www.washingtonpost.com/religion/2023/02/18/asbury-university-revival-kentucky/.

Green, Chris. "The Spirit That Makes Us (Number) One." *Pneuma* 41 (2019) 397–420.

Hollenweger, Walter. *Pentecostalism: Origins and Developments Worldwide*. Peabody, MA: Hendrickson, 1997.

Lloyd, David. *Under Representation: The Racial Regime of Aesthetics*. New York: Fordham University Press, 2019.

McCall, Tom. "Asbury Professor: We're Witnessing a 'Surprising Work of God.'" *Christianity Today*, February 2023. https://www.christianitytoday.com/ct/2023/february-web-only/asbury-revival-1970-2023-methodist-christian-holy-spirit.html.

Monson, Robert. "What to Black America Is Your Revival?" *The Son Do Move*, February 2023. https://pastortrey05.substack.com/p/what-to-black-america-is-your-revival.

Piper, John. "Can I 'Name It and Claim It?'" *Desiring God*, November 2020. https://www.desiringgod.org/interviews/can-i-name-it-and-claim-it.

Strong, Douglas. *They Walked in the Spirit*. Louisville, KY: Westminster John Knox, 1997.

Subject Index

Scripture Index

www.ingramcontent.com/pod-product-compliance
Lightning Source LLC
LaVergne TN
LVHW100517110826
845146LV00002B/674

* 9 7 9 8 3 8 5 2 1 0 4 6 6 *